NEW LEGENDS OF ENGLAND

THE MIDDLE AGES SERIES

Ruth Mazo Karras, Series Editor

Edward Peters, Founding Editor

A complete list of books in the series is
available from the publisher.

NEW LEGENDS OF ENGLAND

Forms of Community in
Late Medieval Saints' Lives

CATHERINE SANOK

PENN

UNIVERSITY OF PENNSYLVANIA PRESS

PHILADELPHIA

Published by
University of Pennsylvania Press
Philadelphia, Pennsylvania 19104-4112
www.upenn.edu/pennpress

Printed in the United States of America on acid-free paper
10 9 8 7 6 5 4 3 2 1

Library of Congress Cataloging-in-Publication Data
ISBN 978-0-8122-4982-8

For my mother, sister, and brothers, and in memory of my father

CONTENTS

A NOTE ON ABBREVIATIONS AND SPELLING

AASS *Acta Sanctorum*

EEBO Early English Books Online

EETS Early English Text Society

MED *Middle English Dictionary* (University of Michigan, 2001), http://quod.lib.umich.edu/m/med

ODNB *Oxford Dictionary of National Biography*, ed. H. C. G. Matthew and Brian Harrison (Oxford: Oxford University Press, 2004), www.oxforddnb.com

SEL *South English Legendary*

Throughout this study, the ash, thorn, and yogh have been silently modernized in Middle English quotations and abbreviations have been expanded. Translations to modern English are my own, unless otherwise specified.

In 1389, English saints began once again to perform miracles, claims the Benedictine chronicler Thomas Walsingham: despite other calamities that year, Walsingham counts it a "happy" one on account of the "renewal of miracles"—*miracula renovata*—by England's own saints.[1] The British St. Alban, for example, cured a London woman named Agnes, who was so "demented by grief that her madness was known to almost all those who were accustomed to throng the streets of London" (272). The Anglo-Saxon St. Etheldreda—or Audrey, the Anglo-Norman name by which she is also known—renewed her miracle-working too. She appeared in a vision to a young man to warn him of the "gravest dangers which would befall the kingdom, unless a merciful God was placated by the pious prayers of the faithful and thus stayed his hand from punishment" (269). The saint instructed the man to carry her message to the prior and monks and informed him that to prove its truth he would be made lame until the feast of her translation, when he would be miraculously healed. His disabled body provided powerful evidence that his story was not "fake and the invention of human cunning" (270): the crowds that rushed to see him poked at his shins and feet with their knives to confirm for themselves that his flesh was "dead." The man also conveyed Etheldreda's prophecy of the devastating heat wave that summer, when it was so hot that the lead on church roofs melted, weather that would have been "still more intolerable" had not St. Etheldreda advised the English to pray for forgiveness. The saint appeared to an old woman as well, the young man's counterpart, as a medium for dire warnings addressed to both monks and laity to "continue their processions, redouble their intercessions, and to pray without ceasing that God would remove the sword which hung over their heads."

Walsingham's periodizing scheme, structured by the renewed activity of English saints, maps an epistemic shift in vernacular literary culture too. While there had been considerable interest in England's native saints following the Conquest, when a flurry of Anglo-Norman and Latin Lives were written, by the end of the fourteenth century this narrative tradition, like the saints themselves, had long been dormant: with the exception of the *South English Legendary* (*SEL*), there is very little interest in them in English-language narrative culture.[2] But within a generation of the revival announced by Walsingham, Middle English narrative and verse traditions were reshaped by attention to native saints. By the 1420s, English saints' Lives include a verse *Life of St. Edith* and a *Life of St. Etheldreda*, paired together in a manuscript associated with Wilton Abbey; John Audelay's carol-form *Life of St. Wenefred*, a Welsh saint whose two shrines, at Holywell in Flintshire and at Shrewsbury, made her a kind of border saint and increasingly an English one; a tail-rhyme *Life of John of Bridlington*, the last English person to be canonized before the Reformation; and a sprawling four-book *Life of St. Cuthbert*. In the 1430s, John Lydgate's aureate double Lives—the *Life of Sts. Edmund and Fremund* and the *Life of Sts. Alban and Amphibalus*—made native saints' Lives a crucial forum for aesthetic display, while his shorter works on Augustine of Canterbury and Ursula register his broad interest, and that of his patrons, in England's native saints. By the mid-fifteenth century, the Lives of some English saints from the *SEL* were translated into prose and appended to a Middle English translation of *Legenda Aurea*. Shortly thereafter Osbern Bokenham compiled his own legendary, which also adds English saints' Lives to the international canon formed by *Legenda Aurea*. Long literary saints' Lives in a Lydgatean mode were still being produced at the end of the century: they include Henry Bradshaw's *Life of St. Werburge*, Edmund Hatfield's *Lyf of Saynt Ursula*, and Lawrence Wade's *Life of St. Thomas of Canterbury*. Such works retained their appeal into the sixteenth century and crossed into the new medium of print, in editions produced by William Caxton, Wynkyn de Worde, and, especially, Richard Pynson.

Where Walsingham represents British and Anglo-Saxon saints as intercessors for England—that is, as figures for a community at the scale of the nation or realm—these vernacular texts present them as figures for communities at a variety of scales, conceptualized in multiple ways. A central thesis of this book is that Middle English legends of native saints served as an important narrative forum for exploring competing forms of secular and religious community at local, national, and supranational scales: the monastery, the city, and local devotional groups; the nation and the realm; European Christendom and, at the end of the fifteenth century, a world that was suddenly expanding across the Atlantic.[3] These forms of community may be distinguished from one another by temporal as well as geographical scale. Some are experienced or produced through fixed units of time: the day, the week, the year, or the reign; some are defined at a larger historical scale by rupture and periodization, as in Walsingham's representation of English national community; and still others are defined as transhistorical, at a limitless temporal scale. The different kinds of community imagined by native saints' Lives partly reflect the diversity of institutions and audiences responsible for their production, circulation, and reception, which included powerful Benedictine monasteries seeking to advertise their place in English history, nunneries trying to reestablish their authority in the wake of censure, royal and aristocratic patrons promoting their religiosity, and urban textual communities eager for vernacular religious literature, among others.

This book seeks to identify and understand this preoccupation with forms of community in fifteenth-century Lives of English saints as a literary phenomenon. While it necessarily attends to the works' several historical contexts, and while it is motivated in part by a historical question about how religious identity came to be understood as relevant to national identity, the main project of this study is to analyze how, as a group, these literary works explore the nature and experience of different kinds of community. They ask, for example, whether local, national, and supranational devotional communities can be understood through the spatial logic of a graduated scale, or whether they might be better understood as occupying a conceptual scale organized by level of particularity or universality. They explore whether such differences in scale—spatial, temporal, or conceptual—help to structure, or further complicate, the relationships between incommensurable forms of community. And they investigate how the scale of some communities allows them to be defined in terms of contact or intimacy, and how the scale of others demands an acknowledgment of difference. In their broadest terms, that is, they are interested in how communities might be understood in terms of heterogeneity, sameness, or a constitutive paradox of difference and relation that Jean-Luc Nancy has called "being-in-common."[4]

In exploring these questions, English saints' Lives take advantage of a signature capability of literary form, whether on the level of line, stanza, or work: its own capacity to draw attention to and play with scale—to contract or dilate, to emphasize proximity or distance, to specify or generalize. A second key argument of this book is that questions about the scale of community and the relationship between communities at different scales are addressed in this corpus through experimental and heterogeneous literary forms. Middle English Lives of England's saints are written in a dizzying array of verse and prose types. There are examples of "epic" legends in Latinate and literary verse, such as Lydgate's two "double" Lives, the *Life of Sts. Alban and Amphibalus* and the *Life of Sts. Edmund and Fremund*. Other long legends—the *Life of St. Edith* and the *Life of St. Audrey*, both conspicuous for their interest in regnal history—are written in tetrameter quatrains employed elsewhere for secular historiography. The genre-bending tail-rhyme *Life of John of Bridlington*, if lackluster as a story, is notable as an experiment in literary form, as is Audelay's St. Wenefred carol. The prose legends of the mid-fifteenth century are differently inventive: the Lives of native saints added to the *Gilte Legende* are rare examples of "de-versification," that is, translations of earlier verse legends into the medium of prose, while the prose *Life of St. Etheldreda* in Oxford, Corpus Christi College MS 120, divides the legend into chapters and so restructures the familiar conversion plot (in this case, the ever-holy Etheldreda's quest to change her social status from a royal lay-woman to a humble abbess) in ways that anticipate the incremental narratives of character development of later prose fiction.

This formal variety accounts for the fact that most of these texts have appeared one-off, eccentric. For all the critical dismissal of literary taxonomies, we still often rely on formal similarity to group texts and recognize them as part of a consequential literary phenomenon.[5] Lacking a shared form or shared model of community, fifteenth-century Lives of native saints have been read almost exclusively in terms of their local institutional significance, and they have never been studied together. Read as a group, however, their formal heterogeneity registers and addresses the challenge presented in the fifteenth century by the shifting relationships between differently scaled communities and overlapping jurisdictions.[6] While their common interest in native saints and their formal variety may at first seem to point in opposite directions—the first a warrant for considering them as a group and the second a caution or limit to doing so—it is in the conjunction of the two that we can recognize this cultural work.

These texts, then, demand an approach to form that finds analytical purchase in variety rather than similarity. They do not constitute a genre or sub-genre, or really even a corpus or tradition, as those categories are usually defined. My chapters track the relationships between the formal qualities of particular texts and the ideas and forms of community they explore, but my argument rests on the multiple forms these meditations take and the cumulative evidence they provide that literary form was a useful resource for thinking about the relationships between communities at different scales. Because this argument inheres in formal variety, it requires that I analyze a relatively large sample of texts.[7] I offer it as a case study for an approach that understands formal variety across a set of texts to map and develop available conceptual models for a given cultural concern, an approach that may be productively extended to other aspects of narrative and expressive culture in the Middle Ages and in other historical periods. In this way, this study of Middle English Lives of native saints may serve as a model for a synchronic approach to other networks of literary forms.

This book thus defines an archive of Middle English Lives of English saints and studies them at the intersection of their conceptual and formal axes. As a work of cultural history, it traces the way that native saints' Lives recognize, disaggregate, and organize the overlapping jurisdictions in medieval England, where civic, royal, ecclesiastical, and monastic jurisdictions were continually contested and remapped. It argues that vernacular legends of England's saints serve to raise and explore questions about how different forms of community—regional, national, and supernatural; religious and secular; intimate and imagined—relate to one another. At the same time, it also approaches these texts as a body of "vernacular theory": that is, as explorations, on the level of form as well as subject, of the categories and relations through which various forms of community were understood, above all different kinds of spatial, temporal, and conceptual scale. As I explain below, to understand the conceptual work of literary form, I borrow an analytical description from political theory, the political theorist Saskia Sassen's account of the complex system of medieval jurisdictions. But I do not argue that the forms of community that structured late medieval England or the historical pressures on them had a determinative effect on the texts in this study, nor that they should be read primarily as responses to tensions between political, religious, or social institutions. There is rather a correspondence, a loose relation, between social practice and structures of thought. Without making literary culture epiphenomenal to historical crisis or change, we can recognize that it shares conceptual structures with medieval social systems and engages on various levels with issues of topical concern.

Taking this as a working assumption, in the following pages I outline some of the central conceptual categories explored in the Lives of English saints in relation to some of the historical phenomena with which they converge. I begin with three linked frameworks for thinking about forms of community in the late Middle Ages in terms of scale: the complex system of jurisdictions and the changing spatial scale of some important kinds of community in the fifteenth century; the various kinds of time produced by, or affiliated with, different forms of community; and the body as a scalable metaphor for communities of different kinds. I then expand upon the approach to literary form I have just introduced. In the final section, I return to a historical register and offer an overview of the elite political promotion of England's saints, as well as some of the definitions of England as a realm, a nation, and a religious community it helped to foster, not as a context for or impetus to the composition of Middle English Lives of English saints, but as a phenomenon parallel to them.

Jurisdiction and Geographical Scale

The vernacular Lives of English saints studied here take up questions about scale that refract marked shifts in both the boundaries and definition of English polity in the fifteenth century. The realm expanded dramatically under Henry V, but his early death jeopardized both newly acquired and long-established French territories. When Henry VI, at last old enough to rule, was crowned in Paris, English commitment to Henry V's legacy had been an open question on practical and political grounds for decades, and the realm shrank as dramatically as it had expanded. Within the archipelago, Owain Glyndwyr's Welsh revolt was quashed early in the century, but political crises at home and the war with France made it impossible to enforce English overlordship in Ireland, which in practice retracted to the Pale. Such vicissitudes of territorial expansion and contraction, the most obvious sources of shifts in the spatial scale of English community in the late Middle Ages, ramified in significance: with the progressive loss of its Continental territories across the fifteenth century, England became, in effect, an island, with political boundaries more coextensive with geographical ones than ever before.[8] The effect of these losses was compounded by the aggregation of European kingdoms, by which Spain and France grew to more or less the scale they now have as modern states. Its own scale inevitably correlative of that of other polities, England contracted to its insular borders in the same period that its European neighbors scaled up. Many of the literary texts central to this study—works by Audelay, Bokenham, and Lydgate, as well as the Wilton Lives of Edith and Etheldreda and the prose Lives of English saints translated from the

SEL—were composed during the crucial period for this shift, from the 1420s to the 1450s.

New World discovery at the end of the century further altered the spatial frame in which English audiences might think about the geographical scale of the communities they inhabited. It is in this context that I read Hatfield's *Lyf of Saynt Ursula*, which offers obsessively alliterative lists of her companions, naming in turn the virgins, kings, and bishops in her company, and in this way presenting the saint's company in terms of atomized and aggregated political and religious communities. The poem offers a striking parallel to, and perhaps meditation on, the paradoxical diminishment and proliferation of discrete places in the wake of New World discoveries: Columbus had, roughly ten years before its composition, named the Caribbean archipelago that we still know as the Virgin Islands in honor of the Ursuline legend. Hatfield's legend, like the Lives of England's saints written in the first half of the fifteenth century, provides intriguing evidence that the expansion of the literary system itself in this period—including an emerging differentiation of literary and nonliterary texts and attendant developments in style and genre, the energetic translation of religious and secular texts into English, and the massive production of prose texts—may be correlative of the re-scaling of medieval communities in the context of England's diminished borders and its expanding global surround.

It is perhaps worth pausing here to note that the cultural products of the Middle Ages, perhaps especially its narrative forms, may be of particular interest to us now, in a period of transition from an age in which the nation was taken to be the normative scale of community to an imagined future in which forms of identity and affiliation are increasingly multiple or heterogeneous. Like fifteenth-century writers, moved to think about the nature of community because of the re-scaling of political and religious groupings in their own day, modern theoretical interest in scale is inspired by epochal shifts in forms of community in a "postnational" and global frame.[9]

In the late Middle Ages, as now, changing definitions and practices may have been more important than shifts in territorial boundaries. Of particular relevance to some of the material in this study is the definition of a principal or general "nation" formulated at the councils of Pisa and Constance in the context of efforts to resolve the papal Schism. At Pisa, a new voting procedure was adopted in which voting was done by "nation," rather than by individual delegates.[10] Although this change seems to have met no significant opposition at first, it became a source of conflict at the Council of Constance: in the debate over whether England or Aragon should be recognized as the fourth voting nation after France, Germany, and Italy, French delegates objected to recognizing England as a "principal" nation on the grounds that it comprised only itself and a small Irish delegation, whereas the other "nations" represented larger and more diverse political communities.[11] Additional evidence from the administration of Pope Benedict VII was adduced: for example, his *Vas electionis*—essentially a tax policy—had divided the Christian west into four regions, with England subsumed under the German nation, and in the *Statuimus*—an administrative structure imposed on the Benedictine order—England was accorded only one province of thirty-six.[12] In this debate, the administrative and territorial scale of England relative to the other "principal" nations was precisely the issue: speaking for the French, Jean Campan argued that since England was not equal even to a quarter of France, it could not possibly represent a fourth or fifth of Christendom. The English delegation countered with their own numbers, offering the dimensions of the island as evidence that it more than matched the territorial extension of France.[13]

Alongside physical size, the English case rested on political and linguistic diversity: England, so the argument went, comprised eight nations—the three nations of the British Isles, plus four Irish nations, along with the Isle of Man and more than sixty additional islands—where five distinctive languages were spoken, the latter a new and distinctive criterion that was crucial to the English case.[14] In a long view, we can recognize this argument as both nostalgic, insofar as it identifies England with an earlier period of Norman colonization of Celtic nations, and proleptic, insofar as it anticipates later consolidations of "Great Britain." But it is also significant in its own right as a definition of the nation predicated on political, ethnic, and linguistic heterogeneity: the "nation" of early fifteenth-century church councils is defined not by the self-identity of a community, but by its capaciousness.

This definition has implications for how differently scaled communities are related. It resists an understanding of the local as either a synecdoche for the nation (that is, as a part that can represent the whole) or as a hyponym to it (that is, as a more specific instance of a general category).[15] From later forms of nationalism, we may expect the local to be embedded in the national through one of these figural-conceptual structures, both of which define relationships between smaller and larger forms of community by using extension or territorial scale to produce a graduated order. In contrast, the definition of "nation" developed at Constance to establish England's status identifies it as *qualitatively* different from smaller communities, including those that it encompasses.

Many of the saints' Lives under discussion here are as interested—often more interested—in communities at smaller and larger scales than "England," however defined. The forms of community addressed by this corpus are genuinely variable, not oriented toward or by the nation as a paradigmatic form of community. Indeed, they can serve to remind us that the nation was not the normative scale of community in this period, and that contemporary efforts to produce it as such, whether in the context of church councils or within English political culture, were often met with resistance. Some individual texts considered here do re-scale a religious or secular community as national: the Wilton *Life of St. Edith*, for example, reframes a saint's life with national historiography in order to construct a dynamic relation between an intimately scaled community of women religious and England as a secular political community. But the nation is only one framework for identity and belonging during this period; it does not possess the indexical status it later comes to have, nor are the texts discussed here best understood as evidence of its emergence as a "master normativity."[16] The scale of this study is "English saints" because medieval writers and audiences across the landscape of English narrative culture turned to the legends of local or native saints to explore some of the several forms of community in which they participated. But my argument is that these narratives were used to map relationships between *various* forms of community in a system not yet oriented by a single paradigmatic or normative communal identification.

Middle English Lives of native saints, then, are preoccupied both with shifts in the scale of various communities, including the nation, and the correspondingly shifting relationships between them. My approach is informed especially by David Wallace's *Premodern Places*, which analyzes different places and, especially, spatial relations, in the premodern period.[17] This project seeks to extend what I take to be a central insight of Wallace's work: that the multiple temporalities and multiple spatial paradigms that we find in medieval texts are ultimately ways of representing multiple forms of community, which structure and are structured by specific kinds of space and time. The Middle Ages are not the only period in which multiple forms of community coexist, of course—it is no doubt true of any period—but such complexity does have a special visibility and purchase in a premodern context, before the nation organizes, if never fully overwhelms, many other forms of community.

Temporalities

Like medieval jurisdictions, medieval temporal paradigms coexisted and overlapped. Sometimes elided into a simple binary of secular time and sacred timelessness, there are in fact many kinds of secular temporality and many forms of sacred atemporality.[18] These are partly a facet and partly an effect of overlapping jurisdictions and forms of community. Different communities are formed by, or are structured in relation to, different kinds of temporality: liturgical time, seasonal time, generational time, regnal time, and so on. It is worth noting that many of these different kinds of time can be distinguished from one another, and thus also coordinated with one another, in terms of temporal scale. A devotional community defined, say, by its weekly Friday pilgrimages to the Shrewsbury shrine of St. Wenefred may overlap substantially—but not fully—with a parish community defined by an annual liturgical calendar, as well as with an urban community defined by a calendar of civic ritual or other local rhythms of secular time. At the same time, if their city saint is celebrated as a patron of English victory at Agincourt, as Wenefred was, members of that devotional community may also come to see themselves as participants in a national community defined through a diachronic royal history. As our own experience of time and community teaches us, in belonging to different communities (defined by work, sex, age, familial and social affiliations), one occupies multiple times (e.g., the academic calendar, familial and national calendars, daily and age-related "body clocks").[19]

   As the examples here remind us, saints themselves variously figure different times. They may be associated with an arrested temporality; a miraculous synchronicity with other persons, phenomena, or times; or the intersection between divine timelessness and quotidian or chronological time. The texts that celebrate them reflect this variety and sometimes develop it as a formal principle. Jacques Le Goff has recently reminded us that *Legenda Aurea*—the ur-text for Middle English legendaries—comprises three primary forms of time: the cyclical time of the liturgy (the temporale), what he identifies as a "linear" temporality in the Lives of the saints (the sanctorale), and the teleological temporality of the eschaton.[20] It models this complex system of times through the formal technology of the legendary. In Chapter 1, I use the *SEL* to show how two of the legendary's defining formal features—its multipart narrative structure and its calendrical ordering—work to coordinate the complex relationships between different communities through the category of time.

The *SEL*'s exploration of community and temporality can help us understand later developments in the cults of native saints and literary works that respond to them. The fifteenth century witnessed new efforts to align local and national temporalities, and especially secular and liturgical ones, by incorporating native saints into the English liturgical calendar. In 1416, Archbishop Chichele mandated devotion to St. Chad (March 2), St. David (March 1), and St. Wenefred (November 3), as well as observation of John of Beverley's feast (May 5) and his Translation (October 25).[21] These saints had conspicuous political currency as objects of royal devotion, and liturgical celebration of their feasts works to sacralize national history and nationalize liturgical time. So, for example, the victory at Agincourt fell on the feast of St. John of Beverley's Translation: to elevate the feast was not only to claim the saint's endorsement of—even participation in—the military campaign, but also to inscribe in liturgical time a signal moment in English history.

A striking example of this project may be found in the Beaufort Hours, whose calendar, which features many English saints, is also a forum for secular history. Important political events are added in marginal notes to the calendar, which includes the feast days newly added to the Sarum rite—Sts. Chad, David, John of Beverley, and Wenefred—as well as saints with well-established national cults, such as Sts. Etheldreda, Edward the Confessor, King Edmund, Cuthbert, and Oswald, and relatively minor or local saints such as Erkenwald, Cuthburge, Frideswide, and Edith.[22] The June calendar, for example, is annotated with entries for the battles at Stoke Field, a final skirmish in the Lancastrian-Yorkist conflict (1487), and at Blackheath, a Cornish uprising against excessive taxation (1497). Just as sacred time comes to host national history through the addition of native saints to the English liturgy, the Beaufort Hours grants national history the achronological status of the sacred, recording events not by year, but by calendar date, on which they are presumably to be remembered annually. Here we see an especially deliberate instance of the construction of a "time of origins," as recent events are located—on the manuscript page—in liturgical timelessness.

In broader terms, Middle English Lives of English saints may help us recognize and understand a significant shift between premodern and modern conceptualizations of the secular, a category I take up especially in Chapters 3 and 6. Medieval Christians understood the secular primarily as a category of time, whereas its stronger association today is with places, both particular institutions such as the university and more abstract spaces like the state or public. An understanding of the secular as a category of time may make possible, even contribute to, the complex system of overlapping jurisdictions that structured medieval social forms. A specific place might host a range of religious and secular communities that correlate with different temporal orders: say, an urban community, organized in part by the mayoral year and in part by regnal time or history, which overlaps with a devotional community defined by local pilgrimage as well as by its relation to a mythic Christian past. Native saints' Lives help us to see how shifting jurisdictions, which remapped differences between the secular and sacred spatially rather than temporally, contribute to the incipient shift from the medieval identification of the secular with the particular, historical, and contingent, toward a modern idea of the secular as "universal"—a massive change that has not yet been fully addressed in recent work on the history or concept of the secular.

Bodies, Embodiment, and Corporate Metaphors

The body plays a particularly important role in saints' Lives and in the ideas of community they instantiate. The saint's body, sometimes explicitly and sometimes implicitly, represents an earthly community. It may do so in ritual practice, as an object of veneration that links diverse people in a shared devotional project, or it may do so symbolically, as the location of sacrifice or sacrality with import for a larger community on whose behalf the saint is understood to die or who are the beneficiaries of his or her exceptional virtue. Saints' Lives are stories in which a body that miraculously retains its capacity to serve as a vehicle for a person's singular agency, even after death, also serves miraculously as a vessel for group identity—often an earthly corporate identity that is understood to transcend the individual lives of its members. At the same time, saints are understood to participate in the communion of saints, and the saint's body is also metonymic of this more universal corporate identity.

The capacity to embody a community in this way is correlative of the saint's miraculous physical integrity and posthumous agency: the fiction of a community as a body likewise extends identity in time, past the lifetimes of individual members, by substituting for their mortal bodies an alternative corporate identity that precedes and perdures beyond any human life. But it also derives from the widespread use of corporate metaphors to conceptualize communities. While the body is often imagined as a bounded space—the limit of individual identity—it is also a remarkably elastic and capacious figure that readily accommodates communities at different scales, such as the *corpus mysticum ecclesia* or the body politic. The saint's body, with its special power to represent and sacralize various forms of community, has an especially tractable scale. In Henry Bradshaw's *Life of St. Werburge*, the saint figures the continuous identity of both a region, Mercia, and England, while Lydgate's St. Edmund symbolically embodies both the abbey to which he gives his name and England, which is sanctified by his death as a far larger religious community. In these works, the saint's body, a figure for two differently scaled forms of community, secures the relationship between them.

While any saint—or indeed any fragment of a saint's body—could figure numinous wholeness, the enduring physical integrity of the saint's body was, from at least William of Malmesbury onward, considered a special feature of English sanctity.[23] Some legends studied here, such as Lydgate's *Life of Sts. Edmund and Fremund,* adopt this trope in a way broadly consonant with the main line of the tradition, while others deconstruct it for a far less monolithic representation of community. As I argue in Chapter 2, the Wilton *Life of St. Edith* does this with special force by exposing how the symbolic capacity of the saint's body depends on its absolute difference from the phenomena of embodiment—that is, from bodily experiences defined by, among other things, vulnerability to pain and mortality. The legend is concerned precisely with the relationship between the saint's symbolic body—especially the symbolic morphology of the body imagined as an enclosed space—and what I will call her phenomenal body, a body defined by its physical circumstances, including forms of physical and affective intimacy that depend on the material body and the experiences of illness and death to which it is subject.

As the Edith legend reminds us, the body lacks both the material and definitional stasis that are often imputed to it to facilitate its use as an ideological and analytical category. The idea of the body as a natural, continuous, and bounded locus of identity has, of course, been challenged on theoretical and other grounds.[24] The Edith legend provides an extraordinary elaboration of this challenge by representing the body's very form as differently constituted by the several communities it inhabits: its alternating appearances as corrupt and incorrupt figure differences between the community of women at Wilton Abbey and the community of the realm. The legend suggests that the fantasy of the body's material stasis is belied, among other things, by the way in which its nature, borders, and constituent parts are produced in reciprocal relation to the specific communities in which it participates. The fiction of the body as bounded and unified—and so as the material basis for a single and singular identity—is challenged by a hagiographic theory of community that acknowledges the heterogeneous communities to which a person belongs and thus also recognizes a corresponding heterogeneity of bodily experience and morphology, insofar as these are informed by different social identities.[25] The individual body, that is, may be recognized as a spatial metaphor through which a person's variable identities and experiences of embodiment, which are contingent on the different communities they inhabit, are presented as a single, coherent, and stable identity.

This study therefore explores narrative representations of the body, including the singular body of the saint, as a species of personification. Like other kinds of personification, the narrative figure of the body gives coherence to experience by attributing a definite physical form to a dynamic identity, whether an individual person or a group of people represented as such by an explicit or implicit corporate metaphor. The difference between these, then, is a question of scale. Indeed, the two kinds of figurative bodies, collective and singular, reinforce one another: the fiction of a unified body politic, for example, depends on the fantasy that each of its constituent members has a single bounded identity. It requires forgetting that the members of the body politic also participate in other communities, which cannot be organized through the imaginary contours of a single (metaphorical) body, and that different forms of community each code the body and its relation to others in distinctive ways. The basic conceptual fulcrum linking the saint's body to forms of community is parsed with particular force in the Life of St. Ursula and the 11,000 Virgins, the story of a British princess and the company of virgins that serves as her collective avatar. In Chapter 1, I lay the groundwork for reading the fifteenth-century materials by analyzing the Ursula legend in the SEL as a kind of vernacular theory of the shifts of scale facilitated by corporate metaphors of identity.

Literary Form as Complex System

To think about communities in terms of the scalable categories of jurisdiction, time, and the body, Middle English native saints' Lives employ a remarkable variety of literary forms, as I noted earlier. Form is not only the medium for thematic articulation of these concerns but also itself an experimental model for exploring them. It works to this end at every level: the line, the individual legend, and the legendary and other large-scale forms. An assumption of this study is that these texts constitute a formal system or network—that is, a set of texts that uses form variably to explore related conceptual and cultural concerns: in this case, the scale and definition of different kinds of community and their relation to other kinds of community.

In its interest in formal variety rather than similarity, my approach departs from those that take form primarily as a mark of genre—that is, as a set of features that pulls texts toward each other through a kind of centripetal force, an approach that cannot account for this corpus. An understanding of genre that privileges identifiable features shared by a group of works has been challenged on theoretical grounds, most influentially in Derrida's "Law of Genre."[26] For Derrida, systems of classification are deconstructed by the nature of the affiliations on which they are predicated: the features that identify items as participating in a genre—the use of a particular stanza form, for example, or the labeling of a nineteenth-century prose narrative as "a novel"—must be external to the genre itself, he argues, because as deictic markers *designating* the affiliation they cannot also be considered the substance of the affiliation. Formal similarities and other marks of genre, that is, *constitute* relationships between texts that are otherwise different: in a deconstructive analysis, they produce categories that have no necessary purchase on the individual items assigned to them.

Literary criticism of the last several generations has developed a view of genre that is corollary to Derrida's, one that emphasizes that genres are so porous, and individual texts so hybrid, that it is a fool's errand to assign texts to genres or to use genres to define literary traditions or trace literary histories. Texts rarely reside fully within a single genre, and definitions of genre are often either too narrow, arbitrarily excluding texts that may be usefully affiliated with the other works they embrace, or so broad that they lose their analytical purchase. It is often assumed, and sometimes claimed, that genre is an especially problematic category of analysis and dubious basis for literary

history in the case of medieval literature because the period lacked an ancillary study of literary texts that identified genres or established expectations
about generic conventions or decorum for their first audiences.

It is, however, only one kind of system, a taxonomy or *closed* system of
literary form, that is challenged on these theoretical and historical grounds,
not a literary system per se, much less the role of form or formal convention
in any such system. Complex-systems theory suggests a way to account for
the *centrifugal* force of form, the way that genres and forms continually mix
with others and migrate to new themes and new audiences, establishing affiliations with other literary conventions and textual traditions.[27] A fundamental principle of systems theory is to refuse to isolate or privilege a single
category of phenomena and instead recognize relationships between phenomena different in kind, scale, and even ontological status. Literary texts
and their forms are cultural products that exist in a complicated network that
includes not only other forms (literary and otherwise) but phenomena of
many kinds: conceptual and ideological (ideas of authorship, political ideolo-
gies, systems of religious symbolism); historical, social, and biographical (the
life circumstances, abilities, and projects of a particular author; natural or
political events; forms of social engagement); cultural and literary (developments in other arts, institutional location of composition, availability and
prestige of particular texts and traditions, the status of a language in relation
to other available vernacular and cosmopolitan languages); and material (the
labor of writing, material conditions of circulation, reception and preservation of certain classes of texts, available media). Literary form is, to borrow
the now-familiar terms of Bruno Latour's "Actor Network Theory," a category
of actant that affects and is affected by other actants in the system.

From this perspective, we can recognize a text's overt formal affiliations
or its formal "hybridity" as a function of a complex system in which formal
features and their significance shape and are shaped by a variety of literary,
social, ideational, and material concerns. The complexity produced by a
system with so many changeable elements, which are ceaselessly combined
and recombined in dynamic relation to one another, accounts for the centrifugal quality of form or genre. Rather than evidence *against* the value of
a system-level account of any kind, the variety of literary forms that characterize a textual tradition in any given historical moment—approached either synchronically or diachronically—can be read as a map of conceptual
and expressive possibilities available for addressing some important cultural concerns.

My approach to literary form as a complex system borrows especially from Sassen's account of the overlapping jurisdictions characteristic of Western Europe before the nation acquired normative or indexical status. Sassen's analysis distinguishes between "capabilities" and "logics of organization": the capabilities of any given component in a complex system often persist even when there is significant alteration to the logics of organization in which it was originally developed. Indeed, at times they make such alteration possible. Different literary forms develop different "capabilities" that derive in part from their aural or visual qualities (e.g., the association and differentiation they make possible through repetition or patterning, their brevity or dilation, or their relationship to other expressive forms such as music or visual art), in part from their distinctive representational strategies (e.g., the level of realism or abstraction they employ, their signature chronotope, the kind and density of imagery or figurative language they employ), and in part from cultural or social factors (e.g., their characteristic linguistic registers, their relationship to other textual traditions, or their affiliation with particular audiences or institutions). Some of these capabilities may be more or less immediately related to some aspect of social praxis contemporary to the form's earliest or most determinative articulation, but they nevertheless persist beyond their immediate historical function through what Sassen calls "path dependency," that is, structures or expectations that keep them current. As elements in a complex system, they are in any case subject to ongoing change since they are shaped, and continually reshaped, by their relationship to many different kinds of phenomena.[28] For this reason, a formal feature developed in one context might work to very different ends in another: so, for example, while Lydgate's aureate style signals the Latinity and hence the linguistic remove characteristic of monastic communities, as I argue in Chapter 5, it is repurposed as a mark of interiority by Lydgate's late successor, Lawrence Wade, in his *Life of Thomas Becket*, as I show in Chapter 6.

Among other things, reading the Lives of English saints across their formal variety underscores that there is no direct correlation between literary forms and forms of community, and especially no analogy between these based on the category of scale. Small-scale forms, that is, are not necessarily used to represent communities at smaller scales, nor are the "epic" qualities of Lydgate's *Life of Sts. Alban and Amphibalus* or Wade's *Life of Thomas Becket* best understood in terms of their interest in England as a nation.[29] Again, because form is a concern on the level of the line, the stanza, the work, and/ or the collection, and because form is a social institution that connects a text

to other texts, as well as to audiences and institutions, no one feature is determinative. Nor are the capabilities of a given form fixed: although I adduce a
topical significance for some forms—aureate stylistics, for example—I understand their use and meaning, like that of all formal features, to be a function of the complex cultural system in which they participate.

My approach is in this regard different from the kinds of historicist for-
malisms that have been so generative in the last several decades. Unlike Fred-
ric Jameson, and a rich vein of medieval criticism that adopts his theory of
form, I do not understand literary forms as lasting instantiations of historically specific formations, constituting a special kind of "archive." Understood
instead as an element in a complex cultural system, with various capabilities
that derive partly from its own representational technologies and partly from
the social institutions and textual traditions with which it is affiliated, form
remains crucial to historical analysis, but not as the calcification of an ideological crisis. By looking at a corpus of texts as a formal system, we can recognize that the use and meaning of specific prosodic, narrative, and stylistic
features vary both over time and within a given historical moment, and they
can be read as explorations—not just resolutions—of cultural and social
concerns.

One advantage of this approach to form is that it avoids reading literature
as "symptomatic" of a more consequential political or social phenomenon. I
have already traced some of the general historical circumstances that made
the legends of England's saints an important fifteenth-century textual tradition, and I offer a more extended account in the pages ahead. But one implication of a systems-theory approach is that such circumstances must be
recognized as only one kind of phenomenon among many others that shape
the production of any particular text or set of texts. Such an approach axiom-
atically resists a neatly linear literary history or narrative of development.
While some texts, such as Lydgate's aureate legends, influence later ones, others, such as the Wilton Lives, do not. And while some texts suggest a response to particular historical circumstances, they also respond to earlier
texts and repeat established narratives, or rely on familiar conceptualizations
of community or temporality, or borrow literary forms from earlier generations: they are subject, that is, to assorted forms of "path dependency," which
produce uneven effects and significant variation. Although the chapters of
this study proceed roughly in the order in which the texts under consideration were written, they present them not as a tradition defined by chrono-

logical development but as an array of texts and formal possibilities within a historical moment that stretches from 1400 to 1525.

Saints for Kings

Partly to mute the explanatory force it might otherwise seem to have, I have left to the last part of this Introduction a discussion of the royal promotion of English saints, which was sometimes a direct and sometimes an indirect impetus to the literary phenomenon traced in this study. Lydgate's *Life of Sts. Edmund and Fremund*, for example, is presented as a memorial to Henry VI's visit to Bury St. Edmunds, while Audelay's St. Wenefred carol notably—perhaps strategically—omits reference to Henry V's celebrated pilgrimage to her shrine. In both cases, the literary text—which can plausibly be understood as the product of political circumstance following the logic of historicist causality—may be better understood as an alternative, or parallel, exploration of how England's saints might provide a forum for thinking about the nature and scale of different forms of community. Here I trace Lancastrian devotion to native saints not so much as background to the discussion of literary texts that follows, but as another important arena in which England's saints were used to think about community at a particular scale, the scale of the realm or nation, and thus as part of a broader inquiry, in which literary culture also participated, into the nature of community.

Royal interest in English saints predates the fifteenth century, and the Lancastrians were inspired in no small part by Richard II's careful cultivation of his affiliation with some native saints, especially St. Edmund, king and martyr, and Edward the Confessor, with whom he is depicted on the Wilton diptych.[30] As Nigel Saul notes, Richard's identification with Edward the Confessor was especially pronounced: Richard impaled his arms with those of the saint according to the iconographic template for a married couple.[31] Lancastrian kings diluted the claim implicit in this affiliation by multiplying the English saints associated with the crown, giving special attention to saints with popular regional cults such as John of Bridlington and St. Wenefred. Though not unprecedented, Lancastrian support for these local cults transformed them into English ones, an appropriation that sometimes met with resistance from more proximate communities and in this way provoked renewed local devotion or vernacular literary production.

Henry IV was especially keen to affiliate himself with local saints in regions where his political support was tenuous. In some cases, he adopted
saints with established royal cults, such as that of John of Beverley, who had
long been identified by English kings as the saintly patron of their claim to
sovereignty over Scotland.[32] Under Henry IV, the cult was reoriented, however, to support the Lancastrian claim to the English crown: a legend circulated that holy oil issued from the saint's tomb for sixty-one days after
Bolingbroke landed at Ravenspur. In 1408 the prince made a pilgrimage to
Beverley, perhaps in response to the growing cult of Archbishop Richard
Scrope, who had been executed for treason in 1405: it was certainly a propi-
tious moment for the display of Lancastrian devotion to another bishop of
York.[33] The king's devotion—presumably accepted by the saint—is a quiet assertion of Lancastrian political authority over the region; at the same time, it
affiliates the sovereign and his subjects through their shared obeisance to the
saint.[34] Both modes of Lancastrian sovereignty, patronal and lateral, cultivated through the king's devotion to John of Beverley were advanced when
Agincourt was won on October 25, the saint's feast. Again, the saint's tomb
was said to have run that day with oil or, as Walsingham has it, with blood.

Lancastrian kings were also on the vanguard of the new cult of John of
Bridlington, a fourteenth-century prior of a venerable Augustinian house on
the North Sea coast and the last English person canonized before the Reformation.[35] Henry IV actively promoted John's sanctification, sending a Bridlington canon to Rome to advance the case in what proved to be an
extraordinarily efficient process: St. John was canonized in 1401, only twenty-
odd years after his death in 1379.[36] Henry IV then supported the construction
of the shrine to which the saint was translated in 1404, and he placed his son
under the protection of the saint, an affiliation that Henry V himself maintained as king.[37] Jonathan Hughes suggests that Lancastrian devotion to John
of Bridlington, like that to St. John of Beverley, was calculated to draw off
some of the enthusiasm for the nascent cult of Scrope. It may have served
more generally, as Susan Wilson suggests, as an appeal to powerful northern
aristocrats, with whom the king was often in conflict.[38] But it also reflected
long-standing devotion: Henry IV had made an offering at St. John's shrine as
early as 1391, as Bridlington emerged as an important object of local and national pilgrimage.[39] In the case of St. John, the royal cult was importantly
complemented by—and drew from—a local cult, a glimpse of which is provided by the *Book of Margery Kempe*: Margery took St. John's confessor as her
own, surely intended as a mark of her own exceptional status, but also an

index of the kind of regional identification that made such saints useful to Lancastrian kings.

No saint was more useful to them than St. Wenefred, a Welsh saint who, according to her legend, was miraculously resurrected after being decapitated by a spurned suitor. Wenefred was celebrated both at Holywell in Flintshire, Wales, the wellspring that was believed to have sprung up miraculously at the site of violence, and at Shrewsbury Abbey, which claimed her relics. Like John of Beverley, Wenefred had enjoyed the devotion of earlier English kings: Richard I had made a pilgrimage to Holywell in 1189, and Edward III had promoted the cult.[40] Richard II, regularly in Chester toward the end of his reign, held parliament at Shrewsbury in 1398, and he visited Holywell then as well.[41] He must have visited Wenefred's new shrine in Shrewsbury Abbey when he was received there on this occasion.[42]

While Shrewsbury was familiar and friendly territory to Richard II, it was marked in the early years of Henry IV's reign by the growing strength of the Glyndwr rebellion and then the Percy revolt.[43] Lancastrian interest in Wenefred may originate in the context of these threats. In Chapter 3, I present new evidence from Osbern Bokenham's *Life of St. Wenefred* that Henry IV commissioned a chapel at Holywell.[44] Although the chapel is otherwise unattested, the reference accords with documented Lancastrian interest in the cult, as is witnessed, for example, by an image of St. Wenefred in one of the windows of the church that Henry IV endowed at the site of the battle of Shrewsbury.[45] Holywell too would have been a worthwhile location at which to assert royal presence and propitiate local communities: Flintshire had been under Henry Percy's jurisdiction as justiciar and it had joined him in revolt.[46] Lancastrian devotion to Wenefred, then, like that to other regional saints, seems to have begun as an effort to override local opposition. An arena of military conflict and political subjection was re-coded as a sacred landscape where sovereign and local subjects were joined in devotion.

The vast historical gulf that separates the legendary Wenefred, who was believed to have lived in the seventh century, and John of Bridlington, a bona fide fourteenth-century prior, has a kind of geographical complement in the distance between their shrines, on opposite sides of Britain. But they were carefully linked in a thanksgiving pilgrimage that Henry V performed after Agincourt, in which he traveled to St. Wenefred's shrine at Shrewsbury, and from there on foot some fifty miles to Holywell, then across the width of Britain to Bridlington and Beverley.[47] The pilgrimage to Holywell provided an opportunity to acknowledge Welsh participation in the French campaigns,[48] and perhaps, in recalling Henry IV's devotions and their political context, to redefine yet again the crown's relationship with North Wales in the wake of Glyndwr's presumed death.[49] But the larger project of the pilgrimage was to identify these local saints—all three credited with the military victory—as participants in a shared project to preserve the English claim to the French throne.

This was an extension of earlier Lancastrian devotion, which placed the king in the same posture or relation to the saint as local communities, asserting his affinity with them as grounds for his sovereignty over them. But in linking several local cults, widely separated geographically, Henry's pilgrimage also fundamentally reoriented them as "English" rather than regional, by interpolating them into a larger abstract idea of national community. At the same time, it grounded the political abstraction of the realm in a concrete geography, as the king traveled to the several shrines that served as the saints' "home."[50] A similar function can be attributed to a second royal pilgrimage in 1421, when Henry V retraced his itinerary from Shrewsbury to Bridlington, this time to drum up support for war taxes and for his new French wife. As a begging tour for his war chest, the second progress claimed regional resources on behalf of England and so advanced the idea of English community rooted in the local cults of native saints.[51] This second pilgrimage, that is, echoed the broader ideological implications of the earlier one, if in a petitionary rather than celebratory mode.

Covering a sizable portion of the realm—from London, northwest to the Welsh marches, then east to the Yorkshire coast—the progress articulated the geographical scale of these cults as national. In doing so, the royal pilgrimages relied on, and developed, some distinctive conceptual capabilities. Most obviously, the re-scaling of local cults as "English" is mediated by the king's piety and especially by his body: his physical presence at each shrine and his movement between them put these formerly regional cults in a spatial relationship to one another through the logic of the body politic. The pilgrimage thus affirmed the ideological force of kingship by asserting the king's body as the mechanism that establishes England as the scale of religious community. That is, it establishes the realm as a paradigmatic spatial organization that governs religious as well as political community. The king's body organizes local cults into a national framework both in its finite material form, through his movement between several local shrines, and in its abstract or notional form, which embraces all these places at once.

Veneration of these saints as English—perhaps primarily as saintly intercessors for English sovereignty—was advanced by high-placed members of the king's retinue, especially those active in the French campaigns.[52] Thomas Beaufort, Duke of Exeter, was on pilgrimage to Bridlington in 1417 when he heard news that the Scots were besieging Roxburgh.[53] William Porter, who campaigned with Henry in France and served as an executor of his will, had images of both St. Wenefred and John of Bridlington included in his deluxe Book of Hours.[54] The most spectacular expressions of devotion are associated with Richard Beauchamp, Earl of Warwick, who had been companion at arms to Henry in his youth and who fought at Shrewsbury and in the Welsh campaigns in 1404 and 1407.[55] His devotion to St. Wenefred and John of Bridlington—which must have inspired or been inspired by the prince's—took extravagant form: his will specified that four gold statues of his own image, each weighing twenty pounds, were to be placed at the shrines of St. Wenefred, St. John of Bridlington, St. Alban, and Thomas of Canterbury.[56] His wife, Isabella Despenser, more modestly left a gown to the statue of St. Wenefred at Holywell.[57] The beautiful chapel built for the earl's tomb at St. Mary's, Warwick—the Beauchamp Chapel—contains windows depicting Sts. Wenefred and John of Bridlington.[58] It is worth noting that Beauchamp, who served as ambassador to the Council of Constance, represents a concrete link between Lancastrian promotion of regional saints and the Constance definition of the nation as a political category defined by the heterogeneous places, people, and languages it contains.

By the middle of the fifteenth century, Sts. John of Bridlington and Wenefred were firmly established as objects of royal devotion, as John of Beverley had long been. Henry VI, recalling Richard II's grant of royal mills to support St. Wenefred's chapel at Holywell, augmented the chaplain's annual income so that daily masses might be said in the saint's honor.[59] Yorkist kings were also devoted to Wenefred, which is unsurprising given that Shrewsbury was an important base of Yorkist support.[60] Edward IV traveled to Holywell and, according to the Welsh poet Tudur Aled, put dirt from the shrine on his crown.[61] In 1465, he too confirmed Richard II's grant to the chaplain there, as did Richard III and Henry VII.[62] Henry V's promotion of the cult of John of Bridlington was also enthusiastically continued by his son and later by Edward IV, who granted exempt status to the priory in 1468 in language similar to that used by Henry V and Henry VI before him.[63] Henry VI spent a week in Beverley in 1448, where he must have made his devotions at the shrine of St. John of Beverley; his progress also took him to the shrine of St. Cuthbert in Durham.[64]

Henry's 1416 pilgrimage sought to redefine regional saints as national ones for his subjects, as well as for his affinity and successors, and to shape an idea of England as a religious community. In the wake of Henry's pilgrimage, any English person's pilgrimage to Wenefred's shrine or to John of Bridlington's might be recognized as devotion to an *English* saint, rather than a Welsh or Yorkshire one. The project of making native saints national—for English people of various statuses—was further advanced by their inclusion in Sarum liturgy: in 1416 shortly after Henry's pilgrimage, as was discussed earlier, Henry Chichele mandated observance of the feasts of St. Wenefred and John of Beverley. Liturgical celebration of these saints—in regions far from their shrines—helped to generalize devotion to these saints as "English." But while communities affiliated with royal power dutifully folded the new feasts into their practice,[65] others responded unevenly to this effort to conscript them as national figures, as witnessed by variations in vernacular textual traditions. Testifying to the success of the Lancastrian promotion of Wenefred as an English saint, a fifteenth-century exemplar of the *SEL* includes a unique verse version of her legend that neglects to identify the saint as Welsh and offers the name of the English king as the single localizing detail.[66] But a late fifteenth-century manuscript of John Mirk's *Festial* shows the limits of this success: localized to Warwickshire, it retains Mirk's original introduction to the St. Wenefred legend, which states explicitly that her feast need not be observed.[67] Mirk had included Wenefred as a local saint, and this copy of the *Festial*, produced well after the inclusion of the saint in the Sarum rite as an obligatory feast, inadvertently refashions her as one.[68] Other manuscripts of the *Festial* register the variable effect of official nationalization of the cult: one preface remarks of her legend that "thow somme knowen it, somme doth not."[69]

Evidence for popular devotion to John of Bridlington is sparse, but this may be attributed to the late date of the cult and the special fervor with which it was destroyed by Cromwell's agents following the participation of Bridlington's last prior, William Wode, in the Northern Rebellion.[70] Devotion to St. John, according to Walsingham, "rested on his humility and his pity for the afflicted" (273), which may account for the enthusiasm of ordinary people for the cult that can be traced in local wills and parish churches across England until the eve of the Dissolution.[71] Such evidence is, in any case, indifferent witness to the effect of Lancastrian promotion of the cult. While John of Bridlington and St. Wenefred were marshaled by English kings as national saints, their cults—like the literary texts studied in this book—speak to varied forms of identification and community.

England as Nation, Realm, and Religious Community

Henry V's pilgrimages made at least two distinctive contributions to the project of fashioning local places into a national geography: they mediated a specifically spatial conceptualization of England, and this spatial conceptualization, in turn, allowed national and religious forms of community to be represented as coextensive. In this way, royal devotion might itself paradoxically dislodge the "realm" as the primary structure for national community: England could be identified as a religious community in addition to, and therefore in place of, its identification with the crown. The relationship between England as a realm, nation, and religious community can serve as a preliminary example of the kind of "jurisdictional heterogeneity" addressed in Lives of native saints.[72]

As we have seen, the relationship between secular polities and their religious analogues was a subject of debate in fifteenth-century church councils, which used the term "nation" to designate communities defined at the intersection of secular and religious jurisdictions. Nor was this the only available understanding of "nation," which had long been a descriptor for ethnic identity (*natio*). The less familiar conceptualization, formulated in the context of ecclesiastical politics, reminds us that the category was not a settled one, that there were competing definitions, and that religious discourses and institutions contributed to theorizing secular political community in the period. The conciliar definition, which differs so importantly from later discourses of nationhood, presents an especially useful challenge to fixed, transhistorical definitions of the "nation" on which objections to discussing medieval political forms under this rubric depend. Far from eliding differences between medieval and modern forms of community, as is sometimes charged, retaining the term "nation" allows us to denaturalize the category in productive ways, as well as to recognize the conceptual capabilities developed in the Middle Ages that contributed to later formations.

The most significant of these was distinguishing the nation from the realm, as Louise Loomis long ago remarked. The English delegation at the Council of Constance argued that not all communities in a nation owe loyalty to one prince, citing Spanish kingdoms that did not recognize the King of Castile as their ruler and French polities—Provence, Dauphiny, Savoy, Burgundy, Lorraine—that were not ruled by the French king.[73] The nation was thus geographically, and therefore categorically, distinct from the realm. Indeed, as the English argument had it, just as the nation comprises areas not subject to a single sovereign, the realm might extend to domains that are not part of the nation. For late medieval England, this was most obviously true of France, but it was also the case for the English king's claim to Ireland and Wales. J. P. Genet notes that the English delegation to Constance was hampered in their claim to be a "nation" precisely by the fact that the king's dominion over these areas did not produce "feelings of consent and homogeneity" that were implied by medieval definitions of the term.[74]

It is worth pausing here to address the terms "England" and "English" as they are used in this project. I use them largely as a matter of convenience, for want of better descriptors, although it leads to unfortunate elisions. St. Wenefred, whose legend is the focus of Chapter 3, is a Welsh saint who is made to represent certain forms of English community, and St. Ursula, long identified as British in hagiographic and historiographic traditions, is only recognized as a native saint in the fifteenth century, in the face of ambiguity about the geographical and ethnological referent for "Britain." The definition of a nation at the Council of Constance could perhaps provide a warrant for my use of England to refer to British, Anglo-Saxon, and Welsh saints: Thomas Polton, the English spokesperson who countered the French case at the council, took pains to blur the distinction between them by referring to "natio Anglicana sive Britannica."[75] But I do not want to give a veneer of authority to an admittedly inadequate term. I use it because it is, generally speaking, the term preferred in many of my materials, and because it may therefore help us recognize how some of the conceptual frameworks established in the fifteenth century have an afterlife in later constructions of English community.

Some of the literary works explored in this study are interested in definitions of English community that are fundamentally structured by the realm: so, for example, the Wilton *Life of St. Edith* pays particular attention to the "French" St. Denis, as Jocelyn Wogan-Browne has noted, in the context of its emphasis on regnal history and identity.[76] But English community is elsewhere conceived in terms oblique to the king's sovereignty. Bokenham's English saints' Lives, for example, follow a geographical logic, and the prose Lives of St. Erkenwald and Edward the Confessor in an important manuscript of *Gilte Legende* present London as a paradigm for national community, as we will see in Chapters 4 and 5. These legends seem to bear out

Sassen's claim that in the fifteenth century ideas of the people or *patria* as the basis for jurisdiction and rights are challenged by alternative ideas rooted in territory.[77]

Interest both in England as a "nation" and in communities at scales smaller and larger than England was no doubt fueled by the fifteenth-century crises in kingship. From the deposition of Richard II to the uncertain start of Tudor rule, the roiling instability of the monarchy threatened the symbolic structures by which the king's body figured national community and the patrilineal order of monarchical succession guaranteed its continuous authority. In this context, English saints might have seemed to promise miraculous rescue not only from natural disasters, as in Walsingham, but also from political ones, by restoring to the body politic the authority, continuity, and wholeness that recent events had revealed it to lack. The long reign of Henry VI is the backdrop for a good portion of the textual tradition studied here. The many ways in which his reign failed to correspond to ideals of kingship or models of sovereignty—from his accession to the throne as an infant and his long minority, to his lassitude regarding affairs of state once he began to rule in his own name, and his intermittent madness, even catatonia—destabilized not only the realm, but also the definitional categories correlative with the ideology of kingship. It had an especially striking effect on dominant tropes of historical time: as the historiographical fiction that the king ensures the continuous identity of the realm became increasingly fraught, some chronicles abandon regnal years as the system of dating in favor of Christian ones. In the Middle English *Brut*, for example, the convention of dating events according to the year of the monarch's rule—such as "And yn the forth yere of King Harryez regne the fifthe"—is replaced during some especially chaotic years of Henry VI's reign with reference to Christian time, as in "And in the yere of grace M cccc xxx^{ti}."[78]

Some fifteenth-century Lives of English saints respond to the crisis in monarchic authority by rooting national community in the person of the saint rather than the body of the king. So John Lydgate's epic *Life of Sts. Alban and Amphibalus*—written when Henry VI was still a child—identifies St. Alban as England's "protomartyr" and founder of "Brutus Albion," the poetic name he gives to England reimagined not as a realm embodied by the king but as a religious community symbolized by the saint. It is worth noting that this phenomenon—like the shift from regnal year to Christic year in some fifteenth-century chronicle entries—presents a curious wrinkle to established cultural narratives about the inexorable process of "secularization" by which ancient religious forms were superseded by more modern secular ones. So, the argument goes, the supranational Christian community of the Middle Ages is superseded by the secular nation. But in the fifteenth century, a crisis in the authority and representational practices of the monarchy may account for a new emphasis on religious definitions of English community: a sacralization of a more secular political form, rather than the secularization of a religious one.

Imbricated with the political instability of the fifteenth century was a phenomenon of particular importance to this study: the increasing coordination of the authority of church and crown, a significant change to the structure of ecclesiastical and secular jurisdiction to which, I argue in Chapter 5, some Lives of English saints respond.[79] An early seventeenth-century Puritan such as William Stoughton might aver that "there is no crime respecting any commandment contained within either of the two tables of the holy law of God but . . . that hath been evermore and is now punishable by the king's regal and temporal jurisdiction" (1604).[80] But in fact the claim to royal jurisdiction over some religious matters was of relatively recent vintage, not immemorial fact. The English king claimed jurisdiction over Stoughton's specific concern, heresy, only in 1401, with the statute *De haeretico comburendo*, the law that made heterodoxy a crime against the crown and hence punishable by death, creating a new arena in which ecclesiastical and royal jurisdiction converged. Along with the important political role of "king-making" ecclesiasts in the fifteenth century, this law marks a new era of active collaboration between church and crown and a blurring of their erstwhile separate jurisdictions, a signal project of Lancastrian kings and the archbishops of Canterbury who supported them.

This project was not uncontested, however. Nicholas Watson's influential argument that antiheresy legislation at the start of the century—above all Archbishop Arundel's Lambeth Constitutions—had a chilling effect on literary production has recently been subject to revision in ways that allow us now to explore how the alignment of ecclesiastical and royal jurisdiction, of which antiheresy legislation is a particularly acute symptom, provoked some of the more consequential developments in late medieval literary culture.[81] Indeed, I argue in Chapter 5 that it can be linked to an emerging definition of the literary as a category of narrative or expressive writing marked by its remove from the secular order.[82] English saints' Lives attest to the way that fifteenth-century efforts to coordinate secular and religious authority provoked an interest in the jurisdiction of the literary itself.

*   *   *

Even well before this period, saints' Lives formed a body of vernacular theory about the relationship between secular and sacred forms of community at different scales. Laying the groundwork for the fifteenth-century texts that are the primary concern of this study, the next chapter offers a reading of the *SEL*, which anticipates these works by more than a century. The *SEL* circulated and was copied in the fifteenth century, and it was an immediate source for some of the texts produced then. The *SEL* begins this study, however, not for those reasons, but because it offers a useful heuristic for two analytical categories central to this project: literary form and scale. In its multipart narrative form, the *SEL* demonstrates the capacity of literary form to model the complex system of late medieval communities and jurisdictions, and in its *Life of St. Ursula*, it develops a paradigm for understanding the shifts in scale that characterize the relationship between communities in this system, especially as these are figured by the scalar relationship between the body and a community understood as an alternative corporate form. It is not its content, that is, but its structures of thought that make the *South English Legendary* an essential starting point.

CHAPTER 1

Conceptualizing Community in the *South English Legendary*

The legendary served as an important forum for meditations on the nature of community in the Middle Ages. This was facilitated by its distinctive formal capabilities as a multipart narrative work, as a large-scale work structured by the category of time, and as a set of narratives centered on saints, figures who link secular experience to absolute, transcendent, or ideal forms of being. The *South English Legendary* (*SEL*), long recognized for its complex exploration of local, English, and supranational forms of community, can be seen as paradigmatic in its use of these formal capabilities to explore variously constituted communities. While the *SEL* is famously concerned with "England the nation," it is also concerned with communities defined by gender or region, as well as by Christianity itself, and this layering identifies relationships *between* overlapping communities at different scales—not just the constitution of a particular community through structures of inclusion and exclusion—as essential to their definition and function. Indeed, it may be this understanding of community that motivates the inclusion of native saints' Lives—legends that are forerunners to the texts at the heart of this study and exceptions to the general rule that English saints only become popular as the subject of Middle English narrative culture in the fifteenth century.

Thanks to generations of scholarship on the *Canterbury Tales*, we already have a nuanced understanding of how a multipart narrative form can serve as a vehicle for representing and theorizing community.[1] The *Canterbury Tales* produces an image of community through the many voices represented by its individual narratives, the wide differences in social class and experience that divide the tale-tellers, and the shared enterprise that insists, nevertheless, on their collective identity. This paradoxical understanding of community—as a framework for individual difference and as a form of collective identity—is above all an effect of the fiction of Chaucer's authorial persona, the one voice that contains the social variety cataloged in the multipart *Canterbury Tales*. The narrator's voice is both the vehicle for the several voices of the pilgrims and the instrument that produces them as a group, a social body animated by a single governing intelligence. That voice can thus be understood as a hyperbolic, or second-order, version of the personae it comprises: the narrator embodies the pilgrim company, just as the Knight may be understood to embody the generic identity of knights and the Monk that of monks. The voice of the narrator, which is a medium for all the other voices of the text, represents—in its capaciousness, its variety, and its obscure origin in a single, coherent (and fictive) physical body—the capaciousness, difference, and nevertheless improbably singular and delimited status of any community. Chaucer thus investigates a signal way that imaginative literature makes community: by giving it bodily form through the fiction of the poet-narrator's own voice.

The *SEL*, which dates some hundred years before the *Canterbury Tales*, does not use an authorial persona to the same degree.[2] Some individual legends—and the collection as a whole in some branches of the textual tradition—have a narrator with an identifiable voice, most famously the "outspoken" narrator identified with the "A redactor" who revised and added to the legendary. But this voice is not developed into a full persona in the way that Chaucer's is, and the variability in voice across the legendary's several individual narratives points to the collective work of producing the legendary, not a collective identity produced *by* it. In the absence of a single controlling intelligence, the legendary's variety seems dispersive, especially compared with the role of the Chaucerian narrative persona in representing— even constituting—the shared aspect of identity or experience that defines community in the face of individual and social variety.

But it may have seemed much less so to medieval readers, for whom hagiography was a crucial genre of identification and community. The legendary—the earliest kind of story collection in English—may be recognized as a formal expression of the idea of the communion of saints, a cornerstone of medieval religious theory and practice. Evidence that the legendary's multipart form was a resource for thinking about the relationships between various forms of community may be found in the *SEL*'s ample textual tradition, which shows considerable variety in the contents, order, and larger structure of the text. The *SEL* models a complex system of varying and overlapping forms of affiliation and jurisdiction by placing into relation myriad narratives that create, acknowledge, or are affiliated with various communities at different scales: regional and national communities; communities organized by sex, vocation, or circumstance; as well as a supervening Christian community represented by the whole. Through the legends they add or exclude, the many different redactions of the *SEL* assemble different sets of communities and thus also reconfigure the relationships between them.

More conspicuous, and perhaps more consequential, reconfigurations are produced by different kinds of time that structure the *SEL*'s multipart form. The *SEL*, like many legendaries, sequences its constituent parts according to the liturgical calendar. But while some versions also follow the liturgical calendar in beginning with legends affiliated with November feasts, others start with January feasts, in accordance with the Julian calendar, a framework for the year often used in secular historiography. In these texts, as we will see, the friction between liturgical and secular temporalities presents an especially complex model of overlapping communities. In all of them, different kinds of community are related to, or differentiated from, one another through the category of time.

In exploring how the *SEL*'s multipart form conceptualizes the relationship between communities, this chapter also develops a framework for understanding the two major mid-fifteenth century legendaries, the *Gilte Legende* and Osbern Bokenham's Abbotsford legendary, discussed in Chapters 4 and 5. More broadly, it establishes a framework for understanding the corpus of fifteenth-century native saints' Lives *tout court*. Indeed, the set of texts addressed in this study might be read on analogy to a legendary, insofar as they together explore a complex system of overlapping groupings and affiliations not only severally, but especially in relation to one another. The legendary as a multipart form and the *SEL* as an exemplary instance of that form at once model the affiliations, differences, and relationships between different kinds of community and provide a heuristic for reading the corpus of individual saints' Lives in similar terms.

This chapter turns at the end to scale as a crucial conceptual category through which the relationships between different forms of community in this complex system are understood. Some communities, for example, might be related by means of their relative geographical scale through the logic of synecdoche, as part and whole. Smaller communities do not, however, always nest within larger ones in a graduated spatial order. Indeed, some are not defined in geographical terms at all and so cannot be mapped through spatial relations, and instead relate to other forms of community through conceptual or temporal scale. Saint's Lives are well suited to thinking about all three categories of scale—spatial, temporal, and conceptual—because of the way they explore corporate metaphors of community: metaphors that re-scale the human body as a community and a community as a body, and thereby recalibrate their spatial, temporal, and conceptual extension. Here too the *Canterbury Tales* is a useful *comparandum*: we have seen how the abstract boundaries of the Chaucerian authorial persona expand to encompass the pilgrim company to which it gives voice. The vernacular tradition examined in this study takes full advantage of the affordances of corporate metaphors to explore the relationship between communities: a saint that figures the corporate identity of a monastery, for example, might also figure the metaphorical body of the nation, and in this way be a means for thinking about the relationship between them. This is indeed the conceptual structure embraced by Lydgate's *Life of St. Alban and Amphibalus*, discussed in Chapter 5, and rejected by the Wilton *Life of St. Edith*, discussed in Chapter 2.

In order to lay the groundwork for analyzing the scalar relationship between the individual body and corporate conceptualizations of community in fifteenth-century saints' Lives, the final section of this chapter turns to one of the most complex and theoretical forms it takes, the *SEL* legend of St. Ursula and the 11,000 virgins. The way that Ursula's company re-scales her body as a figure for their collective identity is familiar from visual representations of the saint, who is often represented large enough to accommodate her retinue under her cloak, like the Virgin of Mercy. The *SEL's Life of St. Ursula* theorizes this movement between scales in its representation of Ursula's boat, which represents two communities fashioned reciprocally: the Ursuline company aboard the boat and a political community comprising the British and English kingdoms, which are joined by the shared project of supplying Ursula with her companions in anticipation of the still-stronger alliance promised by her prospective marriage to the English prince. The relationship between these two communities is explored through a narrative image of the kind of "heterotopia" theorized by Michel Foucault. The *SEL Ursula* helps us to see the degree to which scale informs Foucault's own paradigm, and in turn it helps us to account more fully for the conceptual work that the mobility of scale does in negotiating the relationships between the different forms of actual and imagined community.

Multipart Form and the *South English Legendary*'s Model of Community

Identifying the *SEL* as a paradigmatic multipart narrative may seem risky insofar as it may seem to posit a stable text that can be discussed as such. Its heterogeneous textual tradition has, generally speaking, prompted a critical approach that looks at single legends or sets of legends identified with a specific manuscript or manuscript group.[3] For the same reason, formalist approaches to the legendary are often limited to the level of the line (its hallmark septenary verse) or the legend (its possible relation to the narrative forms of sermons, for example). As distorting as it may be to discuss such a various textual tradition under a single title, it is necessary to do so in order to understand the significance of its large-scale form. By the *South English Legendary*, then, I refer not to a putative original or ideal version of the work abstracted from its textual instantiations, but the formal principles that define it, however flexibly, as a collection—that is, the principles that persist through, and may indeed compel, the variousness of its textual tradition.

I am especially concerned with these formal principles as they were developed by the A redactor, who made significant changes to the text as it is represented by the earliest manuscript, Oxford, Bodleian Library MS Laud 108. We can credit this redactor, who added a prologue and reordered the text, with the formal conceit of a collection. As we will see, the prologue, often given the title *Banna sanctorum*, employs two extended metaphors that make explicit the *SEL*'s formal identity as a coordinated collection. The prologue further specifies the structure of that form by announcing that the legends are sequenced in calendrical order from January 1.[4] The formal principles that inform the work as a multipart narrative, then, do not *inaugurate* the textual tradition we call the "South English Legendary": they are a response to—that is, *a reading of*—early stages of that tradition, evidence of meditation on the conceptual possibilities presented by a single work that comprises many individual short narratives. By attending to its form on this level, I propose, we may better understand how the *SEL* explores community, and in particular how it understands the relationship between different kinds of community—regional, gendered, national, Christian—that are different in kind and scale.

This approach may offer some purchase, in particular, on the status of the legends of native saints, a central question in *SEL* scholarship.[5] Critical analysis of these legends generally discovers a significant interest in national identity, but the legendary itself has seemed to provide weak evidence for it: as many have noted, only about 20 percent of its legends are devoted to English saints.[6] Two questions emerge from this: first, does the *SEL* subsume the native saints within a universalized communion of saints, or does their inclusion reflect a specifically national project of some kind, perhaps also signaled by the legendary's use of English? Second, what is the relationship between England and other earthly communities that the *SEL* also addresses, those defined, for example, by gender or region?

Such questions are, importantly, produced by the *SEL*'s multipart form. It is telling that the preface added in the A redaction develops two conceits, each with the double function of fashioning the miscellaneous texts of the *SEL* into a collection and addressing the community defined in relationship to it.[7] The first is an agricultural metaphor in which the "new fruit" of Christianity is grown in a sacrificial garden, watered by Christ's blood and then by the blood of generations of martyrs; the second is a military metaphor in which Christ is a king arrayed for battle, attended by ranks of archers and backed by his hardy knights. These two violent metaphors ground a community defined by their (prescribed) affective response: "Wel aghte *we* louie Cristendom . that is so dure iboght" (Well should we love Christendom that is so dearly bought; emphasis added), exhorts the narrator (I, 3, 57). At the same time, the two conceits highlight the formal features of the collection as such. The serried ranks of Christ's knights find a close analogue in the stories about them told "bi reuwe" (66) in the collection that follows. The ordering of the legends, in turn, recalls the garden of the "new fruit": it follows the calendar, "as hare dai valth in the yere" (as their day falls in the year), a seasonal and cyclical order commemorating the "herte blod" that waters the seed that Christ has sown.[8] The metaphors that compel the community addressed by the *SEL*—the one interpellated by the injunction to love Christendom—also figure the form of the collection, the narratives that represent an ordered procession of Christ's saints, organized by the cycle of the year, which is defined by both agricultural seasons and the ritual celebration of the life of Christ.

Even fashioned into a collection, however, the constituent parts of the *SEL* retain their striking variety, and this variety challenges the way we might be tempted to conceptualize the collection through the logic of synecdoche: the part standing for the whole. This logic might be suggested both by the structure of the *SEL* as a multipart narrative and by its primary subject: saints, who are often imagined as holy metonyms for the communities formed or addressed by their cults. And indeed synecdoche does structure some *SEL* legends: it is at the heart of the idea of community developed, for example, in the legend of Alphege, in which the saint stands for an urban community and that community, in turn, stands for England. Although Alphege is associated with specific places throughout the legend—Deerhurst, where he first becomes a monk; Bath, where he lives as a hermit and then prior; and then Winchester, where he serves as bishop before he is made Archbishop of Canterbury—the first lines of the legend introduce him as having been born in "Engelonde." England, that is, is the threshold identification that defines Alphege, and it establishes the several local places he inhabits—all within England—as synecdoches for this national community. The opening reference to England thus not only identifies Alphege as an "English" saint, but also establishes the nation as the paradigmatic form and scale of community, one that subsumes smaller communities and inhabits larger ones as parts within a whole.

This synecdochal logic is elaborated in Alphege's martyrdom, in which Alphege comes to stand for Canterbury and then in turn to figure England. When Danes threaten to attack Canterbury, Alphege offers himself as a substitute: he "propherede is owe lyf . forto giue for hore" (offered his own life in exchange for theirs) (I, 151, 87). His ability as one man to stand for an entire urban community is, in a crossing of religious and secular forms of community, a function of his exceptional status as archbishop: given ultimate responsibility for the spiritual lives of the townspeople, Alphege comes to represent them in this martial context as well, to such an extent that his person stands for the entire community, even to the pagan Danes. The logic of metonymy then facilitates another category shift by which the saint figures the still larger and more imaginative community of England. The devil, disguised as an angel, successfully tempts Alphege into escaping from prison by claiming that God wants him to do so in order to "saui Engelond" (I, 151, 102). Although he initially adopts the wrong course of action, Alphege's desire to act "For the loue of Engelond" (I, 154, 186) is ultimately confirmed by his martyrdom. Community is defined in this legend, then, in terms of a graduated sequence—an individual represents a city, which in turn represents a nation. Importantly, this serves to represent religious and secular community as coextensive or isomorphic: the differences between ecclesiastical and civic jurisdictions and between national and Christian communities are obscured through the fiction of a single graduated scale that coordinates different communities in a neatly concatenated chain.

This logic could inform a legendary as a whole, as it does in the 1516 *Kalendre of the Newe Legende of Englande* in which local, regional, and institutional saints figure England metonymically.[9] But the remarkable variety of the *SEL* prevents any one part from standing for the whole, and this resistance to synecdoche on the level of form—the failure of any one legend to stand for the collection—correlates with a resistance to synecdoche as a privileged model for representing community. The Alphege legend is an exception; for the most part, local categories of identity and community do not point to larger ones, which are too heterogeneous to be defined in this way. The *SEL*, that is, recognizes the synecdochic structure of English community explored in the Alphege legend as only one form of community among others—a particular, not paradigmatic, form in a collection that comprises many different forms.[10]

The various ways in which community is represented in the *SEL* quickly multiply. The legend of St. Kenelm defines England in terms of a detailed political geography,[11] while the legend of St. Botolph represents it through an abstract spatial paradigm of pagan wilderness and monastic precinct. The legend of Wulfstan imagines English community in terms of historiography,[12] while others, such as Aldhelm's, give prominent attention to genealogy.[13] While, as we have seen, Alphege takes affect as a structure of community, the legend of King Oswald emphasizes ethics in its central story about his care for the hungry.[14] In addition to the way that these legends use different categories—geography, history, genealogy, ethics, and affect—to define community, they also employ varying conceptual and narrative structures. The *SEL* canvases forms of community represented by an exemplary figure and those represented by an exceptional one, in addition to the model of metonymic representation that we saw in the Alphege legend. So, for example, Thomas Becket is presented as a saintly example for all English Christians and a special model for English ecclesiasts, while Edmund Rich, a later Archbishop of Canterbury, whose legend is imagined as an *imitatio* of Becket, is represented as a saintly exception—a figure to be wondered at, not imitated—as evidenced by his miraculous birth without the blood and "hore" (muck) of childbed (II, 492, 8–10).[15]

The realm, embodied symbolically by the king, is an especially important form of English community in the *SEL* legends of native saints, and even in this special category there is a striking variety. In the Edburga legend, the saint is the daughter of King Edward, the first English king to be anointed as such; before his accession, kings "Bote as it dukes were" (were but as dukes)— that is, they enjoyed inherited right but not sacralized sovereignty. Edward's anointing inaugurates a perdurable tradition: "seththe thei habbeth echon" (they all have been [annointed] since) (18).[16] This continuity has a corollary in the continuity of kings' names: Edburga's father is the first of four kings named Edward, all carefully identified in the legend's opening lines. The legend imagines England as a realm embodied by the anointed king, linked by genealogy to other kings. The legend of Edward the Elder, in contrast, emphasizes the status of the king—even an illegitimate one—as a symbolic embodiment of his people. This symbolic status is made clear by the punishment endured by the English people when Etheldred comes to the throne through Edward's murder, even though the "lond folk of Engelond" themselves "no gult nabbeth therto" (bear no guilt for it) (I, 113, 110). Dunstan, as he reluctantly crowns Etheldred, prophesies: "For more wrechede & sorwe . ther cometh bi thine daye / Into Engelond uor thulke sunne . than me euere iseye" (For there will come more misery and sorrow in your day/ Into England on account of your sin than anyone has ever seen) (I, 113, 111–12).[17] Punishment for Etheldred's sin is visited on the realm, a community understood as an extension of his person and so punished for his transgression, even as the punishment identifies his rule as illegitimate. The rift between the secular polity and its ideal sacralized form is displayed in the blighted body politic.

The fundamental tension between religious and political forms of English community is explored in the legends of Sts. Edmund and Aethelberht as well. St. Aethelberht's ambivalent position as a figure for both is figured by his ambivalent sexuality.[18] Introduced as "the holi king . . . of Engelonde," his extraordinary virtue as a child-king is "queinte," that is, curious or queer (165, 6). He is ever a "clene maide" and "chast thorw alle thinge" (165, 9), suffering at mere reference to the compulsory heterosexuality of kingship: "Him was the worse whan me spak.of ani wiuinge" (it was to him worse when men spoke about taking a wife) (166, 1). He nevertheless heeds the counsel of his barons when they insist that royal chastity is a "luther dede" (an evil deed) (166, 5) that threatens the country with the prospect of political chaos after his death. As Aethelberht sets off to find a bride, "wonder tokne[s]"—an earthquake and an eclipse—herald his destiny (166, 33). When he arrives at the Mercian court, Offa's daughter loves him instantly and innocently ("without ech vilanie"), but her evil mother plots against him (166, 39). The story that unfolds, in a stunning commentary of the fictions of royal genealogy, reimagines the rationale for Aethelberht's suit—the king's responsibility to have an heir in order to secure political continuity—as malicious plot: Offa and his wife are old, the legend notes, and she envies the next generation their youth. She convinces Offa that Aethelberht comes "vor no gode ac vor quede" (for no good but for evil) (167, 7), that is, to usurp his land: the young king, she claims, will be eager for their deaths once married to their daughter.

As with other sainted kings, Aethelberht's thoroughly secular death—his head is cut off by an evil man with whom he had been reared—is understood as martyrdom, and the legend closes with reference to his cult at Hereford. The natural wonders that presage his death point to the contradiction, but also miraculous coincidence, of the king's embodiment of both sacred and secular community, a tension here expressed in terms of sexuality: the irreconcilable demands of saintly chastity and the royal obligation to produce an heir. The legend displays the tension between these imperatives in order to make them sublime: it does not resolve, but instead elevates them by displacing them with portent and sacrificial death. This is, I think, the core structure of the Edmund legend too, which insists on the dual, coincident, and mutually exclusive imperatives that define Edmund as a saint and a king: to protect the nation and to sacrifice himself on its behalf. Again, what is at stake is a definition of English community embodied by a sainted king, developed in a narrative that at once extends an ideology of anointed kingship to sacralize the secular nation and recognizes the (conceptual, historical, and ethical) differences between the monarchy and religious community.

English community, itself variously defined, is, as we have already seen, only one variety of community addressed by the legendary. Others include communities defined by sex and vocation. The legend of Edmund Rich famously invokes a feminine audience, when the narrator, after describing Edmund's constant devotion to the Virgin, teases, "Wele whar eni of you couthe such an hosebonde fynde" (Any of you would be lucky to find such a husband) (II, 496, 100). The legend of St. Margaret identifies an even more specific audience of women: "Wymmen that with other were wanne hi child bere" (Women who are with other women when they bear children) (I, 302, 317), who are encouraged to read the legend to the women for whom they care. Legends with special affiliations with specific vocations do not address them as directly as this, but there are intriguing moments of attention, for example, to the special significance to eggmongers of St. Swithun's miraculous reconstitution of a woman's broken eggs, as well as a striking dilation of the story of St. Mark and the shoemaker, which occupies half of the *SEL* legend, the only event from his vita recounted before the narrative turns to his martyrdom.[19] At the same time, and on an entirely different scale, the many *SEL* legends that find analogues in *Legenda Aurea* (that is, that show a rough correspondence with the Dominican sanctorale) point to a translocal, supranational Christian community, defined by a shared liturgical tradition.

In the variety of communities it comprises, and the different ways they are defined, the multipart form of the legendary represents a complex, rather than rationalized, system of overlapping forms of community. Within the Christian world it imagines, it does not segregate different categories of identity or community; it neither divides one reader from another according to a privileged category of identity nor subordinates one category to another. After all, a member of the *SEL*'s audience may be a woman and an eggmonger, a resident of Worcestershire, and an "English" subject. She would share some of these categories of identity with her husband, some with other women, some with all (or most) members of her town. She participates in many communities: some are larger and some smaller in scale, but they cannot therefore be coordinated with, or made to stand for, one another.

This is true even for regional, national, and supranational communities, which—with rare exceptions such as the *Life of Alphege*—are imagined in the *SEL* not through category shifts from the particular to the general, from hyponym to hypernym, and much less as differences in spatial scale, but as shifts between incommensurable categories. This is thematized in the collection's final legend, the *Life of Thomas Becket*, in the story of Becket's father, Gilbert, a Crusader who is captured in Jerusalem and becomes a favorite of the Saracen prince, Amiraud. One day, Amiraud asks Gilbert about "the manere of Engelond . and of the lawe" (II, 611, 18). The prince's interest in English practice is echoed by his daughter, who also "esste him [Gilbert] of Engelond . and of the maner there / And of the lif of Cristendom . & wat hare bileue were" (asked him about England and the manners there / and about the life of Christians and what their beliefs were) (II, 610, 30). Unlike her father, the girl recognizes that Gilbert hails from two different communities, England and Christendom—the first sign of the perspicacity and sympathy that will make her worthy to be his wife and mother to the holy Thomas. The shift from England to Christendom may seem privileged by the narrative: to marry Gilbert, the girl need not adopt English manners, but she must convert. Yet Gilbert's own answer moves in the other direction, toward a more local, rather than supranational, frame: he tells the girl about England and Christianity, as she has asked, and also about "the toun het Londone . that he was inne bore" (the town called London where he was born) (II, 611, 32).[20] Later, when she secretly follows him after his escape, "London" is the only English word she knows and she uses it to arrive at Gilbert's house and prove her love for him: insofar as community is a phenomenon of affect, it requires a local habitation, even if it is not limited to this place.

The story insists that local, national, and supranational communities are constituted differently: London is defined by place, England by manners and law, and Christendom by faith.[21] They cannot, therefore, be understood in terms of category shifts between the particular and the general, or as a species of synecdoche, as they are in the Alphege legend. All three thus function differently in the story: the intimacies of urban community are the practical condition of the union of Gilbert and his Saracen bride, just as Christian community is its ideological condition, while the question of English custom and law is suspended in this genealogical backstory to become the narrative's central problematic. I will return later to the Becket legend and its interest in how the conflict between ecclesiastical and royal jurisdiction—the conflict between England as a religious and as a political community—is complicated by its relationship to both local and supranational communities. Here let me underscore how thoroughly the legend challenges the synecdochic relationship linking local, national, and supranational communities developed in the Alphege legend. In the Becket legend, as in the legendary as a whole, these categories cannot be coordinated into a hierarchy of value or even stable relationship; instead they coexist as separate, but overlapping categories of identity.

This layered representation of community, presented by the Becket legend on the level of theme, is, as I argued above, presented in the *SEL* itself on the level of form. Its multipart narrative offers an image of diversity and complexity without pretending to a comprehensive accounting or even a representative sampling, which also implies a finite set. From this perspective, the fact that the collection betrays a regional orientation, or that the native saints remain a minority, may be seen to strengthen, rather than dilute, the force of the *SEL*'s representation of a national community, which is, after all, defined not only by that category of identity and history, but also by its complicated relationship to many categories. The nation becomes reified as the primary form of community and affiliation in a later period, of course, but it is not offered as such here.

The complex system of communities imagined by the *SEL* resonates strongly with recent accounts of culture and community in a postnational frame. Arjun Appadurai, in an influential analysis of the accelerated pace of global media and the modern experience of migration, argues that cultures are now "fractal" and "overlapping" rather than "isomorphic."[22] For Appadurai, this is a consequence of the multiple factors that structure global culture—technology, media, finance, ethnic identity, and ideology—in their variable relation to one another and in the complicated patterns of their confluence and divergence. In proposing an analogous definition of community from a premodern perspective, the *SEL* suggests the truly theoretical nature of Appadurai's paradigm and its general applicability: material, expressive, and ideological formations produce a variety of communities, of markedly different scales, that proliferate and overlap in ways that challenge fictions of unified and bounded cultures in general and, in particular, the scalar fiction of the nation as the privileged form that mediates between the local and the supranational.[23]

The *SEL* arrives at this insight through the formal principle of the multipart narrative collection, a collection that puts "regional" saints such as Kenelm in relationship with saints who represent a national community, such as Becket or Edmund or Alban, and with so-called universal saints, such as Katherine or John the Baptist or Sebastian. The relationship between them is not defined by a hierarchy of geographic referent or scale. It is defined instead in terms of time, through the calendar figured by their feast days and those of the temporale.

The Many Times of Medieval Communities

Our hypothetical eggmonger from Worcestershire inhabits different categories of time, just as she participates in different communities: liturgical time, defined by the sequence of holy days; the time of the Christian era, which records her distance from the birth of Christ; the cycle of the seasons, which we might call agricultural time; regnal time, as defined by the king's reign; and the time of her own life span and place in a sequence of generations.[24] As has already been noted, the *SEL* is especially indebted to liturgical time: it is the formal technology of the calendar that comprises its individual narratives into a coordinated collection. The individual legends relate to the whole, that is, primarily as temporal phenomena: individual feast days that together fashion a year.

It is tempting to privilege liturgical time in readings of the *SEL* on this basis, especially when we attend to the collection's form. For example, Thorlac Turville-Petre argues that the calendrical ordering of the legendary obscures a historical rendering of English community to which the native saints' Lives might otherwise seem to gesture: in the absence of a chronological structure linking them, he remarks, the collection can provide "only isolated glimpses of the political development of the relationship between Church and Crown."[25] Such a reading contrasts with a more thematic approach, such as that of Klaus Jankofsky, for whom the audience of the *SEL* inhabits a double sense of time. While the sacrificial violence in the legends of the "Latin" martyrs invokes a typological relationship to Christ and thus an extrahistorical temporality, the Anglo-Saxon saints' Lives address specific historical events and social concerns, creating a complementary vision of the ahistorical and historical, which, he argues, suggests "the continuum of this world and the next."[26]

The two kinds of time at issue—sometimes juxtaposed as "liturgical time" and "historical time"—are encoded in the legendary's form in the branch of the textual tradition that follows the A redaction. This version of the text does not adopt the structure of the liturgical year, which traditionally begins with Advent, as does Jacobus de Voragine's *Legenda Aurea*, which explicitly theorizes the liturgical calendar in its preface.[27] Nor is it structured by the English year, which began on March 25, the feast of the Annunciation. The *SEL* opts instead to begin with January 1.[28] This choice is unusual not just in the context of hagiography, but in vernacular culture at large. The *SEL*'s term for January 1 is "yeresday," and the *Middle English Dictionary* (*MED*) lists three instances from three different moments in the legendary's own textual history (Bodleian Library MS Laud 108; Corpus Christi Coll., Cambridge MS 145; B.L. MS Egerton 1993) as the first three uses of the term; the next witness given by the *MED* is Trevisa's translation of the *Polychronicon* (1387). "New Year's day" is used as early as the *Ormulum* (1200), but that is the only witness given by the *MED* until *Sir Gawain and the Green Knight*. So, on the evidence of the *MED*, the idea of January 1 as the start of the new year is very rare outside of the *SEL* until the end of the fourteenth century. It may well be influenced by the calendars prefacing Books of Hours, which often begin with January, as I address below, but the primary *narrative* context in which January 1 serves as the start of the year is in historiographic traditions that depend on the Julian calendar.[29] What modern scholarship has often understood as antithetical temporal frames—the liturgical and the historical—are simultaneously invoked in the *SEL*'s form, poised between the calendar, with its strong allusion to liturgical time, and historiography, as it marks out the year from January 1.

One effect of this order is that the year is inaugurated by the feast of the Circumcision, the first time Christ's blood is shed, as the legend notes (I, 3, 5). As with a year beginning with the Annunciation or the season of Advent, a year that begins with the Circumcision is structured fundamentally by the paradigm of Christ's life. More than other Christic feasts, however, the Circumcision draws special attention to typology (unlike the Annunciation, say, with its emphasis on prophecy). Jesus is circumcised according to the "olde lay," as the legend has it, a phrase it repeats conspicuously four times in its brief twenty-eight lines. Even this new beginning is set in relation to what precedes it, as well as having a pointed relation to what will follow: as the *first* time Christ's blood is shed, it heralds the Passion and Crucifixion. Time here is caught between past and future, suspended by the atemporal structure of typology, even as the Circumcision stands for the radical division of old and new through the logic of supersession, what Kathleen Biddick calls a cut in time.[30]

If the Circumcision points backward and forward, curiously evacuating the event itself, the second feast in this calendrical organization, Epiphany or Twelfthday, heaps event upon event. It is not only the day on which the kings visit the infant Christ: it is also the day of his baptism twenty-nine years later "to bygynne the niwe lay" (to inaugurate the new law) (I, 5, 6), as well as the day he turned water into wine a year later, and, the year after that, the day on which he fed five thousand men with five loaves. Here the *SEL* uses the cyclical nature of the calendar precisely to describe—not deny—chronology, the progress of time, with January 6 standing for a series of dates in Christ's life linked by ideas of transformation but not fully typological in nature. In the conjunction of the Circumcision and Epiphany as the first two narratives of the *SEL* we can see a paradigm for the complementary presence of historical and ahistorical time, grounded not only in the difference between England and Christendom, as Jankofsky has it, but also as endemic to Christendom itself, indeed, to the theology of an incarnate Christ.[31]

It is also endemic to the form of the legendary, which marries narratives of the past with an annual cycle that obtains in the present and points to the future. Alison Chapman, in a brilliant discussion of the calendars in Foxe's *Acts and Monuments* and the *Book of Common Prayer*, argues that when "a historical narrative is accompanied by a calendar . . . the history makes a far more pressing claim on the experience of time. While the narrative itself shows the unspooling events of times past, the calendar provides a framework for times to come and makes clear the text's intent to shape the future."[32] The Twelfthday narrative is closely relevant here: Christ models the progress of time for readers, for whom the cycle of the liturgical year may also encourage an awareness of such forward movement in the context of their own lives and that of the communities they inhabit.[33] Chapman's argument may be the best framework for understanding the odd choice of January 1 as the start of the year, which may be informed primarily by calendars found in breviaries, which often start with January.[34] The text maps out time the way a calendar itself does: formed by feast days, it is nevertheless a flexible instrument that can accommodate all kinds of time—not only liturgical time, but also the structure of national history that puts the stories of England's past in relationship to the present, and even the unfolding of personal or familial histories that inform more local kinds of community.

From this perspective, the calendrical order of the collection is evidence for Anne Thompson's suggestion, made on the grounds of narrative thematics, that the temporal horizon of the *SEL* is less history or eternity than the day.[35] If historical time alienates the past through its relentlessly progressive nature, and liturgical time paradoxically uses the cycle of the year to point to a time outside the forward movement of chronology, a calendar that marks an intersection between the two provides a paradigm of time to be filled by the individual, who may—like the Christ of the Twelfthday feast—mark significant events and chart the passing of the years against the calendar.[36] Christian typology, as a form of temporal suspension, holds a space open for those who inhabit the present.[37] Importantly, this is at once an individual and communal paradigm: individual experiences are charted against feast days known to all. Perhaps the most important category of time in the *SEL* is the quotidian, which for medieval Christians has an important relationship to both history and eternity but also includes all manner of mundane and personal categories of time.

As I suggested earlier, the temporal form of the *SEL* is correlative of its representation of community. It too is layered, accommodating many different kinds of time, from the seasonal time of agrarian community, with its intimate cycles of human family and local affiliation, to the historical frameworks invoked to understand national community, to the eschatology invoked in the prologue's trope of transhistorical spiritual warfare. Less bounded and fixed than communities defined as phenomena of geography or blood, communities understood as phenomena of time can borrow from it, as the *SEL* does, an open extension that admits multiple frameworks—national and Christian history, human generations and regnal years, agricultural and liturgical seasons, and so on. These overlapping temporalities prevent the subordination of various kinds of community to a single indexical or paradigmatic form of community (such as Christendom or England). The use of time as a structural principle of the *SEL* is thus intimately related to its representation of the several communities in which its audience participates.

The Becket Legend: Formal Closure and Fractured Community

This complex system of heterogeneous forms of community is the central insight of the *SEL*, as well as the central problem of its final legend. Unfixed by a graduated ordering that would place it between local and supranational communities, England emerges as a distinct form of community in the *SEL*, one that lacks the normative status it will later claim. The *SEL* does not, however, simply celebrate the various kinds of communities it acknowledges; in its final legend, it also investigates the conflicts that can emerge between different, especially overlapping, forms of community. The legend of Thomas of Canterbury addresses the irreconcilable claims of ecclesiastical and regnal authority—that is, competing definitions of national community as fundamentally religious or political—a conflict that is compounded by the coexistence of, and intricate relationship among, many other kinds of community that cannot be coordinated with the nation, including local ones such as Canterbury and supranational ones such as monastic orders. Whatever the discursive context for the use of January 1 to initiate the legendary, it serves to designate as the final articulation of its key themes the legend of Thomas Becket, which—like the *SEL* as a whole—acknowledges community as a complicated, layered phenomenon, this time in a tragic register.[38]

This is a formal, as well as thematic, contribution of the *SEL* Becket legend. Critics have often noted that its "length and literary ambition" serve to conclude the whole.[39] The legend also offers extended echoes of the metaphorics of spiritual knighthood in the *Banna Sanctorum* and in this way more specifically creates a bookend for the collection. These echoes surface initially in the account of Thomas's Crusader father, Gilbert, and then in the figuration of Thomas himself as a knight of Christ. The full significance of the

SEL's use of this metaphoric pattern to frame the multipart collection may depend on its evocation of aspects of the Becket cult that themselves point to overlapping forms of community, and that may even provide an etiology for the collection's concern with the complex system constituted by them. The cult suggests at least three contexts for the *SEL*'s representation of a fractured, nonisomorphic community: the international context of the Crusade, the Barons' War, and England's own history of invasion and conquest, all of which may be briefly considered here as part of the text's meditation on the nature of community as it is framed by the prologue and the final legend.

The story of Becket's father, the Crusader who marries a Saracen princess whom he has met while imprisoned by her father, recalls in the idiom of romance the presence of English Christian communities in the contested territories in the Holy Land, and in particular the English Crusading order dedicated to Thomas of Canterbury, the Knights of St. Thomas of Acon.[40] The foundation of this order, after Acre was taken in 1191, is closely contemporary with the composition of the story, which reads like an etiological myth for the order's original commitment to succor imprisoned Crusaders.[41] Conversely, the order's identification of English canons (its original membership) as "knights" anticipates both the military metaphors of the *Banna sanctorum* and the Becket legend's central problematic, the relationship between secular and sacred jurisdictions, which are distinguished in the Becket legend precisely through chivalric metaphors.

While Crusaders, such as Gilbert Becket, and the Knights of St. Thomas are knights of Christ in a literal sense, Thomas Becket becomes a figurative one when he gives up his secular career. When the knights in Thomas's company abandon him during his trial at Northampton, Becket declares that the poor men whom he serves are the true "Godes knights": "other men me habbeth forsake / theose knightes ich louie more" (Other men have forsaken me / these knights I love more) (II, 639, 889–90). So is Thomas himself. In the scene that anticipates his martyrdom, his vestments are elaborately imagined in military terms:

Tho sein Thomas hadde is masse ido . is chesible he gan of weue
Ac alle the othere vestemens . he let on him bileue
Other armure nadde he non . for Holy Churche to fighte
. . . .
A crois he nom inis hond . and wende forth baldeliche
The vestemens [were] is armure . as fel to suche knighte

The crois was is baner . for Holy Churche to fighte
Forth wende this gode knight . among al is fon (II, 641, 953–61)

[When St. Thomas had finished his mass, he began to take off his
      chasuble
But all of his other vestments he kept on
He had no other armor in which to fight for Holy Church
. . . .
He took a cross in his hand and boldly went forth
The vestments were his armor, appropriate to such a knight.
The cross was his banner, to fight for Holy Church
Forth went this good knight, among all his enemies].

In a clear echo of the *Banna sanctorum*, Thomas declares that he is "hardiore" because he is armed with the cross (II, 641, 968).[42]

If such imagery invokes England's participation in international crusade, it also points toward the politics of the Barons' War. Indeed, Becket is so frequently identified as a spiritual warrior in the historiography of that conflict that the *SEL*'s first audience may well have recognized the commonplace military metaphor of the *Banna sanctorum* as a specific reference to him. In the *Life of St. Thomas Cantilupe*, the young Thomas—who would later champion the barons' cause—is asked by his uncle, the Bishop Walter of Worcester, about his future, and the boy responds that he hopes to be a knight: Walter counters that he will be a knight of Christ, the champion of God and of St. Thomas of Canterbury.[43] This affiliation points to more politicized uses of the trope linking Becket to Simon de Monfort's victory at Lewes.[44] Becket's association with spiritual knighthood, then, points to internal contests over the nature of national community, especially the politics and local affiliations of the Barons' War, as well as to the place of England in Christendom's ongoing struggle to define itself in the face of Muslim military power.

The metaphor of spiritual knighthood also, of course, points to the overlapping jurisdictions of royal and ecclesiastical authority: the constitutive tension between the metaphor's tenor and vehicle registers the incompatible claims of secular community (chivalry and the loyalty to the king that it demands) and religious community (the church as an institution with special prerogatives that devolve from Christ himself) that ultimately lead to Becket's death. The *SEL* represents the conflict between them as a historical accident, not a necessary antithesis: as Renee Hamelinck has noted, the *SEL* stages the tension between church and state, which culminates in the Becket legend, as the consequence of the Norman Conquest.[45] The inaugural English saint's Life, the legend of Wulfstan, spans the time before and after the Norman Conquest and illustrates how it fractured the relationship between spiritual and secular authority. When Duke William dismisses Wulfstan as bishop on the grounds that he is too ignorant, Wulfstan strikes the tomb of Edward the Confessor with his crozier, where it sticks fast. When no one else is able to remove it, William and his archbishop repent and urge Wulfstan to reclaim his staff, to which Wulfstan replies with sly impertinence, "ich mot nede do . mine souereines wille" (I must do my sovereign's will) (I, 13, 155)—asserting his ongoing loyalty to the (dead) king he regards as his sovereign under the guise of acquiescing to the reigning one he does not. The legend at once tracks the pre-Conquest coincidence of spiritual and political community—given miraculous witness in Edward's continuing authority over the bishop he named—and identifies their difference under Norman rule, through William's inability to present the crozier to a bishop of his own choosing.

This fault line between secular and sacred forms of community runs to Canterbury. The *SEL Becket* renders the terrible verdict that it is impossible to negotiate the intersection of ecclesiastical and regnal jurisdiction in post-Conquest England. But it does not evince the simple anti-Norman bias of the Wulfstan legend. The Becket legend is surprisingly sympathetic to the king's concerns about his own power and authority, even as Becket's sanctity is defined in terms of his willingness to die for the "righte of Holy Churche" (II, 679, 2114). The legend—at remarkable length, given the narrative expectations set by the rest of the legendary—presents Becket's death as the inescapable consequence of the profound difference between religious and political community, despite Becket's own loyalty and the king's basic goodness. The irresolvable conflict between Becket and the king is the *SEL*'s final demonstration of the coincident, but sometimes incompatible, categories of community given expression in the legendary's multipart form.

The end of the Becket legend offers an apparently compensatory image of a seamless, single community formed through devotion to the martyr during the ritual of his translation. Not only is the king reconciled to his erstwhile enemy, but a markedly diverse community is brought together, a local and living analog to the kind of procession that the *Banna sanctorum* offers as the structure of the legendary:

Vorto honoury thys holy man . ther com volk ynowgh
Of bysscopes & of abbotes . monyon thuder drowgh
Of pryoures & parsons . & of other clerkes also
Of heorles & barouns . & many a knyght therto
Of seriauns & squyers . & hosebondes ynowe
& of simple men eke of the lond . so thykke thuder drowe
That al the contrey ther aboute . & toune wyde & longe
Myghte unnethe al that folk . that ther com undervonge (II, 690–91,
    19–26)

[To honor this holy man, there came plenty of people
Of bishops and abbots, there were many who came
Of priors and parsons and other clerks too,
Of earls and barons, and many a knight came to that place,
Of sergeants and squires and householders plenty
And also simple men of the land, so thickly went there
That all the country around, and the town wide and long
Could barely accommodate all the people who came there].

Here the *SEL* indulges in the fantasy of a community, unified in its devotion to Becket, comprising secular and spiritual estates, rich and poor, rural and urban. Interestingly, the coordination of such diversity into a community is associated with temporal repetition in a striking echo of the Epiphany narrative. The translation of Becket's body occurred on a Tuesday, the legend twice insists (II, 693, 38 and 53), and it was on Tuesdays that most of the consequential events of his life happened:

Alle hys chaunces that he hadde . by Tywesdawes hii come
By Tywesday he was ibore . & of hys moder wombe com
& also as me bryngeth a theof . vorto vonge hys dom
Byvore the kyng at Northhamthone . by a Tywesday
Wyth greot sschame he was ibrought . as al that folk ysay
Vyloker than eny theof . that folk him ther sschende (II, 691–92,
    54–59)

[All the events of his life fell on a Tuesday
On Tuesday he was born, and came from his mother's womb
And like someone brings a thief to receive his sentence

Before the king at Northampton on a Tuesday
With great shame he was brought, as all people say,
More degradingly than any thief, the people humiliated him there].

Born, martyred, and translated on a Tuesday, Becket was also exiled on a Tuesday, informed by God of his impending martyrdom on a Tuesday, and returned to England from exile on a Tuesday (II, 694, 60–68).[46] He is thus to be honored by a Tuesday fast, a ritual commemoration that can reenact the community formed during his translation.

The collection, then, closes by coordinating the diverse communities of the legendary through the sacrificial body of the saint. But this is less a fiction of a national community founded on Becket's sacrifice than a reminder that this unity exists only in the temporary—even extratemporal—performances of ritual. Even the weekly commemoration of Becket's martyrdom, while seeking to reenact this unity, recalls a death that symbolizes the impossibility of fashioning a fully representative, fully integrated English community, given the contested jurisdictions, the local and supranational affiliations, and the irreconcilable commitments of its constituents. Defined in relation to so many different categories of community—ecclesiastical, royal, monastic, chivalric—England has complex and capacious boundaries that resist any literal or material instantiation: hence the (merely) symbolic value of Becket's death.

The Becket legend underscores the remarkable way in which the *SEL* imagines English community as defined by what it does not have in common, rather than by what it does: by the particular categories of identity and community that structure the lives of individuals; by the various kinds of time that pace social, historical, and religious existence; and by the different ways in which communities are imagined—through a representative or exceptional exemplar, or the mapping of place, or an expression of feeling, by the presence of a sacred object or the performance of a shared ritual. The Becket legend—at least in his translation—privileges these last two, but it also provides a kind of conspectus of the rest, and so also a confirmation of the heterogeneity that it pretends to unify. The *SEL*, like the *Canterbury Tales*, is oriented by Thomas Becket, but unlike Chaucer's multipart work, it refuses the metaphorical logic by which a single person, a single persona, can embody or voice the complex system of medieval communities and heterogeneous affiliations—a logic that Chaucer himself may borrow in part from saints' Lives. The *SEL* does not have, cannot have, a controlling narrative voice because it would be antithetical to the way it represents communities as necessarily, ineluctably plural. This quality is explored in the legendary's multipart form, organized through an open paradigm of time, through which the *SEL* develops the genre's capacity to model a complex system of community that preserves, indeed is defined by, a precarious relationship between many different kinds of affiliation and collective identity.

Heterotopic Ursula in the *SEL*

The *SEL* legend that offers the most thorough exploration of community as necessarily constituted by heterogeneous members—and therefore resistant to the metaphorical structure by which it might be represented by or as a body—is the extraordinary *Life of St. Ursula and the 11,000 Virgins*. The legend, in every version, creates a dynamic tension between the singular saint and the company of 11,000 virgins who accompany her, who figure different communities and so also provides a forum for imagining the relationships between them. The *SEL Ursula* offers special purchase on the role that scale plays in this dynamic: it suggests that the inherent elasticity of scale, figured by the mobility of Ursula's boat, helps negotiate relationships between different forms of community. In understanding these relationships in terms of scale, the *SEL Ursula* develops a theory of community that resists the spatial fixity of groups defined by territory or geography, creating instead a nuanced model of "being-in-common," Jean-Luc Nancy's term for modes of affiliation in which individual difference is not subordinated to a notion of shared or homeostatic identity.[47] In this way, I propose, the Ursula legend offers something like the conceptual basis for the *SEL* as a whole.

Ursula is the daughter of the Christian king of Britain, and her renowned beauty and virtue induce a pagan English king to demand her hand for his son. Ursula's father despairs at the news: his daughter has vowed her virginity to God, but the English king is too powerful to be refused. Ursula miraculously learns of her father's dilemma from an angel, who instructs her to agree to marry the prince on two conditions: that he convert to Christianity and that she be provided with ten noble virgins, each of whom—along with Ursula herself—are to be granted a retinue of a thousand more virgins. There is to be a three-year interval before the marriage in which this vast company can celebrate Ursula's virginity. Ursula and her companions dwell aboard a ship off the coast of her father's kingdom, and then they go on pilgrimage to

Rome, where the pope, Cyriacus, who is also British, joins their company. Returning via Cologne, they are martyred by evil pagans, as is Ursula's betrothed, now king, who has come to meet his bride. Through their martyrdom, the virgin company—which already substitutes a collective identity for the singular saint—joins the still larger communion of saints.

It is worth pausing to note that in spite of the geographical referents in the legend, the *SEL Ursula* does not suggest any particular affiliation between the British saint and England, in contrast to the British St. Alban in the *SEL* version of his legend. In lieu of reference to his British identity, Alban is said to be "her of Engelonde," like the Anglo-Saxon saints who are the primary representatives of English identity.[48] The *SEL* Ursula, however, is identified only as British, alienating her from the English community addressed by the collection.[49] Nor does the *SEL* legend evince much interest in the English prince to whom Ursula is betrothed. The significance of the legend to the collection of the whole is not, that is, analogous to that of Becket or the Anglo-Saxon saints, through which the collection integrates English history and culturally specific topical concerns about other forms of community. The *SEL Ursula* is offered for its general, rather than particular, interest to its audience, as a meditation not on Britain or England per se, but on the forms of community that the narrative represents on a more abstract level.

There are at least two different communities, at different scales, figured by the virgin company: their own group, defined by their shared sex and sexual status, and the political community formed through the alliance of Britain and England that resolves the potentially violent difference between them. Both forms of community are predicated on the category of virginity: the necessity of providing Ursula with a company of virgins transforms England and Britain from enemies defined by a hierarchy of military might into participants in this shared project, which is in turn a criterion for the even fuller union of these polities through Ursula's prospective marriage. Ursula's retinue is thus both a figure for, and alternative to, the two nations and the larger political structure they would form through her marriage. But this marital alliance is ultimately unrealized, and its failure identifies the company of virgins, rather than marriage, as the privileged conceptual model for community and, especially, the relationship between communities.

The relationship between the retinue of virgins and the two political communities from which they hail is charged with ambivalence. Its polarity is strong enough to produce *mouvaunce* in the *SEL*'s textual tradition, which oscillates between an emphasis on the girls' beauty—and so on the virgins as a feminine alternative to male political community—and a metaphor that compares them to an army. In some manuscripts, Ursula's father is inspired to build a boat for Ursula on account of her "fairhede," her loveliness: "So glad was the king of is doghter . and of hure fairhede / That he let ham makie a ssip . of gret lengthe & brede" (So glad was the king on account of his daughter and her beauty / That he had a ship of great length and width built) (II, 445, 63–64). Other manuscripts, however, read "ferrade," a military company, in place of "fairhede."[50] In these versions, the king has the ship built on account of his daughter and her *troops*. The metaphor identifies the virgins as an alternative to the invading English army with which Britain is threatened if the demand for Ursula's hand is refused. Insofar as the metaphor in this way equates Ursula's virgin company with the secular communities from which it is formed, it highlights military power as their foundation. But insofar as the metaphor underscores their difference, it identifies the virgin militia—ostensibly less threatening to the British king than the aggression of his English counterpart—as a deeper challenge to the protocols of military might and masculine authority on which the realms depend. This challenge becomes a more absolute alternative to secular political community when the girls are identified by their beauty: the "fairhede" of the 11,000 virgins has no martial value whatsoever, and the British king, already at a military disadvantage, uses his resources to build not a warship for his army, but a pleasure boat for beautiful girls.

The ambivalent relation that Ursula's company has to the political communities by which it is constituted identifies it as something like Foucault's "heterotopia": an "other" place that exists in dynamic relation to a site structured by social norms or political authority. Foucault uses the metaphor of a mirror to explain the essential quality of a heterotopia: like a mirror, a heterotopia provides a displaced image of the place one inhabits, rendering it "at once absolutely real, connected with all the space that surrounds it, and absolutely unreal, since in order to be perceived it has to pass through this virtual point which is over there."[51] A heterotopia thus figures both the *condition* and *limit* of a community, just as Ursula's company is at once a product of and metonym for the British and English realms and a feminine and otherworldly alternative to them that undermines the political imperatives and social practices by which they are defined.

As it happens, the Ursula legend also anticipates Foucault in offering the boat as a paradigmatic heterotopia. For Foucault, the boat, in its finite space and structure, models key elements of territorial communities, at the same time that it stands as an alternative to communities defined by territoriality. It is a paradigmatic heterotopia because it is a "place without a place," at once "closed in on itself" and "given over to the infinity of the sea."[52] The legend develops the boat's ambivalent relationship to structured sites of community once the virgin company is aboard, when it becomes the site of ludic versions of the norms and procedures of secular communities.[53] The girls, watched by men on shore, sing and dance "tresches"—fashionable French court dances contemporary with the legend—until the fateful day on which the boat begins its spiritual itinerary. In their symmetry and elaborate codification, the dances are a hyperbolic, aestheticized version of the diplomatic and military interaction of the two kings. In their evocation of noninstrumental pleasure, however, they also stand as a challenge to the functional, potentially violent, protocols of the kings' interactions. The men's gaze measures the distance between the geographically bounded community they inhabit and the virgins' boat, floating just beyond the jurisdiction of both Britain and England, an extraterritorial community that has no need of the structures of power and capacity for violence that characterize secular polities.

As a mirror of the political communities with which it is affiliated, the boat performs a primary and paradoxical function of Foucault's heterotopia: it displaces political boundaries and marks their insubstantiality, even as it provides a crucial image of their coherence and knowability. Unlike Britain or England, the virgin company aboard the boat is capable of being viewed in its entirety, and it thus serves as a countersite for the *SEL*'s Lives of Anglo-Saxon saints. But where those legends explicitly locate national identity and community in geographical space, the boat is mobile, a figure that fundamentally resists place as a coordinate of identity. This resistance is given an ultimate warrant in the way that the extraterritoriality of the boat prefigures the more categorical extraterritoriality of the heavenly realm the virgin company will come to occupy after their martyrdom.

Indeed, the boat is extraterritorial both in a practical sense—it is outside territorial jurisdictions—and in a more abstract sense implied by Foucault's metaphor of infinity (the boat is "given over to the infinity of the sea"). The *SEL Ursula* can help us to see something implicit in this metaphor: that the infinity of the sea is an effect of the boat's mobility (which is itself correlative of the boat's self-enclosure), a function of the infinite number of places that it can occupy in the sea's unending movement. It is not, that is, an infinity of limitless *expansion*, like the infinity we ascribe to the universe. It is rather an infinity *within a bounded space*, like the infinite points that make up the circumference of a circle. What is important about this distinction is that it underscores the way in which infinities—by definition—operate irrespective of quantitative scale: both a very small circle and a very large one contain an infinite number of points as its circumference. The relatively small community on a boat serves as a heterotopia for a much larger community by virtue of a difference in scale. Foucault's theory of the operations of a heterotopia as an "other place," that is, might also be read as a theory of the conceptual affordances of scale.

The Ursula legend arrives at a related insight, I think, through its narrative linking *mobility in space* to the *mobility of scale* through the figure of the boat. After the girls have spent some time aboard, the boat departs—through no human agency—for Cologne, and it arrives well ahead of the day designated for Ursula's encounter with her betrothed. The extra time allows Ursula and her virgins to travel to Rome: the boat has, as it were, changed the scale of its terminus, from Cologne to Western Christendom, and the narrative itself thus scales up from the city to a more abstract spatial field. The boat, given over to the infinity of the sea, is a heuristic for the spaces of the legend, which expand and contract: as it moves between places, Ursula's retinue— itself too large to imagine—traverses spaces that are themselves at different scales. The legend reveals that one mechanism by which heterotopia refuses a fixed place is its uncertain or unstable *scale*: like a mirror or a boat, to which Foucault compares it, a heterotopia disrupts the normative scale of the community with which it is in relation.

The spatial dislocation that results from and produces movement across different scales is echoed by temporal dislocation. The virgin company is associated not only with the infinity of the sea, but also with infinite deferral in time: the three-year delay before Ursula's marriage to the English prince is finally extended indefinitely when she is martyred rather than married upon their arrival in Cologne. The structure of delay—the temporal suspension between virginity and (prospective) marriage within which the narrative occurs—is crucial to the poem's meditation on community.[54] Like the *Prose SEL Life of St. Edward the Confessor*, discussed in Chapter 4, the Ursula legend conforms to the structure of the "hymeneal," the ritual celebration of virginity in anticipation of marriage, brilliantly analyzed by Kathleen Davis.[55] The hymeneal identifies virginity as both the condition of marital communion and that which must be destroyed to form that communion. Davis shows that the temporal interval represented by the hymeneal is a way that medieval culture theorized community formation through the model of

sexual union: the virginal female body on the threshold of marriage figures
the paradoxical nature of community as a structure of exclusion (defined by
limits, closure, identity) as well as a structure of affiliation (defined by contact, access, intimacy).

This conceptual project is intricately developed in the *SEL Ursula*. The
virginal Ursula represents a sealed, static identity that is the condition of, and
figure for, the community to be formed by her marriage to the English
prince.[56] But precisely insofar as it is figured by Ursula's nuptial body, that
community is identified as materially impossible: Ursula cannot be both a
virgin and a bride. Indeed the double martyrdom of the British Ursula and
the English king violently cancels the ethnic or geographic definition of community offered by their prospective union. The extended ritual celebration of
Ursula's nuptial virginity—the dilation of the liminal time between virginity
and marriage—turns out to prefigure the indefinite suspension of her marriage in collective martyrdom. This is underscored by the nuptial metaphors
that figure Ursula's death as spiritual marriage to Christ: although they are
familiar from other female saints' lives, such metaphors work differently in
the Ursula legend, where martyrdom substitutes for a marriage that the narrative has posited as its end, not one rejected from the beginning. The legend
thus theorizes community as *anticipatory*: neither rooted in the past, nor ever
accomplished in the present, it is necessarily provisional.

Where the *SEL* legends of Anglo-Saxon saints represent England in terms
of ethnic identity, regional geography, or political and ecclesiastical history,
then, the Ursula legend imagines community as a paradoxical condition, a
structure of belonging whose truest form is characterized by anticipation and
mobility. The legend is both the antithesis of and a complement to the Anglo-
Saxon saints' Lives, which—in positioning native identity against Norman
rule—are always in danger of creating a static, and increasingly alienated,
origin for Englishness. In place of the topical politics on display elsewhere in
the *SEL*, the Ursula legend cultivates an idea of community as a fragile, liminal, unconsummated phenomenon, defined by a ceaseless tension between
the heterogeneity of its members and their communal practices.

*   *   *

In its hyperbolic narrative image of 11,000 virgins, each a figure for an intact
and separate identity as well as a member of a collective group, the *SEL*

Ursula provides an especially focused exploration of this definition of community. In this legend, martyrdom renders permanent, and sanctifies, a temporal suspension in which the uneasy but necessary relationship between discrete, singular forms of identity and shared, collective ones can be imagined. The narrative conjunction of hymeneal ritual and the virgin's sacrificial death strikingly rewrites martyrdom not as an act that produces sacred communion, but as one that permanently—infinitely—extends the fragile paradox of being-in-common. The *SEL Ursula*, that is, plays with temporal scale in order to open this constitutive paradox of community, just as it plays with spatial scale in order to place different forms of community in fluid relation to one another, unfixed by an order rooted in territorial extension or precedence based on superior power or authority. It thus contributes to the larger project of the *SEL* by suggesting that the complex system of communities it models is correlative of the elastic scalar relationships between different kinds of jurisdiction and affiliation, and the necessary failure of any one form of community to subsume or erase differences between its members, who also participate diversely in other communities.

This model of community, developed across the *SEL* in its multipart form, is adapted most directly in the fifteenth-century legendaries discussed in Chapters 4 and 5. But it can also serve as a model for the relationship between the various materials analyzed in this study. The next two chapters echo the *SEL* in presenting a local community—a monastic community and an urban or regional one—as categorically different from, rather than metonymic of, the realm. In both chapters, the material singularity of the saint's body—its history of embodiment or its location in a particular place—is essential to forms of intimacy or unmediated affiliation that define local, but not national, communities. The Wilton Lives of Edith and Etheldreda, the focus of Chapter 2, however, depart from the *SEL* in embracing regnal history as an overarching temporal framework, while the Wenefred legends discussed in Chapter 3 extend the *SEL*'s interest in quotidian time by developing it as a way of conceptualizing the secular. Chapters 4 and 5 take up especially the status of territory, tracking the way in which mid-fifteenth-century legendaries use the multipart form of the legendary and urban metaphors for national community to address the contraction of English boundaries and changes to its relative scale. Chapter 6 explores how Lawrence Wade's *Life of St. Thomas of Canterbury* locates the sacred in an even more enclosed space, the private self, defined against an urban or English public where secular and religious jurisdictions are thoroughly integrated—a striking antithesis to the *SEL Becket*. Chapter 7, then, returns to the Ursula legend, to suggest how two versions, that of Edmund Hatfield and Richard Pynson, use distinctive formal means to develop the legend's meditation on the category of scale, already explored as a vernacular theory of community in the *SEL*.

CHAPTER 2

The Phenomenal Bodies of
Anglo-Saxon Virgins

As examples of fifteenth-century Lives of English saints, the Middle English *Life of St. Edith* (also known as the *Chronicle of Wilton*) and *Life of St. Etheldreda (Audrey)*, closely associated with Wilton Abbey, are both early and eccentric. From a historical perspective, they participate in a broad effort by Benedictine institutions to demonstrate the order's historical role in the establishment of English Christianity, as well as its current importance as custodians of the relics of English saints, and in this they anticipate the institutional investments of Lydgate's slightly later *Life of Sts. Alban and Amphibalus* and *Life of Sts. Edmund and Fremund*, addressed in Chapter 5. But where those texts embrace a metonymic logic by which the saint's body figures a corporate monastic community, which in turn might represent a larger English community, the Wilton legends distinguish between monastic and national community, defining the first in terms of affective intimacy and grounding the second more abstractly in the framework of regnal history, in which Wilton Abbey nevertheless participates. They make this distinction by rejecting the symbolic function usually served by the body, and especially the virginal female body, in representing a bounded space. They thus have implications for a historically specific formation—fifteenth-century monastic models of England as a realm—as well as for the more general conceptual structure by which corporate metaphors are used to represent social or institutional groupings. Indeed, as we will see, they challenge any representation of the body as discrete and entire unto itself.

Found together in British Library MS Cotton Faustina B. III, the Wilton Lives work in concert to recognize the body as not only a symbol, but also the site of bodily phenomena, or embodiment.[1] The *Life of St. Etheldreda* strikingly defines virginity as a practice of mediation, rather than a paradigm of stasis, and it represents the virginal body as an agent that brings together different forms of community, sacred and secular, rather than as a figure for an organic corporate entity, monastic or national. The *Life of St. Edith* works in tandem to explore the paradoxical relationship between the body understood in phenomenological terms—especially the body as the instrument of sensory experience, as a product of human sexuality, and as subject to illness and death—and the symbolic value attributed to its morphology, that is, the abstracted idea of the body's shape and structure that allows it to serve as a privileged figure for community.[2] As we will see, the legends' understanding of virginity and the body are central to the way they investigate the relationship between Wilton and England as a question of scale, as well as to how they meditate more broadly on the relationship between the experience of embodiment and the nature of community.

*   *   *

The Lives of St. Edith and St. Etheldreda, which date to the first quarter of the fifteenth century, were written in the wake of official censure of Wilton Abbey for lax administration and the irregular conduct of some of the nuns. The abbey seems to have worked vigorously to reestablish its authority, and its efforts were rewarded in 1425 when John Chandler, Bishop of Salisbury and former Wilton chaplain, issued an indulgence for pilgrimage to Edith's shrine on her feast day, September 16.[3] Although we cannot date them precisely, the legends are surely associated with this institutional project: Edith was the abbey's former abbess, as well as its patron saint, and Etheldreda—queen, abbess, and patron saint of the powerful monastery of Ely—was the figure who could most fully establish the historical and saintly authority of English female monasticism.[4]

Both legends make a related, if indirect, claim for the status of Wilton Abbey by presenting the saint within a sweeping history of Anglo-Saxon England: each poem begins generations before the saint's earthly career and stretches well beyond it through a narrative of her posthumous one.[5] In the *Life of St. Edith*, this national history narrows to focus on the foundation and institutional history of Wilton, which then becomes the point of reference for subsequent events in English history, such as Danish attacks and Cnut's kingship, while the *Life of St. Etheldreda* reframes this history in broader terms.

Together, the legends write the history of English Benedictine nuns as nearly coincident with English history *tout court*.[6]

Indeed, as Carl Horstmann noted long ago, the Wilton Lives of Sts. Edith and Etheldreda may be classified as history writing.[7] They signal their status as historiography in part through their poetic form: the legends are composed in quatrains of four-beat lines that are, as Jocelyn Wogan-Browne has remarked, characteristic of history writing in the southwest of England.[8] The legends' verse form alerts readers to the surprising fact that the saint and the monastery stand above all in *historical* relationship to England, rather than in symbolic or metaphorical relationship to it. Together the poetic form and narrative sweep of the Wilton legends reject the saint's body as an abstracted or transcendent symbol for England and identify it instead as a relic of history. In both legends, but especially in the *Life of St. Edith*, the living and posthumous offices of the saint secure the monastery within the temporal framework of English regnal history.

This insistence on the saints' historical location has to be understood in contrast to corporate metaphors of community in general and the special form that this trope took in the cults of some Anglo-Saxon saints, including Etheldreda. Representing a community as a body—the conceptual framework for many medieval theories of political and religious community—identifies it as a bounded organic form and confers on it the continuous and coherent identity generally ascribed to an individual person. As a figure for a self-identical whole, the body projects the boundaries of a community as intact and fixed, even as it acknowledges their figurative, or fictive, and also potentially mobile quality. Hence the usefulness of the body in representing forms of community that rely on notional affiliation, rather than affiliation formed through contact, communication, or other forms of practice. It is especially useful for forms of community whose notional or "imagined" quality is a function of scale: for example, the modern nation and, in the Middle Ages, the realm and Christian community. A distinctive version of the metaphor obtained in England, which was acclaimed from at least the time of William of Malmesbury for the unusual number of saints whose bodies were believed to have remained miraculously intact long after death and that were therefore understood to figure the corporate identity of England as a sacred community.[9] Like all such figures for community, the perfectly preserved body of an Anglo-Saxon saint imparts a stable form to the changeable and contingent boundaries of the polity, as well as to the still-more variable aggregation of people who inhabit it.

This is a function of the body's symbolic morphology, the body as abstract and conceptual space, which the Wilton legends challenge through their persistent attention to *experiences* of embodiment. Complicating any ready translation of the saint's physical body into a figurative one, the *Life of St. Edith*, in particular, offers strikingly incoherent representations of the saint's relics as both incorrupt and corrupt: at times, Edith's miraculously intact relics serve as a symbol of Wilton Abbey, but at others the saint's body is subject to decay, registering its materiality and recalling Edith's lived experience. In this unresolved contradiction, the *Life of St. Edith* repeatedly underscores the incommensurability of the mortal body and its symbolization. St. Edith may appear in perfect bodily form, especially in her role as patron saint of the abbey, but, to the degree that it has symbolic value, this perfect body no longer hosts the phenomena of embodiment—sense perception, physical intimacy, and vulnerability to pain, illness, and mortality—on which her relationship to that community is predicated.

Indeed, her body retains aspects of embodiment precisely because it grounds her ongoing relation to the Wilton community, sustaining the affective and physical relationships she continues to have with those who survive her. The legend explores how communities constituted through intimacy continue to make claims on the phenomenal body beyond the limit of death. In this way it challenges fictions of affiliation central to many kinds of imagined community. I argue that the spectacular differences between Edith's phenomenal body and her symbolic body track the categorical difference between Wilton and England, and indeed between any community constituted through unmediated affective relationships and those constituted through notional or abstract bonds.

The Wilton legends also clarify the special appeal of the virgin's body as a figure for community. Medieval discourses represent the virginal female body as sealed, intact, and whole, and it is therefore the paradigmatic symbolic body. At the same time, women are, as a class, associated with the phenomena of embodiment: senses, sexuality, procreativity, and material physicality. Sarah Salih has explored the fine line between virginity as a bodily state and a spiritual one in the Middle Ages: virginity was, as she has shown, a flexible category that could, but need not, refer exclusively to the body, one that might be used to identify the body as the location of an ethical identity or to dismiss it as an inconsequential vessel for, or mere representation of, a spiritual commitment that transcends the body.[10] This constitutive ambivalence—the virgin's body as the material form of an immaterial perfection— is the conceptual mechanism that links the phenomenal and the symbolic body. It is thus also important to the figurative work of the virgin's body: that is, the image it provides of a unified and self-identical community that comprises different members, whose physical bodies are subsumed by an abstract communal one. The Wilton legends analyze the logic of this figure by distinguishing between the body's symbolic purchase and its materiality. Even the body of a virgin saint, they insist, is fundamentally divided between its putative wholeness and the experience of embodiment, manifest in the physical traces of its generation, its experiences of sensation and illness, and the ethical practices—related to eating, sleeping, grooming, and so on—that shape it. Even the saint's body, that is, is ineluctably historical.

This chapter seeks to understand how the Wilton legends' surprising investment in the phenomenological body of the virgin saint is related to the construction of England and English history as a framework for religious identity. Edith's body, alternately static symbol and index of material change, points to the dual temporality of Wilton Abbey itself, at once in and out of time. Suspended between sacred perfection and embodied experience, the changing form of her relics differentiate between the monastery as a corporate body and as a contingent assemblage of particular bodies—that is, between an entity that participates in English history at a temporal scale much larger than any individual life span and an intimate community defined by concrete affective interactions between mortal women. The legends thus explore some of the implications of re-scaling religious community to the abstract dimensions of the nation. At the same time, their mixed endorsement of the phenomenology and the symbolic purchase of the virgin's body traces the promise and the limits of corporate identity per se.

Retheorizing Virginity in the Wilton
Life of St. Etheldreda

Like Lydgate's doubled *Life of Sts. Alban and Amphibalus* and *Life of Sts. Edmund and Fremund*, the two Wilton legends constitute a double narrative, if a much looser one, with the *Life of St. Etheldreda* acting as a kind of gloss on the *Life of St. Edith*. It does this by developing and authorizing a theory of virginity that underlies the Edith legend. The *Life of St. Etheldreda* posits virginity not as an end in itself—the assumption of many vernacular saints' Lives—but as a *mean* between earthly and heavenly realms: that is, as a practice that mediates between the experience of embodiment and its symbolic transcendence. Virginity thus serves as an analytical framework—and also, for the nuns who were the legends' first audience, as an analytical *practice*—for thinking about the relationship between phenomenal and symbolic bodies. It is useful for this reason to begin with the *Life of St. Etheldreda*, before turning to the more extended, and apparently incoherent, exploration of this relationship in the Edith legend.

Etheldreda was a much more prominent saint than Edith of Wilton, and she was associated with a much more powerful monastic institution, Ely. As Virginia Blanton has documented, the cult of St. Etheldreda—who is also called by the Anglo-Norman form of her name, Audrey, in the Wilton Life—generated a rich and varied textual tradition in Latin, Anglo-Norman, and English.[11] For our purposes, the most important aspect of the cult was the causal relationship it posited between the miracle of Etheldreda's incorrupt relics and her presumed virginity: Etheldreda was—in legend and in historical fact—married twice, but her corpse was understood to be incorrupt, and this was taken as evidence that she had remained a virgin despite her marriages. Many of the miracles included in her traditional legend demonstrate or call attention to her physical integrity, the category that links virginity and the posthumous incorruptibility of the body: so, for example, skeptical attempts to verify the incorruption of Etheldreda's relics are severely punished, and Danish violence against the monastery fails to destroy the saint's tomb, which remains perfectly intact.

The Wilton *Life of St. Etheldreda* rehearses this theme, but in a muted way. In redefining virginity as embodied praxis rather than bodily stasis, it truncates and conflates miracles that demonstrate Etheldreda's bodily integrity. It also swerves from any association between the saint and a coherent, transhistorical representation of England, such as is found in Malmesbury. Indeed, the legend opens with an account of England's internal heterogeneity, its originary political structure represented not as a unified body politic, but as an aggregation of discrete polities: "Sevene kyndames with inne this lond somme tyme ther were / And sevene kynges wyth inne hem ther regnede also" (Seven kingdoms within this land there once were / And seven kings reigned within them as well) (lines 1–2).[12] This erstwhile political variation within the geographical space of England points, in turn, to historical change, namely the consolidation of six kingdoms under the king of Wessex.[13] When Etheldreda, debating her right to remain chaste with her husband Ecgfrith and her confessor Wilfrid, declares that "this world nys nought / bot ever fals and fyculle and ryght unsadde" (this world is never other than false, fickle and very un-stable) (208–9), it has the authority of history. In the *Life of St. Etheldreda*, England's history is special not because an essential, transhistorical identity is manifest in the miraculous physical integrity of its saints, as in Malmesbury. It is instead a special—that is, a specific—instance of the general truth of the instability of the secular order, against which divine stasis is conceptualized.

Etheldreda thus understands physical integrity, in the idealized form of virginity, not as an embodied image or guarantee of stability, but rather as a "mene" between earthly kingdoms and the heavenly realm in which joy "hath non ending" (219). "Mayden hode," she argues, "is a ryght gode mene / to bring us up to that blessude place" (223–24).[14] In the saint's own voice, the legend defines virginity not as stasis, but as a practice of *mobility*—as movement *between* states. It produces connection, acting against the categorical differentiation, separation, and impermeability that the virgin body is made to represent elsewhere in medieval discourses.[15]

Instead of her body, Etheldreda's tomb, which is miraculously discovered during preparations for her translation, serves as the icon of miraculous per-fection. The substitution of the tomb for the body as a symbol of wholeness is forecast by Etheldreda's own prophecy regarding her death. Although she readily offers other details she has learned in an angelic vision—namely her death by pestilence and her sister Sexburge's election as abbess—Etheldreda only hints at the fate of her body and refuses to explain her meaning fully:

> And sixstene wynter my body shull lye
> In the urthe there as ye shull leyge hit full styll.
> Bot what men wolle do then there by,
> Y nyll yow no thyng now therof tell (397–400)

> [And sixteen winters my body shall lie
> Very peaceably in the earth where you shall lay it.
> But what men will do then thereby,
> I do not want to tell you anything about it now].

Having just claimed that she will not tell "what men wolle do then there by," she nevertheless prophesies that her body will be translated at that time. It might be supposed that what is left unsaid is that it will be found perfectly intact: even the abscess on her neck, which precipitates her death, and the large incision by which it was drained—with "wel gret yssu" (473)—will no longer be visible, a state of physical incorruption that was the most celebrated aspect of her ritual translation. But the miraculous status of her relics cannot be ascribed to men's "doing." Rather, the reference is to the elaborate process by which her future tomb will be discovered: the unspoken part of the prophecy—the part that the saint is determined to mystify—concerns not Etheldreda's body per se, but the material object that will contain and represent it and thereby absorb the body's conceptual role as an abstracted figure of a bounded space.

After a cursory account of Ely's fortunes—a catalog of the abbesses who followed Etheldreda, discussed below, followed by a bare account of its refounding as a college of secular canons and later as a house of Benedictine monks—the poem returns to Etheldreda's original tomb, the site of "mony grete leyghtes" (many great lights) (590) and "meche swetnesse of swete savour" (much sweetness of sweet odor) (591), where sick, blind, crooked, deaf, and dumb people are cured. These miracles prompt Wilfrid and Sexburge, who is now abbess, to move Etheldreda's body to a stone tomb. The men charged with finding the materials for it are at first unable to find anything "sufficiant" (615), but Wilfrid and Sexburge each receive a divine vision of Etheldreda, who tells them that a suitable stone is to be found in the vicinity of a nearby town, once a much larger city. Etheldreda's description of the stone, which turns out to be a Roman sarcophagus, hints that its appearance—the marble is "whyght and clene" (647)—makes it especially appropriate for her body: "Ryght thus hit is, as y yow say. Ye witte well what y mene" (Just so it is, as I say to you. You know well what I mean) (649).

Indeed, when Cynfrey finds the sarcophagus, it is "as whytte as whall" (as white as whalebone) (688). He recognizes it immediately because—it turns out—he had also received a vision, which the Life describes at some length, showing him the tomb he was to find (690–713). This vision builds on the suggestion that the tomb is perfectly suited to Etheldreda's relics: the "semely man" who appears to him explains that it is "kyndliche ywrought for hure every dell" (made for her in every respect according to kind) (709). "Kyndliche" communicates the tomb's justness for Etheldreda's relics: its most obvious meaning here is "effectively," "appropriately." But the word also encodes the idea of an inherent or innate quality, and it thus also emphasizes the surprise of that justness: independent of human intention and effort, the correspondence of the saint's body and the perfectly white, perfectly clean, and perfectly sized stone container is miraculous.[16] The "kyndliche" relationship between a found object and so singular a thing as an individual human body itself constitutes a kind of wonder.

Indeed, the "kyndeliche" affiliation between Etheldreda's body and the tomb suggests an even deeper identity linking them. "Kind," as "nature," also means "essence" or "identity," and the word thus points to the possibility that the relics and tomb are linked by some shared fundamental quality, that they are related to one another by "kynde."[17] It is miraculous not only that a found object should so completely answer to a purpose that cannot have been anticipated when it was made, but also that it should somehow share in the nature of that thing. This implication is developed in the thanksgiving prayer offered by those who are present when the tomb is found, which further elides the difference between the tomb and the body it is to contain. They thank God "that gaf hem grace to funde suche a stone / For hure body so nete and so clene ydyght" (who gave them grace to find such a stone for her body so neatly and cleanly prepared) (716–17). The lines that follow, which describe the tomb's artistry and perfection, suggest that it is the *tomb* that is "so neatly and cleanly prepared" for the body.[18] But the referent for the phrase remains ambiguous, because the body is also neatly and cleanly prepared—by Etheldreda's virtue, by her penitential illness, and by the sixteen years in the grave during which its miraculous power is manifest—*for* this special tomb, which is both a natural wonder and a monument of England's past. When her coffin is opened, her limbs are "white as ony lily floure" (842); they lie "bothe streght and evene" (849); and the wound on her neck is "clene, holl wyth ougt ony douht" (848): that is, her body is itself a perfectly formed white container.

The tomb, then, exquisitely jointed and without flaw, is both a formal and material double for Etheldreda's body:

For that ston was well ygrave, every geyntte,
That holy body to close all holl wyth inne,
Wyth ryght curiose crafte everyche a neynche,
Ther myght no fauht be founden ther inne (718–21)

[For that stone was well carved, every joint,
In order to enclose that holy body entirely within,
With very curious craft every inch,
There might no fault be found in it].

The virginal body, theorized in medieval Christianity as a perfect container for a soul dedicated to God,[19] is here literally subsumed by an object of a similar "kind" that encloses the virginal body "all holl wyth inne"—an object, that is, that can both entirely enclose the body (contain it wholly within) and preserve it in its intact form (contain it within all whole).

When Etheldreda's relics are entombed in the sarcophagus later in the legend, some of this language returns specifically to describe her body. The joints, in particular, are no longer the fittings of the tomb, but the limbs of the body it contains:

> And that ston was yshape as mete for hurre body, y wys,
> And bothe ycorvyn and ygravyd so sotelly,
> That no geynte of hurre body lay therinne amys (878–80)

> [And that stone was shaped as appropriately for her body, indeed,
> And both carved and engraved so subtly,
> That no joint of her body lay amiss in it].

Following immediately upon the information that the tomb was discovered in Grantchester, the city where Etheldreda was born (876–77), these lines identify the tomb and the saint's body as isomorphic. Indeed, they substitute the tomb's physical perfection, the perfection of its form, for the perfection of Etheldreda's virginal body.[20] The concatenated references to joints merge an image of *bodily integrity* (the perfect joints of the tomb fashion a hermetically sealed container) with one of the *articulated body* (the body's joints properly aligned). They thus conflate anxieties about the body as permeable/impermeable with the pervasive concern in medieval culture with the body as "crooked"/"straight," a concern that surfaces repeatedly in healing miracles performed at Etheldreda's tomb.[21]

The story of Etheldreda's translation theorizes the relationship between the body's phenomenal status and its symbolic value. Like matryoshka dolls, the tomb and body form a set of matched containers, one of which houses and represents the other enclosed within it, absorbing its identity in a process that Seeta Chaganti has called the "poetics of enshrinement."[22] This process traces the transformation of Etheldreda's phenomenal body, marked by her lived experience and historical identity (manifest especially by the tumor on her neck), into a symbolic one as "white as whale"—that is, bleached, like whalebone, of its bodily particularity in order to serve a new function. At the same time, it identifies the isometric identity of Etheldreda's body and the tomb—their shared shape, abstracted from the material particularities that would distinguish them—as the basis of their symbolic value. Like the tomb, Etheldreda's body too can now serve as a container for other meanings or identities.

This shift from the phenomena of embodiment to the symbolic morphology of the body is charted again in the miracle of Etheldreda's ring, an episode in the Middle English Life that has no known analogue.[23] As the monks' joy at discovering the marble tomb gives way to anxiety about how to transport it, a carter arrives who has had a vision in which a fair woman—readily identified by Wilfrid as St. Etheldreda—commissioned him to do the job and paid him in advance with a gold ring. Sexburge, recognizing it immediately as the saint's "professhennall ryng" (797), buys it from the carter and takes it to the tomb. The ring represents Etheldreda's individual, embodied identity: as a symbol of her religious vocation, it points to the practices by which that vocation was defined—her cold baths, plain food, waking prayer, and illness, which the legend has rehearsed in detail. The purchase of the ring is a narrative mechanism for marking a shift in its symbolic status, from an object that obligated the historical Etheldreda to a religious profession and hence a specific form of embodiment, to one that, adorning the shrine, represents the symbolic value of those practices.[24]

If Etheldreda's saintly body is like its marble tomb, it is also like—but only like—her body in life. The miracle of the ring inspires Sexburge, Wilfrid, and two unnamed bishops to descend to see the body in its original coffin, where they find it as whole as on the day it was buried:

As whyte, as rody, and as freysshe,
hurre fayre body was ther as hit tho lay,
and wyth ouht ony corrupcion of hurre fleysshe,
Ryght as thaw hit hadde ben leyde wyth in the chest that same day.
Hurre lures weron white as ony lely floure,
y meynde wyth rod ryght as hit was best,
and hurre body was of the same coloure
Ryght semely and sote and eke full honest.
And the grete swellyng, the whiche was her nekke abouht,
was vanysshede away, and nothyng senene,
and the wonde was clene, holl wyth ouht ony douht,
and all hurre body lay ther bothe streght and evene (838–49)

[As white, as ruddy, and as fresh
Was her fair body where it then lay
And without any corruption of her flesh
Just as if it had been laid in the chest that same day.
Her cheeks were white as any lily flower
Mixed with red right as it was best
And her body was of the same color.
Very attractive and sweet and also very proper.
And the great swelling that had been on her neck
Had vanished away and was not to be seen.
And the wound was clean, cured without any doubt
And all her body lay there both straight and even].

Etheldreda's body is at once as if *the same* as it was on the day it was en-tombed and *more perfect*, with the tumor on her neck—the one mark of her human capacity for moral imperfection and vulnerability to illness, the single trace of her historical and embodied experience—entirely effaced. As we have just seen, such perfection, on which the body's abstract form is predi-cated, is necessary to its symbolic capacity, even as it is at odds with an equally necessary liveliness. The legend insists that these are coincident: "Hurre body lay ther as semely in everichemonnes syght, / Ryght a lyve as thaw hit yet were" (Her body lay there as attractive in everyone's sight just as if it were still alive) (850–51). Her body is *so beautiful it is as though it were alive*, the legend claims. But this beauty is clearly beyond the beauty of a living body, that is, beyond the beauty of embodiment, of the phenomenon of having a body. Its very liveliness paradoxically attests that this body is removed from the phe-nomena of embodiment, as Etheldreda's several appearances in visions have already made clear. The fantasy of such a body, whose symbolic value and even vitality are predicated on exemption from experiences of embodiment, is not limited to medieval Christian culture. But if we take the interest in vir-gin martyr legends as symptomatic, we may recognize that the desire for such a body is especially strong, and subject to extensive exploration, in this period.

*   *   *

Once the tomb has taken on the symbolic function of the saint's body, the legend seems to turn to a more conventional representation of the relic's physical wholeness. The narrator, in a style more anecdotal than is characteristic of the rest of the legend, includes a miracle about which he claims to have read when visiting Gostow, the Oxfordshire nunnery (lines 990–1098):[25] once, when Ely housed canons, a secular canon named Cerdic chiseled a hole in Etheldreda's tomb in order to see whether the relics were still whole. When he tried to pull the clothes away from the body with an iron hook on a pole, the implement stuck fast—or was perhaps seized by the saint—and the canon was blinded. Corporate penance by the college earned some mercy from the saint: Cerdic was able to pull his hooked stick from the tomb and the hole he had made was sealed, although he himself remained blind.

Even this narrative, however, is less a witness to the sacred inviolability of Etheldreda's body than an index of its ability to mediate between heaven and earth. So the narrator interjects:

> Bot wyst ryght well that hurre soule was in hevene blys,
> And that hurre body was as hole as he was mayde ybore,
> And that hurre body ever in urthe in gret worship shall be (1096–98)

> [But know right well that her soul was in heavenly bliss,
> And that her body was as whole as when she was a newly born maid,
> And that her body shall always have great worship on earth]

As Etheldreda had argued to Ecgfrith regarding her virginity, bodily integrity—here in the form of her perfectly preserved corpse—is a "mean" between heaven and earth, a mechanism for their relation or for movement between these distinct realms: reference to it literally mediates between heavenly bliss and worldly worship.[26] The parallel between this passage and Etheldreda's understanding of virginity confirms the ideological construction of virginity as wholeness or integrity—again, by linking sexual encratism and the corpse's incorruption—at the same time that it confirms her redefinition of virginity as a form of praxis rather than stasis. The virginal body, in life and death, is retheorized as one that moves between the experience of human embodiment and the body's symbolic value, and thus traces the difference between them.

St. Edith's Symbolic and Phenomenal Bodies

The difference between the phenomenal and symbolic body explored in the *Life of St. Etheldreda* is used in the *Life of St. Edith* to distinguish between two forms of monastic community: the legend suggests that while the monastery may be figured as a metaphorical body, modeled on the symbolic integrity of the saint's body, its status as a community is also defined through practice, especially affective and ethical practices that depend on contact, presence, and other forms of intimacy. This understanding of monastic community, in turn, differentiates the monastery from England, a community whose geographical scale necessarily attenuates relationships between its members.

The legend maps its two models of monastic community most graphically through its incoherent representations of Edith's body as both incorrupt and corrupt. It appears by turns—and sometimes at once—as miraculously intact and as decayed, in witness to the phenomena of her lived experience. The legend first forecasts the wonderful state of Edith's relics in a triple set of triple dreams: the Duke of Cornwall, King Aethelred, and Dunstan each report having three dreams on three successive nights in which they are told that Edith's body should be translated. Edith then appears to Dunstan to announce that her body will be found incorrupt, evidence of God's power over "monnes hele and his hereynge" (man's well-being and his glory) (2460). This is a commonplace symbolic meaning of the intact body in medieval Christianity: that is, as a promise of future resurrection and a representation of the perfected communion of saints. When Edith's body is exhumed in order to be translated to a new tomb, it indeed appears whole, in its perfect symbolic form:

> This blessude body *as hole they hit founde*
> *Ryght as alyve hit was goynge here*, y wys,
> and as sote a savore come ouht of that grounde
> as thaw hit hadde come ouht from paradys (2559–62)
>
> [This blessed body, *they found it as whole*
> *As it was indeed when it, alive, walked here,*
> And as sweet a smell came out of that ground
> As though it had come out of paradise]

The assembled company—which includes the king, the dukes of Cornwall and Dorset, the archbishops Dunstan and Elphege, and the Bishop of Winchester—sees the body "as feyre, as hole, as bryght in ble / as hit was alyve when hit dude here go" (as fair, as whole, as bright in countenance as it was when alive it did walk here) (2565–66). Note the neuter pronoun: the body here is distinguished from Edith herself, as the corporeal vessel that she inhabited. That implicit distinction triggers an apparently antithetical claim, unreconciled with the assertion of physical integrity, that Edith's sensory "organs," especially those of feeling and sight (2567–69), are corrupt. The legend insists at once that the saint's body is both miraculously preserved, in witness to her sanctity, and corrupt, evidence of her embodiment. Its symbolic wholeness, it turns out, does not depend on its material status, which is not whole after all.

The Wilton *Life*'s incoherent representation of St. Edith's relics is still more surprising given that they were not traditionally understood to have remained miraculously intact: unlike St. Etheldreda, she is not included in Malmesbury's list of English saints whose bodies resist corruption, and Goscelin's eleventh-century vita, which is both the primary account of her life and the main source for the Middle English legend, describes a kind of hybrid body, corrupt in some parts and incorrupt in others: "Her extremities were destroyed, from the elbows and knees, and also her face; the rest of the body, together with the thumb, the standard-bearer of the holy cross, as it was called, was quick with firmness and beauty, so that the marvelous grace of God might be praised equally in her blooming and in her death."[27] It is her thumb that receives the greatest attention in Goscelin's legend: St. Dunstan, observing the unusual frequency with which Edith crosses herself, predicts that her thumb will be preserved from material corruption, in contrast to the rest of her body.[28] Against this established tradition, the Wilton legend insists repeatedly on the saint's total physical incorruption. The pairing of the *Life of St. Edith* with the *Life of St. Etheldreda*—the English saint most widely celebrated for the miraculous integrity of her body—further constructs a parallel between them based on this quality.

The Middle English legend, then, rewrites the story of Edith's translation as a story of the miraculous incorruption of her relics, while retaining—with striking disregard for narrative coherence—narrative episodes in which her corpse is identified as partly decayed. The emphasis in the first of these passages is on the corruption of the "organys of the lemys" (organs of the limbs), which Edith used "childlych" in her youth, especially by feeding wild beasts

(2467, 2468, 2470). The incoherence is magnified if we follow the implied moral logic and return to the legend's account of Edith's childhood, where her attention to wild animals is lauded:

> And wylde bestes and folys of flyght
> to here clepyng wolde come full snell.
> And at hurr byddyng thei wolde doun lyght,
> and of hurre hond they wold meyte take (1114–17)

> [And wild beasts and birds of flight
> To her calling would come very quickly.
> And at her bidding they would land
> And they would take food from her hand]

Edith's care of the animals is included in a list of her many acts of charity in the service of God. She feeds the poor, washes and heals the bodies of the sick and maimed, takes the lame and the leprous to church, and intercedes for thieves who would otherwise be hanged (1089–1110). Unlike the care that Chaucer's Prioress lavishes on her dogs, that is, Edith's feeding of wild animals is an extension of, not a substitute for, corporeal works of charity performed on behalf of vulnerable people. Far from being morally culpable, Edith's attentions to wild birds are a precocious form of her future sanctity.

How, then, should we understand the posthumous rebuke of Edith's apparently innocent, even meritorious, care of wild animals, especially its manifestation in the decomposition of her body? Perhaps she is guilty of a category mistake: in feeding the birds, Edith may privilege their physical bodies over their symbolic meaning. Edith's greatest affection is for doves because of their affiliation with the Holy Spirit (1114–20).[29] Or her error may be to elide the symbolic and the material: Edith feeds the doves *because* they represent the Holy Spirit. Perhaps, rather, her error is to predicate her care of animals on their symbolic significance, rather than their physical needs. If the decay of Edith's limbs and sensory organs ascribes moral significance to the material condition of the body, it does so obscurely, with no indication of the nature of her transgression. Indeed, the legend only *seems* to inscribe the ontology of sin on to Edith's body: the absence of any clear moral logic challenges any presumption that the body can be read as a symbol of spiritual status. Her corrupted limbs serve instead as a morally neutral material record

of Edith's childhood, a history of embodiment that is separate from any symbolic meaning that might be attributed to their physical state.[30]

Like the *Life of St. Etheldreda*, then, the *Life of St. Edith* raises fundamental questions about the relationship between the saint's lifelike relics and her
once-living body, between a symbolic body that is miraculously whole and a
phenomenal body whose limbs and sensory organs are subject to decay.
Edith's body can act *as if* it were whole, "as hole hit ys": note that she asserts
her physical integrity as simile.[31] But just as it can no longer feed wild animals, it no longer experiences sensation. Edith's body retains its phenomenal
status, that is, in part through limits on her agency as a saint, figured by the
decay of her sensory organs. The legend thus draws a bright line between the
agency of a phenomenal body (the capacity to interact with the world through
the senses) and that of a saint's symbolic body. The latter is an agent (it heals
people) as well as a sign (it figures God's power and the institutional authority of Wilton Abbey), but its actions do not rely on the senses and are restricted to Christian community. These limits do not diminish Edith's agency
as a saint, but shift it: her symbolic body—again, despite its lifelike qualities—
cannot act as a mortal body because it is a function of an abstract morphology that is separate from, indeed antithetical to, the material body.

Edith's body nevertheless retains the traces of earthly embodiment, a
physical record of her behavior as a child, her sensory experiences, and so
on. The absence of her sensory organs itself marks her body as material.
Even as Edith's body stands as a symbolic double for, and thus also a guarantee and protector of, Wilton Abbey, it remains linked to a particular history
of embodiment. This is evident, above all, in the legend's unprecedented representation of her genitalia as subject to decay, an index of human sexuality
and procreativity against which virginity is usually defined. In a passage otherwise unattested, Edith explains in a vision to Dunstan that the "organys of
my nother lemys" (organs of my nether limbs) have disintegrated because of
her "fader gulte" (2484, 2483). Edith's body is shaped by its sexual generation,
through which the material body comes to be. In a notable departure from
medieval discourses in which the virgin's abstinence is understood to exempt her from human sexuality and generation altogether, Edith's genitals
mark her body as a product of sex, regardless of her own vocation and
virginity.

It is important to note that Edith is not represented as inheriting any
moral culpability from her father: her genitals are not subject to decay *because* he transgresses Christian sexual morality. This is the wrong-headed

assumption of the pagan Cnut, who doubts Edith's miraculous resurrection of a boy, saying,

> Kyng Edgares dougter, yche wene he was,
> y kete bot upon a wenche.
> How shulde he ever have suche a grase,
> whose wolde hym self this well by thence? (3351–54)

> [King Edgar's daughter, I think she was,
> Sired on a lower-class woman.
> How should she ever have such a grace,
> Whoever would judge well of this one?]

Cnut is wrong: Edith has indeed resurrected the boy, proving that her capacity for sanctity is not compromised by her "fadur gulte." By attributing to Cnut's faulty understanding the belief that sin is inheritable, the legend distinguishes the phenomena of embodiment from the moral systems through which such phenomena are sometimes understood. In the place of such fictions of inherited moral identity, the legend insists on a kind of durable physical relationship to a parent, one of the many forms of intimacy that it explores. Her father's "guilt" is manifest materially on Edith's body only to mark her as the product of human generation: the material condition of her body links her to the act through which she was created and thus to her father's (immoral) body.

Against dominant discourses of virginity and of the body as a register of moral status, then, the legend insists on the material condition of the virgin's body against its idealized morphology. Just as the corruption of Edith's organs indexes her embodiment by underscoring the loss of sensory experience—"felyng and seygt ys from hem take" (feeling and seeing is taken from them) (2469)—so the disintegration of her genitals registers family relationships as bodily phenomena. The legend insists throughout on the experience of embodiment, defined in terms of the sensory capacity of the body, its biological connection to other bodies, and the physical dimension of its affective relationships. The sacred integrity of Edith's body thus exists in uneasy relation to the materiality of human embodiment: it has both a perfect, abstract form and a physical presence that is an agent of, and subject to, the senses, sexual generation, and other embodied phenomena.

Community and Corporate Identity

This incoherence is central to the legend's meditation on Wilton Abbey as a community and form of corporate identity. On the one hand, the poem imagines Wilton in terms of a corporate identity secured by the saint to whom it is devoted and at times figured by the miraculous wholeness of her relics. The collective identity of the nuns is, as we might expect, often expressed through their shared devotion to Edith: Edith's translation is celebrated with "song and gladnesse / That *ychemonn made with other yfere*" (song and gladness / that everyone made together with the others) (2581–82), the group joins together to sing the *Te Deum* after many of Edith's miracles,[32] and they intercede collectively on behalf of goldsmiths who have stolen the precious metals that were to be used for Edith's shrine (3595–3601). On the other hand, the legend insists throughout on the phenomena of embodiment, which are not susceptible to symbolic or metaphorical abstraction, as the foundation of community.

A key episode, remarked recently by Jocelyn Wogan-Browne and Cynthia Camp, is a miracle that occurs during Edith's translation, when a monk named Edulf secretly tries to cut a piece of her garment with his knife and accidently nicks Edith's breastbone.[33] The blood runs from the cut so copiously—"as thawe hit hade come from a lyvyng monn / That hadde be lette blode in a quyke veyne" (as though it had come from a living person whose blood had been let from a live vein) (2615–16)—that it soaks her clothes and his, and covers the floor. The monk responds not with fear or horror, but with "sorwe" (2621) at the injury to the lifelike relic of Edith's body, and he sinks to the ground "as thaw he were dede." As he repents, his brothers lift him from the floor and pray for him; when they perform a penitential procession on his behalf, the blood vanishes and Edith's body and her clothing are whole once more. In this miracle, Edith's body testifies to her lively presence in the house; she is there as though "a lyvynge monn," a living person, with a body that bleeds when cut.

The image insists on the ordinary phenomenology of the body—vulnerable to accident, even to the surprising way a small surface cut can bleed out of proportion to the injury—rather than on the significance of the transgression. Indeed, the monk's action is hardly blameworthy: Edith's relics are eminently desirable, after all, and he does not attempt to take part of her body.[34] The cut is an accident, and the body responds as any body, nicked in a "quick vein," might. At the same time, the miracle posits a perfectly whole body by imagining its apparent rupture. As a symbol that depends on its abstract morphology, Edith's body is *necessarily* whole and cannot be compromised by its material condition: if the monk's actions are ostensibly rebuked by the alarming effusion of blood, they are ultimately inconsequential, because Edith's miraculous wholeness is a symbolic abstraction, independent of the material body itself. This symbolic wholeness may represent Wilton Abbey, as Camp argues, though it is worth noting that the narrative more immediately celebrates the community of visiting monks who join together around their hapless brother. The miracle highlights the corporate activity of this other monastic community, *in parvo*, whose collective penance restores to their pristine state the saint's body and the sacred space it occupies.

The miracle curiously anticipates the narrative tropes of an anti-Semitic myth, mentioned subsequently, in which the ambivalence about the symbolic and material body takes its ugliest form: a claim that Jews bleed from the anus every Friday as retribution for their putative role in Jesus' death (4753). In this myth, the failure of Jews to maintain normative bodily integrity is a sign of their exclusion from the corporate body of Christendom. The Edulf incident unexpectedly aligns Edith with the Jews: as the one who bleeds, Edith's is the body that figures a threat to corporate identity.[35] The parallel may signal the "hermeneutic" function of Edith's bleeding body, like the one Lisa Lampert identifies in the representation of Jews in much Middle English literature: like the Jews of the myth, Edith exposes the degree to which the ideal of a corporate Christian community depends on the threat of its rupture.[36] At the same time, the anti-Semitic myth can also be understood as a hateful version of the legend's general interest in the vulnerability of mortal bodies, an interest that equals, perhaps even outweighs, its interest in the fantasy of corporate Christian identity. One young nun, for example, suffers from abundant menses ("blody mensone," 3174) that have so enervated her that she is in danger of dying.

Indeed, if Edith's (sometimes whole) body represents the corporate identity of Wilton Abbey, the legend is otherwise preoccupied with the phenomenal bodies of its individual members, such as the menstruating nun. The stories of Edith's miracle working, especially, are stories of the bodily experiences of individual nuns, whose illnesses, migraines, and menstrual disorders she is called upon to remedy and which thus constitute and demonstrate her agency as saint. The phenomenological bodies of the nuns she cures are not reducible to the abstract morphology of Edith's body, nor are they represented as secondary to it. While the legend at times invokes the body's symbolic status, it qualifies this by identifying the body's greatest representational and analytical purchase in experiences of embodiment, rather than any notional wholeness.

We see this, for example, in the long narrative sequence about the nun Alfyne, who is healed of a blinding migraine when Edith appears and touches her (4570–77) and then, in a second vision, is told by Edith that she will become abbess of Wilton.[37] In the latter, Edith bestows her veil and ring on the young nun (4615–21), a miraculous transfer of the material symbols of her profession that is a prelude to the still more wonderful transfer of Edith's intimate relationship with her own mother, Wultrude, who had succeeded Edith as abbess. Edith grants Alfyne privileged access to Wultrude's tomb, and, in a scene at once terrifying and oddly moving, the dead Wultrude, speaking from there, invites Alfyne to "make [her] dwelling" with her.[38] When Alfyne humbly demurs, Wultrude seizes her hand and pulls Alfyne down so that they lie together on the altar stone (4638–51): the physical intimacy between the deceased abbess and the young nun identifies the monastery as a community that both transcends the life of any individual member and depends on embodied affection between them.[39] This form of community, moreover, responds to the urgent claims of bodily experience, represented in this episode by Alfyne's migraines and failing vision. Its formation through intimate contact with Wultrude's material body thus reflects its purpose as well as its essential structure.

Edith does not cure every sick nun: at one point, she reprimands nuns who pray for her intercession on the grounds that, as a saint, she is obligated to help every Christian, not only the members of her own abbey (4806). What she offers the Wilton nuns is her lifelike presence and companionship, as this reprimand itself—delivered, as it were, in person (4838–43)—recalls. As in her earthly role as abbess, Edith's posthumous relationship to Wilton is an affective, embodied one. Thus in another miracle associated with her translation, Edith's quasi-living presence makes Wultrude and the nunnery "ful glad in hert" (2664), even as it reveals Edith's capacity for formidable anger. A "lady" of the abbey—that is, most likely a nun, though possibly a lay patron[40]—tries to cut off "a litul particule" of Edith's head covering as a relic (2651). This act is described as both a moral and criminal transgression—it is prideful (2657) and a form of theft (2658)—and it receives a strident rebuke from the saint. Edith rears up from her bier and her face registers her disapproval:

Bot that blessud virgyn sodenlyche heve up here hedde,
Ryght as thaw he hadde ben alyve there tho,
and schewede that lady with hurre chere also
that hit nas not the wyll of God, ny for hurre hele,
that he wolde so prowdelyche thedere so go,
or ony pece of hurre blessud clothus to stele (2653–58)

[But that blessed virgin suddenly heaved up her head,
Right as though she had been alive there at that time,
And also showed that lady by her expression
That it was not the will of God, nor for her good,
That she would go so proudly thither,
Or steal any piece of her blessed clothing]

The lady is alarmed and repentant, but also "full glad" of the miracle (2663): she has, indeed, received a striking form of recognition by the saint, in gesture and expression as well as in the words spoken to her. After the encounter, the lady, identified as one Elbright after the miracle is narrated, reforms her erstwhile sinful life, and Edith later reappears to her to applaud her good works and inform her of her heavenly reward. Edith's embodiment is the vehicle for an affective relationship—if initially a terrifying one—with her devotee.

It is only in the final episode of the legend that the symbolic wholeness of Edith's body serves to represent and protect the status of Wilton. When the abbess Algide—frustrated at the difficulty of defending the house's interests to the Bishop of Salisbury—impatiently accuses Edith of failing to look after the nunnery, another nun, Tole, receives a vision of Edith's incorrupt body. In this vision, even Edith's hands and feet—limbs once corrupt—are sound, as the saint declares:

Lowe, see here my hondone and my fete also,
how holle and sounde my body ys,
and how myghty and how quyke ycham nowe also,
For of body ny of leme no corrupcyon ther nys.
Se me and fele me at thy nowne wyll,
and loke that hit be so as y yow say (4886–91)

[Lo see here my hands and also my feet,
How whole and sound my body is,

And how mighty and how alive I am now also
For there is no corruption either of body or limb.
See me and feel me at your own will,
And see that it is as I say to you]

In this last episode of the legend, Edith's symbolic body asserts itself in response to threats to the nunnery's privileges and autonomy. Edith, who has refused to cure individual nuns, defends the abbey as a corporate institution through the symbolic wholeness of her own body. It is notable that even here the legend associates such abstract integrity with the nunnery as an *institution*, rather than as a community.

The legend thus exposes the logic by which a monastery or other institution might borrow its notional integrity from a saint or other paradigmatic body. That Edith's body has been acknowledged as corrupt is no barrier to this symbolic function: saints' bodies—even, or especially, as fragmentary remains—are understood to possess a magical completeness and integrity, through a kind of metonymic and counterfactual thinking. Just as the Eucharist is understood by medieval Christians to be the (perfect) body of Christ, any saint's relic, however small, points to her miraculously whole body. In its final, finally perfect, form, Edith's body instantiates the abstract morphology that allows virginity to be understood as intactness, that allows saints' relics to represent a perfected community, and, more broadly, that facilitates the conceptual work of the body as an organic whole and isolate container of individual identity. But Edith's body elsewhere in the legend retains its phenomenological status: its corruption witnesses a lived history of sensory experience, human generation, and intimate affective relationships. The legend understands community—and in particular Wilton Abbey as a community—far more in terms of its members' radically singular experiences of embodiment than in terms of a corporate identity in which they are imagined to participate.

Wilton Abbey as an Affective Community

One value of the phenomenal body is its capacity for intimacy, and thus for a form of selfhood in which, as Tony Kushner insists, "the smallest indivisible human unit is two people."[41] This kind of selfhood is given material and narrative expression in the very pairing of the Edith and Etheldreda legends, their codicological intimacy. Certainly, their shared preoccupation with the saint's phenomenal body is correlative to their interest in the monastery as an affective community, predicated on embodied intimacy. This is especially clear in the *Life of St. Edith*, in which a key capability of the saint's phenomenal body is the emotional relationship it sustains with her mother, Wultrude, which exemplifies the nature and structure of the Wilton community at large.

Affective intimacy is a principle of community from Wilton's very foundation, which commemorates Elflede, the daughter of King Edward the Elder and his queen, Ecgwyn.[42] Elflede dies when she is two years old, the accidental victim of national history: she drowns in her bath while her nurse is distracted by the "crye and sorwe" of women and children during a Viking raid (451). The child's death and the commemorative foundation of the monastery anticipate Edith's own early death at the age of twenty-three and the devotional practices and administrative role that her mother, Wultrude, adopts in response. As we have already seen in the story of Alfyne's election as abbess, this affective relationship in turn becomes a model for subsequent abbesses.[43] Addressed to Wilton nuns, as well as the abbey's lay residents, the legend uses the mother-daughter relationship to posit a community constituted by physical proximity and emotional intimacy.[44]

Importantly, this conceptualization identifies the nunnery as historical, located in the saeculum, in contrast to the familiar representation of monastic institutions as models of Christian communion outside of historical time (a representation we will explore in Lydgate's English saints' Lives in Chapter 5). In the Wilton *Life of St. Edith*, the boundary separating the earthly nunnery from a sacred realm is itself structured by affect, exemplified by Wultrude's distress at Edith's death. Wultrude's lament for the loss of her daughter's companionship is also, literally, the lament of an abbess for a deceased nun: "My dure doughter, what shall y nowe do? / whom shall y have now to my fere, / when ye arne thus from me go?" (My dear daughter, what shall I now do? Whom shall I have now as a companion when you are thus gone from me?) (1986–88). The antithesis of Wultrude's sorrow is voiced by Dunstan, who emphasizes God's desire for Edith (her "shappe" and her "fayre bewete," 2017, 2018) and their joyful spiritual union—a theological perspective on Edith's death wholly at odds with Wultrude's desperate earthly desire for her daughter. The legend elaborates these separate frameworks for Edith's death by contrasting the grief of the Wilton community to the happiness Edith's death produces in heaven. Wultrude, having lost her "worldly joy," wrings her hands and gnashes her teeth, and the other nuns tear their hair in sorrow,

"Bot the angelus song, and maden gode chere, / and broughton hurre soule up to hevene blys" (But the angels sang and made good cheer, and brought her soul up to the bliss of heaven) (2073–74). The secular world and the monastic community located there are defined by distinctive affective phenomena as separate from a heavenly realm.

Affect is thus also the primary mechanism by which Edith remains part of the Wilton community after her death, above all through her mother's surprisingly persistent concern about her spiritual status. Wultrude's ongoing, unwarranted concern for Edith's soul—"for drede of hurre soule he had gret fere, / albut thaw hit nere no nede" (for dread of her soul she had great fear, even though there was no need) (2115–16)—leads her to sponsor a chantry of twelve poor men that continues "yet in to this day" (2111). Edith's sanctification is signaled unambiguously by the bright light that emanates from her tomb, a sign that should reassure even the most anxious mother, but fails to assuage Wultrude's fears:

> Nought ageyne stondynge that, in that place,
> ofto tyme was ysey full gret leyght,
> there as hurre body enterud was,
> bothe by day and eke by nyght.
> yet had hurre moder bothe dougt and drede
> of hurre doughter soule, y wys, for all that
> and made prestus bothe syng and rede
> and gret penaunce he dud hurre self algate (2117–24)

> [Notwithstanding that in that place
> Often times was seen a very great light,
> Where her body was interred,
> Both day and also by night,
> Yet her mother had both doubt and dread
> About her daughter's soul, indeed, despite all that
> And made priests both sing and read
> And she herself continually did great penance]

Edith appears in a vision to her mother and recounts how she vanquished Satan and ascended to the bliss of heaven, but Wultrude is still not reassured: "in hurre hert full sore he yet dredde, / nought ageyne stondying that he seyge and herde well / that that blessed virgyne hurre doughter ryght well ferde" (in her heart she yet dreaded very sorely, notwithstanding that she saw and heard well that the blessed virgin, her daughter, fared very well) (2153–55). Her distress about her daughter's spiritual status is credited as a "long martirdam" (2166), a form of maternal solicitude so acute that it approximates the experience of physical violence.[45]

Wultrude's actions are not represented as excessive or suspect, as they might be in other saints' Lives.[46] Indeed, she provides an ideal model of lasting grief for other women whose children have died:

> He dude not lyge, as don mony other wymmen
> that atte hurre children dyenge wepon fulle sore,
> and ryght sone after forgetone hem
> and thenk on hem lytull after that more.
> Bot he continuede algate styll in this,
> in doyng of masse of derche and of almys dede,
> and ever he was hurre self in fastyng and in gret preyeris, y wys,
> and for hurre doughter had algate gret drede (2157–64)

> [She did not vary as many other women do
> Who weep very bitterly at their children's death
> And forget them very soon after
> And think about them little after that.
> Rather she continued always still in this,
> In the performance of the Office for the Dead and almsdeeds,
> And ever she herself was fasting and in great prayer, truly,
> And for her daughter continually had great concern]

The emphasis is not, as we might expect, on the value of such devotions for ensuring her daughter's salvation. Instead Wultrude's activity is encoded by the affective urgency of the passage as an expression of undying love. As further miracles witness Edith's sanctity—for example, a woman who steals the gold border of a cloth that Wultrude has placed on Edith's tomb is miraculously fettered by the fabric—Wultrude provides for still more priests to say additional masses (2261–2332). In the context of Edith's evident holiness, endowing such masses, which might otherwise be understood as forms of penance undertaken on her behalf, serve rather as forms of communication with her, across the boundary of death. Wultrude relaxes her efforts only when she realizes that all sick people who come to Edith's tomb are healed (2333–54):

although she was unmoved by other evidence of Edith's sanctity, such as the miraculous light emitted by her tomb, Wultrude is finally consoled by evidence of her daughter's continuing presence and activity, which suggest other forms of contact and access available to her.[47]

The ongoing affective ties between mother and daughter bind Edith to earthly life. Edith herself "nolde not from hurre moder long dwell" (did not want to dwell away from her mother for long) (2126); she appears to her mother "visablelyche" (visibly) thirty days after her death (2133), speaking to her "in hurre owne langage / Ryght as a neyghbure doth to another here / or knyght or squiere to his page" (in her own language, just like a neighbor does to another here, or a knight or squire does to his page) (2134–36). Compelled by her love for her mother to reappear in embodied form, Edith is then available to participate in a wider community as though she were still living. Thus on the same day that she first appears to Wultrude, Edith fulfills a promise to serve as godparent to a child who is born after her death: she appears bodily ("bodylyche," 2212) in the course of the baptism, and she then guides the child's hand to take a candle and holds it for her (2219–24), receiving the child as though she were still alive ("to fonge to the childe as he had yteyght, / Ryght alyve as thaw he yet were") (2227–28).[48] As Wultrude's anxiety suggests, affective ties—as much as, perhaps even more than, her sanctity—structure Edith's ability to transcend death, to move between heavenly and earthly realms. Her appearance as saintly godmother inaugurates Edith's miracle working—giving "grace and hele to every monn that hurre bede" (2256)—and marks her miracles as manifestations not only of sacred power but also of secular affection.

The love between Edith and Wultrude, both abbesses of Wilton, defines the nature of the institution itself. In an early miracle recounted at length, Wultrude cures the blind Beteric by following directives that he has received from Edith in a vision (2735–2842). The miracle is the joint work of both women, daughter and mother, one the patron saint of Wilton and the other its current abbess. The affective relationship between the women links their respective institutional positions, abbess and patron saint, in an analogous intimacy, as their shared miracle suggests. As the effective cause of Edith's miracles, Wultrude is identified as "Seynt Woltrude" (2902) even while she is still living, especially in miracles related to the status of the abbey. So too local people do her "servyse and honour bothe day and nyght" as the earthly proxy for her daughter (2962). The saintly protagonist of the legend, at this point, is the conjoined identity of the saintly Edith and the still-living Wultrude.[49]

Edith and Wultrude's affective relationship is the primary model for the

Wilton community, over and above the symbolic wholeness of Edith's body, which is in any case only intermittent. Where a poem such as *Pearl* represents a daughter in heaven as so remote from an earthly parent that she is properly beyond any concern for her soul, the Wilton *Edith* insists on a still-intimate affective relationship between living mother and sainted daughter, and it offers this relationship as a paradigm for the nature of monastic community. As we've seen, Wultrude's persistent attention to Edith's status after her death has no penitential or moral necessity; instead, it models the fundamentally affective structure of the monastery's relationship to its patron saint. The community at Wilton is constituted by embodied intimacies, even—or especially—with their patron saint.

Edith and England: Territorial and Temporal Re-scaling

Affect is also a key category in Edith's ability to represent the realm of England. She very briefly figures the corporate body politic when she mourns her father's death as a threat to the collective happiness of the realm. The passage was evidently both important and confusing to the scribe, who inserts, as Mary Dockray-Miller remarks, "a series of non-sequential corrections" on the bottom of the folio:[50]

> gret mowrnyng made that mayde tho,
> nought onlyche for hurre self he ne drede,
> bot also for mony another mon mo.
> He sorowede not onlyche for here self, y wys,
> bot also for mony a nother mo,
> for myche rest, ioy, and blys,
> the Reme laste when he was ago (1638–44)

> [Great mourning made this virgin then,
> She dread not only for herself,
> But also for many another person.
> She sorrowed not only for herself, truly,
> But also for many another more,
> For much rest, joy, and bliss,
> The realm lost when he was gone]

Edith's grief is "not only for herself," but also for the realm, which is bereft of "rest, joy, and bliss"—emotional states that mark England as a communal body. At the same time, Edith's feeling on behalf of "many others more" identifies her closely with this corporate entity, an identification conditioned by her royal birth, through which her personal loss and the national one are imbricated. Edith's grief for her father cannot be distinguished from—indeed is an expression of—the realm's collective loss.

Edith's affect, that is, establishes her capacity to embody the realm: it identifies her body as a spatial form that can figure English community as a coherent and organic unity and can localize the body politic's affective and social interests, which constitute the theoretical ground of sovereignty itself.[51] Edith, however, ultimately prefers the alternative affective community of Wilton to the national one she might otherwise embody. When her brother, King Edward, is murdered, Edith is identified by parliamentary acclaim as sovereign. But Edith refuses, and Aethelred—whose mother has murdered Edward to this very end—accedes to the throne, an inauspicious beginning to his disastrous reign, which leads ultimately to the Norman Conquest. Within one understanding of the historiographic framing of the legend, Edith's decision reads as a political, and even ethical, failure, an abdication of royal obligation that results in national crisis.[52] Her seeming indifference to the responsibilities of sovereignty—"he nolde none suche charge upone hurre take" (she did not want to take on such a responsibility) (1741)—is understood by the messengers from Parliament as culpable, even inhuman, intransigence, evidence that "hurre hert was as hard as ony stone" (her heart was as hard as any stone) (1733).

Like Cnut's mockery of Edith's sanctity, their criticism directs attention to alignments that the legend might seem on the surface to assume or endorse: it is an invitation to explore, in particular, the relationship between England and Wilton Abbey, national community and religious community—a relationship explored also through the formal admixture of regnal history and hagiography that characterizes the *Life of St. Edith* as a whole. The messengers' criticism of Edith's decision is rooted in the specific ethical and political perspective of regnal history, within which Edith's rejection of the crown is an egregious mistake. But it is a legitimate, even wise, choice from the perspective of saints' Lives, within which the narrative of England's volatile history that opens and threads through the *Life of St. Edith* supplements a conventional hagiographic emphasis on the inherent instability of secular politics.[53] A religious vocation, even the vocation of someone who would otherwise reign as sovereign, cannot *make* the realm unstable, since it is necessarily subject to fortune: the political history with which the Edith legend is framed demonstrates precisely that there is no security in any worldly rule. Within this framework, Edith's refusal to assume sovereign authority is not a politico-ethical failing, much less the cause of the Norman Conquest, for not even a saint can forestall the essential variability of secular history.

Edith's abdication prompts a broader question about how the relationship between Wilton and England is conceptualized when the legend is nested within English history. The *Life of St. Edith*'s hybrid narrative form, in which the legend proper is dilated by a regnal history that precedes and extends beyond Edith's own life and the history of Wilton Abbey, rescales the geographical and temporal coordinates of the narrative in ways that echo contemporary Lancastrian efforts to rescale other local cults as national. But even as the poem establishes English history as the legend's narrative scale, and thus as a temporal structure relevant to the monastic community to which it is addressed,[54] it parses the difference between Wilton Abbey and England by defining the former as an intimate community, represented by the phenomenal body of the saint, against the abstract corporate metaphors through which the realm was understood.

It will be helpful first to clarify how the legend understands secular and sacred jurisdictions more generally. Medieval Christian commonplaces about the superiority of the divine realm to an earthly one and the limits of royal might compared to the limitless power of the holy, of the sort that inform Edith's preference for a monastic vocation over queenship, are given ample play in the *Life*. Faced with the prospect of ruling England and France, Edith asserts that "here kyndam nas not here, / bot wyth God hit was in hevene blys" (her kingdom was not here, but with God in heavenly bliss) (1747–48). As Dunstan administers last rites to her, he proclaims that for her "mede and meryte" she will be granted the "corone of mayden hode" (2011, 2013), which is far superior to any earthly crown.[55] The relative insignificance of secular rule is a lesson learned by the newly converted Cnut, returning to England after handily defeating enemies who had invaded his own homeland, when he absurdly orders the wind and water to be calm during a storm at sea only to be reminded of how limited his power is:

> "What gode is hit," qd the kyng tho,
> "Forto be a kyng of remys thre?

This tempest obeyeth hym nomore me to,
Shipmon, then hit dothe to the" (3451–54)

["What good is it," said the king then,
"To be a king of three realms?
This tempest submits itself no more to me,
Shipmen, than it does to you"]

Having failed to command the seas, Cnut prays to St. Edith, who does have Christ-like command of the elements: she casually walks over the water, waving it away with her sleeve.[56] Even people are more surely under Edith's control than under the king's: when Cnut orders a shrine be made for Edith's relics, the goldsmiths steal some of the precious metal, defiant or indifferent to the king's command ("of the kynges precepte they token non hede," 3518). But when they attempt to smuggle the treasure out of the church, they are blinded and unable either to leave or to set down the metal: they pace back and forth bearing it "opynlyche" in their hands (3565).

The *Life of St. Edith* nevertheless presents regality and religious devotion as ideally, if not necessarily, compatible, as Cnut's own conversion and subsequent patronage of Wilton suggests.[57] Anecdotes that seem at first to suggest otherwise ultimately serve to prove the point: thus on one occasion the English forces are very nearly routed by the Danes while King Aethelred is at mass, but after the service has ended the king quickly reverses the battle by making the sign of the cross and commanding that his troops do the same (294–97). The king's daily attendance at mass ensures that God grants him "what that he bedde" (whatever he prayed for) (259), marking Aethelred's devotion as the efficient cause of the English victory: "and thus the victory was his, / thorowe help of the Trinite and *of the masse that he dud here*" (And thus the victory was his through help of the Trinity and *the mass that he had heard*) (304–5; emphasis added). The exemplar of devout kingship, defined equally by political responsibility and religious devotion, is King Alfred, who divides every day into three eight-hour periods, measured by wax candles of equivalent size, the first devoted to serving "God hevene kyng," the next for "rest and play," and the last for "his remes governynge" (395–97). Alfred similarly divides his revenues into equal halves: one going to his reign and the other to almsdeeds (408–9).[58]

If sovereignty is not incompatible with devotion, why then does Edith refuse the crown? She does not reject political rule per se, I propose, but the sovereign's symbolic role as body politic: Edith implicitly refuses the re-scaling of her body from its ordinary dimensions to the abstract spatial form of "England." In life, as in her posthumous career as saint, Edith prefers more local forms of embodiment. Hence the bodily metaphor by which the messengers criticize Edith's response to her parliamentary election: her heart is as hard as any stone. Otherwise capable of exemplary emotion, Edith refuses to instrumentalize this affective capability as a form of political authority.[59] In refusing sovereignty, Edith preserves the categorical difference between the phenomenal body and the body re-scaled by the operations of metaphor to represent an abstract corporate entity such as the realm.

The category on which their difference is predicated is, again, affect. The legend's emphasis on the phenomena of embodiment, including physical intimacy, as the ground of the Wilton community precludes the re-scaling of religious community to the spatial or territorial limits of England. Wilton and England cannot be related on a graduated spatial scale, as smaller and larger communities that Edith might embody, the legend suggests, because one is predicated on embodiment while the other depends on the body's symbolic morphology. In a historical moment in which forms of religious community were being re-scaled as national, the *Life of St. Edith* posits an essential difference between the monastery and the nation. This thematic concern places the legend in conversation with the re-scaling of religious community at the council of Constance, for example, at which voting protocols identified the "nation" as the scale of religious community.[60] It also constitutes an oblique rejection of Lancastrian nationalization of regional or institutional cults, a process also contemporary with the Wilton legends.

One risk of identifying religious community with a national one is that its boundaries become uncertain, subject to political and historical contingency. This is a concern addressed in both Wilton legends, which represent England as subject to dramatic shifts in its geographical definition: in the *Life of St. Edith*, for example, the reign of King Egbert—who is said (twice) to have given his name to "England"—is defined largely by his unification of four of the Anglo-Saxon kingdoms. This lack of stable territorial definition is also represented by the movement of the body politic itself in, for example, thematic attention to the king's multiple residences, Wilton, Winchester, Salisbury, and "mony other places mo" (125). Traveling between them, "as a kyng oughte of suche honour" (as a king of such honor ought to do) (125), is a hallmark of ideal kingship: a king's power resides not in territory per se, and may rather take as key indices his own mobility and the mutability of the realm's boundaries.

Perhaps the legend rejects a spatial or geographical re-scaling of religious community because this kind of dynamic territoriality does not correspond readily to the way that monastic institutions represent themselves in cartularies and other documents, which emphasize their foundation and accumulated territory. Indeed, the catalogs of kings and other founders appended to the end of the *Life of St. Edith* (fols. 263r–264r), which might be considered as an integral part of the legend, underscore its affiliation with monastic charters. Or perhaps the dizzying pace at which English territory changed in the early fifteenth century made it a risky way to map religious community: the parameters for dating these legends place their composition either during the dramatic expansion of English territory under Henry V or its equally dramatic reduction during the reign of Henry VI. Whatever the cause, the conceptual and practical differences between England and Wilton are presented in the *Life of St. Edith* as questions of spatial scale, especially as these are figured by the body and as they permit or preclude unmediated affect and contact among members.

Even Edith's miracles are scaled to the monastery, not the realm, which is sometimes an audience for them, but never their object. As news of her healing miracles spreads, "all the reme had gret joy, y wys / of this blessud virgyn Seynt Ede" (all the realm had great joy, indeed, of this blessed virgin, St. Edith) (2361–62). But Edith's posthumous appearances are confined to Wilton, not "England": her miracles are performed on behalf of the abbey itself and, more often, its visitors, specific people present within the community Edith once inhabited (and still inhabits). Unlike the miracles performed by St. Etheldreda and St. Alban on behalf of an abstract national community in Walsingham's *Chronicle*, Edith's actions deepen the intimate affiliations that structure monastic communities.

Edith's miracles do, however, suggest an extension of temporal scale, one that corresponds to the poem's own temporal re-scaling of the saint's Life to match the duration of English history. Temporal scale is an important category in the relationship between the individual body and corporate forms of identity: the phenomenal body is (ordinarily) bounded by death, whereas communities provide forms of identity not limited to the lifetime of a single person. They do this in no small part by imagining the community itself as a living body, thereby promising to extend individual identity either into a

collective past or a promised future. The *Life of St. Edith*, however, establishes the temporal scale of the Wilton community less through the saint's
symbolic body than through her ongoing affective relationship and gestures
of care and healing toward its members. While such forms of intimacy and
the kind of community they create cannot be scaled up spatially, the legend
suggests, they can—at least as miracles—persist beyond the death of a
person.

Hence the legend's formal investment in historiography: as noted above,
Wogan-Browne has identified the legend's verse form—tetrameter
quatrains—as a prosodic signature of vernacular historiography in the southwest. Its poetic form, that is, helps to identify English history as the temporal,
rather than the geographical, scale of religious community. The Wilton Lives
expand the temporal coordinates of hagiographic narrative by borrowing
tropes of royal genealogy from regnal historiography to extend Edith's vita
backward in time, and they borrow tropes of monastic history to extend it
indefinitely forward. The conceptual centrality of temporality, as we have
seen, registers in the phenomena of embodiment—in the form of human affections and bodily experiences—which occur in, and mark, secular time.
The definition of virginity as praxis (acts of mediation) rather than stasis (as
an image or promise of divine timelessness) in the *Life of St. Etheldreda* corresponds to the emphasis on time as well. Predicating the relationship between religious and national community on the category of time, rather than
space, does not make them invulnerable to change, of course. But unlike
changes in the spatial scale or boundaries of a nation, which erase earlier
formations, change across time accumulates as history.

Thus, beyond its role in authorizing Wilton's foundation and privileges,
English regnal history also provides narrative scaffolding for a series of miracles demonstrating Edith's sanctity and the history of Wilton. For example,
after a long digression recounting some of Wultrude's posthumous miracles,
the narrator promises to return to an account of St. Edith's goodness, but
then bizarrely determines to begin with King Aethelred (3243) and proceeds
to offer an abbreviated political history, recapping the murder of Edward,
Aethelred's accession to the throne and disastrous reign, the rapprochement
between Cnut and Edmund Ironside, and Cnut's rule over England after Edmund's sudden death, all in some thirty lines (3245–74).[61] The historical syn-
opsis is the context for the story of Edith's conversion of Cnut and his baptism
at Wilton, which is narrated in some detail.[62] The regnal history then
recommences —with Cnut's death and the accession of Harold—to serve as

the broad context for a local miracle concerning the monastery's property.[63] Edith's miracles are thus presented as points where the history of England and the legend may be stitched together, sizing the latter according to the temporal scale of the former. Re-scaled in this way, the history of Wilton is made coincident with regnal history. The legend underscores this conceit by asserting, twice, the nonce etymology that England is named for King Egbert, whose sister, Alburge, founded Wilton.[64]

A striking example of the legend's careful scaling of its narrative to align with English history is the temporal coordination of Edward the Confessor's reign and a miracle related to the infamous dance at Colbeck (4054–4293). In this well-known story, a group of revelers refuse to end the carol they are dancing in a churchyard, and they are compelled to continue—without rest or food—for a year. Edith and Wilton have an ancillary role in the story, recorded more famously in Robert Mannyng's *Handling Sin*: one of the dancers, a man named Theodoric, travels to England on pilgrimage once the spell is broken, seeking a cure for the shaking and compulsive dancing that still impair him. Theodoric initially chooses England "for knowlage of Seynt Edward" (4247), but he has also heard a great deal about St. Edith, and he comes to Wilton to pray at her shrine. The story of the dancers of Colbeck and Theodoric's pilgrimage and cure are recounted at length, and they entirely occupy the narrative time of Edward's reign, which ends when the miracle story concludes: "The nexste yere after that tho dyede that blssud thing, / Seynt Edwarde that worthy confessour" (The next year then after that this blessed person, Saint Edward, the worthy confessor, died) (4294–95). Very hasty references to Harold Godwinson, the Battle of Hastings, and the changes in lordship and laws under William the Conqueror—occupying fewer than fifteen lines (4296–4309)—introduce the next miracle.[65] The Colbeck carol—dilated miraculously to a full year—models this narrative distension in which Edith's intercession and Edward's reign alike occupy one period of a shared historical paradigm.

Such alignments may serve to remedy historical ruptures caused by political crisis. When Edith cures the horribly deformed Hutchin, whose limbless torso and enormous head make him look like a large mallet (4323), the usurper Duke William, hearing of the miracle, becomes a patron of the nunnery whose resident saint was once herself in line to rule England (4370–73). Discontinuity in royal genealogy is here repaired by Edith's ongoing miracles, as well as by the continuous history of devotion to her and renewed royal patronage of her house. Wogan-Browne has shown that this can be understood as the text's bid to underwrite the legitimacy of Lancastrian kings.[66] But we may also recognize a more conceptual project: to explore temporality, rather than geography, as the basis on which religious community may be scaled as national.

*   *   *

Edith rescues Hutchin not only from horrible deformity but also from dehumanizing metaphoricity. If the cure of his malletlike body with its oversized head inspires William the Conqueror's devotion to St. Edith, it also prevents Hutchin from symbolizing the overmighty Norman king, mismatched with the functionless body politic over which he rules. As a kind of material and historical mechanism for linking religion and national identity, Edith's phenomenal body returns to historical specificity and personal experience the bodies of both the vulnerable and the kingly. In the *Life of St. Edith*, the saint's body is not more symbolic, more abstract, than the ordinary human body: it does not point to a numberless heavenly host or sacralize a body politic in which individual bodies—aside from that of the sovereign—are mere parts of a corporate whole. Edith, saintly participant in a community defined by affect and intimacy, insists on the body's immediate significance as the site of the experience of embodiment. The *Life of St. Edith* posits the experience of embodiment as fundamental to religion and to religious community, and this acts as a limit on the abstraction of the body as a figure for communities of any kind.

It may be worth underscoring that religious community here grounds identity and relationships in the particular, the local, and the embodied, while secular political community is defined by far more abstract ideas of belonging, an opposition that anticipates post-Enlightenment "formations of the secular," in which religious particularity is contrasted to the "universal" claims of the secular state.[67] Religious community is defined in the *Life of St. Edith* as so intimate that it can host, and attend to, embodied phenomena, and it is therefore antithetical to secular communities at a larger spatial scale that obscure such phenomena, partly by being conceptualized as a body.

While the *Life of St. Edith* analyzes, and resists, the scale jumping at the heart of corporate metaphors for community—in which one body stands for many people—it offers in its stead a shift in temporal scale by which the history of a people extends the short life of the individual, or the longer, but still vulnerable, life of an institution such as Wilton Abbey. Written texts have, of course, an important role to play in this, as a key technology for extending the temporal scale of communal memory. The *Life of St. Edith*, in a quiet apology, notes that the past is forgotten if it is not written down, and it addresses its audience of "yong maydens" as agents of cultural memory—they are at Wilton precisely their "bokes to lere."[68]

In the first decades of print, either a printer who recognized the market for native saints' Lives or someone affiliated with the nunnery, perhaps still seeking to establish its cultural authority, had the idea of re-scaling the legend's audience beyond Wilton, and the single extant manuscript was marked up for printing.[69] It is difficult to know whether or why a metropolitan audience would have been interested in a little-known regional saint, patron of an abbey whose population and power were quickly waning.[70] Perhaps they would have identified Edith as an "English" saint and read the repeated representations of Edith's miraculously intact body as a symbol of England's corporate identity. Or perhaps the legend's persistent meditation on Edith's phenomenal body would have encouraged this audience too to attend to the experiences of embodiment that cannot be subsumed into the abstract morphology of the body politic. Certainly the legend's confidence that religious community can be re-scaled to the nation—if only on the axis of time, not space—could have found a receptive audience among some quarters on the cusp of the sixteenth century.

CHAPTER 3

Local Community and Secular Poetics in
Middle English Lives of St. Wenefred

Like the *Life of St. Edith*, Middle English legends of St. Wenefred resist the geographical re-scaling of the saint's cult. John Audelay's carol version of the Wenefred legend, which is roughly contemporary with the Wilton legends, and Osbern Bokenham's ballad-rhyme Life of St. Wenefred, written perhaps a generation later, emphasize the quotidian and familiar quality of the saint and a correlative representation of community as constituted by ordinary social interactions. They thus also echo the Wilton *Life of St. Edith* in their emphasis on the local as the site of belonging and participation, perhaps as a rebuke to the nationalization of Wenefred's cult, discussed in the Introduction, and in particular the geographically expansive fiction of the royal body politic that informed, and was performed in, Henry V's royal pilgrimage to her shrine. The Audelay legend is notably silent and the Bokenham one explicitly skeptical about royal devotion to St. Wenefred.[1] They each present her legend as a forum for representations of bounded, contingent communities, "actually existing" communities defined by physical presence and regular devotional practice, against competing contemporary ideas of England as the spatial scale of religious community.

Such resonances with the Wilton legends make even more striking the Wenefred legends' starkly different representation of the temporal scale of such communities. Where the Wilton legends extend the Life of the saint and the history of her abbey to occupy the time of English history, the Wenefred legends contract the temporal scale of community to an evanescent *now*. And they present this temporal immediacy as a coproduct of the forms of physical contact and access through which they define devotional communities: in this conceptualization, the present and presence are irreducibly linked. This form of community might be called *secular*, in the medieval sense of the term, especially when recognized as an alternative to communities that claim to transcend concrete affiliations or geographical and temporal boundaries. As I remarked in the Introduction, a key difference between premodern and modern conceptualizations of the secular and the religious is their inverse relationship to categories of particularity and transcendence: in premodern thought, the secular is defined by particularity and contingency, in contrast to the transcendence claimed by religion. This is more or less diametrically opposed to post-Enlightenment thinking, which generally defines the secular as a universal ground, a framework that transcends the particular, including—especially—the particularism associated with religious belief and practice.[2]

Middle English Wenefred legends suggest the importance of the local—of finite *places*—to the medieval understanding of communities that inhabit secular time: they figure community as a lived practice in a specific place. I begin with Bokenham's mid-fifteenth century *Life of St. Wenefred*, which overtly rejects Lancastrian models of English community, before taking up Audelay's Wenefred poems, composed some twenty-five years earlier than Bokenham's during the high point of Henry V's devotions to the saint. Bokenham's opposition to the cult's royal appropriation, as well as his resistance to a Benedictine idea of England as a sacred national community with which he was manifestly familiar, can help us better understand Audelay's more elusive meditation on secular community.

In a more pronounced and intricate way than the Wilton legends, the Wenefred legends use poetic and rhetorical form as important resources for conceptualizing community. Their signature formal features—namely, Audelay's use of carol form and the direct colloquial speech that is a hallmark of Bokenham's style—also represent more conspicuous experiments in, or departures from, the mainline of vernacular saints' Lives. The carol form of Audelay's Wenefred poem, which is crucial to its representation of temporal and spatial finitude, is in itself a distinctive prosodic choice and is still more experimental when recognized as a component part of the elaborate pastoral and lyric sequence in Oxford, Bodleian Library MS Douce 302, the single extant manuscript of Audelay's work. As Susanna Fein has recently taught us, the book presents a large-scale multipart formal structure, despite its apparently eclectic assortment of texts.[3] Bokenham's *Life of St. Wenefred* cannot claim the same level of formal complexity or ingenuity: it is part of a relatively conventional legendary, and it is composed in rhyme-royal stanzas, like

Chaucer's St. Cecilia legend and many post-Chaucerian "literary" saints' Lives.[4] But Bokenham's rejection of aureate style—the conspicuously Latinate vocabulary and ornately alliterative lives associated with this stanza form in the fifteenth century—and a concomitant embrace of direct address, collo-quial language, and personal anecdote bear importantly on his conceptual-ization of community as a phenomenon of everyday interaction.

Insofar as these two legends explore secular forms of community through significant engagement with registers of form and style, they also open ques-tions about the relationship between literature and the secular. Their pro-sodic and narrative features—narrative persona, lexis, stanzaic form, and so on—are oriented toward exploring the capacities of poetry to address local or quotidian experiences of community. I thus turn at the end of the chapter to a consideration of how we may read these vernacular legends for a secular poetics.

Secular Community in Bokenham's *Life of St. Wenefred*

There is a robust corpus of Middle English Wenefred Lives. In addition to the Lives by Audelay and Bokenham—each extant in only a single manuscript—there is a verse legend attested uniquely in a fifteenth-century copy of the *South English Legendary* (*SEL*), Oxford, Bodleian MS Bodley 779, as well as a prose legend by John Mirk included in his *Festial* (both of these are discussed briefly in the Introduction).[5] William Caxton printed two further versions: a short one in the *Golden Legende* and a longer legend printed as a separate booklet.[6] All these vernacular legends tell roughly the same story as the two twelfth-century Latin Lives of St. Wenefred, one by the Shrewsbury monk Robert Pennant (Robert of Shrewsbury) and another anonymous vita that may have been written by a monk of Basingwerk.[7] Wenefred is a devout girl who has promised her virginity to God. One day, home ill while her parents attend mass, she is visited by the local prince Caradoc, who is overcome with desire and demands her love. Wenefred, fearful for her chastity, escapes from the house and is pursued by her irate suitor, who strikes off her head. A spring surges at the spot where Wenefred falls, and Caradoc sinks through the ground to hell. Wenefred's head rolls down the hill to the door of the church, where her spiritual mentor, Beuno, is saying mass. When he has finished the liturgy, he places Wenefred's head on her body and asks the congregation to pray that she be granted the grace to live the religious life to which she had dedicated herself. Wenefred is miraculously restored, with a thin scar around her neck as the only bodily marking of her martyrdom. She is professed and maintains a close affection for Beuno, sending him missives via her spring once he has moved elsewhere. She finally founds her own house of nuns, which she governs piously until her death by natural causes. Her wellspring continues to flow in wondrous abundance, and in it can be seen stones covered with red spots, a second material memorial to Wenefred's violent (if temporary) death.

Osbern Bokenham's Wenefred legend is found in the volume of saints' Lives recently discovered in Sir Walter Scott's library at Abbotsford House and identified by Simon Horobin as Bokenham's "long lost" legendary, the collection of saints' Lives to which Bokenham refers in the prologue to the *Mappula Angliae*, a geographical treatise excerpted and translated from Ranulph Higden's *Polychronicon*. The Wenefred legend is the last extant item in this book, though legends of other saints whose feasts fall in November surely once followed.[8] It would have been conspicuous nevertheless for its length: running some ten folios, it is the fourth longest legend in the collection. This is partly an effect of the legend's personal and anecdotal style: Bokenham recounts conversations from his own pilgrimage to Holywell and adds other incidental comments in the course of the story. This "chatty" persona is familiar from Bokenham's *Legendys of Hooly Wummen*.[9] In those legends, it is a narrative means by which saints and their stories are identified with specific patrons. Here, it is a forum for a distinctive emphasis on the local, the everyday, and the personal—phenomena that point toward secular experience and community. The devotional community oriented by St. Wenefred is defined above all by proximity, including the proximity of the mundane and the sacred.

Like the Wilton *Life of St. Edith*, Bokenham's Wenefred legend is especially interested in affective proximity and in forms of community rooted in the claims of human affection, which confer special value on secular experience. This is perhaps most evident in the dilated representation of her parents' grief when Wenefred is killed. Bokenham adds an otherwise unattested lament, in which they mourn the loss of their daughter as an earthly—that is, secular—source of comfort:

> Alas the whyle that we were born
> Of oure doughtyr this syth to see
> Alas alas now haue we lorn

Alle the ioye of oure antiquyte
Alas we hopyd she shuld haue be
Oure singuler comfort & oure solas
But now ys al goon. Allas allas. (215v)[10]

[Alas, the time that we were born
To see this sight of our daughter.
Alas, alas, now have we lost
All the joy of our old age.
Alas, we hoped that she would be
Our singular comfort and our solace,
But now is all gone. Alas, alas.]

When Beuno hears "of this carful cry the soun"—not the words, but the *sound* of their voices, which registers emotion more viscerally—he comes running. Unlike most versions of the legend, in which Beuno restores Wenefred primarily in order that she may live to pursue her religious vocation, Bokenham's version privileges the consolation that her resurrection offers her devastated parents. Although Beuno's own hope had always been for Wenefred to be sanctified as "Goddys wyf of heuene"—a privilege she earned by dying to defend her vowed virginity—he is moved to undo her martyrdom by their sorrow.

To be sure, Wenefred's resurrection is warranted in Bokenham's version too by her vow to live as a consecrated virgin. But it is also designed to restore the ties to family and community severed by her death. Beuno specifically tells the assembled company to pray not only on account of "Hyre awow . . . but your comodyte" (her vow . . . but also your solace) (216r)—that is, the comfort that she offers to them by her earthly presence, her presence in the saeculum. Indeed, this can be the *only* warrant for her resurrection: Beuno's prayer explicitly recognizes that Wenefred is already in "blysse wich thou [God] hyre to bouth" (bliss which You provide to her). She is already God's spouse (216v), and thus she has "no necessyte" for the "felashyp" of her family and neighbors (216r). Wenefred's resurrection is in defiance of this Christian truism and in deep sympathy with the claims of human affection: it is as if the Pearl Maiden were to leave the procession of the Lamb to rejoin the grieving Dreamer, privileging his desire over the divine. Later, whenever Wenefred shows people the white scar ringing her neck, she asks them to be thankful that God "lengthyd hyre lyuys space" (lengthened the space of her life) (216v), a sharp departure from the urgent prayer of most virgin martyrs to join their heavenly Spouse.

Wenefred's martyrdom, then, is staged—remarkably—as a demonstration of the claims of secular community, especially in the intimate forms of family and neighborhood. Beuno's ministrations as he tries to resurrect Wenefred continue this theme. Weeping, he kisses her head again and again before placing it on her body, where he continues to kiss her and, in a striking detail, blow softly into her nostrils.[11] These physical gestures of love and healing are given the narrative prominence we might expect to be given to his prayer, which is all but passed over: the legend merely notes perfunctorily that he "w[ith] his mantel curyd yt [the body] dede blysse" (blessed the body with his pastoral garment)(216r). Wenefred is resurrected, in Bokenham's version of the legend, through the affective force of her parents' grief and Beuno's gentle attentions to her mortal body, supplemented only vaguely by the thaumaturgic power of his blessing.

This insistence on secular contact and access, as opposed to sacred transcendence, has both a topical political significance and a broader conceptual one. It anticipates an anecdote about a chapel commissioned by Henry IV that serves as an explicit rebuke to Lancastrian appropriation of St. Wenefred and an implicit rejection of a sacralized form of national community.[12] The legend carefully describes the origin and architecture of the chapel:

Kyng herry the fourte for the tendyr loue
Wich that he had to this virgyn pure
Dede maken a chapel ouer the welle abowe
Myhty and strong for to endure
On thre partys closyng yt in sure
And that no man presumyn shuld to come ther ny
A gret grate ys sette on the fourte party

Ffor pleynly hym thouhte aftyr his entent
In to that welle wich clepyd ys holy
That ony man shuld goon was not conuenyent
Syth men myth water han sufficyently
Hem wyth to wasshyn euene therby
Wich at the grate yssuyth owt so sore
That knedeep yt ys at the fallyng or more (217v)

[King Henry IV, for the tender love
That he had for this pure virgin
Had a chapel made above the well
Mighty and strong that it might endure
Enclosing it securely on three sides
And so that no man should presume to come near
A great grate is set on the fourth side.

For plainly it seemed to him, according to his intention,
That it was not appropriate that any man should go
Into that well that is called holy,
Since people could have water in sufficient amount
To bathe themselves just nearby
As it issued out of the grate so vigorously
That it is knee-deep or more where it falls].

The very abundance of the water issuing from the spring—a material manifestation of the saint's fulsome grace—seems to the king to license limited access to it.[13] Royal architecture thus marks off and mediates the space of the sacred.

The chapel may be intended as an act of devotion—Bokenham credits it to the king's "tender love" for Wenefred—but it nevertheless constitutes a violation of the sacred. Bokenham recounts a recent miracle, told to him by his innkeeper, of a white friar from Coventry who makes an annual pilgrimage to Holywell to bathe his legs and body in the waters as protection against illness and sudden death.[14] One time, seeing the fair, clear water in the well, the friar thrust his arms through the grate as far as they could go and prayed to Wenefred for a token of her friendship ("of hyre frenshyppe sum tookne," 217v). When he pulls them out, the friar's arms are covered with red spots—a simulacrum of the bloodied rocks in the spring that highlights the materiality of his body. There are "diuers opynyouns" about the meaning of the spots: some observers think it is a "signe a veniaunce / ffor his presumpcyoun"; others think it is "a specyal tookne. . . . That in Wenefredys grace syngulerly stood he." The spots are still there when the friar wakes up the next morning, and after he sings mass in the chapel, he descends to the well and thrusts his arms in at the grate again, praying that Wenefred remove the spots if they signal her favor and leave them if they are a form of punishment. The friar is immediately healed, in a modest but pointed echo of the more spectacular restoration of the saint's own body after its violent encounter with Caradoc.

The miracle designates the *creation* of boundaries marking off a sacred space, not their transgression, as illegitimate: indeed, like the well itself, whose plentiful waters spill out of the enclosure, the miracle challenges the very idea of spatial distinctions between the secular and the sacred.[15] It endorses unmediated contact with the sacred—not just devotion, but physical access, to the saint. This is manifest on the level of narrative presentation: the poet's claim to have heard this miracle from his host during his own pilgrimage to Holywell is at once a guarantee of its truth and part of a broader emphasis on the saint as a source of community formed through presence or other forms of intimacy.

The mediating function that the king has arrogated to himself in building the royal chapel is thus unnecessary at best and at worst sacrilege. The miracle casts the king's "tender" love for the virgin as a shadow of Caradoc's rash lust, and, like the saint's violent death at Caradoc's hand, its effect is to render Wenefred temporarily unable to comfort those who love her: the grate that separates her devotees from the well's salvific waters has affective consequences that echo those of her beheading. Other works by Bokenham have been read as evidence of Yorkist partisanship: Richard of York's sister Isabel was one of his patrons. Shrewsbury, the site of Wenefred's shrine, had strong affiliations with the Duke of York, and Bokenham's pilgrimage there may be related to his Yorkist affiliations.[16] It is dated in the poem to 1448, which provides the legend's *terminus post quem*. The criticism of Lancastrian appropriation of the cult can be read in terms of Bokenham's Yorkist patrons, and perhaps specifically the contest between Lancastrian and Yorkist factions for Welsh support in the 1450s.

But the legend's concerns extend well beyond immediate political contingencies to a broader exploration of the oscillating relationship between local and national forms of community and identity. The anecdote of the friar's cure at Wenefred's well, as we have seen, insists on local identity, contact, and immediacy. Tellingly, Bokenham and the friar both visit Holywell not as Englishmen visiting an English shrine, as Henry V visits it, but as members of other local communities, Clare and Coventry, by which they are identified: their pilgrimages preserve at once their own regional identities and that of Wenefred's cult. The legend's rejection of Henry V as a figure who mediates their access to the shrine and identifies it as English should be recognized as part of a larger thematic that privileges lateral affiliations between small-scale communities over vertical ones organized by shifts in conceptual scale from the local to the national.

It is important that although it depends on physical presence and personal contact, the form of community imagined in Bokenham's Wenefred legend is not restricted to a local population: it accommodates anyone—or anything—that makes a pilgrimage to the well. Bokenham mentions (and dates) his own pilgrimage to Holywell to attest that the rocks found in the well still display red spots commemorating Wenefred's martyrdom. He cannot, however, personally confirm a related claim that new stones introduced to the well will acquire the spots: he himself has "no evydence" for this:

> But oonly relacyoun of men in that cuntre
> To whom me semyth shuld be yeuyn credence
> Of alle swyche thyngys as ther doon be
> ffor whan y was there myn hoost told me
> That yt soth was wyth owte drede
> ffor hym self had seyn yt doon in dede (217r; emphasis added)

> [But only accounts by men in the region
> To whom should be given credence, it seems to me,
> About all such things that happen there.
> For when I was there my host told me
> That it was true, without doubt,
> For he himself had seen it done in deed].

Those who doubt this miraculous phenomenon are challenged to bring their own clean stones to the well, mark them in some way, and return after a time to verify that they have acquired the spots. At issue is the truth value of the legend, to be sure, but also the value of *presence* emphasized throughout the legend: while Bokenham's limited access to the well prevents him from attesting to the miracle, his personal acquaintance with the host at his inn constitutes a form of knowledge; and others can confirm the miracle through their own unmediated access to Wenefred's well.

The miraculous bloodying of imported stones sacralizes the translocal, the contact between two places understood in terms of their local particularity. Like the miracle of the friar's red spots, the transformation of the stones can be read as resistance to Lancastrian nationalization of the cult: it witnesses a circuit of the sacred that is not routed through the king's body or an abstract idea of English community. The miracle, predicated on and manifest in material form, emphasizes rather the importance of contact and intimacy, forms of

affiliation that cannot be mediated by the king or any other symbolic structure.[17] Knowledge about the miracle parallels the miracle itself in this regard:
it derives from Bokenham's own historically located pilgrimage and his personal relationship with his host. That is, it depends on a translocal epistemol-
ogy, rooted less in one person's experience than in his contact with others.

The "translocal" is a category developed in postcolonial and globalization
studies, where it refers to phenomena not mediated by empire or nation, and
it is important to note its different structure and implication in this premodern context. Because the nation does not function as the normative scale of
community in the late Middle Ages, its absence as the mediating middle term
lacks the political force it has in a national or postnational frame. What is
more significant is the rejection of a transcendent structure of any kind,
whether one attributed to a religious order, such as Augustinian canons, or to
secular sovereignty—any structure that would mediate the relationship between the saint and the pilgrim, or between Shrewsbury and other local
places. The legend imagines instead relationships constituted by proximate,
often physical, contact: the water on the friar's skin, the story shared by a
personal acquaintance, the pebble brought from home, the warm breath
blown into the nostrils of someone's beloved daughter. The emphasis on the
local does not simply resist Lancastrian devotional politics; it is also key to a
counter theory of community, one that rejects abstract ideas of communion
altogether for communal forms that depend on immediacy.

The legend signals an interest in the translocal from its opening lines,
which specify the story's geography. The passage amplifies a brief reference in
Bokenham's main source, Pennant's *Life and Translation of St. Wenefred*,
which locates Wales between the kingdom of "Anglia" and the "Ocean sea."[18]
Bokenham supplements this with the description of Wales from Higden's
Polychronicon:

> At the west ende of Brytayne the mor
> lyeth a Province. a ful fayr cuntre
> Wich aftyr Policronicas lore
> Buttyth on the gret Occyan see
> Wich ys distinct in to partys thre
> And in oure Wulgare. now ys clepyd Walys (214v)

> [At the west end of Great Britain
> Lies a province, a very fair region

Which according to the teaching of the *Polychronicon*
Abuts the great ocean waters
And which is divided into three parts
And in our vernacular is now called Wales].

Along with the tripartite division of Wales, Higden is the source for an account of Welsh history and economy to which Bokenham alludes in a two-
stanza *occupatio* that follows, before he dismisses "Topographye" as a subject
on the grounds that it is not "the principal cause of this labour."[19] This passage, and especially the explicit reference to Higden, links the Wenefred legend to the *Mappula Angliae*, the treatise on English geography from the
Polychronicon that Bokenham translated as a companion text to his Lives of
native saints.[20] It is significant here for the way the sequence deftly frames the
Wenefred legend in terms of regional description, even as it disavows chorog-
raphy as its proper subject. In citing, then rejecting, "topography" in favor of
a saint's Life, the legend signals that it maps regional difference through the
spiritual and affective communities organized by the saint, rather than either
ancient kingdoms or current economic practice, as Higden does.

In its affiliation with the *Mappula Angliae*, this passage also heralds the
legend's representation of Britain as an aggregate of local places and overlapping jurisdictions. As I argue in the next chapter, the *Mappula* represents
England not as a single coherent national community, but as a space configured by multiple, sometimes competing, frameworks, each of which organizes individual places or regions (rivers or roads, ecclesiastical and secular
jurisdictions) somewhat differently. This emphasis on England's variegated
geographies, in lieu of an abstracted and undifferentiated idea of the body
politic, is developed across the several native saints' Lives of the Abbotsford
legendary. The contribution of the Wenefred legend in particular is to conceptualize England as constituted by discrete local places—Shrewsbury, Coventry, Clare—and the relationships between them formed by regional
pilgrimage: in this model, ordinary devotional practice, not the ritual religiosity of kings, organizes the relationships between different English cities and
regions.

These relationships depend on—indeed, they are the effect of—physical
presence or other forms of contact, and they are therefore singular, contingent, ad hoc, even though they are grounded in the sacred. Those "there present" at Wenefred's resurrection are granted sight of numberless miracles
"with here owyn eyne" (with their own eyes), a privilege still available to all

who make a pilgrimage to the shrine: "& so moun yet tho / Wich thedyr on pilgrymage lyst for to go" (and so too might still those who want to go there on pilgrimage) (216v).[21] The miracle of the stones brought from elsewhere insists, in a conventional way, on the timelessness of Wenefred's martyrdom. What is distinctive is that this transcendent time depends on an experience that is literally *contingent*, an experience of physical contact, which opens the self (and objects of the natural world) to the timelessness of the sacred.[22] This special form of timelessness makes possible a community that is open to new participants from a wide geographical area and across time—a paradigm of community that is correlative of the nonfinite nature of Wenefred's martyrdom, manifest in the continual bloodying of rocks introduced to the well. While it is a framework for participating in sacred timelessness, this community remains an assemblage of individuals, in shifting relationship to one another, not a self-identical or bounded whole that might be imagined as a corporate form. It is neither secured by an idea of territorial belonging nor instantiated as a static entity based on some fixed feature or category of identity.

It is formed instead by practice, in lived—that is, secular—time. This is an important alternative to, and perhaps purposeful revision of, Lancastrian efforts to coordinate sacred time, especially liturgical time, and national time by adding British saints such as Wenefred to the Sarum liturgy. For Bokenham, the sacred waters of the well shrine make Wenefred's martyrdom miraculously available across time. But while the legend thus defines sanctity in terms of timelessness, it is accessed through concrete material and personal contact that takes place in historically specific moments. Hence Bokenham's careful dating of his own Holywell pilgrimage to 1448: he knows about the miraculously bloodied rocks, he says, "As experience me tawt the soth to seyn / The yer of grace to spekyn pleynly / A thousand foure hundryd & eygthe & fourty" (as experience taught me, truth to tell, / the year of grace, to speak plainly, / 1448) (217r). Because the idea of community formulated in the legend depends on participation, performance, and presence, it necessarily occurs in a precise interval of secular historical time.

The legend's commitment to the secular finds curious expression in an admitted "dygressyoun" from the legend. Where most vernacular Wenefred legends interrupt the diegetic time of the narrative to tell of future miracles at the well, Bokenham breaks the narrative chronology to comment instead on the punishment of Caradoc's kin, who are condemned by his deed to "lych doggys euere whoule & berke" (always to howl and bark like dogs) until they are led to Holywell or Shrewsbury to be cured (217r), another detail derived from the *Polychronicon*.[23] The anecdote serves as a vehicle for reminding the audience of the need to repent in this life:

> By wiche punysshment men moun conceyue
> Ho gret displesaunce beforn the face
> Of god yt ys frowardly to weyue
> By final unrepentaunce from his grace
> Wherfore yche man whyle he hath space
> *In this werd here* for no maner synne [emphasis added]
> Ffrom hope of mercy loke he neuere twynne
>
> Ffor doctours seyn that yet neuer was synne
> So greuous don *in this lyf* sothly
> That yf the doere ther of wold blynne
> And wyth a contryt herte cryin god mercy
> He shuld yt han for judas treuly
> Schuld not han be dampnyd thow he cryst betrayid
> Had not his herte by wanhope ben afrayd (217r)
>
> [By which punishment people might understand
> How great a displeasure before the face
> Of God it is to turn away wickedly
> From his grace by an ultimate lack of repentance.
> Therefore every person while he has space
> *Here in this world* should seek never to abandon
> Hope of mercy on account of any sin.
>
> For theologians say that truly there was
> Never such a grievous sin done *in this life*
> That if the doer would cease thereof
> And cry mercy of God with a contrite heart
> He would not have it. For Judas truly
> Would not have been damned though he betrayed Christ
> Had not his heart been made afraid by despair].

In Audelay's version of the legend, as I discuss below, the series of miracles associated with the well, which witness its extratemporality, finds a formal analogue in their placement at this point in the narrative, where they interrupt chronological sequence, looking beyond Wenefred's resurrection, which is yet to be recounted. Both the miracles and their narration, that is, bisect the progress of ordinary, secular time by opening it to sacred event. Bokenham's moralizing digression, in contrast, sticks resolutely to mortal, historical, secular time "in this life," which is the time of repentance.

The idea that the saeculum is the time to repent is a pastoral commonplace, one that finds expression in the Lives of repentant sinners, such as Mary Magdalene.[24] But it is very unusual for this moral to be associated with the saint's *persecutor*: the caricatured evil of the saint's murderer is an unlikely platform for serious pastoral reflection on secular life as the framework for ethical and devotional practice. Bokenham's use of Caradoc to this end thus underscores secular practice as a key thematic. His Wenefred legend is focused above all on the value and significance of mortal life, to which the saint is recalled *even after her martyrdom*.[25] Perhaps its most striking expression is Wenefred's last earthly request: the single "bone" that she asks of Elerius, head of the religious house where she ends her life, is to be buried by her spiritual mother, the abbess Theonye, Elerius's own mother (218v). In her dying moments, Wenefred's first thoughts are on human companionship; her prayer to her heavenly spouse comes second.

The counter theory of community that Bokenham develops in this legend finds a correlative in a counter poetics. Bokenham's plain style contrasts, especially, to the aureate poetics of John Lydgate, one of Bokenham's most important literary influences. As we will see in Chapter 5, Lydgate defines his aureate style as timeless, as transcending the secular order, by associating it with the saint, especially in the conceit that identifies the ink with which he writes with the "aureate licour" of the saint's blood. Bokenham's casual self-presentation and use of personal anecdote, which are broadly characteristic of his work but have distinct thematic resonance here, may be read as a pointed rejection of the high style of Lydgate's legends, with which Bokenham was certainly familiar.[26] It is worth noting that this departure could potentially have been recognized as such by contemporary readers: Kathleen Scott identifies the marginal decoration in the Abbotsford legendary as the work of the same artist who decorated the pages of a manuscript of Lydgate's *Life of Sts. Edmund and Fremund*.[27] The production, and quite possibly the audience, of Bokenham's legendary and Lydgate's English saints' Lives intersected. The very similarities in visual decoration that link their texts highlight Bokenham's general avoidance of the sort of highly aureate diction that, in the Lydgate manuscript, is often presented as a verbal analogue of the beautiful surface of the page.

Bokenham's Wenefred legend is not entirely void of aureate vocabulary but it is lightly used and generally confined to surprisingly infrequent passages describing Wenefred's devotions. The first time the characteristically Latinate and polysyllabic vocabulary of aureate poetry surfaces in the legend—in a rhyme triplet of "comunycacyoun," "conuersacyoun," and "exhortacyoun" in the ninth stanza—it serves as a marked elevation in style. But even these are relatively common terms, certainly ones familiar to the legion of mid-fifteenth-century readers of devotional prose. As in Lydgate's Lives, aureate diction here points to an extrahistorical realm, but in Bokenham's Wenefred that realm is a rare counterpoint in a narrative much more conspicuously concerned with the historical time inhabited by the gossipy narrator himself.

Especially telling in this regard is the contrast between Caradoc's aureate formulations and Wenefred's own polite and capable, but unornamented, speech. Wenefred's first words to Caradoc, responding to his question about her father's whereabouts, are "syre for sothe at the cherche ys he / Wherfore wyth hym yf ye owt wyl doo / abydyth awhile y shal hym clepe you to" (sir, forsooth he is at church. Therefore if you have any business to do with him, abide a while; I shall call him to you) (215r). Her simple courtesy is answered in a grandiloquent style that self-consciously echoes aureate poetry: Caradoc demands that she assent "to the lust of my plesaunce," a phrase that may parody Lydgate's conspicuous use of the objective genitive.[28] Wenefred in turn ventriloquizes Caradoc's artificial style as she pretends to accede to his demands: in an attempt to escape from him, she excuses herself "ffor the embesshyng of my symplynesse" (215v), that is, to dress up her plain appearance. Her phrase at once imitates the awkward genitive structure of Caradoc's demand and parallels the explicitly manufactured beauty that she proposes. Importantly, the term Wenefred uses for such artificial decoration—embellishing—is a term of vernacular poetics, one that Bokenham himself uses in the Legendys of Hooly Wummen, where he refers to a high style "enbelshyd wyth colours of rethoryk" associated with Geoffrey of Vinsauf's Poetria Nova.[29] Indeed, the account of Wenefred's initial encounter with Caradoc may be read as a programmatic account of instrumental and self-consciously literary language, in which rhetorical complexity and ornamentation are morally dangerous.

Bokenham's Wenefred does, however, adopt the rhyme-royal stanza form characteristic of the aureate tradition. This is a self-conscious choice, as Bo-kenham's metapoetic identification of the legend's verse form suggests: he re-fers to it by the contemporary technical term "balade" (217r).[30] This formal stanza, which elsewhere signals elite cultural status and literary aspiration, is repurposed as a vehicle for ordinary speech. Bokenham presents the anec-dote of the white friar, for example, as reported speech, with repetitions and idiomatic locutions almost worthy of Chaucer: "This frere quod myn ost this relygious man / Oo tyme but late whan he was here" ("This friar," said my host, "this religious man, one time just recently when he was here") (217v). The anecdote is bracketed by another reference to Bokenham's innkeeper at its conclusion. "Lo syre quod my ost so god me spede / This story ys soth wich y you haue told / Wherfore to reportyn yt ye may be bold" ("Lo, sir," said my host, "so God speed me, the story which I have told you is true. Therefore you may be confident in reporting it") (218r). This is not a Chaucerian pose of objective reportage: there is no layer of irony here. It is rather a truth claim rooted in interpersonal relationships, as well as an insistence on poetry as the vehicle for this relationship, not despite but *because* of its historical, limited, and particular quality—that is, its secularity. And it uses the disorienting juncture of colloquial speech and high-style stanza form to draw attention to its use of direct quotation, a rhetorical mark of the legend's own capacity to inhabit a secular present.

Throughout the legend, the use of *balade* rhyme is given visual form on the page: brackets track the rhyme scheme and emphasize the formal pat-terning and repetition that define it (see Figure 1).[31] The brackets point to meaning that inheres in sound alone—like the inarticulate "sound" of Wene-fred's parents' lament—and specifically to sounds in proximity, a physical proximity that can be readily traced with a pen. Indeed, we may see the brackets as a graphic insistence on rhyme as an aural image of proximity. In the context of Bokenham's careful imitation of the rhythms of ordinary speech, we may even discover in the legend a parallel between repetition in rhyme and repetition in spoken language, linked as figures for proximity and the personal relationships it makes possible. That is, just as the repetition in the host's reported speech—"this frere . . . this relygious man"—signals Bo-kenham's unmediated relationship to him, and thus to a series of direct per-sonal relationships that link him to the miraculous event (the white friar is known to the host, whom the narrator knows in turn), so formal repetition (both rhyme within the stanza and the repetition of stanza form itself) is

The lyf of Seynt Wenefrede

Figure 1. Osbern Bokenham, *Lives of Saints*, Abbotsford Manuscript, fol. 214v.
By courtesy of the Faculty of Advocates Abbotsford Collection Trust.

identified by the brackets as a register of proximity. Bokenham's poetic corresponds, that is, to an idea of community defined—like rhyme—by affiliation and contact *in time*.[32]

On the level of theme and form, then, Bokenham's legend points to an idea of community that is contingent in both the general and etymological senses of the term—community that is not fixed, necessary, or inevitable, a community that is not determined in advance by birth, blood, or nation, but is rather dependent on proximity, on touching (*contingere*: to touch together, to come into contact). In contrast to the notion of national community figured by the king's symbolic body, Bokenham's St. Wenefred legend points to a community rooted in accidental, material, and local relationships: that is, a secular community, as that category was defined in the Middle Ages. This is true even of relationships with the saint herself, whose shrine is not to be marked off from ready, even casual, access. This secular form of community is not defined against the sacred; indeed, it is authorized by the sacred and is a conduit for it. But it refuses a sacralization of community per se, and it is located in the secular lives of Wenefred's devotees—in the specific, finite time that they inhabit, and especially in their affective human relationships—whether the passing acquaintance of a friendly innkeeper or the enduring love for a daughter.

If Bokenham's legend counters the abstract representation of England as a body politic on which, for example, Henry V's 1416 pilgrimage depended, it does nevertheless echo that event in defining a community through physical presence and the networks linking different regions that are created by human movement between them. The vectors of pilgrimage in Bokenham's Wenefred legend, which all point to Holywell, are the centripetal complement to the idea of community mapped in Henry V's pilgrimage. As we saw in the Introduction, Henry's pilgrimage presented the king's body as an abstract mediating structure and supervening figure for the nation, in accordance with the ideological metaphor of the king's body politic. At the same time, however, Henry's pilgrimage staged the importance of his bodily presence at the shrines of native saints. This was in part a matter of politics: as James Doig notes, despite the accelerating production of royal writs to communicate with different regions or cities, Henry V understood that "personal contact between king and subject" remained "critical."[33]

But it also has broader implications as an alternative to earlier discourses in which the miraculously intact bodies of native saints, re-scaled as embodiments of England, establish its notional—and unlocated—boundaries. This capacity, which might accommodate the instability of actual territorial boundaries, no doubt accounts for some of the fifteenth-century appeal of such saints. Although premised on an analogous understanding of the king's body politic, Henry V's pilgrimage in practice represents England not through such corporeal figures of spatial extension, but through the king's serial presence at different local places. It thus defines English community through syntagmatic relations, not synecdochic ones: that is, through the contiguity of places, rather than an abstract spatial paradigm. From this perspective, Henry's pilgrimage may be seen to parallel the Wilton *Life of St. Edith*, insofar as it values the role of physical presence as the foundation of community, even as it seeks to map a far larger structure of affiliation.

As we have seen, Bokenham's meditation on presence and proximity as the foundation of community is worked out in the prosody of his Wenefred legend, as well as in its narrative argument. The legend offers an especially useful case study for examining the link between literary form and a form of affiliation and collective identity. This is especially true of its attention to rhyme as a form of proximity in both its graphic realization on the manuscript page and its echo of the legend's thematic concern with access and with sound. At the same time, the legend's relationship to Lydgate's work—through the shared use of ballad stanza, as well as through the codicological associations that suggest intersecting histories of production or reception—helps to highlight the significance of Bokenham's narratorial persona, colloquial style, and the use of direct quotation as elements of a practical, or vernacular, theory of community that departs from influential contemporary alternatives. Bokenham's poetics of proximity and his avoidance of Lydgatean aureation are both at heart concerned with the scale of community: its local, or translocal, quality, as well as the limits and possibilities entailed in a form of community predicated on physical presence and (literally) contingent affiliations.

Literary form is especially well suited to thinking about community, Bokenham's legend suggests, because it is especially well suited to thinking about temporality and spatial scale. Audelay's St. Wenefred carol, to which I now turn, similarly uses form to develop a theory of community, in this case emphasizing stasis and repetition rather than proximity. It also plays with temporal scale, as the choice of form suggests: the carol is a formal vehicle for dilating the secular present, the unbounded but nevertheless evanescent moment that characterizes secular time.

The Secular Present in Carol Form

Like Bokenham, John Audelay champions Wenefred as a categorically local saint. She was indeed part of his own "neighborhood": Audelay resided at Haughmond Abbey, an Augustinian priory not far from Wenefred's shrine at Shrewsbury. His carol version of her legend addresses an audience of pilgrims who visit her shrine every Friday. This emphasis on her regional cult runs athwart its nationalization by Lancastrian kings, but the carol is not necessarily opposed, as Bokenham's is, to royal appropriation of St. Wenefred. It is even possible that Audelay originally wrote the carol in the hope of being named priest of the chantry that Henry V intended to found at the shrine. Although it was to be housed at the conventual church, plans for the chantry specified that the priest could be a secular cleric, as Audelay was.[34] Other poems in the Audelay manuscript celebrating the Lancastrian devotional program (e.g., the "Salutation to St. Bridget," which praises Henry V's support of Syon) and the king's military triumphs (extolled in the carol addressed to the infant Henry VI) may perhaps have once formed a sort of dossier advertising Audelay's suitability to serve as a priest for a Lancastrian chantry dedicated to St. Wenefred.[35]

Audelay's Wenefred carol nevertheless departs importantly from royal nationalization of the cult. Whether through his own immersion in a regional cult or a more studied response to its political instrumentalization, Audelay's carol, like Bokenham's later legend, defines community in terms of contingent relationships made possible by, and dependent on, physical presence. The emphasis on the cult's essentially local nature is especially pronounced in the series of miracles that occupies the middle of the carol: Wenefred is credited with the miraculous survival of a child caught under a millstone, her spring ceases to flow when her shrine is used to store wine, a man is unable to retrieve a coin that has fallen in the well. Given its provenance—from which we can infer that the poet and his primary audience knew of royal promotion of the cult—the carol's exclusive interest in quotidian and local miracles must be read as an alternative to the dynastic and national miracles attributed to Wenefred in this period. The victory at Agincourt loses out here to a nameless Englishman unable to retrieve his lost groat from the well, an inadvertent offering to a saint invoked with such careful calculation by his sovereign.

Audelay was a secular poet in a specific vocational sense: he was a secular canon and a chantry priest.[36] His pastoral responsibilities lay in this world, this temporal order, and were preoccupied with the mortal and contingent— that is, secular—life of his fellow Christians. Although we are likely to classify him as a "religious" poet, on the grounds of both his profession and the themes of his work, Audelay himself would have defined his status as a secular priest in opposition to a "religious"—that is, to a monastic—vocation, characterized, at least in theory, by its remove from the world. This opposition, between secular and monastic vocations, important as it was, could nevertheless be fuzzy, and it is worth noting that Audelay inhabited a border zone between them. Haughmond Abbey, where he resided when the manuscript containing the Wenefred legend and all his known writings were produced, was a house of Augustinian canons.[37] The Augustinians were a nonmonastic religious order: they lived in a community, under a rule, but were primarily engaged in pastoral care, in parishes or private chapels, doing the work of secular priests. They are, that is, a *quid medium*, as Erasmus would say, between the monastic and the secular.[38] Some houses were closer to the monastic end of the spectrum, and others had a more pastoral orientation, although they are all finally "secular" in the strict sense that they follow a secular liturgy.[39] Haughmond Abbey seems to have a more "secular" orientation, judging by the high percentage of salaried priests, which, as historians have noted, gives topical significance to Audelay's satire of "our gentle Sir John" (144), the all-too-worldly priest in *Marcolf and Solomon*.

We know that Audelay was a chantry priest living at Haughmond Abbey because he tells us so in his book, Oxford, Bodleian Library MS Douce 302, a compendium of pastoral materials that comprises all of Audelay's known writings. His vocation as a secular priest is part of his self-representation as a poet, developed through the extended pastoral and penitential themes that occupy his writing. Indeed, as Fein argues, the apparently miscellaneous materials in MS Douce 302 are organized into a complex whole specifically through Audelay's poetic persona and a sustained emphasis on penitence.[40] Put differently, we might say that the collection is presented as such by its secular address: Audelay, in the persona of an aging secular priest-poet, is concerned with the moral amendment "here," a term he uses repeatedly. Like Bokenham's Wenefred legend, Audelay's multipart and multiform work, which includes verse instruction on the mass and the works of mercy, passion meditation and other devotions, satire on the ecclesiastical orders, and admonitions to the laity about their obligations, as well as hagiographic materials in several forms, is structured by secular time.

Hence the pervasive invocation of the present moment that he and his audience occupy. In the epilogue to the *Counsel of Conscience*, the poet asks God to reward those who "here mysdedis *here* will amend" (their misdeeds will amend here) (11); he encourages his readers to take him as an example "while ye han space *here*" (26); and later he prays that "In this world *here* levyng" he himself will have his "payne" and his "purgatory" (477–78; emphases mine). Again, this emphasis on the saeculum is a temporal corollary of the penitential themes that structure the book: it is the limited time in which it is possible to remedy transgression. The poems thus work ceaselessly to inhabit the present: "Prays fore me *that beth present*-- / My name is Jon the Blynd Awdlay" (Pray for me, you who are present. My name is John Audelay the Blind) (506–7), he writes at the end of the *Counsel of Conscience*, in a formula he uses many times throughout the book.[41]

If the pastoral themes are partly a reflection of Audelay's preoccupations as a secular priest, they are also—like Bokenham's interest in the local—part of a conceptualization of devotional community whose temporal location is the elusive present of secular time. Where Bokenham's anecdotal style and direct quotation identify contact and access as key to this conceptualization, the carol form of Audelay's Wenefred legend points to an open, porous, present as its defining quality. This dilated present, as we will see, derives from both the associations of the carol with dance—a mode of performance that itself occupies and extends a fleeting "now"—and its circular structure, which repeatedly interrupts narrative time with a burden that draws attention to the moment of performance. It relies, that is, on specific formal capabilities of the carol.

The secular present of the poem is also constituted by the poet's self-naming, as we have just seen in the signature closing of the *Counsel of Conscience*: Audelay's address to his audience as "present" locates them in a temporal framework inhabited by the poet, "Blind Audelay," as he calls himself some sixteen times in the book.[42] The use of his proper name sets Audelay in the vanguard of literary writing in this period: Robert Meyer-Lee has identified the inscription of the poet's name within his work as an index and feature of a new self-conscious attention to the literary in the fifteenth century. Audelay's self-references do not serve, however, as a hinge between a historical world and extrahistorical literary one, as do those in "laureate" poetry.[43] Instead, the presence of the poet—represented in terms of his aging and disabled body—is the work's most concrete and specific representation of human mortality, vulnerability, and finitude. Audelay represents himself as a poet subject to, even a paradigm of, human mortality, which is in turn the basis of his affiliation with others.

While the very inclusion of Audelay's carol within a pastoral compendium such as MS Douce 302 highlights its secular address, its placement in the sequence of texts is a further indication of its claim on earthly temporality. It is conspicuously separate from the other carols in the book, which all participate in a carol sequence presented as Christmas texts.[44] The Wenefred carol—the only other example of that poetic form in the book—is placed instead in a group of devotional materials loosely related through their shared interest in female spirituality and dominated by Marian poems that feature a marked rhetorical and formal emphasis on immediacy and intimacy. The series starts with a salutation poem built on the *Ave*, which begins, "Hayle, Maré, to thee I say, / Hayle, ful of grace, God is with thee," and ultimately modulates into a poem addressed to Jesus: "O Jhesu, fore these Joys Fyve, / O Jhesu, thi moder had of thee" (91–92). After a few short devotions, there are two more salutation poems addressed to Mary, the second of which is in Gabriel's voice and is followed by a verse paraphrase of the *Magnificat*, Mary's salutation to Jesus. These poems are the model for four more poems of salutation addressed to St. Bridget of Sweden, St. Wenefred, St. Anne, and the Holy Face, all of which are structured by an anaphoric greeting, a fiction of direct address that recalls the paradigmatic moment of intimacy between the human and divine in the *Ave*. In these poems, each line repeats a greeting that bridges the earthly realm and a divine one: a human speaker hails a holy figure and speaks to her from his or her position within secular time. Other pieces in this section—most notably the drawing of St. Veronica's sudarium that precedes the "Salutation to the Holy Face" (27v)—underscore the interest in immediate presence correlative to the poetic form of the salutations.

Audelay's Wenefred carol is embedded in the middle of this section, between the "Salutation to St. Bridget" and the "Salutation to St. Wenefred," and the formal logic of the salutation poems provides a heuristic for Audelay's unusual choice of the carol as the vehicle for a saint's Life. Like the salutations, the Wenefred carol employs direct address as a structural feature: its burden is "Wenefrede, thou swete may, / Thow pray for us bothe nyght and day." But this similarity is limited to the burden: Audelay's carol is otherwise a narrative poem, offering a relatively complete version of the Wenefred legend. Unlike Mary and the other female saints addressed in this section of the manuscript, Wenefred is both a second-person addressee in the carol's burden and the third-person subject of the story recounted in its verses. Where the salutations continually voice a crossing from the secular present to the timeless domain of the sacred, the Wenefred carol oscillates between a similar structure of address and the story of Wenefred's earthly life.

The alternation between narrative stanzas and the refrain is an essential capability of the carol as a form. The burden interrupts narrative progress and offers unchanging, static comment on, or counterpoint to, that progress.[45] It can thus serve as a vehicle for representing a heavenly timelessness, in contrast to the progress of secular narrative time in the verses. But in the case of the Wenefred carol, the refrain is used to represent perpetual action *in time* rather than its divine transcendence.[46] Note that the speaker (or speakers) of the carol address the saint not to pray for her (future) intercession, but to announce, in a continuous present, that she prays for them: "Wenefred, thou swete may / thow pray for us both nygt and day" (Wenefred, you sweet maiden, you pray for us both night and day). The refrain is an account of ongoing, indeed, daily activity. It points to the kind of secular *now* that preoccupies Audelay throughout the book and that subtends the salutations in particular: an insistence on the present as the temporal framework of contact or communication, even—or especially—with the divine. The refrain is formally and thematically the agent of this: in each iteration, it insistently halts the forward narrative movement of the carol and opens the story to the current moment of reading or performance. Although the burden gives the carol a characteristic recursive structure, its repetition works less to loop the poem back and propel it forward than to foreground the poem's location in, and creation of, the temporality of its own utterance.

We might recognize the carol's denial of progressive linear time—a general capability of the form—as an extension of its historical affiliations with dance in the round.[47] The evocation of the present in Audelay's Wenefred carol may register an even more fundamental debt to dance: that is, its insistence on the moment of performance, a metonym for secular time more generally, which is characterized by evanescence, presence, and contingency. Secular time is activated in the poem whenever it is read, as the plural first-person "us" of the refrain is given definition and currency in this act, whether it takes the form of private reading or public recitation. In turn, the temporality of the performance provides a referent for the continuous present of "thou pray for us." The relationship between the narrative stanzas and the refrain is thus defined less by a contrast between progressive time and static timelessness than between the legend's past and an open present.

The different parts of the carol coordinate, rather than distinguish, these times: the category of the day—a basic unit of secular time—is also the temporal category that structures Wenefred's saintly intercession.[48] That intercession is ongoing, uninflected by distinct periods. Even the moment of its origin is obscured: martyrdom conventionally marks the saint's entry into heaven and the start date for her intercessory capacity. But Wenefred, resurrected by Beuno, continues an earthly life after her martyrdom. So too, from the perspective of the speaker and the audience, the present tense of the refrain obscures historical distance separating the carol's performance from its story: time in the carol-form legend is not organized by a difference between past and present, but arcs between them. The refrain's direct address and its repetition throughout the narrative of Wenefred's life deny any temporal boundary separating Wenefred from the speaker and audience; they occupy a single expansive secular time.

This secular present, analogous to the present moment emphasized in Bokenham's narrative voicing, offers a useful contrast to the historical, sequential, linear paradigm of time that the Lives of St. Edith and of St. Etheldreda borrow from vernacular historiography. The Wilton *Lives*, like the chronicles they imitate, posit a continuous and unified temporal frame, even as they narrate consequential moments of historical change such as the Norman Conquest. As Peter Osborne argues, periodization does less to divide time than to coordinate it into a coherent syntax, and in this way it can be as totalizing as eschatalogical or other forms of sacred time.[49] Putative moments of rupture inevitably produce an argument about the course of history: we have seen, for example, how Walsingham's identification of the *miracula renovata*—the renaissance of miracle working—at the end of the fourteenth century periodizes the activity of native saints in order to make sense of English history. The secular present in Audelay's carol is, in contrast, truly contingent, its cyclical structure having so elliptical a relationship to any large-scale historical frame as to be essentially undetermined.

The central narrative symbol of this open present is Wenefred's sacred well. The well's symbolic function registers, on the level of theme and narrative form, in the proleptic account of the spring's continuing existence "to this day" that interrupts the chronological account of Wenefred's life. In other versions of the legend, the miracles attributed to the spring connect sacred past to an unmarked present; Audelay's carol effaces the difference between them still more forcefully by moving the miracles from their conventional place at the end of the legend to the narrative moment of the wellspring's first appearance, where they bisect the linear narrative of Wenefred's life. The final miracle in the series specifically thematizes interruption: the well water ceases to flow when the chapel is used to store wine. When the wine is removed, the spring erupts again with a "hedus bere," a terrific noise (93).[50] As in Bokenham's legend, the thematic emphasis on *sound* points to the poem's own form: the deafening roar made by the waters as they begin again to flow implies the gentler sound that the spring usually produces in its ceaseless course, which is given formal expression in the measured musicality and unbounded temporality of the carol.

Other miracles in the series conspicuously occupy an undefined—that is, continuous—present. The wonders, which have a paradoxically mundane quality—an unrecoverable coin, a child who survives a close call with the mill wheel, saintly displeasure at the inappropriate use of the church as a storeroom—are set in an abstract present underscored by their ordinariness. Their everyday quality connects them to the lives of Wenefred's late medieval devotees, who are not separated from them by any notable historical distance or difference. The formal principle of the carol, in which narrative time is interrupted by the burden, is thus echoed by its narrative structure, as the story of Wenefred's death and resurrection is punctuated by the unmarked, quotidian time illuminated by the minor miracles that occur at the well. Like the refrain's address to Wenefred in the secular present, the miracles figure an everyday time, represented by childhood accidents and lost items, in a striking representation of the unbounded, even abstract, quality of secular time.

The significance of the miracles as an evocation of a special kind of secular present becomes still clearer if we compare Audelay's carol to other vernacular versions of the Wenefred legend. In most versions, Wenefred's beheading interrupts the liturgy: when Caradoc strikes off her head, it rolls to the church, where Beuno is saying mass. He and the other congregants leave the service to investigate, but they return to the church and finish the liturgy before Beuno restores Wenefred's head to her body. Audelay elides this sequencing of martyrdom, liturgy, and miraculous resurrection by having Beuno resurrect Wenefred immediately, even before Caradoc is swallowed by the earth. Where, in most versions of the legend, Wenefred's resurrection is deferred by the liturgy—with the special timelessness it represents—in Audelay's carol the story of her martyrdom and vocation is interrupted instead by the catalog of the notably quotidian miracles that happen at her well after her death.

The carol's burden, with its invocation of the "now" of performance, and its central image, the well with its continual outpouring of water, together work to define this secular present in terms of a paradoxically dynamic stasis: an endless movement located in a single place, which is itself so delimited that the movement it hosts reads almost as its antithesis, like a spinning dot whose size and speed make it appear still. Even as it is defined by dynamic activity, this form of the present occupies a kind of parenthesis that separates it from diachronic progression. The carol, that is, invokes a present that is dynamic, despite its brevity, its uncertain relation to past and future, and—especially—its notional isolation from linear chronology. It identifies this present as partly an effect of its finite location, the well.[51]

This local place and the special kind of secular time with which it is affiliated define a particular kind of community, explored in the carol's closing stanzas. In contrast to the spectacle of royal pilgrimage, Audelay—who was likely in residence at Haughmond Abbey when Henry V visited Shrewsbury in 1416 and 1421—figures devotion to Wenefred's shrine as an ordinary and local phenomenon. Shrewsbury is the first community named, and it is defined by weekly pilgrimage to her shrine, housed in the nearby Benedictine abbey:[52]

> Glad mai be al Schrosbere
> To do reverens to that lady
> Thai seche here grace and here mercy
> On pilgrymage ther evere Fryday (157–60)

> [Glad may be all Shrewsbury
> To do reverence to that lady,
> They seek her grace and her mercy
> On pilgrimage there every Friday].

The reference is more immediate still in the next stanza, narrowed to those "present" in the moment of the carol's actual or imagined utterance: "we prayn the, al that beth present" (we, all who are present, pray you) (169). The insistence on local presence is not provincial; indeed, Audelay insists on the heterogeneity of the community that forms around Wenefred and her shrine: "Mone a merakil ther hath be syne / Of dyvers pepul in fer cuntre" (Many a miracle has been seen there by diverse people from distant regions) (147–48). The word "cuntre" can refer to a small or large community: the line can be understood to refer to Welsh and English devotion to the saint, perhaps even to supranational devotion, or it may refer to different regions within England, along the lines of Bokenham's legend, that is, to a translocal community devoted to the saint.[53] Importantly, this phrase forms the b-rhyme of the carol and so plays a structural role in linking this stanza to all the others.

This heterogeneous community is necessarily defined by presence, the phenomenon of being in a specific place at a given time: that is how it is constituted as a community despite its variousness. The poem takes advantage of its oral and performative qualities—indeed, its reliance on the basic quality of sound—in its definition of community as those who are "here present": everyone who can hear that phrase is addressed by it. Like St. Wenefred's bell—a massive bell dedicated to the saint and inscribed with a prayer requesting her intercession—the carol calls to, and speaks for, those devoted to the saint in the limited but radically inclusive soundscape that it creates, a local space that nevertheless has indeterminate borders, since they are established by sensory access—that is, by the singular embodiment of its addressees.[54]

In this way, the carol recalls the representation of Wilton in the *Life of St. Edith* analyzed in the last chapter, a *comparandum* that can help us recognize this form of community as an alternative to larger-scaled and therefore more notional ones. The Wenefred legend, too, theorizes the body in terms of its materiality, which is underscored by the miraculous transference between the saint's body and the red-spotted rocks that bear witness to her martyrdom. Unlike the spring, whose transparent purity and lack of solid materiality seem to cancel the fact of Wenefred's embodiment, the rocks insist on the basic physicality of the body. Audelay's carol transfers this emphasis to the community formed through devotion to the saint, which is defined by its members' own physical presence. This commitment to embodied presence presents an alternative to the kind of imagined English community advanced by royal promotion of the cult and the inclusion of Wenefred's feast in the Sarum liturgy.[55] The poem and the well in the poem define a community that depends on presence, available primarily to local men and women—surely the only ones able to make a pilgrimage to her shrine *every* Friday—but not defined by ethnic or regional identity and including anyone in attendance. This form of community refuses any normative instantiation or definition: ever forming and reforming, it is as contingent as it is capacious.

This community ultimately becomes the voice of the poem, as the first-person collective "we" replaces "Shrewsbury." The lyric voice thus itself comes to constitute the plural community described in the preceding stanzas:

Wynfrede, we thee beseche,
Now ryght with herfilly speche,
That thou wilt be our soulis leche,
Thee to serve, both plese and pay (163–66)

[Wenefred, we beseech you,
Now truly with worshipful speech,
That you will be our souls' healer;
May it both please and profit to serve you].

Even in the movement toward a collective voice, this community is not homogenized or regularized. In the poem's final stanza, it shrinks to its vanish-
ing point, the singular, mortal individual, represented by the poet himself:

I pray youe al, pur charyte
Redis this carol reverently,
Fore I hit mad with wepyng ye.
Mi name hit is the Blynd Awdlay (175–78)

[I pray you all for charity
Read this carol reverently
For I made it with weeping eye;
My name, it is the blind Audelay].

The community tapers from the nonce collective hailing from far countries
to Audelay himself, whose identity is particularized by both his name and his
blindness—that is, both his social identity and his physical body. His particularity is paradigmatic of secular experience itself: in its movement toward
increasingly local, ad hoc devotional practice, the carol offers the blind
Audelay—the historically specific and singular individual, whose vulnerable
mortal body represents humanity more generally—as the paradigmatic devotee of Wenefred's cult.[56] The speaker poet is the final figure for the contingent, fragile human community that inhabits the carol's present.

For, as the oscillation between the singular and collective first person in
the carol's final stanzas suggests, the community imagined by the poem is an
assemblage of mortal humans, with particular physical and spiritual identities. The creation of this community, which brings together individuals limited to and by their own mortal bodies, is a function attributed to the saint.

Like the monastic community conceptualized in the *Life of St. Edith*, this one does not assume a corporate form, as an abstract body that promises a collective identity beyond the embodied life of its members. Where the Wilton community persists nevertheless thanks to the saint's ongoing care of its members, this one has an implicit future in the weekly pilgrimages that will presumably persist beyond Audelay's individual lifetime, or that of any reader. That future community is also, in the terms of the poem, a structure that exists only in a contingent, secular present, and it is necessarily constituted by singular individuals. Again, this is an idea of community closely related to the poem's form: the carol's iterability, its circularity, its evocation of the moment of performance, perhaps even the affiliations with dance that identify it as an embodied form, allow it to address a community not as static or transcendent, but as contingent on temporary, temporal, physical presence.

This type of secular community may be related to the urban geography of the cult. The monastery that housed Wenefred's shrine lay just across the river from the city of Shrewsbury, and the final stanzas of the poem track physical movement from city to shrine—from an urban space to a religious one.[57] This religious space is, in some ways, a site of community in a transcendent mode, a space defined in the Middle Ages in terms of the monastic removal from secular concerns. At the same time, however, the shrine itself is defined by local presence and thus spatial particularity. This is, in part, a function of its status as a major shrine, the saint's "home," which, as Ben Nilson has explained, is different from the geographically unfixed aspects of a saint's cult, expressed, for example, through the mobility of relics.[58] In Audelay's carol, such geographical specificity is also a function of the representation of the shrine as an object of urban pilgrimage and its essential relationship to the secular arena adjacent to it, which the carol itself traces.

Audelay's poem, as we have seen, shares with the Wilton Lives of Edith and Etheldreda a definition of community as an embodied phenomenon, but it does not coordinate the female saint's Life with the regnal structure of English history, as those legends do, even though Wenefred had recently been made a conspicuous part of Lancastrian royal identity. In both cases, literary form is correlative of the work's conceptualization of religious and national community: the carol form of Audelay's Wenefred poem registers a fundamental resistance to the chronological organization of time that structures the national and institutional histories that the Wilton *Life of St. Edith* uses as a narrative frame. It is significant in this regard that Audelay's carol is specifically identified as a written form: at the close of the poem, the poet narrator prays for grace for everyone who *reads* it. The poem in this way asks to be compared with other textualizations of native saints' Lives, including national and monastic historiography, as well as narrative hagiography. The reference stages the carol, governed by a pervasive fiction of oral performance, as an alternative to the genres that usually host the legend in textual form.

Audelay's carol also eschews Wenefred's liturgical place in a communion of saints. There is no reference whatsoever to her feast day, the royal and national import of which had recently been enhanced by its inclusion in the Sarum liturgy. The local paraliturgical tradition of weekly Friday pilgrimage to the Shrewsbury shrine is an alternative to the annual national celebration of the saint, and these frequent, regular, and voluntary celebrations of Wenefred's daily intercessions form a community very different from the one posited by official liturgical observance. As a community formed by habitual and embodied participation, it hosts relatively ordinary saintly favor of the sort exemplified by the miracles at the well shrine—protecting children, assisting in the recovery of lost items—rather than miraculous irruptions of sacred power that might ground an abstract, transhistorical community, such as the marvelous military victory at Agincourt that Henry V attributed to the saint. The temporal scale of devotion, the paradigm of weekly pilgrimage, and the special intimacy and familiarity between the saint and the members of the community devoted to her—each of which is explored through a formal quality of the carol—are mutually constitutive, alike cause and consequence of the other.

But the poem's most fundamental, if implicit, critique of the English community figured by Henry V's Shrewsbury pilgrimage lies in Audelay's own role as the saint's paradigmatic devotee. The somatic metaphor of community in which one body stands for others—including both the royal body politic invoked in the king's thanksgiving pilgrimage and saintly body that figures a national religious community—is challenged by Audelay's insistence on his proper body, signified by both his name and his blindness. The local community on which the poem insists, contracted in the final stanza to the poet alone, rebukes imagined communities through its emphasis on the singularity of the mortal body. Of course Audelay's body is figurative too: the metonymic relationship that Audelay claims for his body, its capacity to represent the community of those devoted to the saint, supplants the body politic as the referent for the Wenefred cult and the form of community it sustains. But

Audelay's body represents, rather than symbolizes, this community: his blind, deaf, and aged body remains one member among many who inhabit the plural first person of the carol's burden. Like the *Life of St. Edith*, Audelay's Wenefred Life insists on a finite community in order to refuse the rescaling of individual bodies into the abstract form of corporate identity.

*   *   *

Audelay's carol is an especially clear example of one of this book's central arguments: that, in the fifteenth century, literary form was a crucial resource for conceptualizing different kinds of community and especially for thinking about community in terms of scale. It is, of course, a special capacity of lyric forms to draw attention to the contribution that their stylistic and structural features make. The carol may thus be a useful heuristic for thinking about the conceptual contribution of literary form in other texts addressed in this study. The tetrameter quatrains in the Wilton legends, for example, may not invite formal analysis to the same degree that the carol form does, but we can nevertheless recognize them as an important resource for thinking about the nature of community: they structure a progressive and expansive narrative—one capable of tracing a long historical arc and recognizing simultaneous and sequenced events across a dilated temporal framework—that has an essential relation to the form of community imagined in the legend.

This is not to say that any poem in tetrameter quatrains imagines this form of community, just as the carol form itself does not necessarily produce a secular community of the sort developed in Audelay's Wenefred carol. On the contrary, Audelay's carol sequence found elsewhere in the Douce manuscript has a complex relationship to liturgical time, heralded by its Christmas affiliation. It may be helpful to repeat here two premises of this study: first, that form is best understood in terms of capabilities, some of which may be endemic but some of which are historical. That is, some inhere in specific features (e.g., the tension between the stanzas and burden in the carol), while others are an effect of literary tradition, audiences' expectations, relationships to other available forms, and other factors. Their significance (and this is the second point) is best understood in terms of other available formal choices: close reading establishes the thematic concerns of a text and sometimes makes visible the conceptual resource provided by form, but the latter emerges more fully through comparative analysis across texts with different forms.

The Secular Poetics of Saints' Lives

Where Audelay concatenates the complex, experimental form of his Wenefred legend (as a carol that participates in a large-scale multipart work) with
a notion of community predicated on human vulnerability, sociality, and familiarity, Bokenham develops a similar conceptualization of community
through an informal idiomatic and anecdotal style that is highlighted by a
stanza form that elsewhere lays claim to literary seriousness. Both works
identify the Wenefred cult with the temporal rather than the supratemporal,
and with the local rather than the supralocal. And both poems are important
evidence that saints' Lives were a useful forum for conceptualizing community in terms of its members' particularity, rather than some kind of homeostatic similarity. They each insist on the variegated nature of human affiliation
and on the raw fact of mortality as the temporal limit of communal identity.
Their signature formal features—the carol's refrain and Bokenham's colloquial style—are central to this, as is their shared use of a personalized lyric
voice to fashion the open present of secular time.

Together they trace a spectrum of what might be called secular poetics.
Other late medieval definitions of the literary identify it as supratemporal, as
in Chaucer's idea of a transhistorical symposium of *auctoritas*, populated by
Homer, Vergil, Ovid, Lucan, and Statius, at the end of the *Troilus*, or John
Lydgate's aureate vision of a poetry that transcends the ordinary social and
political world, to which we turn in Chapter 5.[59] The secular poetics of Audelay and Bokenham in contrast insist on the temporal, the contingent, the finite. Audelay and Bokenham should be recognized as developing a distinctive
vision of the literary that rejected contemporary ideas of poetry as transhistorical or transcendent. Indeed, in the context of Audelay's frank endorsement of the instrumental use of literature, his ambitious poetics challenge
not only medieval but also modern definitions of the literary.

As we have seen, Audelay's poetry is profoundly secular in the medieval
sense: rooted in urgent ethical and, especially, bodily contingencies. It is
therefore also thoroughly instrumental: it is in the service of a pastoral program designed specifically to address the secular lives—that is, the mortal
lives—of Audelay's audience. It may be tempting to dismiss these texts as
"nonliterary" precisely because they define themselves in terms of their instrumental value, in accordance with their specifically religious and ethical
function. At the same time, their evident interest in poetic form seems to me

grounds for considering these Lives not as the antithesis of "literature," but as evidence for a competing understanding of the literary, one defined by its usefulness as an instrument of secular life, rather than by its capacity to transcend geographical and temporal boundaries.

We may see an interest in the instrumental value of literature further manifest in a number of these legends' features. They are notably interested in the creation of community through the literary text, signaled by references to the audience of an (imagined) oral performance of the poem. Above all, they define literature as instrumental in terms of its ability to console or comfort—poetry as palliative—nowhere more poignantly expressed than in Audelay's signature references to his own mortal body. As throughout the Douce manuscript, the poet's references to himself as "Blind Audelay" in the Wenefred carol—"Mi name hit is the Blynd Awdlay" (178)—identify his blindness as the sign not of a prophetic gift, but of the perfectly ordinary fragility of the human body. Audelay's concern with this fragility, the mortal human body in its acutely historical existence, is closely related to the secular commitments and instrumental quality of his poetry. His self-presentation as impaired and thus embodied serves as a vernacular theory of what literature does and what it is: his poems enact an *ars poetica* that insists on literature's special capacity to express, and sometimes assuage, a shared mortal condition that lies at the root of all forms of human community.[60]

Like their formal choices, then, the idea of literature developed in the Middle English Wenefred legends corresponds to the forms of community they recognize and those they reject. In the context of contemporary efforts to define the nation as the temporal scale of religious community, as in the Wilton legends, or to insist on its transcendent, unfixed, pervasive, or immemorial status, as we will see in Lydgate's native saints' Lives, Audelay and Bokenham explore communities rooted in the present moment of concrete social interaction.

Beyond any topical significance this may have in the context of Lancastrian efforts to enlist St. Wenefred as a figure for England, this interest in the secular—in the finite, social, and historical—may help us understand both the appeal and challenge of the secular during this period. Perhaps it can also help us refine our understanding of the relationship between the secular and the literary. The Wenefred legends reflect the premodern understanding of the secular as the location of the particular, against its modern affiliation with the general or universal and a concomitant assumption that it provides a neutral or nonhierarchical ground of human affiliation. Indeed, these legends provide a small window on the historical shift from the premodern understanding of the secular to the more familiar modern one.[61] Their interest in secular community—community constituted by human particularity and difference, and therefore a forum for the desire to transcend the limits of individual identity—may be a useful model for addressing the current questions about the nature and role of literature as "secular." At the very least they suggest that we might advance our historical understanding of the status and operative definitions of the literary by attending to the various ways in which texts are presented, or received, as topical or timeless, rooted in or aloof from contemporary concerns, addressed to immediate or imagined audiences.

CHAPTER 4

Englishing the *Golden Legend* and the Geography of Religious Community

The St. Wenefred legends discussed in Chapter 3 and the Wilton Lives of St. Edith and Etheldreda discussed in Chapter 2 all exhibit a thematic and formal emphasis on the saint's singularity. In the *Life of St. Edith*, singularity is correlative of the saint's embodiment and specific historical location, the latter underscored by the poem's affiliation to vernacular historiography, which is signaled in part by its tetrameter quatrains. In Audelay's Wenefred carol, the saint's singularity is manifest in her intimate relationship to the community formed every Friday through local pilgrimage, an occasional community that is, as we have just seen, figured by the legend's carol form. Devotion to saints in the Middle Ages often emphasized a distinct quality that linked the saint and devotee: a shared name, for example, or a specific kind of intercessory power, such as was attributed to St. Christopher, who offered protection from sudden death, or St. Margaret, patron of childbirth.[1] Hence the idiosyncratic appearance of saints' Lives in miscellaneous volumes, sometimes in small clusters and sometimes singly, from which we may infer a habit of thought in which saints were above all figures for particular needs, particular modes of identification or devotion, or particular communities.

The singularity of the saint may seem axiomatic: saints are, by definition, exceptional. Yet a countervailing truism emphasizes their function as figures of communion: in the first place, there are lots of them, and their vast number is an image of an undifferentiated Christian community. The most important formal vehicle for this idea is the legendary, in which the singularity of each saint is subordinated to their collective participation in a heavenly communion. In the mid-fifteenth century, vernacular writers turned to this formal structure to think about English saints as members of a pan-Christian community, and thus also to think about local, regional, and national communities in relation to supranational religious formations. There are two full-scale English legendaries produced in this period, parallel though apparently unrelated projects: the *Gilte Legende*, which presents a translation of *Legenda Aurea* supplemented by a set of Lives translated into prose from the *South English Legendary* (*SEL*), and the legendary attributed to Osbern Bokenham, recently discovered in Sir Walter Scott's library at Abbotsford House, which is also a translation of *Legenda Aurea* with the addition of English saints and others of special interest to Bokenham.[2]

Through their comprehensive form, both of these works explore the idea of a saintly communion that eclipses individual investments and identities. Yet they also take advantage of the legendary's multipart structure to add supplementary material of interest to some audiences, and in this way they testify to the tenacious appeal and practical authority of such idiosyncratic investments. Most strikingly, both collections add a significant number of native saints' Lives to the sanctorale materials they inherit from *Legenda Aurea*. The Abbotsford legendary includes the Lives of Alban, Aldhelm, Augustine of Canterbury, Botolph, Cedde, David, Dunstan, Etheldreda, Felix, Gilbert, John of Beverley, Wilfrid, Wenefred, and Wulfstan. The *Gilte Legende* in its original form adds only the *Life of St. Alban* to Jacobus de Voragines's *Legenda*,[3] but the *SEL* Lives redacted in prose that were incorporated into some versions of the collection include those of Aldhelm, Alphege, Augustine, Bride, Chad, Cuthbert, Dunstan, Edmund of Abingdon, Edmund king and martyr, Kenelm, Oswald Bishop, Swithun, and a longer legend of Thomas of Canterbury. One book, British Library MS Additional 35298, further adds the Lives of Edward the Confessor, Erkenwald, and Wenefred.[4]

This addition of native saints' Lives to Middle English translations of *Legenda Aurea* indexes the legendary's importance in this period as a formal technology for representing a national community in relation to a supranational Christian one. As translations of *Legenda Aurea*, both collections point to their audiences' desire to participate in a shared, supranational Christian community via what was arguably the most important narrative work in the Western Christian world, a multipart collection of stories that addressed the layered and multiform communities that linked Western Christians across boundaries of kingdoms and regions. The very choice of the Latin *Legenda Aurea*, a pan-European textual tradition, rather than the *SEL*, which was still being copied in the early fifteenth century, is evidence of the appeal of this supranational textual community, and its translation into English can be seen as an effort to recalibrate the affiliation of English audiences to this community.[5] At the same time, the addition of English saints' Lives suggests a paradoxical correlative: a sense that national identity was germane to religious identity.

This chapter explores how the relationship between England and Christendom is defined in these two collections in spatial terms, and in particular how they position England as a geographical category that mediates between local cult sites and a Christendom that transcends location. This is most evident in the case of the Abbotsford legendary: long before its recent discovery, scholars knew of the existence of such a work from the prologue to Bokenham's *Mappula Angliae*, his translation of a cartographic description of England excerpted from Ranulph Higden's *Polychronicon*. This companion text is evidence on its face that England had become a point of identification for Bokenham and his readers: the Lives of native saints are to be read precisely through the spatial paradigm of England and specific references to English places that surface in them.

The *Gilte Legende*, in contrast, offers England as the middle term in a conceptual, rather than geographical, schema. It is the hypernym of local communities (that is, it represents a category shift from the particular to the more general) and hyponym of a supranational Christianity (that is, from the perspective of Christianity, it represents a category shift from the general to the more particular). It echoes Bokenham's legendary, however, in the thematic and formal attention given to *place* as a defining category for this conceptualization of England. The most interesting articulation of this idea is to be found in British Library MS Additional 35298, whose three uniquely attested legends offer the city as a spatial paradigm for national community. While the *Prose SEL* legends remain somewhat nostalgic for England's claim to France, the trio of additional legends in British Library MS Additional 35298 offers London as a forum for thinking about England's new insularity.

*   *   *

That two Middle English translations of *Legenda Aurea* were produced independently in the mid-fifteenth century is perhaps less surprising than that there was no full-scale translation prior to 1438, the date assigned to the *Gilte Legende* in Bodleian Library MS Douce 372.[6] The enormous popularity of Jacobus de Voragine's collection is often measured by its rapid translation into other vernaculars, including French, German, Spanish, Italian, and Dutch; it had been a medieval "best seller" in other languages for well over a hundred years when the English translations were produced.[7] The delay can be explained in part by the availability of French translations, especially Jean de Vignay's, which would have satisfied some of the need for a vernacular version of *Legenda Aurea* for pastoral and devotional purposes. So too did the *SEL*, which includes some materials translated from *Legenda Aurea*.[8] By the end of the fourteenth century, John Mirk recognized the need for a Middle English handbook for temporale and sanctorale feasts, and his *Festial* is largely based on *Legenda Aurea*. But it provides only a sizable sample, not a full-scale translation, of Jacobus's compendium, and the Lives are presented as the sermons of a parish priest.[9]

The translation projects of the mid-fifteenth century, then, witness a significant turn to the legendary as a form, and they show a special interest in that form as a context for English saints' Lives. They are anticipated in this by the *SEL*, discussed in Chapter 1, which constitutes both a precedent for these works and a direct influence on one of them: as noted above, it is the source for the *Gilte Legende*'s native saints' Lives. Like the *SEL*, the *Gilte Legende* and the Abbotsford collection use the formal technology of the legendary in order to present multiple, nonisomorphic communities—including religious community at local, national, and supranational scales. The communion of saints in these legendaries, as in their thirteenth-century precedent, comprises multiple categories of identity and affiliation—a variousness that the multipart form of the legendary is especially well suited to represent.

I want to underscore, however, that this conceptualization of community is not an immanent quality of the form. The legendary can be used to different ends, as it is, for example, in the *Kalendre of the Newe Legende of Englande*, in which the iterative structure of the multipart legendary is used to represent a far more monolithic national community. It is instead a *capability* of the form, realized in both the *SEL* and the fifteenth-century legendaries.[10] The similarity between the *SEL* and the fifteenth-century legendaries and the turn to the *SEL* as a source for the legends supplementary to *Gilte Legende* register a desire to explore multiple, overlapping, and variously scaled communities through the multipart form of the legendary; they are not evidence of a reflex embedded in the form itself. Indeed, the legendary's ability to represent the varied relationship between different communities is inevitably altered in the centuries that separate the *SEL* from its mid-fifteenth-century successors, above all in two signal differences I explore in this chapter: a marked shift from a temporal to a spatial framework for thinking about the relationship between communities at different scales, and the concomitant development of England as a point of identification that mediates between local and supranational forms of community.

The *Gilte Legende* and the Abbotsford legendary nevertheless echo the *SEL* in inviting the reader to identify with England as just one of many forms of community. Even as they encourage the reader's identification with native saints on the basis of their Englishness, this affiliation does not moot other categories of identity or forms of community represented in the ample collection of narratives. Folded into large collections such as these, native saints' Lives have a lateral relationship to other legends, which are associated with other forms of community. In this way, native saints and the readers affiliated with them through shared Englishness are recognized *by the form of the legendary* as members of a supranational communion. In the *Gilte Legende* and Bokenham's legendary, the relationships between these kinds of affiliation and community are conceptualized through the categories of geography and place.

This may reflect the rapid shifts in the scale of English community relative to other Western European polities, discussed in the Introduction. Especially relevant here are the losses of England's Continental territories during Henry VI's minority and early rule, through which England's actual borders increasingly approximated the visible geographical boundary of its own coastline. The realm was nevertheless still figured in terms of its historical claim to France,[11] and the debate about how energetically to pursue this claim—in effect, a debate about the scale of the realm—was the most consequential political concern in the period during which the Middle English legendaries were composed. The Treaty of Tours in the 1440s confirmed the unavoidable fact of England's diminishing scale, its Continental holdings reduced to half the territory claimed by the crown at the start of the century. At the same time, as we also saw in the Introduction, the definitions of the nation developed in the context of conciliar politics expanded England's scale, in part by detaching it from the person of the king. In this historical moment, it would have been difficult to know whether St. Michael's Mount (Mont Saint-Michel) was, or might one day be, part of England, or whether St. Faith of Conques or the Irish St. Brendan—whose Lives are among those added to *Gilte Legende*—was (still) in some way an "English" saint. Indeed, it would not have been entirely clear whether England names the king's realm, or a general "nation" defined by ethical, political, and linguistic diversity, or, as from the vantage of realpolitik, a small island, separated from the Continent by a "little sea" that it no longer controlled.[12]

Whatever its impetus, a spatial conceptualization of England is developed in the midcentury legendaries through the distinctive capabilities of the legendary as a multipart narrative form. Beyond their own formal boundaries, moreover, both collections are affiliated with works that give extended thematic attention to the geography of national community: Bokenham's *Mappula Angliae*, and the *Libelle of Englyshe Polycye*, a polemical poem contemporary with the midcentury legendaries and a textual first cousin to two of them. The *Mappula Angliae* is presented explicitly as a companion text to some of the English saints' Lives included in the Abbotsford legendary. The affiliations of the *Libelle* are not quite as intimate, but they nevertheless index the relationship of its concerns to those of the legendaries: indeed, one copy is found alongside Bokenham's *Mappula Angliae* in British Library MS Harley 4011. Another is found in Huntington Library MS 140, which also includes a prose legend of St. Ursula (discussed in Chapter 7), which is, in turn, grouped in Southwell Minster MS 7 with some of the *Prose SEL* Lives of English saints as an appendix to Mirk's *Festial*.

Both the *Mappula Angliae* and the *Libelle of Englische Polycye* are preoccupied with England as an island, defined by its finite geography, which the first work measures in geographical terms and the second figures through the metaphor of the walled city. By turning first to the spatial representations of England in these works, we will be better able to discern the conceptualization of England developed in the formal structure of the mid-fifteenth-century legendaries.

Spatializing England: Island, City, See

The *Libelle of Englyshe Polycye*, composed sometime between 1436 and 1438, responds explicitly to England's increasing insularity, its re-scaling as an island nation.[13] Although it advocates keeping Calais, the *Libelle* is otherwise resigned to the recent loss of England's Continental territories: "exhortynge alle Englande to kepe the see enviroun and namelye the narowe see," it argues not to retake former territories, but rather to defend the sea itself as England's border. Indeed, the sea is represented less as England's new boundary, diminished from the more expansive ones it had recently known, than as an immutable, even inevitable border, a natural analogue to the fortifications of a city:

> Kepe than the see abought in speciall,
> Whiche of England is the rounde wall,
> As thoughe England were lykened to a cite
> And the wall environ were the see.
> Kepe than the see, that is the wall of Englond,
> And than is Englond kepte by Goddes sond;
> That, as for ony thinge that is wythoute,
> Englande were than at ease wythouten doute (1092–99)

> [Protect then the surrounding sea especially,
> Which is the encircling wall of England,
> As though England were comparable to a city
> And the wall around it were the sea.
> Protect, then, the sea that is the wall of England,
> And then England shall be protected by God's favor;
> So that, whatever happens externally,
> England would still be secure without doubt]

The image notably occludes England's recent history of Continental conquest and loss. It posits instead the durable isomorphism of England's geographical and political boundaries: the sea as the "round wall" of England. By imagining its jurisdiction as limited by the sea in this way, the poem conceptualizes England in terms of spatial or territorial extension. While this may seem commonplace from a modern perspective, it represents an important departure from traditional monarchical models of jurisdiction and authority, which are correlative of obligation, not territory. The realm, that is, is defined in terms of the interpersonal structure linking king and subject. In secular contexts, territorial jurisdiction was, as the poem's city metaphor indicates, primarily an urban phenomenon: the citizen, unlike the subject, is defined by his relationship to a specific *place*.

On one level, the poem's conceptualization of England as "likened to a city" betrays the psychological pressure of the ongoing conflict with France, which it curiously invokes through a striking inversion of scale. Compared to a walled city threatened by siege, England is figured through tacit analogy to Harfleur or Rouen, whose capture had secured Normandy earlier in the

century.[14] Now England itself has become the walled city, through a shift in
scale so extreme that the governing literary figure, synecdoche, is itself re-
versed: rather than a city representing the realm in which it is found, the
whole of England is figured as a single city, protected by but also confined
within its island borders. The image, not least as a suppressed memory of
England's sudden isolation from a Continental geography that it had recently occupied, establishes urban territoriality as the spatial paradigm for
England.

An additional and more optimistic etiology for the *Libelle*'s urban analogy surfaces in its exhaustive description of commodities whose exchange
defines England's relationship to other communities. Catalogs of the goods
produced by other nations occupy a full quarter of the poem, well more
than 300 of its 1,164 lines. The lists provide a forum for satirical comment
on other nations, as many scholars have noted: as, for example, the poem's
dismissal of Italian commodities: "Apes and japes and marmusettes taylede
/ Nifles, trifles, that litell have availed" (Apes and novelties and monkeys
with tails, frippery, trinkets that are useless, ll. 348–49).[15] But the discussion of trade also serves as an extended gloss on the metaphor of the city.
England's insularity is inflected by a mercantile emphasis on the city as a
center of trade, a node in a translocal network.[16] The city in the *Libelle* is
thus paradigmatic of a national community defined through discrete geography and jurisdiction, and relationships of exchange with, and difference
from, other communities.

These two genealogies for the city metaphor, military and mercantile, are
complementary: the catalogs of heterogeneous commodities produced in
other countries identify such diversity as external to England, which is imagined, in contrast, as markedly homogeneous—as "one hoole Jurisdiccion and
libertie," as London fashioned itself.[17] The urban metaphor, in figuring England as a small-scale political community, represents it as just such a unified
space: the oceanic "wall" that circles England circumscribes an undifferentiated and finite community. Following traditional political theories, this community is unified through the person of the king, who embodies and thus
ensures their common will and identity. So the *Libelle* offers Edgar as an exemplary English king on account of practices that produce a uniform polity:
in winter, Edgar traveled throughout the country to enforce his law, ensuring
coherence within the realm, while in summer, he would ready a large navy,
some 3,600 ships (918), and "saile and rowe environ all alonge / So regaliche
aboute the Englisshe yle" (933–34). The correlative of England's status as an

island is the internal homogeneity of the realm, an organic unity represented by the king's body politic.

Bokenham's *Mappula Angliae* shares with the *Libelle* a preoccupation with England's status as an island nation, but it represents this fixed geography as a template for multiple overlapping spatial paradigms, defined by different features of the natural and human-made landscape and different forms of jurisdiction. The text refers repeatedly to England as "this island": "This yle Albyoun" (7) or "this yle Brytayne" (9).[18] This insularity is correlative of England's geographical eccentricity, its separation from Europe: following a well-established conceit emphasizing England's marginality, the *Mappula Angliae* declares that it is called "Anglia of angulus, the wch is a Cornere, ffor Englonde, quod he [i.e., Higden], stant in a Cornere of the worlde" (Anglia, from Latin "angle," which is a corner, for England, he says, stands in a corner of the world).[19] The conceptual framework linking eccentricity and insularity is made concrete in the *Mappula*'s description of England's geographical disposition: it is "in the west ende of the worlde anempste Germayne, Fraunce & Spayne betwixt the Northe & the West, disseuered & departed from the seid countrees wt the see" (in the west end of the world, across from Germany, France, and Spain, between the north and the west, cut off from and separated from these countries by the sea) (7). Its insularity confers on England borders so absolute they sever it from the rest of the world. Thus Bokenham, citing Isidore of Seville's *Etymologies*, explains that "Brytayne stant wt-in the Occiane as thaughe hit were in a nother worlde" (Britain stands within the ocean as though it were in another world). While its extension can be calculated, as it is in chapter 3 of the *Mappula*,[20] England escapes the spatial logic, and the relative scale, determined by the Continent.

In the *Mappula*, the enclosed and delimited geographical boundaries of England circumscribe a notable diversity, produced by its variable and violent history.[21] The island comprises "as many dyuerys peeples as hit hathe dwellers, so many hit hathe dyuersites of toungis and languagis" (as many diverse people as it has inhabitants, it has so many diversities of tongues and languages) (30); these are not "alle pure, but sum ben mixte & medlid on sundry wys" (all pure, but some are mixed and combined in various ways) (30), differences that may be indexed especially in terms of different regional dialects. This diversity is identified as a consequence of England's long history of ethnic difference and conquest: although some have been vanquished entirely, the various people who have inhabited the island in different historical periods correspond now to different regional groups:

And so now at thus dayes, the Pyctis & the Danys vttirly distroyed, Brytayne is oonly Inhabyted wt these V naciouns, as wt Scottis yn Albayne, wt Britouns yn Cambria or yn Walys, wt Flemmynges yn West-Walis, wt Normannys & Englysshe men myxte and medlyd yn all the Ile aftir (29)

[And so now in these days, the Picts and the Danes having been utterly destroyed, Britain is only inhabited by these five ethnic groups, with Scots in Albany, with British in Cambria or in Wales, with Flemish in West Wales, with Normans and English men mixed in all the rest of the island].

This history of displacement, compounded with England's island status, has particular consequences for the "English," that is, the "residue peple of ynglyssh men inhabetynge Loegrie, as an insulan peple ferre run from hur ffirste institucioun" (the remaining people from the English men inhabiting Logres, as an island people far flung from their first origin). They are

by hire propir mocyoun inward wt-owtyn only straunge or foreyn styrynge owtewarde . . . redely and sone mevid to contrarye thyngis, that is to seyne, now to willyn O certeyn thynge, & wt-owtyn ony grete abydynge or taryinge, that wille forsakyn, to wyllyn evyn the contrary. In so moche that they been euer ynpacient of reste, loueris of solicitude & bysynesse, & lothyn alle ese & ydelnesse. In so moche, as seithe William de pontificibz li. 3, That when they hane vttirly depressid hur outward enmyes, they brosyn eche other & faryn lyke an empty stomake the whiche wirkythe vpon hit-selfe (31–32)

[by their own inward motion, without any external or foreign outward incitement . . . readily and soon moved to contrary things: that is to say, now to will a certain thing, and without any great waiting or delaying, forsake that will to will just the contrary, to such an extent that they have been ever impatient of rest, lovers of industry and busyness, and hate all ease and idleness. To such an extent, as says William [of Malmesbury], *De Pontificibus*, bk. 3, that when they have utterly defeated their external enemies, they batter each other and fare like an empty stomach that works upon itself].

Confined to the finite space of the island, the English people—remnants of successive waves of invasion and conquest—inhabit it restlessly and self-destructively, like a body that turns on itself. The inward turning of the empty stomach is a literally visceral image of insularity: of a space that achieves its singularity through the absence of contact, exchange, or external stimulus of any kind. Enclosed within the insular borders of a territory to which they are not native, the English are self-consuming. Rather than defining self against other, England's island borders define the self *as* other. The *Mappula*, as a consequence, recognizes the centripetal orientation of national space—oriented inward from its boundaries—as the source of division and internal violence. And it further recognizes the human body, a privileged metaphor for the integrity of a community, as an apt vehicle for representing the costs of such isolation.

This *in malo* notion of insularity has an *in bono* complement: sacred bodies whose intactness does not produce self-consuming hunger, but transcendent completeness. Bokenham is hesitant to vouch for other marvels that he reports, but the wonderful preservation of so many saints' bodies—England's singular (and insular) privilege—is an exception. So, in the *Polychronicon*'s account, which Bokenham acknowledges that he "dar. . .well sey & hope for trewthe" (dare well say and hope is true),

> Hit is to be considered deuovtly how moche cleere brightnes of goddis mercyfulle pite hathe syngulerly Illumined & iradied the peple of Ynglond from the bygynnynge of the feithe recevid, that no-wheere of no peple in oo prouynce be foundyne so many seyntis bodies liynge hool aftur hur dethe, incorupt & hauynge the similitude & the examplary of finalle incorupcioun, as byne in Yngelond: and he exemplifi-ethe by seynt Edward and synt Edmund kyngis, seynt Alphege & seynt Cutberde bischopes (11)

> [It is to be devoutly contemplated how much clear brightness of God's merciful pity has singularly illuminated and irradiated the people of England, from the beginning of the reception of the faith, that no-where is there any people in any province where are found so many saints' bodies lying whole after their deaths, incorrupt and presenting the appearance and model of ultimate incorruption, as there are in England: and he shows this by the examples of St. Edward and St. Edmund, kings, and by St. Alphege and St. Cuthbert, bishops].

Bokenham adds John Constaunce, a bishop who lies uncorrupt at Worcester, St. Etheldreda (Audrey), "wife twyes queen & maydoun" (11), and Joan of Acre, whom he names here "boldly by auctoryte of experyence" (11). The "other world" of England is, in the context of these saints, an image of the eschatological future, where the "final incorruption" of the body will no longer be the special privilege of these saints, or the special privilege of England, but the material form of salvation and the undifferentiated communion it promises.

In the secular world, however, neither England's insularity nor the wonderfully incorrupt bodies of its saints produces a homogeneous space. The *Mappula* comprises a series of chapters that each describe England according to a different spatial paradigm: in chapter 3, its geographical dimensions; in chapter 6, its three principal regional divisions; in chapter 7, its "collateral Iles"—that is, England as one island in an archipelago; in chapter 8, its highways, which figure England as a networked space; chapter 9, its major rivers, the natural analogue of roads, as networks of commerce; chapter 10, its shires, a spatial organization determined by local secular administration and law; chapter 11, its "famous" cities, a spatial organization determined by urban centers; chapter 13, rather late in the text, England as divided into "reigns," the ancient heptarchy and royal partitions; and chapter 14, England as figured by bishoprics, that is, by ecclesiastical jurisdiction.

Bokenham follows the *Polychronicon* closely in all of this, but the effect is quite different here, where the whole work, not a small part of a long one, is devoted to the plural spatial organizations that figure England. The pernicious isolation of the island body, cut off from external contact or resources and thus vulnerable to the inward corrosion of the stomach "turned against itself," finds some remedy in sustained attention to the multiple jurisdictions and other spatial organizations it contains, which significantly qualify any representation of England as an undifferentiated space or organic unity.

Out of the several spatial logics traced in the *Mappula*, religious jurisdiction is the only one in which English saints appear. In chapter 14, having described in the previous chapter "the partycyoun & the diuision of the temporalle rewle and gouernaunce of thus lond by knygis" (the partition and division according to secular rule and governance of this land by kings), Bokenham, following his source, turns to the "spiritualle policies of this londe by bysshopes, and of hur sees and of the boundis of hire Jurisdiccions" (spiritual administration of this land by bishops and of their sees and of the bounds of their jurisdictions) (24). It is here that we find reference to Felix, the Suffolk saint whose legend is mentioned in the prologue as an occasion for the text: the description of the religious jurisdictions in Essex explains that "the provynce of Est-ynglonde, the which conteynythe Northe-folke & Sowthe-folke, had firste but oon bysshope, whose name was Felix, the wch kepte his sees XVII yere at Dunwyche" (the province of East England, which contains Norfolk and Suffolk, initially had only one bishop, whose name was Felix, who kept his see seventeen years at Dunwich) (26).[22] Cedde is mentioned too, in the description of the see at Litchfield, of which Cedde was the fifth bishop (27).[23] There is a brief reference to St. Edward, in a description of how the Danes oppressed the land for two hundred years, from "the tyme of the seyde Egbert on-to the tyme of seynt Edwarde," but even saintly kings show up primarily in the context of ecclesiastical jurisdiction: a reference to "seynte Oswalde the kynge regnynge yn Northehumbirlonde" (27) surfaces in the account of the see of York left vacant after the death of King Edwin.[24] The *Mappula* represents English saints, then, and the framework of ecclesiastical jurisdiction to which they are confined, as a categorically separate form of national community, one not necessarily in tension with the several forms of secular community it limns, but different from, and largely indifferent to, them.

Mapping the Scale of Religious Communities

This representation of religious community as a discrete spatial form, separate from the secular jurisdictions with which it overlaps, is corroborated by the Abbotsford legendary, which confines itself to religious communities and jurisdictions. Where England has definite spatial limits in the *Mappula*, in the Abbotsford legendary it is limited less in size than in "jurisdictional heterogeneity."[25] The legendary places the geography of English devotion in relation to supranational communities, both particular ones such as the Augustinian order and the general community of Christendom. But this more expansive geographical reach has as its functional corollary a more exclusive focus on a single spatial paradigm: England as a religious space, defined by the landscape of its native saints' Lives. As we will see, the most striking symptom of this is the absence of saintly kings, an omission that allows the legendary to disaggregate English religious communities from political or secular jurisdictions, past and present.[26]

The Abbotsford legendary, only recently discovered, needs some

introduction, and it is especially important to my argument that its relationship to the *Mappula Angliae* be clarified. It is in the *Mappula* that Bokenham
refers to an "englische boke" containing the Lives of St. Cedde, Felix, Oswald,
and Edward that he had compiled from "legenda aurea and other famous
legendes": the treatise is presented as an extended gloss on the obscure geographical references in these legends.[27] Despite the regrettable loss of some
single folios scattered throughout the book, and what was perhaps a more
substantial loss at its end, the Abbotsford legendary, which contains legends
known to be Bokenham's, corresponds closely to the description in the *Mappula*: it is a translation of Jacobus de Voragine's *Legenda Aurea*, supplemented
by a number of English saints, including those specifically named in the
prologue.[28]

It is nevertheless important to consider that the Abbotsford legendary
may not in fact be the book to which Bokenham refers in *Mappula Angliae* or
a copy identical to it, despite these correspondences. The legendary could
represent a somewhat, or perhaps significantly, altered collection of Bokenham's hagiography.[29] We know that Bokenham repurposed his compositions
freely: several of the legends in the *Legendys of Hooly Wummen*, especially
those addressed to particular lay readers, were very likely one-off works that
were subsequently compiled as a legendary of female saints for a house of
nuns, and then adapted yet again for the omnibus Abbotsford legendary. The
Abbotsford book—dated some twenty years after the *Mappula*—could itself
be a later assemblage of saints' Lives, rather than the one that initially inspired Bokenham to translate Higden's treatise.[30] Being wary of an overhasty
identification of the Abbotsford legendary with the collection mentioned in
the *Mappula* can help us identify more precisely the similarities and differences in their conceptual frameworks: namely, that while both disaggregate
religious community from other ways of mapping English geographies, the
Mappula presents this kind of community as coextensive with both secular
jurisdictions and insular topography, while the Abbotsford legendary presents English religious community as at once more categorically separate from
the realm and more thoroughly imbricated in local and supranational Christian communities.

The most striking evidence of the first is the exclusion of England's saintly
kings from the Abbotsford legendary, including Oswald and Edward, the two
named in the prologue to the *Mappula Angliae*.[31] It is possible that the legend
of a saintly king featured on a now-missing folio, but this seems unlikely.
With the exception of the section lost from the manuscript's end, almost all

of the missing pages contained the beginning of a major Christic or Marian feast, and the most likely explanation for their loss is that these important legends featured miniatures or some other deluxe decoration whose aesthetic value led to their removal from the book. It is just possible that a very short legend of Edward the Confessor appeared on the folio that contained the beginning of the Epiphany narrative, as Simon Horobin has suggested: the Deposition of Edward fell on January 5, between the feast of St. Basil on January 2 and Epiphany on January 6.[32] But this is unlikely given that Edward's main feast, commemorating his Translation (October 13), is not included.[33] There is greater uncertainty regarding St. Oswald, as there are two St. Oswalds, the holy king Oswald of Northumbria and the Bishop of Worcester, and it is risky to assume a priori that Bokenham refers to the former rather than the latter in the *Mappula*. Indeed, for the reasons outlined above, we may rather assume his greater interest in the bishop. In any case, neither legend is extant in the Abbotsford legendary. If it did once possess an Oswald legend, it must have been the saintly king, whose feast fell on August 5: there is a missing page between the Invention of St. Stephen, on August 3, and the feast of St. Dominic, on August 5, that could have held his legend.[34] This missing leaf is somewhat more mysterious than the other lost pages. It is the single exception to the general rule that missing folios correspond to major Christic or Marian feasts. It is also the single instance in which the extant folios are numbered continuously across the lost page, which seems to suggest that it was cut out before the others were excised.

The intriguing possibility that the life of St. Oswald, king and martyr, was removed at an early moment can return us to the more secure observation that the Abbotsford legendary lacks a significant interest in saintly kings: even in the unlikely event that it did originally possess a Life of St. Oswald and possibly of Edward the Confessor, it has no St. Edmund, no St. Kenelm, no St. Edward, king and martyr, nor does it have minor saintly kings, such as St. Alkmund, included in Mirk's *Festial*, or St. Walstan, whose cult enjoyed a vogue in the mid-fifteenth century and who was venerated not far from Clare Priory at Cavenham and Earl Stonham.[35] The Abbotsford legendary is interested instead, as Horobin notes, in the "foundation of the early church and lives of its bishops."[36] It maps England, that is, by see, episcopal jurisdiction, which nevertheless deepens a diachronic representation of national community, insofar as these legends provide a forum for English history, and places England in a broad European ecclesiastical geography.

In general terms, the omission of the Lives of saintly kings may be seen as part of a larger rejection of contemporary efforts to coordinate secular and spiritual authority, which is the focus of the next chapter. Bokenham's legend of John of Beverley, for example, omits the well-known miracle that first made him a royal and national saint. In the story, found in Latin vitae and in the *Kalendre of the Newe Legende of Englande,* King Aethelstan prays to the saint for a sign of England's dominance over Scotland, and when Aethelstan strikes a stone with his sword, it leaves a large divot.[37] This saintly approval of English sovereignty over Scotland was invoked repeatedly from the twelfth century through the fifteenth century: English armies went into battle against the Scots under the banner of St. John.[38] Bokenham's version of the legend neglects this miracle altogether, confining itself to one in which the Holy Spirit shines so brightly on John as he prays that a deacon is burned by the fierce heat, his shriveled face later healed by John's touch. Like his Wenefred legend, discussed in Chapter 3, Bokenham's *Life of John of Beverley* thus rejects the appropriation of a native saint to guarantee royal authority or to sacralize political community—even when this function was a long-established aspect of the cult. Figuring John of Beverley's piety as so absolute that it cannot be approached even by someone with the pastoral responsibilities of a deacon, and omitting altogether his very visible role as patron saint of English sovereignty over Scotland, the Abbotsford legendary insists on a sharp delineation between English religious community and the realm. The St. John legend indexes a fundamental resistance to the coordination of sacred and political orders that threads through the collection, as we saw, for example, in the miracle of the Carmelite friar's access to Wenefred's well, discussed in Chapter 3. Indeed, this project supersedes whatever topical or partisan importance such anecdotes may have.

The Abbotsford legendary's focus on religious community does not, however, produce England as a homogeneous space; instead, it produces a centrifugal map of overlapping communities that cannot be confined to the island nation. The English legends in the collection point to several varieties of religious community—monastic, ecclesiastical, and popular—which in turn index some of the spatial paradigms through which English places are linked to pan-European Christianity. Thus while a saint such as Botolph (114v–115r) is represented as an "English" saint (the legend focuses on the abbey that he founds in the fens of Suffolk as part of the early history of England's conversion), he is also affiliated with other non-English Augustinian saints, such as William the Hermit (63r–63v) and Nicholas of Tolentino (181r–183v), a recently canonized member of the order. By refracting the

English affiliations of a saint through other affillations, as Botolph is associated with the international order of Augustinians, the multipart narrative form of the legendary creates a layered map of religious communities, whose boundaries do not coincide or serve as firm borders.

This project is facilitated by thematic attention to the place of England in a pan-European Christendom. Here too Botolph is a useful example: Botolph, a descendant of Saxons, bemoans the weak presence of Christianity on his "natal sool" (native soil) and therefore travels to Saxony to learn monastic discipline. The saint's return to an ethnic origin—as a Saxon who travels to Saxony—is compelled not by the claims of blood or territory, but rather by access to portable knowledge and habits of Christian discipline that might be retrieved from there and brought to England. When Botolph returns to England seeking to found his own religious house, he is offered several endowments of land, but he does not want anyone to be "excludid from his heritage" (114v), and so he asks that the king instead grant him "grounde untilled wast wilde" (untilled land, a wild wasteland). The abbey is thus located in fenland, a place outside human use, knowledge, or rights: this founding institution of a nascent English church, located in English landscape but external to English history, explicitly depends on Christian belief and practice borrowed from a supranational religious institution. The legend conceptualizes the relationship between local English cults and Christendom as a relationship between territorial specificity and the boundary-crossing, pan-European categories of Christian practice and knowledge.

A similar structure obtains in the *Life of St. Wilfrid*. Wilfrid departs from Lindisfarne because he realizes that "the wey of vertu youyn of scottys was not perfyht ner sufficient" (the way of virtue established by the Scots was not perfect nor sufficient) (204v). Traveling through France on his way to Rome, Wilfrid so impresses a bishop, Dalfinus, that Dalfinus wants to take him as his adoptive son and heir, and he promises Wilfrid "the gouvernaunce of a gret part of France." But Wilfrid presses on to Rome in order to learn "thynggys wich he myht not lernyn in his owyn cuntre." On his return, he remains with Dalfinus for three years, and again the question of the bishop's heritage is raised. Partly because Dalfinus is murdered by Queen Bathilda and partly because "goddys eternal provydence" had determined that he should serve as a bishop in "his owe cuntre," however, Wilfrid cannot remain. Before returning to England, he is consecrated in Paris, an index of England's continued dependence on the more authoritative ecclesiastical structure found on the Continent. This is a recurrent theme in the story, in which Wilfrid is forced to resort to Rome because of flawed understanding of key Christian rites, including the Roman system for determining Easter, and irregularities in ecclesiastical appointments, including the loss of his bishopric when King Ecgfrith comes to power. This does not undermine the importance of his local presence in England, however, which is carefully invoked in the legend's final reference to his shrine at Ripon "on the south syde of the awter" in St. Peter's church, which is "adornyd wyth an Epitaphie of twenty vers conteynyng the substaunce of his lyf" (205r). Although the narrative operates within the framework of a supranational Christendom, whose claim on Wilfrid is repeatedly staged, his body and "life" are finally given a fixed geographical location in England.

The native saints' legends in the Abbotsford collection do not simply identify England as a more local place within the expansive boundaries of Christianity. Rather, they encode various geographies that overlap and diverge in a complex system. St. Botolph is ultimately identified with three Benedictine abbeys where his relics come to rest: Thorney, Westminster, and Ely. The last links him to other Ely saints—St. Etheldreda (Audrey) (117v), for example—and more broadly to a cluster of saints associated with "East England," including Cedde and Felix. Together these Lives at once reference a local devotional community and indicate variegated relationships to a supranational one. Felix, for example, is born and consecrated in Burgundy, but comes to England because he believes that it is "more meritory to prechyn to hethen peple" (72v), while Botolph, as we've seen, is born in England and travels to Saxony in order to learn Christian doctrine and monastic practice.

Where the *Mappula Angliae* represents England through its topography, its cities, its shires, and its ancient kingdoms, as well as its religious jurisdictions, then, the Abbotsford legendary spatializes England through the several communities—spiritual and geographical—of late medieval Christianity, few of which map onto the boundaries of the nation. Thus, while the *Mappula Angliae*'s mixed and complex model of England's overlapping, nonisomorphic jurisdictions of political and religious authority is bounded by its insular geography, the Abbotsford legendary presents English communities in relation to pan-European Christian ones, through which they shift in relative scale. It does so through its own fine-grained sense of the various affiliations to different regions, different institutions, different histories by which these communities might be distinguished, even as it maps them on to a shared English geography.

One unusual and perhaps telling representation of the relationship between England and a broader geography is found in the *Life of St. Thomas Becket*, which is especially well suited to the project of intercalating England in a complex world map: it begins with the captivity of Thomas's father, Gilbert, by a Muslim ruler, and Becket himself is exiled to France after Clarendon, familiar episodes that Bokenham's version rehearses. What is distinctive about Bokenham's legend is reference to economic relationships, and particularly "commodities," as a primary way in which England is defined in relation to other places—which is, notably, also how it is defined in both Bokenham's *Mappula Angliae* and the *Libelle of Englysche Polycye*, which are found together in MS Harley 4011. When Maud, the Saracen princess who is to become Thomas's mother, asks Gilbert about his homeland, he answers first by explaining the "conditions and commoditees" of England and London (21r), as might the poet of *Libelle of Englysche Polycye*. More striking are the interpretations of the pregnant Maud's vision of the Thames pouring into her lap. One wise man gives the reading found in the source text for the vision, the vita by Guernes de Pont St. Maxence, which explains that water represents people and the dream is a prophecy that her child will govern many people.[39] A second man gives an interpretation without precedent in this source: he explains that the water represents the "plentevous habundaunce of grace" (plentiful abundance of grace) for "as al Ingelonde is refresshid and comfortid by the plentevous commoditees of divers marchaundises and richessis which ben conveyed in by Thamyse flode bodily . right so shal it be watrid and embawmed by the plentevous habundaunce of graces which shul issuen from thy childis brest gostely" (just as all England is refreshed and comforted by the plentiful commodities of diverse merchandise and riches that are conveyed physically by the Thames River, just so shall it be watered and embalmed by the plentiful abundance of graces that shall issue spiritually from your child's breast) (22r). The Thames figures the grace offered by the saint through an analogy between the merchandise it transports to London and the abundant spiritual good that Thomas will provide—an analogy that recalls the economic practices that define England in relation to other polities in the *Libelle of Englysche Polycye*.

*   *   *

Thematic attention to the landscape of English religious community is even more pronounced in the Lives of saints from the *South English Legendary* that are translated into prose and incorporated into some copies of the *Gilte*

Legende. The *Prose SEL* legends are, as other critics have noted, preoccupied with shrines and other sites of pilgrimage:[40] Dunstan's body lies in a "full worshipful shryne" at Glastonbury where he has effected many great miracles (184), Kenelm lies at Winchcomb in a "worshipful schyryne in the abbey that his fader Kenulf had made" (211), the purple vestment that Aldhelm once hung on a sunbeam is still at Malmesbury (182), and Thomas of Canterbury was born in London "where Seint Thomas of Akers chirche is nowe" (285). The interest in such details is marked enough, Manfred Görlach suggests, to render the legends a "pilgrim's guide to the shrines of English saints."[41] This mapping of English devotional community is determined by localities *interior* to it, from which this space is projected centrifugally, in lieu of borders that circumscribe it. Like a line drawing of a constellation, England is the abstract figure formed by the spatial relation between concrete places—Winchester, Canterbury, London, York.

Such geographical detail is a distinctive feature of the English saints' Lives in the *Gilte Legende*, which telescopes between a generic geography of Christendom in its other saints' Lives to the close focus with which its English legends identify, for example, the shrine of Frideswide—"hir bodye lyeth at Oxford in a fulle worshipfulle shryne in the pryery of Blake Chanons that nowe is clepyd the churche of Seynt Frydeswyde" (her body lies at Oxford in a very holy shrine in the priory of Black Canons, which is now called the church of St. Frideswide) (155). This difference in the specificity of geographical references is especially vivid in the case of the non-English saints that are part of the cluster of Lives translated into prose from the *SEL*: St. Leger, St. Faith, St. Michael, St. Brendan, St. Bride (Brigit), and Theophilus. Those which may, in muted fashion, represent England's historical and strategic claims are sometimes figured in the broad terms of those claims—for example, St. Bride is "bore in Yrelond" (143)—but they lack the more precise locations given in the legends of Anglo-Saxon saints. The enormously popular St. Faith, whose relics—as English pilgrims well knew—were enshrined at a Benedictine monastery at Conques on the route to Compostella, is not even explicitly acknowledged as French.[42] The geographic references in her legend are entirely generic: Diocletian and Maximian, familiar persecutors in vernacular legends, search for Christians in "diuerse londes"; they come to "the towne where this holy virgyn Seint Feith dwellid"; other Christians "fled away oute of the towne and hid hem for fere in dicchis and pittis in the contrey"; the bodies of Faith and those martyred with her are buried by devotees "in the most worshipful place that thei myght" (225–26).

As these generic representations suggest, there is no an explicit rationale or programmatic frame for the inclusion of non-English (that is, non-Anglo-Saxon) saints in the *Prose SEL*. They may implicitly figure English polity in its expansive, imperial mode: St. Faith has a French compatriot in St. Leger, and the archangel Michael is closely associated with Mont St. Michel, which the English had attempted, in vain, to capture by siege in 1423 and again a decade later.[43] The Irish saints, Brendan and Bride, may represent another domain in which the English king, as Lord of Ireland, claimed—but had in fact progressively lost—authority.[44] The multipart narrative form of the legendary, which puts discrete legends in paratactic relation to one another, allows multiple definitions of English community to coexist, in unresolved but unavoidable relation to one another.

Indeed, if the *Gilte Legende* was supplemented by the *Prose SEL* Lives of French saints such as Faith reflexively, in what is essentially a mini-legendary of English saints embedded within it, it is significant that they do not explicitly represent an English claim to France. As we have seen, the Faith legend does not in fact represent France at all, but an unlocalized Christendom. Thus while these legends have a weak association with "England" by virtue of their textual proximity to the Anglo-Saxon saints' Lives and their shared reliance on the *SEL* as a source, they are just as readily recognized as part of the pan-European communion of saints attested in the *Gilte Legende* as a whole. Like the legends that derive from *Legenda Aurea* that populate most of the legendary, the *Prose SEL* Lives of non-English saints figure a geographically unspecified Christian community, which is then oriented by the English saints' Lives, which offer specific locations as spatial coordinates. In contrast to the *Mappula Angliae*, in which national community, imagined as a body that devours itself from within, has an inward orientation, the *Gilte Legende* projects English community outward from the cities and shrines named in the *Prose SEL* Lives of native saints. Whatever notional boundaries are limned in this way open readily to the forms of religious community represented in the collection as a whole.

*   *   *

Like the Abbotsford legendary, then, the *Gilte Legende* puts English community into relation to both local and supranational Christian communities through a spatial framework. In both collections, the nation is the middle term, and more specifically the medial position on a graduated scale in which the local (city, shrine, region) stands as the hyponym to England, which in turn serves as an instantiation of a more general hypernym, Christendom at large. This mediating function may be understood as a correlative of—or as a capability derived from—the contemporary elasticity of England's spatial definition, from its shrinking territorial boundaries to its expansive definition as a "nation" in the context of ecclesiastical politics. In the legendaries, England's relation to other forms of community is defined not through fixed and measurable categories of extension or proximity, but the relative and thus variable category of scale: it lies somewhere between the geographical specificity associated with the bodies of native saints and the generic landscape of the other forms of Christian community. This may be usefully compared to the representation of England as a walled city in the *Libelle of Englysche Polycye*: as we have seen, in that text England's island isolation makes its scale, as a relative category, especially labile; in the Middle English legendaries, on the other hand, its scale is labile because England, whose boundaries are historically and continually subject to change, exists in relation to many other forms of community at various scales.

This flexibility of scale and affiliation is produced, above all, by the assemblage of legends: it is a product, that is, of multipart narrative form. But it is also worth noting that the flexible geographical and conceptual scale through which the two midcentury legendaries think across different forms of community finds a striking analogue in the native saints themselves, whose mobility—often a sign of sanctity—often effects movement between scales. Take again the example of Bokenham's *Life of St. Botolph*. In it, Botolph's relics are gathered up after the Danish invasions and dispersed to several places: his heart is sent to Ely, other relics are sent to Thornsby, and some are kept with other "regal reliques" and later given by Edward the Confessor to Westminster Abbey (115r). Vulnerable to national history, the relics move to multiple local sites, ultimately including one that signals the saint's claim to be an "English" saint as well as a regional one.

Or take the *Prose SEL Life of St. Edward Martyr*, a narrative rife with images of the local represented by particularizing details (e.g., "thaye buryed this holy body in a churcheyerth of oure ladye at the este ende of the sayde churche, where nowe is a fayre chapelle of oure ladye" [they buried this holy body in a churchyard of Our Lady at the east end of the said church, which is now a fair chapel of Our Lady], 160). In this legend, such specificity correlates closely with movement between localities. Edward, murdered at the command of his wicked stepmother, is first buried in "a desolate place of the wode, that no man shulde knowe where he were become" (159). But when his followers seek the body, in order to bury it in a more sacred place, "a grete lyght in the wode lyke a pyller of fyre strecchyng up fro that place to hevyn" (a great light in the woods, like a pillar of fire stretching up from that place to heaven) (160) reveals its location. It is interred in the Lady chapel at Warham, in the passage quoted above, while the place in the wood where the body was discovered is marked by a "fayre welle," called St. Edward's well and renowned for the miracles that have taken place there. These miracles in turn, as witness to his sanctity, lead to the translation of Edward's relics to Shaftesbury. Like the pillar of light, which links the earthly finitude of the saint's body to a boundless sacred, the movement of the saint's relics *between different places* is coordinated with movement *between the different scales* through which those places are known: from the abstract "wood" to the altar in Warham, defined by its particular placement within the church and its cardinal orientation, to the comparatively generalized reference to Shaftesbury, which lacks the site-specific details of the Warham shrine.

As it happens, many of Edward's miracles involve curing crippled people: the murdered king—whose body is sacralized by its wonderful movement between places and across scales—restores the mobility of those devoted to him.[45] His stepmother is his antithesis in this regard: when she repents her crime and sets out to ride to his shrine, her horse will not move. The contrast between her immobility and the mobility of the saint's body, which escaped its first burial and manifests its sacred status by restoring the bodily mobility of others, highlights the intrinsic mobility of scale: the special liberty made possible by movement across different spatial paradigms. Like Caradoc in the St. Wenefred legend, the wicked queen represents the local as a bounded and therefore alienated place, cut off from other places, whereas the saint, properly enshrined at last, is associated with a local place that lends definition to, and thus helps to produce, space on a larger scale.

Urban Models of Community and Citizenship

The spatial representation of England developed in the *Prose SEL* legends takes on a more specifically territorial quality in the set of three additional saints' Lives—of Edward the Confessor, Erkenwald, and Wenefred—incorporated into the copy of the *Gilte Legende* in British Library MS Additional 35298.[46] Their emphasis on a territorial definition of community can be linked, broadly, to ideas of urban jurisdiction, and it may thus be recognized as a conceptual affordance derived from the London cults of these three saints. Like the *Libelle of Englysche Polycye*, these legends use the city to imagine England's topographical and jurisdictional borders as isomorphic. But where the *Libelle* represents the city as a self-identical space defined against a bewildering variety of foreign merchandise, they offer it instead as a model for internal diversity within a single geographical space, emphasizing urban experiences of proximity, difference, and mobility. They also invoke citizenship—the distinctively urban framework that identified belonging, identity, and rights in terms of a specific geography—as a model for participation in other kinds of communities.

The *Gilte Legende* tradition as a whole has London affiliations, and the spatial sense of English community that I identified above as characteristic of the *Prose SEL* Lives may be informed in a general way by urban territoriality.[47] The most interesting evidence for this is to be found in the *Life of St. Alban*, part of the *Gilte Legende*'s original sanctorale.[48] The legend's narrative interest in Verolamium as a city, especially during the course of Alban's persecution, helps to establish "citizenship" as a central metaphor of Christian belonging.[49] Drawing on a specifically urban vocabulary of community and privilege, the metaphor is grounded, literally, in Alban's body: on the night of Alban's martyrdom, "ther was sene a clere beme come fro heuene strechinge right downe vpon the sepulcre of Seint Albone, and aungels alle the night descendinge and goinge vp ayein" (there was seen a clear beam come from heaven stretching right down upon the sepulcher of St. Alban, and angels all night long descending and going back up) (707–9). The "spectacle" draws a "concours of peple," as urban spectacles do, drawn by its "nouelte" (712, 715). One member of the crowd, who turns out to speak for them all, announces their general conversion to Christianity, and he specifically contrasts the burgesses' "unprofitable werkes" to the work of praise performed by "the citezenis of heuene," that is, the angels who busily traverse the beam of light (720, 722). Citizenship is not just a privilege of angelic communities, however: once the people of Verolamium, inspired by this sight, seek out Amphibalus in Wales and receive baptism, they too are identified as citizens—"citesenes of that citee" (835).[50] Their citizenship in a secular city, that is, is made the consequence of spiritual citizenship, in a telling inversion of the latter's conceptual dependence on civic rights and privileges.[51] The corporate body of Christian community in the Alban legend is coterminous with the city itself: "And soo fro that day forward," the legend concludes, "*all the pepull of that cyte* knewen welle that they hadde worschypped veyne and false goddys, and nowe with all theyre studyes and wyttes they study to loue and worschyp Crist the sonne of God" (*all the people of that city* knew well that they had worshipped vain and false gods and now with all their attention and wits they study to love and worship Christ the son of God) (1054–58, emphasis added).

The legend's representation of citizenship and urban space reflects the importance of theories and practices of medieval citizenship to an understanding of rights as correlative of territory, a conceptual linkage that has been explored brilliantly by Saskia Sassen.[52] In broad terms, citizenship links the special value of place to abstract ideas of participation and identity. Thus within the Alban legend, the city and the concept of citizenship serve as resources for thinking about community as a function of a specific place, or produced within a geographically delimited space. Just as the medieval city affiliated the categories of territory and rights, the Alban legend links a territorial or spatial idea of England to a spiritualized idea of citizenship. It is through metaphors of citizenship that special privileges and shared identity (which are abstract and metaphorical) are conferred by Christianity and mapped on to the geography of England. By making participation in an urban community a privileged image of participation in a heavenly one, the legend predicates English Christian community on specific spatial coordinates analogous to the way that medieval cities confer citizenship.

This urban paradigm of community is extended in the three legends unique to British Library MS Additional 35298, as we may see most readily in the *Life of St. Erkenwald*. Although the story begins with Erkenwald's monastic foundations—a male community at Chertsey and a female one, headed by his sister Ethelburge, at Barking—the main focus is on his London cult, localized by his shrine at St. Paul's. The tension between these three communities helps to establish territory as an essential aspect of the form of community the saint embodies. Erkenwald dies at Barking Abbey, and the nuns want to keep his body, but the monks of Chertsey also lay claim to it, as do the canons of St. Paul's, who insist that bishops are always entombed in the city of their see. In the meanwhile, the "people of the cyte" themselves seize the body, and the monks and nuns pursue them, making "grete lamentacion that so precyous a body shulde be take awaye fro them" (51). There is a terrific storm, and as Londoners approach the city they are unable to cross the bridge. The nuns read this as confirmation that they have seized the body illegitimately. But the candles held by the Londoners remain miraculously lit despite the rain, and they claim that they have the body by right and will fight to keep it, insisting, "ye shalle rather bete downe the wallys of oure ctye than to haue awey oure patrone fro us" (you shall sooner beat down the walls of our city than take our patron away from us) (51).

In this narrative, Erkenwald seems at first to represent a nonterritorialized sense of community. The Londoners claim not to be bound by the city walls; their devotion to Erkenwald exceeds this space, just as his cult—of devotional significance to Barking and Chertsey abbeys—cannot be limited to London. But Erkenwald's body ultimately reterritorializes this urban community by confirming the saint's command over geographical boundaries: the assembled crowd prays for a sign to know where the body should lie—the religious say the litany, while the laity say the *Paternoster* and *Ave*—and the water divides, opening the path to London. On the way to be enshrined in St. Paul's, Erkenwald refigures the city's boundaries, both its walls and the river, as the limits of the community constituted by his sacred body. In this way, the legend conceptualizes jurisdiction, community, and affiliation in terms of urban space.

Urban space and sacrality are also mutually defined in another miracle. A man who refuses to observe the saint's feast happens to set down the load he is carrying against the wall of St. Paul's behind which Erkenwald's relics are enshrined. As he complains that saints' days are merely occasions for idleness, he is suddenly panic-stricken for no evident reason and begins to run; he falls into an open grave and the accident causes him to lose his ability to speak. For this man, the wall of St. Paul's is part of the cityscape, a place to rest his burden; he ignores, to his peril, the shrine housed within the cathedral on its other side. The wall, that is, does not mark off sacred space; it is part of the fabric of an urban space that hosts a religious community to which the man ought to belong. The miracle stages his failure to understand the nature and organization of this space, punished tellingly by his mad run into someone else's grave—a confusion of the basic spatial separation of the living and the dead, and even of the ontological difference between self and other. The man's inability to communicate after the accident in turn indexes the effect his failure has on his participation in any kind of community, urban or religious. Lest the lesson implicit in the narrative be lost on some readers, it is announced by an old man, who states that the man is "not worthye to be nombrid among true cristenne men, nor to be buryed in cristen beryels" (not worthy to be numbered among true Christian men, nor to be buried in Christian burials) (55).

In a miracle with a happier ending, a prisoner hears the bells ringing "thurgh alle the cyte as the custome is" (55) on Erkenwald's feast day. When he learns of the cures attributed to the saint, he breaks out of prison and joins "moche people resortyng to the churche that the relyques of this holy seynt restyn in" (numerous people heading to the church in which rest the relics of this holy saint). At the tomb, the prisoner's conversion is complete; he prays to be free not from the metal chains he still bears, but from the chains of sin, confessing to the saint that he has long sought the "losyng of my body, which shulde haue come to the longe ago for to haue had the losyng of my soule" (the freeing of my body, who should have come to you long ago in order to have the freeing of my soul). His turn from his physical to spiritual state occasions a corresponding turn from earthly to spiritual jurisdictions: he had been "sore turmentid with the fere of temporalle dethe ayenst the kyng, but hiderto I neuer ferid the ieopardy of the spiritualle dethe ayenst my moste souereyne lorde kyng of hevyn" (sorely tormented with the fear of mortal death before the king, but before now I never feared the jeopardy of spiritual death before my most sovereign Lord, king of heaven) (55). Just as his jailers arrive at the tomb, his chains fall away "with a grete sowne" (a loud sound) (57)—clanging that echoes the bells that had first called him to the shrine.

This miracle, like that of the panicked man, is also about urban space and community, and here too the place of St. Paul's in the city is essential to the event. The prisoner hears the city's bells rung; he participates in a collective pilgrimage to Erkenwald's shrine where he more fully joins, or rejoins, an urban community. This London community is an alternative to one constituted through royal authority: the prisoner has transgressed against the king's law, and royal jurisdiction has put his life in jeopardy, but his participation in this city community effects his release. This story might have been told as a contest between royal and ecclesiastical jurisdiction—that is, as a story about sanctuary, which would also exempt the prisoner from temporal punishment.[53] The prisoner himself compares spiritual and temporal jurisdictions, arriving at the Christian truism that the first is more consequential than the second, a lesson preached by the bishop as well. But instead of ecclesiastical jurisdiction, the miracle highlights the city itself—its soundscape, population density, and, above all, the collective devotional practices it hosts—in representing the religious community also figured by the saint.[54]

In this legend, then, religious community is constituted by urban space and the devotional practices of citizens, who are the necessary complement to the numinous or symbolic function of the saint's sacred body. Thus when clerics decide to translate Erkenwald's body to a more ornate tomb in secret, hoping to avoid the crowd that would surely congregate to witness the event, God himself alerts the people, who "resortid theder wounderly faste" (66) and lift the massive cathedral doors from their hinges, transforming the ritual into a demonstration of their collective identity. This miracle is echoed by another in which a painter, in danger of failing to finish decorating the tomb in advance of the saint's feast, shuts the people out of the chapel so that he can work uninterrupted. This time, the saint himself appears and beats the artisan with his staff: Erkenwald here embodies the peculiar jurisdiction of the citizens themselves, the authority they secure by force of their collective energies and demands.

There is one miracle in which Erkenwald is presented as an English, rather than a London, saint, and it can help us understand how the legend construes the relationship between national and urban community. A woman with a withered hand had prayed to many saints and gone on many pilgrimages to find a cure "but it plesid almyghty God to reserue hir to his holy and devoute confessoure Seinte Erkenwolde" (but it pleased almighty God to reserve her for his holy and devout confessor, St. Erkenwald) (59). The narrator makes explicit the logic that governs this arrangement:

> O thou holy Arkynwolde, that arte blessid among alle seyntis, for Peter and Powle with many other seyntis refusid to yeue helth to this woman because that thu shuldist appiere the more gloryous among Ynglisshmen when thaye sawe the to yeve helthe and comforte to this woman

> [O though holy Erkenwald, who are blessed among all saints, for Peter and Paul, with many other saints, refused to give health to this woman so that you should appear the more glorious among Englishmen when they saw that you gave health and comfort to this woman].

Peter and Paul are also London saints: the association between St. Peter and Westminster is emphasized in the *Life of St. Edward the Confessor* that accompanies this narrative in British Library Additional MS 35298, and St. Paul of course is the patron of the London cathedral where Erkenwald is enshrined. As major universal saints, their authority evidently exceeds Erkenwald's, their provincial colleague to whom they seem faintly condescending (the miracle they reserve for him is a relatively minor one, after all). But they lack the particular affiliation with English people that St. Erkenwald has by virtue of his own Englishness.

Erkenwald's relation to an English religious community, based on a shared category of identity, is fundamentally different from his relation to a London community, based on proximity and practice. The relationship of the miracle of the woman with the withered hand to the miracles associated with Erkenwald's shrine suggests that local, national, and supranational religious communities form something like a Venn diagram, with the saint at the point of intersection: Erkenwald is a London saint, an English saint, and a Christian saint. The relationship between these differently scaled communities is not metonymic, with the city representing the nation, as in the *Libelle*, for example, or the *Life of St. Edward the Confessor*, discussed below. Erkenwald's London affiliations are not contained within the larger context of Englishness, nor can his Englishness be represented by his London cult; much less can the specificity of these two forms of community be generalized in terms of a pan-European communion of saints. The urban and English communities that Erkenwald represents are separate, neither subordinate nor superior to the other. The overlap between them defines Erkenwald's special meaning for readers who identify themselves as citizens of London and as English subjects, without asserting any particular relationship between these categories of identity. It is this idea of community that the legend derives from the experience of city life, where proximity fashions all kinds of intentional and adventitious forms of affiliation, which together militate against any fantasy of a homogeneous community or shared identity.

Being-in-Common in the *Life of St. Edward the Confessor*

Although the *Life of St. Edward the Confessor* posits a different relationship between urban and national community from the *Life of St. Erkenwald*, it similarly resists homeostatic ideas of communion. Indeed, it can be read, I want to propose, as an exploration of community that anticipates in broad terms Jean-Luc Nancy's definition of "being-in-common" or "being singular plural."[55] The legend theorizes an ideal community in which the self is not subsumed into a collective identity; rather, community, theorized in terms of its necessary diversity, depends on the singularity of its members. Indeed, that singularity is a coproduct of community, a phenomenon of "being-in-common," in which difference is produced through, not in spite of, affiliation. While there are other possible sources for these ideas about identity and community, the legend's thematic interest in Edward's London cult suggests that its formulation here, as in the *Life of St. Erkenwald*, owes something to the experiences of proximity and contact that characterize city life. The legend opens by presenting Edward as an exemplary king, but he ultimately comes to define community in terms of the city's capacity to contain a heterogeneous population, while also rescaling this capacity as characteristic of English community more broadly.

The Edward legend initially defines kingship in terms of proper respect for sacred space, the violation of which is a clear sign of political illegitimacy or malfeasance. Thus when the infant Aethelred, who will become Edward's father, defecates in the font when he is baptized, it presages the threats to the church's liberties that will characterize his reign and that of his two older sons, Edmund Ironside and Aelred, who come to the throne in spite of their younger brother's clear mandate. Under their illegitimate rule, England is subject to external violence in the form of Danish attacks, as well as more intimate kinds of vulnerability: "in his dayes no man durste truste other ne opyn his herte to his neighboure" (in his day, no man dared trust another nor open his heart to his neighbor) (4).

Edward's kingship is defined, in contrast, by consent and the restoration of communal feeling: when Aethelred consults his people about which son they would like to rule after his death, they enthusiastically choose Edward, though he is as yet unborn. Their choice, confirmed by royal assent and formal oath, is followed by general joy at Edward's birth:

> when this childe was bore then alle this londe was fulfylled with grete ioye, trustyng to God to haue som grete benefete by hym in tyme comyng that were so mervelously kendelid with love to chese hym kyng in his moders wombe (3–4)

> [when this child was born, then all this land was filled with great joy, trusting to God to have some great benefit in the future from him by whom they were so marvelously kindled with love as to choose him as king while in his mother's womb].

Taking advantage of an established pun linking *kindelen* (from Old Icelandic *kynda*), "to light or tend a fire," and *kindelen* (from Old English *kindel*), "to give birth to," the passage suggests a reciprocal birthing of the king and the joyful national community his advent produces, which is "kindled" with love when Edward is still in the womb.[56] When Edward at last accedes to the throne, after the long disastrous rule of his brothers, national community is restored to an organic whole as if by miracle:

> O gode Lorde, whate ioy and gladnes was than in Yngelonde, for when the olde felicite of this londe was allemoost dispeyrid, than was kyndelid ayen by the comyng of the blessid kyng Seinte Edward. Then receyvid the comyn people rest and pees, and the lordis and the gentilment reste and wurship, and holy Churche receyuid then alle his hole lybertees ayen (7)

> [O good Lord, what joy and gladness was then in England, for when the old happiness of this land was almost forsaken, it was then kindled again by the coming of the blessed king St. Edward. Then the common people received rest and peace, and the lords and the gentlemen rest and reverence, and holy Church received then all its full liberties again].

Here the dual etymology of "kindle" defines this miraculous restoration as the product of both human *techne* and natural generation. The restoration of the church's liberties, and thus the reconstitution of English religious community "all whole," is at once a correlative and an image of the restored integrity of the realm itself.

But this community is not defined by some kind of hermetic identity or homogeneity, as we might expect from this passage or from the emphasis in Edward's cult on his virginity. Edward takes the Virgin Mary as his model: just as she was virgin and mother, he will be virgin and husband, taking a wife to satisfy the will of his people but remaining chaste in accord with his own piety. This chaste marriage—rather than Edward's virginity—provides the legend with its central paradigm of community, one in which the singular self is preserved in its difference: "He was belovid of hir and not broken, she was belovid of hym and not touchid" (he was loved by her and not broken, she was loved by him and not touched) (10). The self remains singular, uncompromised even in the shared condition of "spoushed," retaining its full integrity even as desiring agent and as object of love.

The conceptualization of community embedded in this image of a marriage in which the self remains "unbroken" recalls Kathleen Davis's analysis of erotic union and political community, discussed in Chapter 1.[57] Davis, as we saw, argues that the "hymeneal," or ritual celebration of virginity on the eve of marriage, figures inviolate selfhood as the paradoxical ground of community, represented by sexual union, its most intimate form; and she observes that this paradox is acknowledged only as a crisis of transition, in the threshold moment of (nuptial) ritual. The representation of chaste marriage in the *Life of St. Edward the Confessor* is, I want to suggest, an exploration of this paradox as an extended, rather than liminal, state: that is, it represents singularity not as that which is lost in the formation of community, but as that which is *preserved* by community in its ideal form. It is worth noting that the legend explicitly rejects an instrumentalized understanding of sex as procreative: the narrator notes a rumor, which the story has already shown to be false, that Edward refused to have sex because he fears fathering more tyrants. Rather than a threat to royal lineage, Edward's encratism is a conceptual model for being-in-common: a model of community in which individual difference is not subordinated to a shared identity, which Nancy calls "being singular plural," and which the legend describes with abstract lyricism as being "beloved and not broken."

As Edward's indifference to producing an heir underscores, this ideal of community is antithetical to kingship. The paradox of "being-in-common" that informs his chaste marriage seems instead to find its genealogy in the urban experience of physical proximity in a space that necessarily hosts difference. This is illustrated especially in the posthumous miracles that occupy much of the legend, which represent on an urban scale the cycle of social division and restored community initially imagined in the legend on a national scale. Many of the miracles are associated with Edward's shrine at Westminster, which is tellingly represented as the center of urban community rather than the cult site of sacralized kingship.[58] Thus in a miracle of "how vengeaunce was shewid to a damselle that blasphemyd Seinte Edwarde" (33), the girl's transgression lies precisely in her rejection of Edward as an urban saint. A London matron, a silk worker engaged to embroider garments for the Countess of Gloucester, was afraid that she might not complete the work in time, and she asks the "yong damyselle that was hir felowe" whether it would be worse to work on St. Edward's feast day or to displease the countess. The girl disdains the Confessor's feast altogether, saying, "'Is not this Edwarde whom the chorles of the cuntre wurshippith as he were a God?' And saide: 'Whate haue I to do with hym? I wolle no more wurship hym than a chorylle if he were'" ("Is not this the Edward whom the peasants in the countryside worship as though he were a God?" and said, "What do I have to do with him? I will no more worship him than if he were a peasant") (33).[59] The matron is appalled by the girl's blasphemy and beats her, then beats her still more when the girl refuses to recant. The violence leaves the girl palsied; her mouth is so distorted that she is unable to speak; she gnashes her teeth and vomits "lyke a boore" (34)—a bore or a boar, either like the churls she has mocked or their animal inferior. Seeing her in this state, the matron weeps, not because of the harm she has done but because she believes the girl's condition is further divine punishment for her lack of respect for the saint. The matron, that is, thinks she has justly punished one whom God rebukes in still more awful form.

The case is soon "knowyn in the cyte," and among those who throng to see the girl is a neighbor who suggests that she be taken to the saint's shrine at Westminster, where she is restored after a great deal of prayer. The miracle is preoccupied with the conditions of urban community, in the form of artisanal association (constituted by the women's shared labor), as well as neighborhood (constituted by proximity and acquaintance), by which the girl's condition is widely known in a short time. The two women figure the categories of identity, shared and differentiated, that undergird these two kinds of community: they inhabit a community defined by their shared sex and one defined by their shared class status, but they come from different generations and function as different narrative types, the wise matron and the heedless maiden. These forms of urban community are set against national communities structured by aristocratic birth and property, which are put into relief by the shadow presence of the Countess of Gloucester.

Importantly, St. Edward figures both a London community and an English one in this narrative. The miracle represents as categorically false the maiden's belief that her urban identity separates her from her rural countrymen. In the context of the saint's feast, she is, or should be, part of a shared national community, defined by a common devotional obligation. The miraculous cure of the girl, which remedies this category error, reframes the intimacy of urban community—measured in temporal terms by the speed with which the girl's fate is known and in spatial ones by ready access to Westminster where she is cured—as a model for participating in a national community. The miracle, that is, has a didactic and a deictic function as a model for a shared national identity, embodied by St. Edward, that the girl had wrongly disavowed. It identifies her transgression as a failure to recognize Edward as a national saint, one who establishes her affiliation even to nameless "churls," against whose rural and class status she otherwise defines herself. Importantly, while her London identity is the basis of her error, it is also the means of her correction and her reintegration into the urban and national communities from which she has been alienated by both neighborly and divine vengeance.

*   *   *

Like the *Libelle of Englysche Polycye*, then, the Lives of the London saints in British Library MS Additional 35298 think about national community through the model offered by the city. As an enclosed or bounded space, the city can figure the more abstract, and elastic, borders of England, as it does in the *Life of St. Edward the Confessor*, or it can serve as an alternative to national community with which it intersects only spatially, as in the *Life of St. Erkenwald*. Both of these conceptual capabilities rely on the special way in which urban community was defined in terms of a specific geography; their importance in these texts points to emerging redefinitions of the nation based on territory, rather than ethnic affiliation or the king's personal rule.[60] As a privileged figure for thinking about England as a coherent geographical space, in which overlapping paradigms of community might be mapped, the city proves especially useful for thinking about the relationship between secular political authority and religious jurisdictions, a concern I take up in the next chapter.

The Place of the Reader and the Poetics of Proximity

Before turning to that topic, however, I would like to take up again the question of how community is conceptualized in this corpus on the level of form. I argued at the beginning of the chapter that the multipart narrative form of the legendary allows various associations to obtain between different narratives and the different kinds of community to which they correspond. I turn now to a different level of form—the basic distinction between verse and prose—to suggest its significance for the idea of community developed on the macro-level of the legendary as a whole. Here too there are interesting resonances between the *Prose SEL* legends and the Abbotsford legendary, as well as important differences. As we will see, the juxtaposition of verse and prose in both collections shapes the experience of reading as another forum for defining identity through the categories of place and space.

Let us first consider the *Prose SEL* legends, which are, as noted earlier, "de-versified" versions of *SEL* Lives. The use of prose for these Lives may seem at first their least remarkable feature. But as Görlach has remarked, prose redaction of a verse text—a movement between formal registers that may be compared to translation between languages—was uncommon in late medieval English literary culture. The production of English prose in the fifteenth century, one of the signature literary developments of the period, was predominantly through translation from French and Latin. Prose writers rarely turned to verse texts in their own vernacular as sources. The main body of the *Gilte Legende* itself witnesses this preference for translating across linguistic, rather than formal, boundaries: the existence of a vernacular legendary in English verse was overlooked or ignored by the translator, who chose the *Légende dorée* rather than the *SEL* as his base text. The choice of the *SEL* as the base text for the legends of English saints—rather than either Latin or Anglo-Norman vitae—is thus significant. So is their "de-versification," which cannot be ascribed simply to the fact that the main corpus of the *Gilte Legende* is in prose.[61] Medieval readers, who were well accustomed to books that mixed prose and verse, had no fixed expectation of formal consistency.[62] Even within a legendary presented as a unified collection, there was no overriding pressure to occupy a single formal register: so, as we will see, Bokenham's roughly contemporary legendary features mixed forms. The *SEL* itself is formally heterogeneous, if in a limited way, interleaving its signature verse form, the septenary couplet, with stanzaic forms.

On the most basic level, the use of prose signals a preference for ordinary, accessible language that is also entailed in the use of English. Its real significance, however, is as a formal marker by which the *Prose SEL* Lives distance themselves from the liturgical calendar. As a departure from both liturgical Latin and the self-consciously literary verse also used in this period for the Lives of some of these saints, the workaday prose of these Lives signals their quotidian instrumental value, identified in the brief prologue as the collection's primary aim:

Here biginnyth the meroure and the liuynge of holie martres and of seintis that suffriden here in her liuis grete peyne and passioune in encresinge her ioie in the blisse of heuen, to excite and sterre symple lettrid men and women to encrese in vertue bi the offten redinge and hiringe of this boke (I.3)

[Here begins the mirror and the living of holy martyrs and of saints who suffered here in their lives great pain and passion to increase their joy in the bliss of heaven, to excite and stir simple literate men and women to increase in virtue through the frequent reading and hearing of this book].

The legends are accounts of the "living" of the saints, exemplars who can "excite and stir" ordinary audiences to virtue in their everyday lives. The slight incoherence with which the audience is defined as "symple lettrid" men and women is a mark of the collection's broad address: all those who might read or have read to them legends ("redinge and hiringe of this boke") in straightforward vernacular prose, an audience both simple and lettered, who represent the broad spectrum between those categories.

The address to this audience's personal and idiosyncratic ethical lives also registers in the identification of individual legends as chapters ordered by cardinal numbers, rather than by the calendar dates of the saints' major feasts. This formal innovation emphasizes the legendary as a multipart form comprising discrete narratives: the numbered chapters produce an orderly sequence that makes it easier to track inclusion, substitution, and omission than do references to saints' days.[63] And they further distance the legends from liturgical practice: the calendar of feast days is no longer offered as the organizing logic of the collection, nor do the legends, presented as chapters, refer to, or represent, liturgical time. There is, to be sure, a vestige of the earlier temporal structure of the legendary: the legends in the main body of the *Gilte Legende* do in fact follow calendar order, and the collection begins, as does *Legenda Aurea*, with St. Andrew, whose November feast stood at the start of the liturgical year. But, absent reference to feast days, this order is detached from the liturgy and the special temporality it creates and represents.

Perhaps tellingly, the best evidence for the merely residual quality of calendar order is the inclusion of the *Prose SEL* legends as a group, even though they were almost certainly adapted from an *SEL* structured by the calendar.[64] In British Library MS Additional 11565, they follow the Becket legend, the most internationally famous English saint, whose Life seems to solicit the Lives of other native saints.[65] In the two other manuscripts, they are inserted roughly halfway through the collection, amid the July feasts, a placement that likely reflects the happenstance exigencies of book production: Görlach suggests that the exemplars on which they were based had appended the *Prose SEL* legends to the end of the first of two volumes, and that this placement, an accident of the process of compilation, was preserved in the extant copies.[66] Because the *Prose SEL* legends fall in slightly different places in these two books, this seems to have happened on two separate occasions. In all three manuscripts, the *Prose SEL* legends, clustered together and inserted in the collection irrespective of feast dates, decisively replace the logic of the calendar with the logic of the chapter.

This shift from calendar to chapter is perhaps the most striking departure from the *SEL*, which—as we saw in Chapter 1—uses the medium of time to put different legends and the different forms of community they represent in relation to one another. In the *SEL*, as in other legendaries that present saints' Lives in calendar order, references to feast days project their audience into the communal time of ritual, a shared or collateral time. The logic of the chapter is more personal, as is suggested by the table of contents, a modern textual technology that anticipates audiences who will read at will in the collection—precisely as the prologue recommends—in an effort to identify with the saints according to their own ethical and devotional lives.[67] In this way, the numbered chapters isolate readers in time and instead mark their spatial location in the material book, defined by how far an individual reader or audience has read, or the chapter they choose to read today. In turning away from liturgical time, the *Gilte Legende* points toward a more individual, idiosyncratic form of time: the time of reading itself.

In a general sense, readerly time and liturgical time may both be considered forms of atemporality—an atemporality made possible by the material text, on the one hand, and an atemporality made possible by Christian theories of sacred time on the other. These two forms of timelessness have very different implications for community formation. Where liturgical atemporality grounds a Christian community at large, the readerly interval of the chapter may be shared at most with an intimate textual community and is unrelated to the temporality of those beyond this finite group. In the context of English saints, the special timelessness of the liturgy is important to national or dynastic cults precisely because it suspends them from history, making them the ground of perpetually performed forms of national community.[68] Hence, as we saw in the Introduction, the early fifteenth-century addition of native saints to the realm's dominant liturgical rite, which lent a sacred timelessness to national history in the wake of dramatic political instability. In substituting the atemporality of the reader's textual experience for the atemporality of the liturgy, the *Gilte Legende* is able to present the English saints of the *Prose SEL* as available, but not necessary or normative, models for its Anglophone audience.

A useful contrast is provided by the fourth textual witness to the *Prose SEL*: the copy appended to Mirk's *Festial* in Southwell Minster MS 7, dated shortly after 1500, which includes the legends of Saints Oswald, Dunstan, Edmund Rich, Edmund king and martyr, Edward king and martyr, and Faith.[69] As a sermon handbook in intention and form, the Southwell *Festial* reclaims these legends for liturgical practice.[70] Indeed, this set of *Prose SEL* legends includes only those saints celebrated in the Sarum rite, while regional saints, such as Frideswide and Kenelm, are omitted. A similar process of selection is evident in the main body of the *Festial*, which excludes the legend of St. Alkmund, patron of the church at Lilleshall where Mirk himself likely preached, but retains the legend of St. Wenefred.[71]

The Southwell Minster *Festial* is in fact even more selective than this: it registers a clear preference for martyred kings and bishops. Thus the martyred kings Edmund and Edward are included, but not Edward the Confessor. This preference endorses the symbolic role of the king as an embodiment of national religious community, which is sanctified by his sacrificial death. The selection of *Prose SEL* legends added to the Southwell *Festial* conceptualizes England as at once a realm and a religious community, figured by martyred kings and bishops, and it affiliates this representation of England with the liturgy and thus with sacred timelessness.[72] Formal affiliation and thematic development here work reciprocally: the liturgical framework provided by the *Festial* solicits the legends of martyred kings and bishops, who together figure the nation as a sacred community, one in which political and religious community are closely identified with one another.

The *Prose SEL* legends as incorporated into the *Gilte Legende*, in contrast, strategically reject a temporal paradigm, preempting the calendar with an arbitrary sequence of chapters whose logic is spatial rather than temporal. The reader of these collections is positioned with reference to the particular textual *location* she inhabits, a location determined by the chapter of the book being read. Rather than a relation to daily, or annual, or historical, or eschatological time, as in the *South English Legendary*, the reader of the *Gilte Legende* has a *place* within a text, in a sequential order that may, but need not, be the order of reading—a place that may or may not correlate to time because it may be reached by linear progression or by random selection. A spatial framework, that is, obtains for the experience of reading the saints' Lives in this collection, just as it structures the relationship between native saints' Lives and the other materials it includes.

While the *Gilte Legende* encourages the reader's idiosyncratic response, the Abbotsford legendary uses a mix of verse and prose to limn the writer's distinctively personal affiliations, which in turn index the heterogeneity of the religious communities represented in the collection. The choice of form in this collection reflects the uneven and contingent composition of individual legends, thus standing as a haphazard expression of different kinds of association. As noted above, some of Bokenham's saints' Lives, originally written for specific lay patrons and later gathered into a collection of female saints' Lives for a house of nuns, are also included in the Abbotsford legendary.[73] The compiler has taken care to alter these legends to fit their new textual location: Horobin notes, for example, that the names of specific patrons have been scrubbed from them, and the legends have each been inserted into the collection according to feast day. But their use of verse—a vestige of the personal affiliations and specific circumstances that informed their composition—is retained. Other legends in the collection similarly signal Bokenham's personal experiences, and notably his physical access to the saint, in their use of verse: for example, the legend of St. Vincent, to whom a chapel at Clare Priory was dedicated (46r–47v); and, as we saw in the last chapter, St. Wenefred, to whose shrine Bokenham had made a pilgrimage.[74] The Etheldreda legend, also in verse, may have been written for a specific patron or circumstance—certainly its ethical address recalls similar passages in the *Legendys of Hooly Wummen*. Or it too may have a connection to Bokenham's own travels: he asks for her intercession "in especial" (120r) as the translator of her legend.

The distinctive formal qualities of these legends are given special visibility through their mise-en-page: their rhyme schemes are traced in red ink and their stanza divisions marked with small initials.[75] The contrast with the prose texts in the collection, with their blocks of text, is conspicuous and significant (as you can see, for example, in Figure 1 in Chapter 3, the page on which the Wenefred legend begins). In Chapter 3 I argued in reference to Bokenham's *Life of St. Wenefred* that such brackets, tracing the affiliation between rhyming words and marking out the intimate space of the stanza, delineate an aesthetics of proximity. From the perspective of the book as a whole, we can now see that this aesthetics, graphed on the manuscript page,

also serves as an index of the personal affiliation or attachment that Bokenham or his patron had to the saint, or an index of their participation in a
community that the saint represents, just as the prosodic form of the *Life of
St. Wenefred* reflects Bokenham's participation in the devotional community
formed by pilgrimage to her Shrewsbury shrine. The special proximity of
rhyme signals and parallels a proximity of interest or identity, as, for example,
a name shared by saint and patron, or familiar access to a chapel or shrine, as
in the Vincent and Wenefred legends.[76] The Abbotsford legendary uses literary form to mark the degree of intimacy or attachment that the poet or his
first audience has to particular saints and to their communities.

   This acknowledgment of personal commitments, encoded in poetic form
and its textual presentation, both complements and challenges the presentation of the legendary as a single integrated work. The specific interests of
Bokenham's own "special friends" that register in these formal qualities mod-
ify the claims, inherent in the macro-form of the legendary, to represent the
"communion" of saints. Where the *SEL* and the *Gilte Legende* use literary
technologies of unity—respectively, a governing prologue and sequential
chapter numbering—as frameworks within which to acknowledge the constitutive heterogeneity of communities, the Abbotsford legendary explores an
analogous heterogeneity through a formal variety that recalls the multiple
and idiosyncratic affiliations of the poet and his audience. Like the legends of
MS Additional 35298, which insist on the diversity of the communities that
one inhabits or encounters in an urban space, the Abbotsford legendary explores the coexistence of multiple communities as a function of the idiosyncratic, singular, and contingent affiliations and identities that the poet is
called upon to voice.

CHAPTER 5

Secular, Religious, and Literary Jurisdictions

As we saw in the last chapter, the geographical conceptualization of English community witnessed by fifteenth-century legendaries is often developed through a collateral interest in overlapping jurisdictions and other spatial paradigms. Particularly striking evidence of this is offered by an addition that the *Prose South English Legendary (SEL) Life of St. Edward the Confessor* makes to the traditional story: it folds into itself the legend of the bishop Wulfstan, which is usually presented as a separate legend altogether. As we saw in Chapter 1, the Wulfstan legend stages the relationship between secular and ecclesiastical jurisdiction: when Wulfstan is ordered to give up his bishopric by the new Norman archbishop Lanfranc, Wulfstan sticks his pastoral staff in the tomb of Edward, the sovereign who had elevated him, and no one is able to remove it until Wulfstan is allowed to reclaim his rightful post. Where in the *SEL* the story demonstrates the church's uninterrupted authority across the political rupture of the Conquest, in the *Prose SEL Life of St. Edward*, it attests to the separate but interlaced jurisdictions of church and crown. This idea is produced, and paralleled, by the legend's hypotactic narrative, the story of a king that envelops the story of a bishop whose authority persists, regardless of political regime.

The complex relationship between religious and secular jurisdiction explored in the *Prose SEL Life of St. Edward* structures other English saints' Lives written in the middle decades of the fifteenth century as well. This chapter argues that this relationship is a central problematic in representations of national community in the *Prose SEL* and in John Lydgate's ambitious double Lives contemporary with the *Gilte Legende*: the *Life of Sts. Edmund and Fremund*, written to commemorate Henry VI's Christmas visit to Bury St. Edmunds in 1433, and the *Life of Sts. Alban and Amphibalus*, written at the request of John Whethamstede, abbot of St. Alban's, in 1439. In a period characterized by the de facto coordination of ecclesiastical and royal jurisdictions, Middle English Lives of English saints were an important resource for conceptualizing their difference. These texts explore and develop models for understanding the relationship between political and religious communities, on the scale of the nation, in the context of increasing efforts to confound them.

Of course, there had long been some convergence between political and ecclesiastical authority: Arundel's double role as Archbishop of Canterbury and Lord Chancellor, for example, had ample precedent.[1] But, along with other related phenomena, the special visibility of Arundel in the establishment of the Lancastrian regime, and of Archbishop Chichele in its maintenance, made this coordination yet more fundamental to the conceptualization of English community. Arundel's important role in supporting Bolingbroke is too well known to require extensive rehearsal here, as is the long-standing historiographic assessment of him as "the leading figure of the new reign."[2] He lent crucial authority to Henry's claim to the throne, both in the parliamentary context in which it was formally made and, especially, in the ritual of crowning.[3] R. L. Storey has argued that Arundel's assertion from the pulpit that the usurpation had a divine mandate was instrumental in neutralizing the anxieties of English subjects, schooled in the belief that rebellion was a sin that merited excommunication.[4] As Paul Strohm and others have shown, this merging of the authority of church and crown was significantly advanced by efforts to respond to the threat, real or imagined, of heterodoxy.[5] Indeed, in the wake of recent scholarship that questions the efficacy of the Lambeth Constitutions in censoring vernacular religious writing, we may recognize as more consequential their role in developing a practical and symbolic arena where ecclesiastical and royal jurisdiction converged.[6]

Such efforts to coordinate ecclesiastical and royal interests had both practical political consequences and a broader conceptual one: a newly emphatic understanding of English polity as coterminous with English religious community.[7] We can take as a symbol of their coincidence the holy oil of Thomas Becket "discovered" by Richard II and used by Arundel to anoint Henry IV.[8] Becket's martyrdom famously registered the *impossibility* of reconciling the claims of ecclesiastical and royal jurisdiction: it marked two fundamentally different forms of community that coexisted but whose separate claims could not be fully resolved into a neat hierarchy or rationalized order of some other kind. Arundel's use of the oil of St. Thomas of Canterbury—which Richard II had touted as a sign of his own regality—to anoint Henry IV was not only a means by which he transferred sacral authority from one king to another, nor only a confirmation of the political authority of his own ecclesiastical position; it also re-signified England as a national community in which fundamental differences between religious and political jurisdiction had been suspended.

However significant the figure of Thomas Arundel in this development, Henry Chichele, who enjoyed a thirty-year career as archbishop, did still more to consolidate the relationship between crown and ecclesiastical authority. He was, Jeremy Catto writes, "the most experienced embodiment of the fusion of the two authorities," one whose "first principle was close co-ordination with royal policy."[9] It was Chichele who mandated liturgical celebration of Sts. Chad, Wenefred, David, John of Beverley, and George in the Sarum rite, which Chichele promoted as "a national liturgical standard."[10] Like Arundel, Chichele also advanced the coordination of church and crown through official responses to religious nonconformity: in 1428, his forceful suppression of an apparent Lollard rising included a procession through London headed by Henry VI: "The visible unity of church and state," Catto notes, "both at prayer and in defense of the faith, encapsulated Chichele's notion of a vigorous public religion."

Incorporated into the *Gilte Legende* sometime in the last decade of Henry Chichele's long tenure as Archbishop of Canterbury, the *Prose SEL*, with its faceted representation of political and ecclesiastical authority as fundamentally different, can easily be read as a rejoinder to contemporary efforts to merge them. Indeed, the centrality of this theme offers another broad framework for understanding why the *Gilte Legende* was supplemented with legends from the *SEL*, which serves as a resource for a complex representation of overlapping forms of community, as we saw in Chapter 1, as well as a source of native saints' Lives. It is also telling in this regard that two manuscripts of the *Gilte Legende* substitute a long version of the Becket legend translated from the *SEL* for the shorter version of the legend translated from *Légende dorée*.[11]

It may seem surprising to suggest that Lydgate's Lives of native saints do similar work. Given its presentation as a memorial to Henry VI's devotion, the *Life of Sts. Edmund and Fremund*, especially, appears to promote the king's special affiliation with a royal saint in a way that may at first seem fully consonant with Chichele's vision of a national community in which church and crown are seamlessly conjoined. As many scholars have noted, however, a monitory tone threads through the poem, a caution, I argue, concerned less with kingship per se than with the coordination of church and crown through which Lancastrian kings and their "king-maker" bishops advanced their authority and political legitimacy.[12]

Concern about this coordination structures the form, as well as the theme, of Lydgate's Lives. These works, in stately rhyme-royal stanzas with a self-consciously literary vocabulary, are monuments of Lydgate's aureate style. Their aesthetic seriousness registers in their length as well, which allows for formal division into books. They thus make a claim, as Robert Meyer-Lee has argued of Lydgate's Life of Our Lady, for the cultural value of Benedictine aesthetics.[13] Here they do so in the context of narrative poetry that explicitly seeks to define English national community, the stories of St. Alban, England's "protomartyr," and of St. Edmund, the Anglo-Saxon king martyred on the altar of secular history. The national community figured by these saints, each the patron of an important Benedictine house, is modeled on the monastery: the Lives imagine England as a transhistorical community, exempt from the secular order, just as the privilege of "exemption" insulated powerful monasteries from ecclesiastical and royal authority. Where the Prose SEL, like the Abbotsford legendary, seeks to preserve a distinction between ecclesiastical and secular jurisdictions that was in fact being steadily eroded during the fifteenth century, Lydgate's native saints' Lives represent the nation—like his verse itself—at a remove from them both, as the monastery had been and still claimed to be.

Many forms of religious jurisdiction, including monastic exemption, had specific geographical boundaries, and in this way concern about the relationship between political and religious authority also helped advance the shift from temporal to geographical definitions of national community that we traced in the last chapter in the context of medieval citizenship and the phenomena of urban experience. Unlike the realm, which was usually theorized in terms of fealty owed the king rather than in terms of territory per se, monastic and ecclesiastical jurisdictions were mapped onto the landscape. Like the city, these forms of jurisdiction, which are often anchored by the shrines of English saints, supply a conceptual framework for definitions of national community in terms of a fixed geography. At the same time, an idea of national space as such came into view as differences between multiple jurisdictions—secular, ecclesiastic, monastic—were eroded. In particular, contemporary efforts to represent the crown and the church in terms of a single unified national community posit coextensive boundaries for secular and religious jurisdiction and thus also contribute to the conceptualization of

England in spatial or territorial terms. Even the texts considered here—all of which are associated on some level with monastic institutions threatened by this coordination and addressed to lay audiences that might also have found it claustrophobic—insist on the difference between these jurisdictions in a way that nevertheless preserves, even advances, the fantasy of their isometric boundaries suggested by the merging of royal politics and ecclesiastic authority.

The emergence of the nation as a paradigmatic scale of religious community, that is, may be in part a conceptual coproduct of the fifteenth-century coordination of secular and religious jurisdictions and responses to it. In Lydgate's legend, as we will see, St. Alban centers the isomorphic secular and religious communities that constitute "Brutus Albion." The saint functions in this way even on a local scale: the British Roman city of Verolamium is the future site of St. Alban's Abbey, which will house the saint's shrine, an over-lapping geography of secular history and monastic space organized by the saint's body. This two-fold local community, in turn, models a national one, which is similarly structured by a doubled spatial paradigm. This doubleness is encoded in the poem's signature name for the nation, Brutus Albion, which identifies it as both a secular polity, founded by the Trojan Brutus, and a Christian community, Albion, founded in Alban's martyrdom. A primary image of their shared boundaries—a shaft of light that emanates from the saint's body and illuminates all "four parts" of Brutus Albion—is, tellingly, borrowed from the *Prose SEL Life of Edward Martyr*. Lydgate's legend shares with that work a geographical conceptualization of England projected from the body of the saint to abstract boundaries that contain and organize secular and religious forms of national community.[14]

Lydgate's Lives and the *Prose SEL* nevertheless adopt strikingly different formal structures with which to respond to the merging of ecclesiastical and royal jurisdiction. The straightforward prose of the de-versified *SEL* legends is the formal antithesis to Lydgate's poetry, with its self-consciously literary vocabulary, ballad stanzas, and subdivision into books, all hallmarks of their aesthetic ambition. As I argued in the last chapter, the de-versification of the *Prose SEL* legends distinguishes them from a national liturgy, which was an important forum for folding secular history into sacred time. Lydgate's development of the self-consciously literary saints' Life is a diametrically opposed response to the same historical phenomenon: its conspicuously artificial language, as we will see, registers a remove from the secular order altogether. While the form of the *Prose SEL* distances it from the sacred time of the liturgy, Lydgate's aureate Lives aspire to a literary realm removed from secular history.

Indeed, in their hyperliterary quality Lydgate's legends posit a third jurisdiction, a third location, for England: the jurisdiction of literature itself. The end of this chapter explores how the project of thinking about English community through the Lives of England's saints contributed to nascent ideas of the literary. Where traditional cultural histories have argued that the idea of "literature" is a product of the "secularization" of a religious textual culture, Lydgate's native saints' Lives point to the increasing coordination of crown and church as an important impetus to an emerging definition of the literary as a category of writing whose aesthetics signal their independence from topical exigencies or use-oriented "projects."[15] Audelay's embrace of a secular poetics grounded in literature's instrumental value finds its antithesis in Lydgate's fantasy of a rarefied literary realm preserved from the secular order.

As we will see, in both its abstraction and its monastic genealogy, Lydgate's idea of the literary as a separate jurisdiction conduces to a collective identity for "Brutus Albion." In this it may be contrasted to the more heterogeneous community associated with the chaptered prose of the *Prose SEL*, which—as we saw in the last chapter—facilitates and highlights the variable relationships that particular readers may have to the saints' legends and the communities they represent. Where the *Prose SEL* offers a readerly model of being-in-common, Lydgate's aureate legends develop a fantasy of national communion, structured by two complementary jurisdictions that doubly embrace English community.

Contested Jurisdictions in the *Prose SEL* Lives of English Saints

The difference between religious and secular jurisdictions is already a significant concern in the original *Gilte Legende*—so important, in fact, that it persists even in the face of textual loss. The *Life of St. Germanus* is missing a sentence in all exemplars,[16] and it thus jumbles together the story of a pagan British king who rejects Germanus with a reference to the king's cowherd at work:

> He [Germanus] preched in a tyme in Bretayne so that the kinge of
> Bretayne forbade hym his hous and hys felawshippe, and thanne the

kingges cowherde hadde ledde his bestes to pasture. So as the Saxenes faught ayenst the Bretones and they saw that they were fewe, and as they saw the seintes passe by the waye they called hem to hem (II, 521)

[He preached at one time in Britain on account of which the king of Britain forbade him his house and his fellowship, and then the king's cowherd had led his beasts to pasture. So when the Saxons fought against the British and they saw that they were few, and as they saw the saints pass by the way, they called them to them].

The missing passage explains the relationship between Germanus and the cowherd, who later becomes king and, so the legend claims, forefather of all subsequent English kings. Mary Jeremy long ago suggested that the omission was intentional, evidence that the translator was a "staunch Englishman" who "could not tolerate this slur upon the royal lineage," or who perhaps feared that his readers—such as Margaret, Duchess of Clarence, patron of the prose *Life of St. Jerome* included in the Lambeth *Gilte Legende*—would not tolerate it.[17] What is more certain, and more striking, is that the interest of this legend, centrally concerned with a contest between secular rule and religious power, was so strong that it overrode this failure of narrative coherence.

In the legend, the king forbids Germanus food and lodging, in a kind of domestic exile, but the saint nevertheless preserves British sovereignty in the face of Saxon incursions. The British, seeing themselves overwhelmed by the invaders, seek Germanus's counsel; he converts and baptizes them, and on Easter they cast aside their arms and purpose to fight "thorugh right brennynge charite of faithe" (II, 521). When the saint shouts "Alleluia," the troops answer the same "with one voys," and the sound is cataclysmic: it seems to their enemies "not only that the hills had falle upon hem but heuene alle hole" (not only that the hills had fallen upon them, but heaven all whole), and they flee. If a pagan Britain is helpless against the pagan Saxons, a Christianized Britain—a national community defined by religious rather than ethnopolitical identity—is miraculously invulnerable to them.

The anecdote draws an obvious contrast between the authority and jurisdiction of king and saint. The king has real, but limited power: he can deprive Germanus of sustenance, but cannot repel the Saxons. Conversely Germanus is subject to the king's authority with regard to his daily existence, but his power to protect a Christianized Britain from threat by a non-Christian force is awesome, far exceeding the king's insufficient military power. The narrative in this way distinguishes between the secular jurisdiction claimed by the king and the spiritual one claimed by the saint, and it locates national community within the latter—grounded in religious identity and practice, where it is preserved from secular contingency. Indeed, an alternative explanation for the missing passage may be found in the way in which this story of Germanus's Easter victory through prayer rather than military power glosses the significance of Britain's Christianization: the reference to royal lineage that was omitted, inadvertently or intentionally, is rendered inconsequential by the story's investment in a definition of England in terms of religious identity, rather than monarchical succession. Hence its equally incoherent elision of British and English identity through a story in which the English/Saxons *fail* to colonize the island.

*   *   *

The interest in the distinct jurisdictions of the secular polity and religious community witnessed by the Germanus legend may help us account for the expansion of the *Gilte Legende* to include the *Prose SEL* Lives, in which this theme is explored more extensively and more subtly. The legend of Edmund of Abingdon inaugurates the series.[18] As in the *SEL* itself, Edmund is represented as a second Becket, who—like his predecessor—"rewled and maynteyned the right of holy Churche. And therefore the devyll of helle had grete envy unto hym for his holy guydyng and sette debate betwene the kyng and hym, the which kyng was Kyng Harry that was Kyng Ihons sonne" (had authority over and maintained the right of holy Church. And therefore the devil of hell had great envy unto him on account of his holy guidance and fomented debate between him and the king, who was King Harry who was King John's son) (138). The genealogical reference—oddly deferred to this passage late in the narrative—underscores an incidental way in which Edmund's legend is in imitation of St. Thomas's: they are linked by the name of the sovereign who contests the church's jurisdiction during their tenure as archbishop. Nephew to and named after Henry II, Henry III takes up his antagonistic role in the legend, which reiterates the constitutive difference between secular and sacred forms of English community: as the legend has it, "this kyng dyd to Seynt Edmond leke as hys unkylle Herry dyd to Seynt Thomas, for alwey he was sturdy ayenst holy Churche" (this king did to St. Edmund just what his uncle Henry did to St. Thomas, for he was always aggressive toward holy Church) (138). The religious past of England is configured by a typological repetition of Becket's sacrifice, as Archbishop Edmund, like St. Thomas, dies in an effort to preserve the church's "lybertyes and fraunchyes" against the encroachments of a king named Henry.

The trope of *imitatio*, which confirms Edmund's sanctity, then, also affirms a fundamental structural tension between ecclesiastical and royal authority. Martyred to preserve the church's rights against the encroachments of secular power even as he insists on his loyalty to the king, St. Edmund—like St. Thomas—preserves a non-identical relationship between ecclesiastical and royal jurisdiction that is enacted in and sacralized by his death. As a typological iteration of the contest at the center of the Becket legend, this establishes the incommensurate and irreconcilable jurisdictions of church and crown as a constitutive feature of English community.

This may easily be interpreted topically, with reference to contemporary England, ruled by a latter-day (though more conspicuously pious) Henry, in which the jurisdictional differences between church and crown had been challenged in a different way. But it can also be seen as a more conceptual exploration of the relationship between religious and secular community, which the legend differentiates on the basis of temporality. The genealogical gloss explaining that King Harry was King John's son invokes the diachronic temporality of kingship, grounded in royal lineage, that informs—for example—dating by regnal year in some chronicles and legal discourses. This secular chronology is juxtaposed with the synchrony of typological repetition. In one of the most explicit formulations identifying him as a second Becket, Edmund has a vision of the martyred archbishop in which St. Thomas encourages him "to suffre dethe [rather] than lese the fredome of the Churche and to take that ensample of hym" (138). Edmund falls to his knees, eager to kiss Thomas's feet, "but he denyed hytt. And then [Edmund] kyssed the mouth of Seynt Thomas and he vanysshyd awaye." Here, the typological relationship between Edmund and Thomas is expressed in part through the latter's miraculous presence to his successor.

This alternative temporality overtly challenges the hierarchical or vertical forms of community associated with the linearity of regnal succession. Thomas's exemplarity initially implies a relationship of temporal and therefore also moral or spiritual precedence, which Edmund seeks to acknowledge by kissing Thomas's feet. Thomas's rejection of this obeisance is a denial of (temporal) priority, and it creates a nonhierarchical relationship between them, expressed when Edmund kisses Thomas instead on the mouth. The two men's shared willingness to die for the church's freedom constitutes a radical similarity: hence Edmund's identity as a "second Thomas." Linking such horizontal affiliation with sacred synchrony, in contrast to diachronic history and vertical hierarchy, the legend constructs a template for the conceptual differences between a religious community and a secular polity: they are distinguished by their different temporal structures, even as they occupy and so constitute a shared national space.

Like the *Life of St. Germanus*, the *Prose SEL* sometimes represents secular and religious jurisdiction as coextensive, especially in the legends of saints who supplement the king's military role as defender of the polity. In the *Life of St. Oswald*, the saintly bishop rebukes King Athelstan when he is about to flee from the Danes, saying, "Sir kyng, where is thye noble herte become? Drawe owte thye swerde"—words that in the early 1440s may have carried a topical political sting. Even as such narratives imply the shared boundaries of the secular polity and religious community, they distinguish between them: here through the irony of the fainthearted king schooled in warfare by the pious bishop. In contrast, narratives that might suggest the full identity of the realm and religious community are muted in the *Prose SEL*: the *Life of St. Edmund, King and Martyr*, for example, is conspicuously short and undistinguished. It is a mere fifty lines in Hamer's edition, less than a sixth of the length of the *Life of Edmund of Abingdon*.

The *Life of St. Edward, King and Martyr* is also notably abbreviated. It is concerned primarily with Edward's wicked stepmother, who has him killed in order that her son Aethelred may accede to the throne (in saints' Lives, as in fairy tales, stepmothers are "selde gode," as the legend knowingly observes). The remainder of the traditional legend—which recounts the sorrows that come to the land when Dunstan is forced to crown Aethelred—has been transferred to the *Life of St. Alphege*, Archbishop of Canterbury: the political consequences of Edward's martyrdom, usually central to his legend, are placed within the narrative jurisdiction of an ecclesiastical saint.[19] Indeed, the story of Alphege's election as Archbishop of Canterbury—the narrative occasion for a digression explaining royal genealogy—is thereby presented as an event that organizes secular history and pins it to the landscape of English sanctity:

That tyme was Ethelrede kyng of Ynglonde and Seynt Edward the Martyr was hys brother. And Seynt Edwarde the Confessoure was the sonne of Athelrede, that lyeth nowe at Westmynster in a fulle worshipfulle shryne, where oure lorde shewith daylye for hym many a grete myracle (165)

[In that time [of Alphege's election] was Aethelred king of England and St. Edward the Martyr was his brother. And St. Edward the Confessor, who lies now at Westminster in a very holy shrine, where our Lord daily shows a great miracle on his behalf, was the son of Aethelred].

At the same time, Alphege's unanimous endorsement "bye alle the clergye of Ynglonde" (165) figures a unified national religious community that is coextensive with the realm. The legend thus coordinates religious community and secular polity, but does not present them as one. The *Prose SEL Life of St. Alphege* in fact revises the *SEL* legend so that Alphege does not die for England's sake when the Danes attack, as he does in that text, but "for oure lordis sake" (166).[20] In the *Prose SEL* version, religious community subtends or secures the fragile polity, but it is not identical to it.

Religious jurisdiction grounds England as a secular polity in a more literal way as well. It supplies, as I suggested earlier, a territorial definition of community, in contrast to the interpersonal and corporate models (practices of fealty and the idea of the body politic) through which kingship was usually theorized. As we saw in Chapter 4, the short *Life of Edward Martyr* focuses on the martyred king's body and its capacity to signal its own geographical location: the king's murder and the whereabouts of his body are unknown until the corpse emits a pillar of light. Found by this means, the body is translated, and a well, called St. Edward's well, springs up where it had first rested. The episode plays with scale to root national community in a specific geography: when at first hidden, the king's body figures a place so local, so finite, it cannot be discovered. It is finally revealed by the beam of light that stretches beyond earthly territoriality, to represent English community as, quite literally, transcendent, even as the body itself remains located in a particular place.

This episode, as I noted above, is the source for the shaft of light that illuminates the boundaries of the nation in Lydgate's *Life of Sts. Alban and Amphibalus*. In both legends, the miracle marshals religious jurisdiction, localized by the relics of a native saint, as a resource for a territorial representation of English community.

Secular and Sacred Jurisdictions in Lydgate's *Life of Sts. Edmund and Fremund*

The contest between secular and religious jurisdiction has a different institutional cast in Lydgate's Lives of English saints: where the *Prose SEL* follows its source's interest in ecclesiastical history, Lydgate's *Life of Sts. Alban and Amphibalus* and *Life of Sts. Edmund and Fremund* represent religious community instead in terms of the monastery—a reflection of Lydgate's own vocation and the role of the abbots of St. Alban's and Bury St. Edmunds in commissioning these legends. Lydgate's focus on monastic jurisdiction has a bifurcate significance: it constitutes the legends' most urgent topical concern—the exemption of Benedictine monasteries from ecclesiastical and secular jurisdictions—and it is the vehicle of a paradoxical metaphor for English community. On one hand, Lydgate's Lives locate England, like an exempt monastery, at a remove from the secular world. On the other, they also use monastic exemption, a form of jurisdiction defined by discrete places with fixed boundaries, to represent English community in geographical terms.

In producing spaces independent of secular and ecclesiastical authority, monastic exemption serves as a vivid example of the complex system of medieval jurisdictions. In the *Prose SEL Life of St. Aldhelm*, the pope honors the saint's virtue by granting the privilege of exemption to Malmesbury—"that no bishop of Englond shulde haue ado there nor the kyng neyther to lette them of ther fre eleccion, but for to chese ther abbot amongis themself" (187)—but even the pope's authority is challenged by the fact that it is Aldhelm himself who enforces these privileges: before his death, he curses those who wrong the abbey or encroach on its rights. The legend thus reiterates the separate jurisdictions of *ecclesia* and crown—neither bishop nor king can impede the monks' election of their abbot—while complicating this binary model by recalling a more variegated landscape of authority and community.

It is important to remember that ecclesiastical and monastic institutions represent different, and sometimes antagonistic, forms of religious community. While Benedictine abbeys and their abbots had—and retained—considerable economic and political stature in the fifteenth century, their privileges were challenged in practical ways by increasingly powerful archbishops, and in potential ones by a debate about monastic reform that gained traction in this period both in England and at international church councils.[21] Richard Davies suggests that Archbishop Arundel took special interest in his visitations of religious houses, which he performed himself;[22] and abbots were at pains to ensure that these visits did not encroach on their traditional privileges. When Arundel came to Bury St. Edmunds in 1400, as John Ganim recounts, the monks carefully staged his entrance into their precincts in order to neutralize any suggestion that he came in an official supervisory capacity.[23] More threatening still was the reform agenda advanced by Arundel at the Council of Pisa and pursued by a generation of reformist ecclesiasts at Constance and Basel. The articles of reform presented at Pisa asserted that "many abuses and excesses" were to be found in the order and called for a return to piety and simplicity.[24] This reformist protocol dovetailed with Henry V's own criticism of the order's wealth and display, which prompted an official inquiry of English houses in 1421.

Concerns included the privilege of wearing episcopal regalia and a corresponding independence from episcopal jurisdiction, rights enjoyed by the abbots of Bury St. Edmunds and St. Alban's since the twelfth century.[25] The reform measures formulated at Oxford for the Council of Pisa recommended revoking the privilege of the mitre, and the English delegation, which included this recommendation in its Concordat, put their proposal on the agenda at Constance as early as September 1414.[26] Also considered were proposals to revoke all exemptions dating from the Schism and to require mandatory consent of all affected parties for future ones.[27] These reforms, which found a strong advocate in Chichele, were intended in the first place to curtail papal power, but they also threatened to limit monastic privilege.[28]

Nigel Mortimer has recently shown the effects of such efforts on Bury St. Edmunds, Lydgate's house.[29] Contests over the authority of the abbey were especially charged during the tenure of Abbot William Curteys. In the early 1430s, William Alnwick, Bishop of Norwich, assigned an archdeacon, Clement Denston, to review clerical tax status within the abbey precincts, to which Curteys responded by prosecuting Denston on false grounds. On the larger stage of church councils, both Abbot Curteys and Abbot Whethamstede—Lydgate's patron for the *Life of Sts. Alban and Amphibalus*—worked actively against efforts to reform the order. Mortimer cites a 1435 letter from Whethamstede to Curteys about the threatened abridgment of monastic privilege; Curteys himself planned to travel to the Council of Basel to make the case for exemption.[30]

As his patrons worked to protect the order's historic privileges, Lydgate took up the concern with monastic exemption in his self-consciously literary Lives of English saints, developing in the *Life of Sts. Edmund and Fremund* what Ganim calls a "poetics of exemption."[31] As the *Life of Sts. Alban and*

Amphibalus suggests, monastic exemption allows Lydgate to theorize national community as invulnerable to historical contingency, persisting in
some constant or static form because it is independent from the secular
order. This national community, "Brutus Albion," in turn restores the difference between political and religious community effaced by Lancastrian kings
and their archbishops. As this doubled name and their separate (literary) genealogies suggest, the vision of English community that Lydgate develops is
not a homogeneous community in which the jurisdictions of crown and
church have been integrated, but a duplex one, in which an idealized political
structure makes possible a new form of religious community that reveals, but
also remedies, its shortcomings.

The *Life of Sts. Edmund and Fremund* likewise differentiates secular and
religious community. It does so especially through its double narrative: the
story of King Edmund, whose Christian devotion prevents him from fighting
against the invading Danes, which is followed by the story of Fremund's conversion from a religious recluse to a military leader who repels the Vikings.
This narrative diptych, that is, defines England by pairing the martyred king
Edmund, who embodies a sacralized religious community, and Fremund,
who restores the secular polity. I argue that the addition of the Fremund legend to the story of Edmund's willing martyrdom is best read neither as a rebuke to nor naive praise of Edmund's Christian pacificism, but rather as a
doubled image of England that asserts fundamental differences between secular and religious forms of community. By doubling its saintly protagonist,
the legend establishes the separate necessity and authority of these two forms
of community and makes them irreducible to one another.

If St. Alban and St. Edmund both represent a historical English Christian
community, they also represent a categorically extrahistorical one.[32] The
monasteries named for, and devoted to, these saints provide a conceptual resource for imagining a community that is at once rooted in a specific place,
defined by a fixed geography that is anchored by their shrines, and theorized
as removed from the secular order. In Lydgate's ambitiously literary version
of their Lives, St. Alban and St. Edmund host England as this third form of
jurisdiction, modeled on the exempt monastery.

*   *   *

As in earlier versions of the legend stretching back to Aelfric, Lydgate's *Life of
Sts. Edmund and Fremund* initially emphasizes the king's symbolic capacity

to embody national community. King Edmund is martyred when he refuses to fight against the pagan Danes who invade his kingdom. He is first shot through with arrows; his head is then cut off and tossed into brambles, where it is guarded by a wolf. When the missing head is sought by Edmund's people, it calls out "here, here, here," and is restored to his body, which becomes miraculously whole once again. This miracle serves in Lydgate's poem—as it had long served—as a figure for the miraculous integrity of the body politic.[33] Lydgate elaborates the correlative political theory in an idealizing passage on the king as head of this body:

> Thus first of prynces the notable excellence,
> And of the cherch the preued perfeccion,
> And of the iuges thauyse prouydence,
> And of knyhthod the marcial hih renon,
> And of marchantis the hih discrecion,
> With al the residue in oon ymage knet,
> Wer by kyng Edmund in ther dew ordre set.
>
> Of this ymage prynces stood as hed,
> With ther two eyen of prudence and reson,
> To ther sogetis for to takyn heed,
> That thei nat erre by no deuysion (855–65)
>
> [Thus first of princes the notable excellence
> And of the church the proved perfection,
> And of the judges the well-advised providence,
> And of knighthood the martial high renown,
> And of merchants the high discretion,
> With all the remainder knit in one image,
> Were set in their due order by King Edmund.
>
> In this image princes represent the head,
> With their two eyes of prudence and reason,
> To attend to their subjects,
> So that they do not err through any division].

The head that Edmund loses in martyrdom and regains as a sign of his sanctity is explicitly coded as a figure for the realm. Note that by presenting the pun "hed/heed" (862, 864) as *rime riche*, the essential relationship between the king's person and his role is given formal as well as semantic expression. Edmund's status as the body politic is nevertheless identified as an artifact of "policy" (870)—that is, an institutional construct, rather than a natural fact: the realm takes on the borders of body only when sutured together "in due order" by the king. This transformation of the implicit image of the body politic found in earlier analogues into an explicit theoretical account of the metaphor itself identifies the body politic less as an organic quality of royal personhood than as a political structure given bodily form merely as a rhetorical device.

Edmund's position in this paradigm is therefore not necessary after all. While the hierarchical political structure described here is endorsed throughout the legend,[34] Edmund himself disavows his position as "head" of the political body and the obligation to "take heed" on behalf of his subjects. His embrace of a Christ-like passivity and concomitant failure to rebuff the Danish invaders have been read as a caution to, or even prescient criticism of, Henry VI, who proved to be similarly disinclined to carry a battle standard. But Edmund's monkish piety is not presented as a model for kingship—which is formulated in this passage precisely as a foil to his choice—but as evidence of his sainthood, an identity that grounds England as a religious community *rather than* a realm. Lydgate's poem, that is, uses the contradiction between the obligations of kingship and those of sanctity to create a bilateral representation of England as both a political community located in secular history and a more abstract religious community exempt from it.

Lydgate thus revises a signature capability of the legends of saintly kings, which elsewhere represent the convergence of secular and sacred jurisdiction. Edmund's sacrificial death is a response to Danish invasion on a conceptual, as well as narrative, level. His decision to die as a martyr rather than defend the realm as a sovereign makes him invulnerable to military or political event: thus when a bishop counsels Edmund to fake apostasy in order to save himself, Edmund replies, "there anoieth noon aduersite / Where domynacion hath noon interesse" (no opposing power vexes where its rule has no claim) (1625–26). By sacrificing his own kingship—a categorical denial of the "interesse" of political authority—Edmund transforms the Danish invasion from a threat to England's identity as a secular polity to a confirmation of its identity as a Christian nation. It is in this way that Edmund's death imitates Christ's death as the paradigmatic sovereign act—the performance of a supervening authority indifferent to any earthly power.

In distinguishing between England as a realm and as a religious community in this way, the *Life of Sts. Edmund and Fremund* departs from recent influential theories of sovereignty, as well as from its sources and analogues. As Giorgio Agamben has it, the sovereign exists at the *intersection* of the secular and sacred because he is external to both forms of law.[35] Agamben has Continental models, not English ones, in mind in this definition: like those over whom he ruled, the king in medieval England was, in fact, subject to common law. As the legend of St. Edmund recalls in all versions, the English king can place himself fully outside of secular power—and even then only outside of secular power identified as categorically illegitimate—only through his own sacrificial death. In this act, he achieves a more absolute sovereignty than he enjoys as king: he is subject to no earthly law. But this kind of sovereignty is limited to this negative formulation: it is constituted not by power, but by *freedom from* subjection, by a status in which "domynacion hath noon interesse." In this paradigm, the secular and sacred are not adjacent jurisdictions, with a border inhabited by the sovereign who eludes them both, as Agamben has it. The sacred is rather a negative impression of the secular: borrowing familiar tropes of Christian inversion, powerlessness is coded as victory, the total failure of secular agency as total spiritual freedom. Hence the poem's identification of martyrdom itself as a form of sovereignty: the poem celebrates Edmund, along with St. Sebastian to whom he is compared, for the "tryumphes of ther passiouns," which entitle them to "Cleyme hih in heuene to regne in ther estate" (Claim high in heaven to reign in their estate) (1804, 1806). And, again, his death is represented as "Wynnyng a tryumphe, most souereyn of renon, / As kyng and martir wher he may not mysse / Eternaly for to regne in blysse" (Winning a triumph, of the greatest glory, as a king and martyr where he cannot fail to reign eternally in bliss) (2029–31). Sanctity constitutes a form of sovereignty through the absolute renunciation of secular authority.

This is a notable departure from other versions of the Edmund legend, in which the king's martyrdom sacralizes the political fiction of the body politic. Thus in Aelfric's *Passion of St. Edmund*, the king's martyrdom confirms his role as the embodiment of the realm, and once his head is restored to his body, English community is reconstituted as whole, in spite of the historical and narrative framework of Danish invasion and overlordship. But Lydgate's legend distinguishes between secular jurisdiction, which Edmund has abandoned to become a martyr, and the corporate identity of an English religious community he comes to embody through his sacrificial death. Like the martyred king, this sacralized community too inhabits a zone of freedom "out of subieccion, with al extort seruage" (free from subjection, with all coerced bondage/tribute) (1660). Edmund's martyrdom has not guaranteed England's mystified wholeness, as it does in Aelfric; instead, the saint has secured its "franchise" (1681). The poem attributes to the sacrificial body—but not the sovereign body—the capacity to secure a form of corporate identity that is not subject to secular time, history, or mortality.

This religious community, that is, is exempt, a status—as I have suggested—that Lydgate theorizes through analogy to that of exempt monasteries like Bury St. Edmunds. Lydgate establishes monastic exemption as a resource for imagining England's exemption from the secular order by linking the maintenance of monastic jurisdiction to the status of England. This is the work of book 3, which is largely devoted to miracles that address political and ecclesiastical challenges to the abbey's privileges and transgressions of its boundaries.[36] In the first, the tyrannical Sweyn seeks tribute, not sparing territories "Confermed off seyntes ffredam nor ffranchise" (2954). He demands tribute specifically from East Anglian communities that "Cleymed franchise off Edmund ther patron" (2963). The saint appears to his chaplain Ayllewyn and instructs him to insist that their freedom from such levies were "stablysshed off antiquyte" (3029). In case the lesson is lost on contemporary rulers, secular or ecclesiastical, Lydgate makes it plain: "Neuer tirant durste putten assay / Off seynt Edmund to breke the franchise, / But he were punysshed withoute long delay" (No tyrant ever dared to test St. Edmund by breaking the franchise but he was punished before long) (3159–61). St. Edmund protects legal privileges as well as financial ones: in the next miracle, a sheriff, Leoffstan, tries to seize a woman who has taken sanctuary at Edmund's tomb. She cries out to the saint, "Keep and conserue thy iurediccion / Fro this tirant" (Keep and protect your jurisdiction from this tyrant) (3193–94), and when Leoffstan persists in holding court there, a fiend possesses him and he dies. Even the following miracle, in which a bishop hastily punishes eight thieves who conspire to strip St. Edmund's shrine of its rich decoration, is a lesson against usurping the abbey's own authority in such matters: the bishop repents his merciless judgment for the rest of his life. The punishment of the impious Osgothus in the fourth miracle coincides with Edward the Confessor's visit to the abbey "Tencresse ther franchise and ther liberte" (3329); at the king's request, the abbot prays and Osgothus's wits are restored.[37] The series concludes with the miracle of a bishop who tries fraudulently to seize St. Edmund's relics for St. Paul's but finds that the body cannot be moved. As it is carried back to Bury, all those who are ill are "maad hool" (made whole) (3426), and bridges that have collapsed are miraculously repaired so that the martyr might return to his rightful place, where he himself "lith hool now in his shryne" (lies whole now in his shrine) (3451).

These miracles have a strong topical resonance with Bishop Alnwick's 1430 inquiries into heresy within the abbey's jurisdiction.[38] In defense of his own authority over such matters, Curteys appealed to Whethamstede, the papal deputy, who confirmed the abbey's exemption from episcopal oversight. Alnwick, however, persisted in bringing charges against the chaplain Robert Bert, subverting Curteys's claim to autonomous jurisdiction. The *Life of Sts. Edmund and Fremund* reveals continuing anxiety that the abbey's historical privileges will be undermined by new legal protocols for rooting out heresy: hence Lydgate's insistence that Edmund himself was a scourge of heretics: "Lollardis that tyme fond in him no confort. / To holi chirche he was so strong a wal. / Hated fals doctryn in especial" (heretics in that period found no comfort in him, he was such a strong wall for holy Church and especially hated false doctrine) (934–36).[39] Concern about the abbey's jurisdiction in the face of a national policy against heresy and international calls for reform registers in Lydgate's representation of the saint who secures its privileges through his exemplary behavior and his vigilant enforcement of orthodoxy.[40] There is a topical political lesson here for Henry VI: the poem cautions the king to observe and protect the abbey's privileges. But the more interesting work of book 3 is to use monastic exemption to figure a community entirely beyond the purview of secular authority, one embodied by St. Edmund.

Hence the *Life*'s inclusion of so many miracles in which St. Edmund protects the monastery's franchise, on which this idea of England is predicated. In this capacity, Edmund repeatedly performs a militant role as a saint that he had rejected as king. When he appears to Sweyn, it is as a knight carrying the banner to be borne by Henry VI, as described at the beginning of the poem (3081–85, cf. prol., 49–59). The vision explicitly identifies the monastery as a metonym for England—defended by the saint who has resumed his kingly identity—and St. Edmund, who had refused to fight pagan invaders as king, becomes an oppressor of foreign enemies. Thus, the poem prays to him toward its close:

> Be thow our swerd, al foreyn ffoon toppresse
> Our sheeld, our pauys castel off surete,
> Our portecolys, boolewerk off stabylnesse,

Gate off dyffence, so kepyng the entre
That noon enemy may breke our liberte (3524–28)

[Be thou our sword, all foreign foes to oppress
Our shield, our fortified castle of security,
Our portcullis, bulwark of stability,
Gate of defense, so keeping the entrance
That no enemy may destroy our freedom].

St. Edmund's role in protecting the liberties of the monastery—placing its "franchise" under the "wynges off my proteccion" (3022, 3024)—is here extended to the realm at large, "our liberte."[41] Re-scaled to the nation, the freedom that the monastery enjoys—freedom from "al trybut and al exaccion" (3023)—is manifest as protection from external military threat.

*   *   *

In producing a double identity for England, as both realm and religious community, the *Life of Sts. Edmund and Fremund* (re)establishes the kind of open, complex system of jurisdictions that was being steadily eroded in Lydgate's day through the integration of royal and ecclesiastical authority. The legend's interest in this "jurisdictional heterogeneity" is developed above all in its most striking formal innovation: its double narrative structure, comprising the Lives of two saints. Between the story of Edmund's sacrifice in book 1 and the series of miracles in book 3, the poem tells the story of St. Fremund, a holy hermit who—despite his sacred vows and moral objections—becomes Edmund's reluctant successor as king. Fremund's triumph as militant king is a baffling denouement to Edmund's Christian pacifism and Christ-like passion.[42] The incompatibility of the two legends—the different values and structures of causality that inform them—points to incommensurable forms of community, whose fundamental differences cannot be resolved neatly in a single narrative frame. The legend has two protagonists and tells two stories, that is, because it is about two forms of national community.

These forms of community nevertheless have a reciprocal relationship to one another, figured by their copresence within a single formal structure and by their striking complementarity. Edmund's identification with England as a sacred realm, defined against the secular one he has sacrificed, is mirrored in the poem's careful narrative chiasmus by legend of St. Fremund, whose martial valor, itself a sacrifice of his religious vocation, makes him the saintly embodiment of England as an earthly political community. Rather than contradictory models of kingship, Edmund and Fremund represent complementary models of England, as a religious community and as a secular polity. The contradictions produced by yoking these two saints' Lives together do not signal an ideological impasse, but rather constitute the very project of the legend, which rejects the fantasy of the body politic's organic unity for a doubled image of England.

Lydgate's other double saints' Life, the *Life of Sts. Alban and Amphibalus*, has a similar project, but adopts different narrative and thematic means. The two saintly protagonists are not inverse images of one another, and their stories do not produce the palindrome-like narrative structure that the legends of St. Edmund and Fremund do. Instead, Alban and Amphibalus are first paired through their shared status as young noblemen, and later as catechumen and spiritual teacher. Rather than distinguishing between sacred and secular jurisdiction via its two protagonists, as the *Life of Sts. Edmund and Fremund* does, the *Life of Sts. Alban and Amphibalus* distinguishes them through England's relationship to two different supranational forms of community: the Roman empire, which informs England's identity as a secular polity, and Roman Christianity, to which Amphibalus and then Alban are converted, precipitating the mass conversion and martyrdom that define the nation as Christian. These different forms of community are linked through a typological structure: Britain, founded by Brutus, is refounded as Christian Albion by its "protomartyr" Alban.[43] Indeed, just as Britain's Trojan origin is superseded by a Christian one that it has anticipated, so the Trojan myth of *translatio imperii* has itself been superseded by the story of Christian conversion. The logic of typology, in which (earlier) non-Christian forms are preserved even as they are perfected, produces England's doubled identity, secular and Christian, as "Brutus Albion."

The poem inaugurates this typological relationship by representing Roman imperial chivalry as an anticipation of monastic Christianity. Book 1 defines the Roman empire as an ideal political community, and it explains how Britain, weakened by "fals divisioun" (1.126)—much like that plaguing England during the minority of Henry VI—is easily conquered by Caesar.[44] Rome's success as an empire is an effect of its "prudent pollicie" of centralization (1.181): the empire effectively suppresses local identity and action, most prominently by making chivalry an imperial practice. To become a knight one must go to Rome. Roman chivalry involves quasi-monastic discipline:

the knights are sworn to chastity, religious observance, and obedience. They promise to "Withdrawe ther hond from lucre and couetise, / Speciali t'eschewyn ydilnesse" (withdraw their hand from profit and covetousness and especially to avoid idleness) (1.379–80); to "hold vp trowth, suffre non outrage, / Cherissh poraill, do no violence" (to uphold truth, suffer no outrage, cherish the poor, do no violence) (1.388–89); and to "withdrow ther hond fro guerdoun and fro meede" (withdraw their hand from reward and payment) (1.402). As a token of their "clennesse" (1.448)—that is, the chastity and discipline of their bodies—they undergo a ritual shaving and bath when they are received into the order of knighthood, echoing rites of baptism and monastic tonsure. The parallels between imperial chivalry and monastic practice are made explicit after Amphibalus, and then Alban, convert to Christianity, which is repeatedly identified as the "knyhthood of willful poverte" (knighthood of voluntary poverty) (1.865): imperial chivalry as an idealized discipline at once prepares Alban for Christian conversion and is replaced by it.

In Lydgate's poem, conversion to the new religion paradoxically enables the recovery of an ethnic identity, and ultimately a native community, that had almost been eradicated through the homogenizing protocols of empire. In spite of the ritual shaving, bathing, and tonsuring meant to transform them into imperial knights, the British princes and nobles remain identifiable to Pope Zepherynus. In an anecdote borrowed from Bede's account of Pope Gregory, who marvels that the beauty of English slave boys makes them appear more like "angels" than "Angles" ("non angli sed angeli"), the visible gentility of the young noblemen makes "the blood knowe of Briteyn" (1.301) and inspires the pope to convert them. This invention of British "blood" at once reverses and then exceeds the paradigm of *translatio imperii*. Turning back to their own origins, rather than adopting an originary authority from elsewhere, Britain as the "receiving" community of this process of *translatio* gains its own ethnic identity, even as it claims the cultural and political authority of the classical past.

If Englishness is rooted initially in the blood of ethnic affiliation, it is ultimately rooted in the blood of martyrdom. The Christian Alban—whose Trojan genealogy is invented by Lydgate—figures the superior claims of religious violence and the community it founds. The events of the legend are repeatedly presented in comparison to Trojan history: Alban's death is a "gretter conquest than was the siege of Troie" (2.351), the people of Verolamium grieve more deeply at the martyrdom of their kinsmen than the Trojans lamented their own (3.463–69), and Alban's martyred body is more valuable to Albion than the Palladium was to Troy (3.1374). This hyperbolic comparison to the Troy story seeks to establish the ground of English religious community more categorically than the secular political community grounded in the authority of Trojan origins. The impetus for this fantasy of England as a religious community, with a superior claim to a mythic origin, is not far to seek. Written ten years after Henry VI was crowned at Westminster but before he began visibly to rule in his own name, the poem may be read topically as a response to the political instability of a realm whose king, after a long minority, was still only on the cusp of adulthood.[45] Although closely connected by typology to the secular polity founded by Brutus, "Brutus Albion" is a sacralized community whose identity is ensured by its protomartyr and thus independent of historical contingencies of the kind that troubled mid-fifteenth-century England.

It is important, however, that the poem, with its double invocation of *translatio imperii* and Christian supersession, does not *substitute* religious community for a secular polity but *distinguishes* between them. Like the *Life of Sts. Edmund and Fremund*, the *Life of St. Alban and Amphibalus* defines English community through a double jurisdiction.[46] Here too the monastery provides a key paradigm for its religious form, as the monasticism manqué of Alban's knighthood suggests. Although Lydgate does not narrate the founding of "the heldest abbey in Brutis Albioun" (the oldest abbey in Brutus Albion) (3.1540) until much later in the poem, St. Alban's, named like the nation after the saint, figures implicitly as a metonym for it from the beginning.[47] Alban's monkish discipline, after all, links him most immediately to the monks who reside in the monastery dedicated to him. It is significant in this regard that the native Christianity that Alban embodies is strikingly independent from both ecclesiastical and political authority: even the pope disappears from the legend after he has converted Amphibalus, and he has no direct interaction with Alban himself, who is not converted until he returns to Britain.[48] Albion, like St. Alban's, enjoys an independent jurisdiction.

As the center of both St. Alban's and Albion, Alban's sacred body secures the monastery's role in figuring a national community. The narrative's action takes place in Rome and Verolamium, the imperial and the colonial city, not the nation. Aside from the name "Brutus Albion" the only representation of the nation as such depends on Alban's martyred body, in an image that derives, as I mentioned earlier, from the *Prose SEL Life of Edward Martyr*: on the night Alban dies, a column of light ascends from his body, illuminating "alle four parties" of "Breteyn" (2.2010). In this miracle, Alban's body literally makes the nation visible. It is made still more coherent in Lydgate's vivid image of Brutus Albion embalmed with Alban's blood:

> Be glad and mery, this title is riche and good,
> Lond of Breteyn, callid Brutus Albioun,
> Which art enbawmyd with the purpil blood
> Off blissid Albon, prynce of that regioun (3.1366–69)

> [Be glad and merry, this title is rich and good,
> Land of Britain, called Brutus Albion,
> Which is embalmed with the purple blood
> Of blessed Alban, prince of that region].

The metaphorical body of Brutus Albion, produced through its reciprocal identity with Alban, is illuminated as a coherent space by the shaft of light issuing from his body and preserved indefinitely by his embalming blood. In the paradoxical image of an embalmed yet living nation, the sacrificial blood that guarantees Alban's own extrasecular transcendence also guarantees the continuing vitality of the nation. Alban's blood, we should recall, is specifically "British," identified as the material basis of an ethnic community that persists, regardless of England's political identity, and which also grounds a religious community invulnerable to historical change or circumstance. Both images, we might note, identify the spatial boundaries of English community, secular and religious, as isomorphic. And St. Alban's Abbey—"where thou art shryned" (where you are enshrined) (3.1543), as the poet reminds the saint— serves as the specific geographical point of reference, a kind of medieval LORAN station, for the double jurisdictions that define Brutus Albion.

This geography, predicated on a legendary Britain, turns out to embrace Wales as well: one contribution of the Amphibalus legend is to create a second, intimately related, location of the sacred. His story, following Alban's martyrdom, focuses on his flight to Wales, followed by a thousand Verolamium citizens who convert to Christianity. They are pursued with murderous vengeance by some of their fellow citizens, who slaughter all the converts except one who lags behind due to his frail health. This man is healed by Amphibalus on his return to Verolamium, an event that foreshadows the miraculous restoration of the bodies of the 999 martyrs, who ascend to heaven as a company (3670–3704). The mass slaughter of Amphibalus's followers is repeated at Verolamium: this time, an even thousand are killed. The

miraculous bodily integrity of those martyred in Wales, along with the reiter-
ation of their mass martyrdom at Verolamium, produces Wales as a constituent part of "Brutus Albion." The poem compares the martyrs explicitly to the
Anglo-Saxon St. Edmund: their bodies, like his, are guarded by wild animals—
an eagle as well as a wolf—and then made miraculously whole. Brutus Albion
comprises separate religious and secular forms of community, but these layered jurisdictions are coextensive with one another in a territorially expansive
idea of England that homogenizes important geographical, ethnic, and historical differences between England and Wales.

*   *   *

In both the *Life of Sts. Edmund and Fremund* and the *Life of Sts. Alban and
Amphibalus*, as we have seen, England's disparate jurisdictions are manifest
in the doubling of the narrative, which is to say they are manifest in the scale
of the poem. The concatenated stories that extend the narrative allow Lydgate
to explore the relationship between multiple communities in various relationships to one another. This chapter has focused on the primary division
between religious community and secular polity, but these two basic categories each contain several different communities at different scales. In the *Life
of Sts. Alban and Amphibalus*, these include the urban community of Verolamium; Britain, first a Roman colony and then a nation in the ethnic sense;
and Rome itself, a cosmopolitan secular empire. These are overlaid with "Albion," the Christian community founded in Alban's martyrdom, which comes
to embrace Wales through the martyrdom of Amphibalus's converts, as well
as St. Alban's, the monastic community that tends the saint's shrine and imitates his virtues; and Christian Rome, which supersedes the secular empire
but not a native English community.

Aureation and the Jurisdiction of the Literary

In both of these poems, then, England is defined by the jurisdictional heterogeneity it hosts, which the narrative accommodates through its doubled and
dilated structure. I turn now to another form of jurisdiction that preoccupies
these poems—the jurisdiction of literature itself—and the formal features
through which this is explored.[49] Perhaps the most obvious of these is their
scale, itself a measure of their literary ambition, their claim to aesthetic

seriousness and value. Their length allows them to be divided into books, an internal division that recalls major classical works, as well as venerable English vernacular productions such as Chaucer's *Troilus*, which is an important intertext for both of them. But it is especially on the level of lexis—the use of an "aureate" vocabulary—that Lydgate makes a claim that literature inhabits a jurisdiction of its own. Their Latinate vocabulary marks these poems as monastic productions—that is, again, as products of an institution theorized as exempt from the secular order.[50] The self-consciously literary style of Lydgate's legends, which is also a self-conscious reference to the linguistic remove of monasticism, signals their separation from variable structures of earthly authority and the accidents of history. Aureation identifies literature itself as exempt from the secular order.

In the *Life of Sts. Edmund and Fremund*, this alternative jurisdiction too is modeled on the monastery and thus closely affiliated with England imagined as a religious community. This association informs the legend's opening stanza, in which the poet calls on St. Edmund to fill his pen with "Thyn heuenly dewh of grace" (Thy heavenly dew of grace) (122) and represents the poem, like the monastery, as an arena defined by the saint's authority:

> And blissid martir my stile do so dresse
> Vndir thi wengis of proteccion
> That I nat erre in my translacion (124–26)

> [And blessed martyr, do so place my style
> Under thy wings of protection
> That I not err in my translation].

Just as the miracles recounted in book 3 insist on Edmund's special jurisdiction over the monastery, and thus its freedom from episcopal and political oversight, so the prologue makes Lydgate's aureate language a sign that the poem inhabits a special arena, also secured by the saint's body. Indeed, the saintly "wings of protection" that here ensure freedom from literary error reappear later as a defense against secular encroachments on the abbey's franchise: when Edmund appears to Ayllewyn and instructs him to defend the abbey's right, he proclaims that "Ther ffranchise is to stonde in auantage . . . Vnder the wynges off my proteccion" (Their franchise is to stand in a privileged position . . . under the wings of my protection) (3022, 3024).[51]

The claim for literature's ability to transcend secular jurisdictions and contingencies also inheres in Lydgate's conspicuous Chaucerianism, the elaborate displays of deference to the earlier poet that are also part of aureate poetics. Such gestures are themselves a Chaucerian inheritance, borrowed from the end of the *Troilus*, where Chaucer bids his "litel bok" to "kis the steppes where as thow seest pace / Virgile, Ovide, Omer, Lucan, and Stace." The literary tradition to which Chaucer's poem aspires occupies an eternal present, its kinetic energy not arrested even by a kiss of homage. Lydgate recalls these lines at the end of the *Life of Sts. Edmund and Fremund*: "Go litel book. Be ferfful, quaak for drede" (Go little book. Be fearful, quake for dread), begins the envoy (3572). The poem makes a claim to an extratemporal literary order simply by being presented as a part of this Chaucerian tradition. The aureate vocabulary and Chaucerian genealogy of Lydgate's work—features that may seem as antithetical to a modern critic as the conjoined legends of Edmund and Fremund—make related, notably doubled, claims for poetry's exemption from the saeculum.

The parallels between the poem's thematic concerns and its formal qualities in the *Life of Sts. Edmund and Fremund* are echoed in the *Life of Sts. Alban and Amphibalus*. That poem too identifies the jurisdiction of the literary with the sacrificial body of the saint, which Lydgate represents as the source of aureate poetics. St. Alban's embalming blood is a close analogue to the "aureate licour" that St. Edmund offers Lydgate, just as the poet's prayer to the saint to "cast doun thi liht t'enlumyne my langage" (cast down thy light to illuminate my language) (1.96) anticipates Alban's miraculous illumination of Brutus Albion, a conspicuously literary polity. So too is this poem at once subject to Chaucer and liberated by him from the constraints of its historical moment: the formal qualities of the *Life of Sts. Alban and Amphibalus*—from its invocation of the saint as an alternative to a classical muse (1.1–28) to its division into books—corroborate the poem's dense allusions to Troy to identify *Troilus and Criseyde* as a key source of literary authority.[52] The Chaucerianism of the *Life of Sts. Alban and Amphibalus*, which is more pervasive than the incidental allusions to Chaucer in the *Life of Sts. Edmund and Fremund*, identifies it too as part of an extratemporal literary tradition. Lydgate does not simply restore England's jurisdictional heterogeneity through the figure of Brutus Albion; he offers Brutus Albion as a literary figure that *as such* provides an alternative jurisdiction.

This definition of literature as a separate arena of cultural endeavor and an imaginative space defined by its remove from the social world is not limited to the Lives of English saints: Lydgate explores it across many genres, religious and secular.[53] Saints' Lives may nevertheless have a special role to play in its development because they so often offer a parallel thematic concern: the opposition between the realm inhabited by the saint and the secular world that shadows it. The saint provides access to exalted language that doubles in an aesthetic register the saint's own distance from the jurisdiction of secular authority. Thus in Lydgate's *Life of Sts. Edmund and Fremund*, the poet prays that the saint supply the "colors" necessary to "enlumyne" the legend (line 9).[54] They are not merely the colors of classical rhetoric, however, but the jewel tones of Christian virtue and martyrdom, identifying lexis and style with bodily practice and materiality: Edmund is the "saphir of stabilnesse" (sapphire of stability) (line 121), the "richest rube, rubefied with blood" (richest ruby, reddened with blood) (line 127), an "amatist with peynes purpureate" (amethyst purpled with pains) (line 134), and an "emeraud trewe of chastite most cleene" (true emerald of most pure chastity) (line 135). Above all, the poet prays to the saint to "send doun of grace thi licour aureate" (send down by grace thy golden liquor) (line 141), a "heuenly dewh of grace" (heavenly dew of grace) (line 122) that will fill his pen. Such descriptions of the poem's language draw attention to, and claim value for, its highly wrought surface: the elaborately worked poetic language, distinguished from ordinary speech by rhetorical "color," and the aureate rhetoric that are manifestations of the saint's grace. Such passages identify poetry, like the saint in glory, as a phenomenon of a sacred realm that transcends the secular world.

As a crucial forum for aesthetic display in the fifteenth century, aureate hagiography suggests that one provocation for the emerging conception of the literary as extrahistorical, removed from particular concerns or contingencies, was the increasing coordination of ecclesiastical and royal politics. In this historical context, Lydgate elaborates an idea of the literary that borrows from theories and institutional structures of monasticism, above all the idea that the religious life was separate from the saeculum and the monastery was—or should be—exempt from secular jurisdiction. While it responds to the particular pressures on the monastic houses with which Lydgate was affiliated, however, the development of a "poetics of exemption" in a vernacular poem may also suggest a more general desire for an alternative to a nascent ecclesio-political jurisdiction. It is perhaps no coincidence that the definition of literature as occupying, or constituting, its own jurisdiction takes its most influential form—Sidney's claim that literature makes a "golden world" with no truth claim on our brazen one—in the Elizabethan period, in the wake of a much fuller articulation of the conjoined jurisdiction of church and state. The idea of literature's remove from historical exigencies emerges here not— as in many cultural histories—through the "secularization" of religious litera- ture, but as a way to imagine an alternative to a secular order increasingly characterized by the coordination of secular and ecclesiastical power.

A longer historical view can help us recognize that one of the most inter- esting contributions that the *Life of Sts. Edmund and Fremund* and the *Life of Sts. Alban and Amphibalus* make to this emerging definition of the literary is a capacity to protect, or even create, a distinction between the secular and the sacred. In the *Life of Sts. Edmund and Fremund*, the poet acknowledges his own inability to represent the sacred in order to announce that it falls within the purview of the poem itself:

In this mater toforn as I you tolde,
Because it is unkouth and wonderfull,
My speritis feeble and feynt with yeeris olde,
And my corage appallid and maad dull
Myn eyen derkid and with the mystes full,
This is to seyne, the myst of unkonnyng
Troubleth my wit to wrihte so hih a thynge.
. . . .
Who shal speke or telle the grete myht
Of our lord God or shewe his gret poweer? (2129–35, 2143–44)

[In this matter as I told you before,
Because it is unfamiliar and wonderful,
My spirits, feeble and faint with old age,
And my courage weakened and made dull
My eyes darkened and filled with mists,
This is to say, the mist of unknowing
Troubles my wit to write so high a thing.
. . . .
Who shall speak or tell the great might
Of our lord God or show his great power?]

The poet, limited to the secular order by his mortal body, requires the agency of the saint to produce a poem that exceeds it. The poem, in turn, instantiates the difference between secular and religious realms through its own literary quality. But Lydgate's aureate poems insist nevertheless on their dynamic relation to the secular world, inhabited by both the poet and his audience, including the king addressed in the *Life of Sts. Edmund and Fremund*. Literature is imagined as separate from the secular world precisely in order to model jurisdictional heterogeneity as the ideal form this world might take.

CHAPTER 6

The City and the Inner Precincts of the Sacred

In his carol celebrating Thomas Becket, John Audelay imagines something like the collapse of Christian community were it not for the martyrdom of England's most famous saint:

> Then no child criston schuld be,
> Ne clerke take ordere in no degre,
> Ne mayde mared in no cuntre,
> Without trebeut in the kyng dangere.
>> I pra you, seris, al in fere,
>> Worchip Seynt Thomas, this hole marter (19–24)

> [Then no child should be baptized,
> No cleric take orders at any level,
> No maid married in any region,
> Without exaction under the king's control.
>> I pray you, sirs, all together,
>> Worship St. Thomas, this holy martyr].

Had not St. Thomas died, the king's "dangere"—both his personal will and the authority of royal jurisdiction—would have conditioned the basic pastoral practices necessary to Christian community: the christening of children, the marriage of daughters, and the ordination of priests. In a proleptic vision of the Reformation, the first four lines of the stanza imagine an England in which the church and the religious lives of Christians are subject to the monarch's will and authority. But Thomas did die for "Hole Cherche ryght" (7), and the carol's burden turns the poem and its audience—a local community that acts "in fere"—back to a celebration of the saint for the sacrifice that preserved its separate jurisdiction.

As was discussed in the last chapter, the jurisdictions of church and crown that are violently differentiated in the Becket legend coalesced in the fifteenth century through official responses to the threat of heterodoxy and the active role that powerful ecclesiasts took in secular politics.[1] The Becket legend's awkward fit with contemporary ecclesio-political culture may account for the curious inattention to it in the fifteenth century: no poet took the legend as the subject of a sweeping historical poem like the Wilton *Life of St. Edith* or a self-consciously literary one like Lydgate's aureate legends.[2] The only productive vernacular form for the legend in this period is the carol. Because the feast of St. Thomas falls on December 28, between Christmas and Epiphany, it was sometimes folded into carols celebrating the Christmas season.[3] By accident or design, carol form obscures the degree to which the Becket legend runs athwart the late medieval imbrication of ecclesiastical and royal authority. St. Thomas carols reference the central theme of the Becket legend, but their form obviates a full narrative that might raise difficult questions about its currency.

They also take advantage of their Christmas setting to direct attention away from the end of Thomas's life to its beginning: thus the final line of the last stanza of Audelay's carol identifies the "fader and moder [that] him gete and bere" as saints in heaven.[4] This reference points implicitly to Becket's London cult, a central feature of which was the veneration of his parents, whose tombs in the Pardon Churchyard were objects of pilgrimage in their own right and important locations for London civic ritual.[5] Other cult sites included the church of St. Thomas of Acre, where the saint was believed to have been born, and St. Mary's Colechurch, where he was baptized. Indeed, although St. Thomas is usually remembered as the preeminent *English* saint, he was also a patron saint of London, an affiliation heralded in the seals of the mayor and the city corporation, on which his image appeared with that of St. Paul.[6] The motto inscribed on the city's seal was *Me que te peperi ne cesses Thomas tueri* (Do not cease, Thomas, to protect me who bore you). A fragmentary *Life of St. Thomas* printed by John Rastell in the early sixteenth century makes a similar claim:

Nowe reioyce englond & thou London specyall
of thys holy martyr and patron seynt thomas
whych had in hys begynnyng origynall[7]

[Now rejoice, England, and you, London, especially,
On account of this holy martyr and patron St. Thomas
Whose origin was here at his beginning].

The legend was printed in Cheapside "next to Paulis gate," on London's own intramural pilgrimage route for supplicating or thanking St. Thomas.

The St. Thomas carols, which direct attention to this London cult, substitute urban community for the legend's traditional emphasis on the contested jurisdictions of church and crown. In this, they anticipate an "epic" poem that belatedly provided St. Thomas with a literary Life in the vernacular: a long aureate legend, internally dated to 1497, by Lawrence Wade, a Benedictine monk affiliated with Christ Church Priory.[8] Wade's *Life of St. Thomas* may be read as a re-scaling of the St. Thomas carols: it re-weights the legend to focus on the city, at the expense of the jurisdictional contest between king and archbishop, through narrative dilation rather than lyric elision. London is the initial narrative locus of the legend, and the phenomena of city life set the terms for the poem's representation of the sacred. Although the vita by Thomas's companion, Herbert of Bosham, is Wade's primary source for the Council of Clarendon and subsequent events, the poem opens with the romance narrative taken from John Grandison that recounts the story of Thomas's parents, the London citizen Gilbert Becket and the Saracen princess who falls in love with him when he is imprisoned by her father.[9] Identified by this narrative as the story's key setting, the city comes to model a public distinct from both ecclesiastical and royal jurisdiction.[10]

As it mutes the contest between church and crown through this emphasis on the city, Wade's legend positions the boundary between the secular and the sacred at the borders of the self. This too is an effect of urban community, the poem suggests: the city, where a person's identity is constituted in relation to familiars and strangers alike, produces a special sense of interior identity.[11] The story of Becket's mother, in particular, creates a strong, almost causal, relationship between residence in a metropolitan London and a private self that is defined by erotic and devotional commitments. In doing so, it scales religion to the individual body: that is, not as a practice of community, but as a form of selfhood. The legend identifies this interior location of religious devotion as an epiphenomenon of urban life and a complement to urban citizenship.

This inward orientation of religion, its contraction to the secret places of the heart, may also be seen as correlative of the increasing coordination of secular and religious jurisdictions: the private self is a necessary complement to a public arena in which religious community and secular polity have become indistinguishable. Like Lydgate's Lives, Wade's legend presents the nation as the scale of religious community: England sets the practical boundaries of religious jurisdiction, and their coincidence with political boundaries is a sign of an essential compatibility. But Wade's poem takes a rosier view of this conjoined ecclesio-political jurisdiction than do the midcentury saints' Lives considered in Chapter 5, which may reflect the close affiliation between Christ Church Priory and the politically energetic Archbishop John Morton.

Wade's *Life of St. Thomas*, written on the cusp of the sixteenth century, is thus witness to the emergent shift by which religion came to be identified as a "private" experience, defined in contrast to a "secular" public. The poem and its context suggest that this public culture, at the end of the fifteenth century, is not best understood through the so-called subtraction thesis, in which the secular emerges when religion is somehow diminished or dissolved altogether. Instead, the conjoined jurisdictions of church and crown, the "two swords" whose difference had long been central to the Becket legend, produce a public culture against which religion comes to be defined as private. The single manuscript witness of Wade's legend offers some surprising support for this hypothesis by linking it to Thomas More and thus to *Utopia*, the period's most influential account of a secular public.

*   *   *

We may approach this legend, like the other materials in this study, through the lens of literary form. Wade's aureate poetics both recalls and revises Lydgate's Lives, whose stanza form and lexis he adopts.[12] The poem's first reference to St. Thomas hails him as "the blisside laureatt martir dere" (line 6): "laureate," a key word of aureate poetics that was shortly to become a hallmark of the literary in general, refers in the first place to the laurels of martyrdom.[13] It is then linked explicitly to the poem's aesthetic register in the second stanza: the poet prays to Thomas as "Cristys ffamous clerke" (9)—that is, as an ideal example of Wade's own vocational identity—that he serve as the "swett meane" (sweet mediator) (10) of the poem's production, an echo of the Lydgatean trope of invoking the saint as muse.[14] I argued in the last chapter that Lydgate's aureate style constitutes an argument on the level of form that literature participates in, or parallels, a monastic remove from the secular, and that the Latinity of Lydgate's poetic vocabulary, in particular, recalls the linguistic form that this remove took. Wade uses aureate poetics similarly to signal a remove from a secular world—in this case, however, to the inner precincts of the self. The poem's aureate style in general and ballad stanzas in particular—in both their difference from the stylistic register of public discourses and their affiliation with some genres of prayer—serve as formal indexes of inwardness.[15] By invoking the private uses of aureate poetry, rather than its institutional affiliations, Wade's poetics—a poetics of interiority rather than "exemption"—provides an example of formal features repurposed to a new end through their association with different elements in a complex cultural system.

Coordinating Jurisdictions

From its opening address to "ye virtuous souerayns, spiritualle ande temporalle / And all ye deuoute people, bothe more ande lesse / Thatt thys now shalle here" (1–3), Wade's *Life of St. Thomas* appears to have been composed for a specific occasion, perhaps the completion of the majestic central tower at Canterbury Cathedral, Archbishop Morton's ambitious architectural project, in which the prior of Christ Church was also involved.[16] The single extant copy of the poem, in Cambridge, Corpus Christi College MS 298, may in turn date to a more famous, if ultimately less consequential, event: the visit of Emperor Charles V to London in 1522, which is celebrated in London pageants collated with the legend, amid other materials related to the priory and the archbishopric (123v–128v).[17] Or perhaps the legend was copied on the occasion of the emperor's earlier visit to Canterbury, when he met hastily with Henry VIII and Catherine of Aragon, his aunt, on the eve of the Field of Cloth of Gold, when the legend's opening address to both temporal and spiritual sovereigns would have been especially appropriate.[18]

Whatever the poem's original occasion, its dual address to secular and religious "sovereigns" recalls the legend's traditional emphasis on the relationship between regnal and ecclesiastical jurisdictions. Significantly, it does so not to identify the central narrative crisis, but to name its own broad audience, a community comprising the heads of both arenas that anticipates the poem's efforts to efface the differences between them. The legend itself acknowledges their opposition, as it must: Thomas is here, as in other Becket legends, the "archymartyr off Ynglonde victorious," who dies "ffor the churchys ryghte" in "Cristys were" (7). The metaphor of two armies confronting one another on a battlefield at once sets church and crown in a horizontal spatial relation—that is, in separate places—and in a vertical conceptual hierarchy, with Christ's spiritual army elevated over its literal counterpart, the secular power of the crown.[19] The poem itself is identified as a mechanism for the "encrese" of the saint's fame in upholding the "liberty" of the church: as the medium of Thomas's story, it is itself a jurisdictional instrument that helps to maintain the separate authority of the church.

But the difference between religious and secular jurisdiction is compromised elsewhere by the poem's quiet demonstration of their compatibility. They are, in the first place, isomorphic: in Wade's version of the legend, religious community derives its borders from the secular polity. While sacred authority is sometimes represented in the Life in abstract and universal terms, as in Thomas's youthful vision in which a lady gives him keys to the "celestial paradise," Thomas himself instantiates this sacred realm within the limited jurisdiction of the nation: he is the archmartyr of *England*. The central contest in the story is not between the king and the pope—as the Becket legend was later understood—but between the king, as head of the secular polity, and the archbishop, as head of the English church. The representation of this contest itself posits the coincidence of religious and secular forms of English community, which is confirmed by Becket's death: the spiritual realm in which he serves as "God's knight" maps onto the dimensions of England itself, the place made "victorious" by his death.

The spatial coincidence of English secular and religious communities is developed in the debate at Clarendon, which constructs sovereignty in geographical terms, rather than the interpersonal ones traditional to medieval theories of kingship.[20] The third article of the king's statute, for example, would prevent clerics from leaving the realm without license, making England—Thomas claims—like "a prison" for clerics, with the archbishop in particular "in wors condicione / Thene parsons priuatt" (in worse condition than private persons) (992, 993–94), who have the right to come and go as they like.[21] In both its assertion of the king's right to regulate movement across geographical boundaries and its tacit acknowledgment that subjection to the king may be compromised by physical distance, the statute assumes that secular sovereignty is to some degree territorial. Thomas's response underscores this: he emphasizes "terrestrial" kingship, in opposition to Christ's universal sovereignty, which is not territorial precisely because it is not limited, or proper, to any particular place. A cleric's authority derives from Christ's infinite domains, Thomas argues: he thus "owethe to be obeyed here in especialle / Before eny other kynge or prynce terestrialle" (ought to be obeyed here especially, before any other king or terrestrial prince) (1005–6). This argument is rooted in the priest's sacramental privilege, on the grounds that the priest in the performance of the Eucharist holds in his hand "the lorde off alle socoure" (706). The implicit scalar argument here is telling: royal authority cannot encompass the authority even of an individual priest, given the limitless sacred his hands can contain. Christ's sovereignty over the king is thus manifest spatially: "owr kynge is lorde over yow & *off your londys alle*" (734), Thomas asserts. A priest is only vulnerable to civil law when he is "putt aparte" by the church and abandoned to "seculare Juredictione," which is more limited than Christ's sovereignty, which exceeds but observes the territorial extension of royal authority.[22]

Through this spatial paradigm, the legend identifies the nation as the hyponym to a sacred kingdom, whose abstract or universal forms of community, authority, and sovereignty are instantiated more particularly in a secular realm. Both the definition of the king's sovereignty as territorial and the spatial coincidence of religious and secular community are conceptual coproducts of this graduated scale, in which Christ is universal sovereign, his kingdom larger and therefore higher than the earthly kings over whom he rules. It is helpful to compare Wade's legend in this respect to Lydgate's *Life of Sts. Alban and Amphibalus*, in which secular and religious forms of "Brutus Albion" are coextensive but categorically different. In Wade's *Life of St. Thomas*, in contrast, the necessarily finite realm is incommensurable with the infinite jurisdiction of the sacred, but it is nested within that expanse through a broad similarity between the king's sovereignty and God's. A secular polity is subordinate to the universal jurisdiction of the church because the "hy souerantee" (high sovereignty) of the clergy extends over all "Goddys people" (1031) including kings and princes (1034–35); Thomas rejects the king's claim to have the right to name archbishops as an attempt by an "ilonde smalle" (small island) (1096) to usurp the authority of the "hole churche vnyuersalle" (1094).[23] But the nation nevertheless attains a kind of paradigmatic force by structuring the boundaries that Christ's universal church takes on earth: secular jurisdiction confers on the sacred its territorial presence and its operative scale.

The representation of sacred and secular jurisdiction in spatial terms thus also defines the limits of clerical authority, for while Christ's jurisdiction is universal, that of priests—"dukes off cristene knyghthodde" (dukes of Christian knighthood) (1037)—is not. Clerical authority too operates in a finite space, as the legend's frequent use of a deictic "here" underscores.[24] Put in spatial relation to "terrestrial" kingship, religious jurisdiction maps onto the boundaries of secular sovereignty, assuming the scale and boundaries of the nation.[25] This mapping is also an effect of the representational space of the narrative, which is configured by political boundaries, as in the account of Thomas's movement across national boundaries when he is exiled to France and later returns to England.

While the sacred is placeless, then, religious community and jurisdiction are localized. When Thomas is forced to leave Pontigny so that the abbey will not be punished by Henry II, King Louis despairs that religion itself has lost its earthly footing:

> O relligione, where shalle we the fynde?
> Whiche we belefte dede to the worlde wythowytyne dowte,
> The worlde now ferynge, ffrom the thow haste cast owte,
> Recevyde as ane exile in causis for the churche.
> Alasse, o relligione, why hast thow thus now werche! (1326–30)

> [O religion, where shall we find you?
> Which we left dead to the world, without doubt,
> Now fearing the world, you have cast out of yourself
> One received as an exile in the church's cause.
> Alas, o religion, why have you done thus now!]

Religion in the form of monasticism, ideally defined by its separation from the world—indeed a refuge from it akin to the escape provided by death—has come to fear the world, and, in a line whose syntactic confusion models its sense, has cast out its most worthy refugee, and thus cast away its own status as refuge.[26] Thomas is "ane exile in causis for the churche" in a double sense: he was an exile in the church's cause while resident at Pontigny and he is now exiled from that place of refuge—a quite different idea of how his predicament is "in causis for the churche." Thomas's utter abandonment marks religion as nowhere, somehow no longer separate enough from the "world" to be located within it ("O relligione, where shalle we the fynde?"). This wretched placelessness, produced when religious community is perversely subject to secular power, is given grotesque expression at the moment of Thomas's martyrdom in the impossible image of "children sleynge there father wythyne her spiritualle modire wombe" (children slaying their father with the womb of their spiritual mother) (2022). The church's difference from political jurisdiction should make it, like a womb, inaccessible to military violence, to which it is nevertheless vulnerable as a localizable space.

Thomas's martyrdom realigns sacred and secular community and allows the placelessness of the sacred to revert to its absolute form, the universal sovereignty of Christ. Thus while his death is carefully dated in the secular time of royal and ecclesiastical events (2027–30), news of it travels through a kind of timeless vacuum, reaching Jerusalem with impossible speed through the medium of a monk's posthumous appearance in a vision—an index of the extraterritorial and extratemporal nature of the sacred. The monk, who died on the same day as Thomas, appears to his superior, reporting that as he was borne up to heaven he saw "a grete man," accompanied by angels, patriarchs, prophets, and saints, who stood before the Lord as a "martir laurealle" (laureled martyr) with blood still running from his wounds (2063).[27] The poem contrasts the medium of the vision, by which news of Thomas's death travels with miraculous speed, to the earthly media by which news of the vision itself travels through secular time and space: oral report finally arrives in England, delivered "wyth his owne propyr mowyth" (with his own proper mouth) (2093) by the patriarch of Jerusalem, who has traveled (south, according to the poem) at ordinary speed. Thomas's martyrdom, which manifests the difference between the universal jurisdiction of the sacred and the terrestrial jurisdictions of king and clergy, manifests in turn their different temporalities.

Defined against their ultimate referent, the two forms of earthly authority are more readily recognized as similar to one another, and this similarity is underscored by the graphic metaphor of Becket's murder as patricide, which figures them as human bodies in generational relationship to one another. The church, embodied by its clerical representatives, acts as father to lay sons: this is, of course, a hierarchical relationship, but also one that insists strikingly on a shared identity linking the two forms of community they represent. This is developed in the connection the legend draws between the martyrdom as metaphorical patricide and its disruption of the actual relationship between Henry II and his son, "the olde kynge & the yonge kynge" (2249).[28] Thomas's death is such an egregious violation of the church's liberty that the hierarchical order internal to political community is also disturbed: although the king is genuinely contrite, and although he dutifully and willingly performs all the necessary "exterior" penance, his son embarks on a "sedicious were" (2248) against him. Unable to find comfort anywhere—he "wnethys wyst whethere / To flee for comforte" (hardly knew where to flee for comfort) (2250–51)—Henry makes a pilgrimage to Thomas's tomb, where he subjects himself "lowly" to corporal punishment, "roddys disciplyne," by the "hole conuent" (2260).[29] In addition to this physical subjection, the king openly renounces the statutes of Clarendon, which had usurped the church's paternal authority and liberties. Having resumed, in the form of his own body and the body of law, his proper status as an obedient son to the fatherly church, the king receives news the next day that his son and his ally, the Scottish king, have been taken. The threats to the king's sovereignty have been miraculously resolved by the saint whose paternal authority over him—performed by the monks of the cathedral in their corporal punishment of the wayward king—has been reestablished. The superior authority that the legend claims for the church over the crown is, however, less interesting than the homology between them suggested by the imbricated genealogical relationships through which this authority is represented: the archbishop is (spiritual) father to a king whose responsibility for his death makes him vulnerable to the aggression of his own son. The logic of the narrative, which glosses the threat of civil war as an effect of Thomas's martyrdom, further identifies the boundaries of religious community with those of the realm.

Thus Becket's lay career and friendship with the king are not represented, as they are in other versions of the legend, as a confusion of the secular and sacred later violently differentiated by his death, but as a demonstration of their fundamental compatibility, restored by it. Thomas, early in his career, easily straddles secular and religious domains. He follows "the pompe off secular lore" (173), even as his "inward" virtue enables him to resist the "ragys sensualle / Off flowrynge youthe" (sensual rages of flowering youth) (170). The brief period in which he follows "alle cowrtly gyse" (all courtly habit) is, in the very next line, "sodenly" ended as Thomas goes "by hyme-sylff alone . . . Enspirede so wyth grace," to Theobald, Archbishop of Canterbury, who gives him orders (177–78). This is a conversion moment, to be sure, one that echoes his mother's conversion to Christianity, as I will argue. But Thomas does not shed his preconversion commitment to the king or the secular world. Rather he himself is an agent that coordinates religious "wisdom" and secular authority through the affection he inspires in the king: "Lyke as oure Thomas in wysdome dyde encrese, / So euer in favor off veray entere affection / The kynge hyme hade, off princely hyghnes" (Just as our Thomas did increase in wisdom, so ever the king had him in favor of very full affection, by princely noblesse) (198–200). The legend gives attention to, and assumes the rightness of, Thomas's doubled legal role, as head of the consistory court of Canterbury and chancellor of England: Thomas proves in his own person that it is possible, even desirable, to coordinate ecclesiastical and royal law. He inhabits this dual role as a sign not of divided jurisdictions, but of the coextensive and coordinated relationship between them, a relationship that also projects the nation as the normative scale of religious community. Even the legend's depiction of the king's and Thomas's matched wills—"The kynge ever styffe to susteyne his powur ryalle, / The archbishoppe in lyke wyse ever as styffe as hee / The church to preseue and kepe hytt in lybertee" (The king ever unyielding in sustaining his royal power, the archbishop in a similar way always as unyielding as he to preserve the church and keep it in liberty) (628– 30)—presents them as embodiments of two forms of English community of equal force and scale.

*   *   *

If religious and secular jurisdictions exist in such even relation to one another, what accounts for the debate about them and its violent denouement? The translation of Edward the Confessor—itself symbolic of the coincidence of English religious and secular community both as the elevation of a royal saint and as the shared project of Becket and the king—is followed abruptly by the section title "De initio dissentionis inter Regem et archiepiscopum" (following line 587). The crisis is attributed to personal vice: "mene of the churche," who "gave theme inordinately wnto vicious trespass" (591, 592), namely a priest accused of homicide and Phillip de Broyes, who flouts the authority of a judge. Phillip is duly punished: he is beaten "fulle sore" with rods, banished, and stripped of priestly status (622–23). But the king, angry "with alle the churche" (618), is not satisfied in the absence of punishment by "handys temporalle" (625). Henry's argument is that, in the absence of temporal punishment, a criminal would be "More proner to be noyfulle by hys cursyde lyvynge" (more inclined to be dangerous on account of his wicked lifestyle) (644). Hence, "after spiritualle payne a bodily sholde sewe" (after spiritual pain, a bodily one should follow) (645), through the "sharpe ponyshment of law temporalle that is so smerte" (658). The king's summons thus represents "lawe cyvylle" in terms of a future orientation, aimed at the social good: the criminal priest, unpunished by temporal justice, is likely to become a bane to society. The physical punishment of secular justice is not retrospective, but prospective, a correction of the individual body in order to ensure the stable functioning of the collective social body in the future.

The authority of temporal law and its compatibility with religious jurisdiction are largely endorsed by the legend. The worsening of relations at
Clarendon—like the egregious clerical misbehavior that precipitated it—is
represented as a consequence of individual vice, the "malicious compasse"
(1117) of the church's "enymyes" (116). Thomas himself is anxious "to honour
his prince ryalle" (1131), as well as to preserve the church's liberties, and he
fails only because "false brethren" who side with the king deepen the divide.
The other parties to the debate—even those who "ffavorde [the king's] grete
hye parsone"—are credited with authority and transparency: "experte / In
bothe lawes," they "openly and notte in secrete coverte / Shewyde thatt alle
suche by there dome ande reasone / Sholde nott take exile nor in monastery
punycione" (openly and not in a secret plot showed that according to their
judgment and reason all such [criminals] should not take exile nor punishment within the monastery) (660–63). Indeed, the king's position preserves,
in a way, the special status of religious authority: "open transgressione" (672)
is such a violation of the "grete dygnytee & priuylage" (651) of religious orders
that the criminal is, or should be, permanently removed from them, "sent to
the handys off the temporaltee / Ande euer-more after as seruantys ther to
bee / In perpetualle seruytute wnder the shrape correccione / Off temporalle
iustice" (sent to the hands of temporal power and forever after to be as a servant there in perpetual servitude under the sharp correction of temporal justice) (669–72). The subjection of a criminal monk or priest to royal justice is
not primarily a manifestation of the king's jurisdiction, but rather *itself* a
form of punishment for a transgression that has already violated the boundaries that marked his vocation as exempt from secular jurisdiction. The blurring of the jurisdictions of church and crown, then, is the consequence of
individual moral or legal transgression, not a structural tension or fundamental antithesis.

The most substantive theoretical difference between the king's position
and the archbishop's at Clarendon is that the king understands English community to be subject to a unified set of laws whereas Thomas understands
there to be a distinction between secular and religious law. The king's position takes as precedent the "law of Moises," which identifies a single law to
which all are subject:

Thatte alle transgressours wythowtyne eny ordyr off excepcione
Bodely sholde be ponysshede after the qualitee off ther transgresse,

Body for body, ey for ey, thus recevynge the grete payne talyone,
As the peple, so the prest, after goddys iuste flagycione (674–77)

[That all transgressors without any category of exception
Should be punished bodily after the nature of their transgression,
Body for body, eye for eye, thus receiving the great pain of equal
    retribution,
As the people, so the priest, after God's just demand].

The church's law provides, Wade implies, a merciful alternative to this impla-cable logic. The legend later invokes a binary of Jewish vengeance and Chris-tian mercy familiar from anti-Jewish discourses,[30] but here it employs a gender binary opposing a motherly church to a fatherly Moses: "Our mother, alle-holy churche, is mother in generalle" (681). That is to say, she is mother to both "kyngdome & prysthode," the maternal superstructure that contains "Two kyngys, two lawes, two Juredictions, two constrayntys wyth-alle" (682–83). The two laws are not Jewish and Christian law, represented as a punish-ing father and the merciful son who supersedes him, but secular and ecclesiastical law, defined in sibling relation, alike subject to the church's ma-ternal authority. The legend can imagine them on this synchronic plane be-cause, again, it defines the tension between them not as structural but as ethical, a question not of contested jurisdiction but of individual morality. The only division between them happens at the level of the individual person, subject to two forms of "constraint": "one for the body ys, / Another for the sowle, to brydylle the mynde / And neyther off theme superfluous may be" (one is for the body, the other for the soul, to bridle the mind and neither of them may be superfluous) (687–89). Even this division is identified as a kind of complementarity by being located in an individual person, as the irreduc-ible unit of which communities are formed. Although it is only implicit, this account of the relationship between the two laws—as siblings under the au-thority of one parent, or as two aspects, bodily and spiritual, of one person—lays the conceptual groundwork for understanding secular and religious jurisdictions as coordinated or coextensive.

There is a change of speakers when the poem shifts from Mosaic law to the Mother Church, a rhetorical shift from the king's position to Thomas's. At least, that is the case in Wade's source, Bosham's vita; in Wade, the change is only lightly indicated. It occurs in a break between stanzas, the second of which opens with a formal address to the king ("My souerane lorde, kynge and prince beloved dere," 680). This speech is not attributed to anyone, nor is there any clear marker of a change in speaker.[31] In the absence of any narrative indication of a new speaker, the arguments for Mosaic law and its Christian revision are only weakly distinguished from one another, and they are even more weakly associated with the two parties at debate. Only later does the speaker insist that "we off the churche" are subject only to Jesus as king (691–93), and "wndyr noo kynge terestrialle" (695), who derives his power from the divine king to whom they are more immediately subject.

The legend's refusal to identify the different parties at debate and distinguish their arguments from one another furthers a striking overlap in the two positions being debated. In endorsing the jurisdiction of secular law over the body, in contrast to the soul's subjection to spiritual law, the archbishop's position seems largely compatible with the king's claims for some form of jurisdiction over criminal clerics. The proximity of their positions bears out a central argument of the legend: that the two "swords" of temporal and spiritual law are "Bothe Joynede in one, ande noo rebellyone in theme may bee" (Both joined in one, and no rebellion may be in them) (746): "Iff one cannott helpe, another may supplee / Off thes twoo lawes the executione playne" (If one cannot help, another may supply the open execution of these two laws) (747–48). The difference between them makes them complementary, even necessary, to each other.

                              *   *   *

Although my primary interest is in the conceptual, rather than topical, significance of Wade's insistent representation of religious and secular jurisdictions as compatible and coextensive, it may be worth locating the poem, which has received almost no critical attention, within its historical context. Wade was a monk of the priory of the most powerful cathedral in England, a monastic community that enjoyed an intimate relationship to the Archbishop of Canterbury, and this institutional affiliation gives us some historical purchase on the legend's representation of tensions between secular and religious jurisdictions as the consequence of personal failures of loyalty or restraint, rather than symptoms of a more fundamental or structural incompatibility between the different forms of community they articulate.

A topical reading is invited by the legend itself. Precisely as the crisis over the two forms of jurisdiction comes to a head, the legend insists on its currency as both a moral exemplum and an event that occurs in a temporal framework that includes the narrator and his audience. The king, "in his hott wylde mode" (799), demands that Thomas return all "Municiones & honours" (801) he has received from him and then abruptly departs from Westminster, with some bishops in his train. The narrator pauses to identify these "false brethrene" (816) as the source of the greatest contemporary peril, addressing his audience with an uncharacteristic rhetorical question: "how dothe hit yow seme?" (how does it seem to you?) (816). The continuing relevance of this ethical and political danger ushers in a shift in the presentation of the narrative: the events recounted seem to affect the speaker and his audience, as though they inhabit the same historical moment as that in which the action occurs:

> As chaff blowne away by course off the wynde,
> Soo forsoke the bisshoppys owr blissede Thomas here,
> Except a fewe *wyth ws* lefte behynde,
> Ande they only taryde prevely fore fere.
> *Alone we abode, alone we satt here,*
> By many dayes abydynge the kynges goode grace,
> Hopynge off comforte, thus alone taryede owr Thomas (827–33;
>   emphasis added)

> [As chaff blown away by course of the wind,
> So the bishops forsook our blessed Thomas here,
> Except a few who remained behind *with us,*
> And they only tarried secretly for fear.
> *Alone we abode, alone we sat here,*
> For many days waiting the king's good grace,
> Hoping for comfort, thus alone tarried our Thomas].

The events of the past bleed into the present, as the legend's audience is identified by the plural first person with the fearful few who remain with Thomas. The suspension of the debate creates a temporal envelope in which the legend's audience, perhaps contemporary monks of Christ Church, find themselves alongside Thomas's original companions as he departs from Clarendon: "so fro the courte *we* toke *owr* way" (1141; emphasis added).

Although Wade borrows this plural first-person voice from the eyewitness account in Bosham's vita, it cannot be dismissed as an act of faithful or rote translation. The legend contains many departures from his source, not least the versification of the legend. Moreover, while Wade elsewhere explicitly refers to

Bosham as his source, he does not do so here. In fact, Wade takes care to differentiate the collective first-person narrator from Bosham as both author and
Thomas's historical companion. As Thomas leaves Clarendon, Bosham is introduced as a character and a source, *rather than* as the poem's narrative voice:

> Forsoithe, in owr iorney owr holy blessede prelatt
> Above alle manere sore trobulyde was in mynde;
> Musyng by hyme-sylffe, frme alle company segregate
> Rode alone, and spake to none, agayne his olde custome kynde
> The cause off this thought to owt-seche ande fynde
> A disciple off his, thatt wrote this story here,
> Presumede ande sayde: "lorde, whatt is hitt thatt yow chaunge yowr
>   chere?" (1142–48)

> [Forsooth, in our journey our holy blessed prelate
> Was sorely troubled in mind beyond measure;
> Musing by himself, separate from all company
> Rode alone, and spoke to none, against his old accustomed nature.
> The cause of this thought to seek out and find
> A disciple of his, who wrote this story here,
> Ventured to say: "lord, what is it that causes you to change your
>   expression?"].

As the story departs from the closed space of the court, it enters an arena in
which contemporary monks and any reader of the legend may participate.
Addressed by and as the poem's "we," they ride along with Thomas, as it were,
privy to the conversation that ensues between him and Herbert of Bosham.
The contrast with the narrative presentation of the debate at Clarendon as a
discrete historical event is quite marked.

The first-person plural voice thus identifies a transhistorical group comprising Thomas's companions in the poem and the contemporary monks of
Christ Church who are addressed by it.[32] This is anticipated by the identification of Bosham himself as "a brothere off Cristys Churche in Cantorbury" in
the headnote to the poem, an affiliation for which historians find no other
evidence.[33] Later in the legend, when a rapprochement is attempted between
the king and Thomas after his exile in Pontigny, this group of Thomas's most
loyal followers, past and present, sees through the ruse and recognizes Thomas's immanent fate, foretold to him in a dream:

We this heryng consydrede wyth sobyr mynde colde,
Before shewyde to *ws* off *owr* Thomas the nocturnalle vysyone,
Ande anone *we* coniecte hys dreme fylle to a trewe conclusyone
(1433–35; emphasis added)

[*We* considered this message with a solemn, cold mind,
the nocturnal vision shown to *us* earlier by *our* Thomas,
And soon *we* surmised that his dream led to a true conclusion].

Late medieval custodians of Thomas's relics, Wade and his brothers share an-aleptic knowledge of his martyrdom with Thomas himself. In local terms, such moments establish the spiritual authority of Christ Church Priory, while in broader ones, they open the legend to the present, suggesting its general relevance to late medieval England.

The poem underscores its currency toward its close. When the king fi-nally renounces the statutes of Clarendon, the harmonious relationship be-tween secular and religious authority is restored, as is proven by the era of peace it ushers in. The poem's own historical moment, however, requires an-other Thomas:

Butt here is to be sorowede, alas, whatt dayly now do falle:
Soche dedly statutys or worse to be thowght wyth alle
Inducte by sofferance—wherefore, Crist knowythe, hitt is neede
Now off a new Thomas or soche ane othere, for that his blode to
    sheede (2265–68)[34]

[But here is to be mourned, alas, what daily now occurs:
Such deadly statutes or worse ones, if broadly considered,
Established through acquiescence—wherefore, Christ knows, there is
    need
Now of a new Thomas or such another, to shed his blood].

This is followed by surprisingly perfunctory references to Thomas's posthu-mous miracles and his canonization, all in a single stanza (2283–89). The saint's role as intercessor or object of devotion is not the legend's concern; indeed, there is no mention whatsoever of the saint's translation or his shrine.[35] The story's contemporary significance lies rather in the need for an-other "actiff spiritualle knyghte" (2066), a person who might embody both temporal and religious authority, both "active" and "spiritual"—key terms for two kinds of jurisdiction that had once been represented as antithetical.

Wade very likely tips his hat here to John Morton, Archbishop of Canterbury from 1486 to 1500, and Lord Chancellor for most of that time.[36] Sometimes criticized for his harsh implementation of royal policy, Morton was also lauded for his concern with "good order and sound government."[37] He was known especially for his efforts to protect and increase the liberties and jurisdiction of his office, including securing papal authority to conduct visitations of abbeys that had been formally exempt from episcopal oversight. He used this authority to standardize ecclesiastical oversight of monasteries, leveling the uneven pockets of jurisdiction produced by the exempt status or international affiliations of some houses.[38] Christopher Harper-Bill, the leading scholar of Morton's career, suggests that the archbishop's efforts to expand the power of his office was a symptom of, and response to, the "increasingly nationalist" profile of the church.

Harper-Bill identifies two of Morton's most visible and consequential conflicts regarding jurisdiction: one with the monks of Winchester and another with the Bishop of London, Richard Hill.[39] The Winchester case—which concerned *sede vacante* visitations, a lucrative practice that occurred during the vacancy of a see—is representative of Morton's many attempts to regularize practice while also increasing his privileges and his purse.[40] Among the most profitable revenues generated by such visitations were those to the episcopal *mensa*, the fund that supported the archbishop's personal expenses.[41] There was a protracted contest over these revenues at Winchester: St. Swithun's Priory had been granted *sede vacante* revenues from two parishes, East Meon and Hambledon, in an exception to the general rule that such income was claimed by the archbishop.[42] When the see became vacant in 1492, the priory expected to receive revenues as per this standing privilege, but the money was seized by Morton's agents. In 1494, Morton appealed to the pope, who confirmed in general terms the conventional privileges due to the archbishop. There was, however, no specific reference to the case at hand, and the monks of Winchester contested its application to their case, complaining to Rome that "Morton's power in England was so great that none dare stand against him."[43] In the process of eliminating historical monastic privileges in the guise of regularizing ecclesiastical jurisdiction, Morton—like his predecessors Arundel and Chichele—exposed and produced tensions along fault lines within the church.[44]

Wade represents these fault lines—embodied by "false brethren" who require an "active spiritual knight" to rein them in—as more consequential than the one between secular and religious jurisdiction that is usually the focus of the Becket legend. The topical address of the *Life of St. Thomas* may extend to specific controversies such as the one with the Winchester monks. In a passage discussed at greater length below, for example, the episcopal *mensa* appears as a private and secret devotional practice performed under the cover of night, rather than as the financial boon due to the archbishop's office.[45] The *mensa corporali* includes Thomas's almsgiving, his washing the feet of poor men and feeding them, and providing for his prebendaries. These "mawndes" represent "the thre masses done att the blessed fest Natiffe / Off oure redemere, swett Crist Jesus" (the three masses done at the blessed feast of the Nativity of our redeemer, sweet Christ Jesus) (276–77), thus representing Thomas's own sacramental rebirth at his consecration. Most important, they identify his office as archbishop in terms of humble charity, rather than privilege or luxury. Together with the legend's censure of the "false brethren" who betray Thomas, the allegorical *mensae* may comment implicitly on the controversies—not limited to Winchester—surrounding Morton's legal battles to secure *sede vacante* privileges. Morton's petition to the pope to reaffirm these privileges represented the monks of Winchester as betraying the archbishop's traditional prerogative—that is, as "false brethren" out for their own gain.

This local context points to a broader and more consequential issue that we encountered in different form in Chapter 5: the contest between monastic and ecclesiastic institutions, especially when the latter are closely affiliated with the crown, which is in this instance presented from the ecclesiastical perspective. Although he was himself a Benedictine monk, like Lydgate, Wade's priory enjoyed a relationship with the archbishop very different from that of Bury St. Edmunds or St. Alban's. As the priory of Canterbury Cathedral, Christ Church was closely affiliated with the archbishop, and Wade's prior seems to have had an especially good relationship with Morton.[46] Wade grants the monastery no special claim on the sacred: in the *Life of St. Thomas*, it is an institution, like any, embedded in the secular world, and monks are administrators and institution builders, not unlike ecclesiasts.[47] If the king of France cannot find "religion" when Thomas is forced to leave Pontigny, it is partly because the Cistercian house, despite all the debilitating forms of asceticism practiced there, is as much a part of the saeculum, and as subject to its demands, as anywhere else.

Monasticism does, however, provide a *metaphorical* vocabulary for representing the private devotional life of ideal Christians such as Thomas, a secular ecclesiast by day who performs his monkish devotions "secretly at night." The location of the sacred in the private self (*mensae* as acts of devotion that take place out of public view), rather than in an office (*mensa* as archepiscopal prerogative), is the central focus of the representation of Thomas's practices. The identification of religious authority with inner disposition rather than office or public self-presentation is a recurrent theme in this period, with obvious utility in the ecclesio-political culture of late medieval Christianity, in which institutional authority and privilege were grounded in forms of piety (poverty, humility, dispossession) antithetical to them. It has, however, a special point in reference to Morton, given his well-known, often controversial, pursuit of such privileges.

Other controversies in which Morton was embroiled resonate similarly with the poem's thematics. Morton's famous quarrel with Richard Hill, Bishop of London, grew so heated and personal that Hill's party posted a citation against Morton on the door of St. Paul's—high enough to be out of reach so that Morton's men could not remove it—and may have started rumors that the archbishop had been excommunicated.[48] Although Morton ultimately prevailed, and Hill was dead when Wade wrote the Becket legend a couple of years later, the "violence, arrests and mutual recriminations" between the Bishop of London and the archbishop may hover over the legend's representation of an embarrassing squabble among archbishops and bishops over who should consecrate Becket as archbishop. The Archbishop of York believes it is his prerogative, but he is countered by Henry of Winchester on the grounds that the see of London is vacant. The Bishop of Rochester then also makes a claim on the grounds that he holds the office of chaplain to the Archbishop of Canterbury. These differences are resolved as suddenly as they appear, overridden by the bishops' shared desire for "peace & unytee" (243), but the happy outcome points nevertheless to the rash and petty grab for precedence—by every bishop present—that precipitates it.

Morton had served in the double role of archbishop and chancellor for ten years when Wade wrote the *Life of St. Thomas*: he embodied the coordination of ecclesiastical and secular power that the poem takes as an ideal. Morton had attained the status of Bachelor of Both Laws as a student at Oxford, and as he grew in prominence, he served as both Dean of the Court of Arches—the ecclesiastical court for Canterbury—and Master of the Rolls at Chancery.[49] It is no wonder that the *Life of St. Thomas*, written toward the end of his formidable career, insists on the compatibility of the "two laws." With a political career that spanned the end of Henry VI's reign, and then the reigns of Edward IV and Henry VII (after his exile during the reign of Richard III), Morton was an enduring figure of English political culture, with a career that far outlasted the kings he served.[50] Wade's poem can be read, at least in part, as an endorsement of his status as "active spiritual knight," and, more broadly, of the conjoined ecclesio-political jurisdiction that he embodied.

The City and the Inner Precincts of the Sacred

Rather than a structural antithesis, tensions between secular and ecclesiastical authority in Wade's legend, as we have seen, are the effect of individual moral failure or internecine quarreling. Re-scaled as local failings, they find a correlative in the identification of the sacred as private, a familiar feature of late medieval religion. Wade, like other late medieval writers, is interested in an interior self as the domain of religious devotion. This "privatization" of late medieval devotion has many genealogies: in women's devotional practices, in lay enthusiasm for a more active role in their own religious lives, and in the theologies that emphasized meditation, to name some that have received important scholarly attention.[51] Wade's legend participates in this broad cultural development and suggests another genealogy for the inward turn of late medieval religion: that is, as a coproduct and complement to the increasing coordination of religious and secular jurisdictions and the public culture it produced. The legend conjoins these two phenomena by grafting onto Bosham's vita the romance story, taken from John Grandison's *Life*, of Becket's father, Gilbert, and his mother, Maud (also called Matilda), a Saracen princess.[52] Grandison's story focuses on London and gives prominence to the private self. The city, as a paradigmatic secular space, and erotic love, as a paradigmatic form of interiority, are both important to the unlikely endorsement of the coordination of church and crown in a legend traditionally dedicated to elaborating the irreconcilable opposition between them.

It is Maud's love for Gilbert that provides the crucial link between affective interiority and religious identity. Gilbert Becket is captured during pilgrimage to the Holy Land by a Saracen admiral, who imprisons him for a year. Maud, the admiral's daughter, falls in love with Gilbert, and her singular feeling for him—she "synglarly hym lovede alle erthly mene above" (35)—is a model for the devotion that a Christian (man) should feel for God, following a familiar hierarchy of obligation by which women are devoted to men and men to God. So when Maud shows "all her herte" to Gilbert (45), its full content is her love for him, which has as a secondary effect her willingness to convert to Christianity; Gilbert in turn shows Maud "all his herte" on the day after they marry (109), which is his sudden intention to undertake another pilgrimage to the Holy Land. In this chain of affective orientations, Maud's love for Gilbert is an earthly model for religious devotion and for the inward location of this feeling: Gilbert's religious desire, like Maud's desire for him, is confined within the heart. The concatenated structure linking Maud's love to Thomas's spiritual vocation identifies the latter as private, even when it takes the form of pilgrimage.[53] Spirituality is not a practice that takes place in a public space, the legend suggests, but a feeling or commitment located in the interior of the self. The boundary between the secular and sacred, that is, lies at the border of the body, not between the church and crown.

The story of Thomas's early career further advances this representation of a private spirituality defined against a public culture in which secular and religious authority have merged. One index of this merging is the concomitant convergence of religious and secular ethics, which moots the traditional conversion narrative, a primary vehicle for articulating their difference. Thus in earlier Becket legends, Thomas, who enjoys worldly success and its attendant luxuries, abandons secular pleasures and prestige for his spiritual vocation, and he mortifies his body to atone for his earlier life. Wade, in contrast, represents Thomas as saintly from before his birth and, more surprisingly and more importantly, represents his access to the privileges of his position as signs of virtue. Lacking the reversal characteristic of a conversion narrative, Wade's legend relies here too on Maud's story to establish a paradigm for an internal change, in this case by creating a parallel between her conversion to Christianity and the change produced by Thomas's consecration. In both, there is a change in external appearance, but it is an inconsequential manifestation of a more significant internal transformation. Maud arrives in London in "vyle aray" (61)—her appearance is such that the "childrene off the cite" trail after and taunt her (64–65)—until she is "newly arayde" by a kind woman in whose care she is placed while Gilbert consults with the Bishop of London. Although Gilbert explains that he has only "dissymylyde wyth hyrre condicionally" about marriage (87), the bishop declares her arrival a divine portent, and she is baptized and they are married without more ado.[54] Maud is already transformed through her desire in ways that make her a suitable bride for Gilbert; her reclothing is merely the external sign of the affective and religious changes that have already occurred.

Thomas's consecration echoes Maud's conversion, which acts as a kind of threshold narrative for it. Thomas, too, casts away his old clothing—here the purple robes of secular power—as a sign of a more consequential internal transformation:

> Castynge away hys purpylle wedys alle
> Sondenly changed newly forthe-wyth anone,
> Bothe lyfe & conuersacioune acordyng to his palle,
> To be as a myrrore unto his subjectys alle;
> Gave hyme to prayor, wache & contemplacione—
> Thus renewyde his life offe a godly inspiracione (247–52)

> [Casting away all his purple clothing
> Suddenly changed newly in a very short time
> Both his life and conversation, in accordance with his vestment,
> To be a mirror to all his subjects;
> Gave himself to prayer, vigil, and contemplation—
> Thus renewed his life through a holy inspiration].

Whereas Maud's desire to convert precedes her baptism, Thomas's transformation is precipitated by sacramental ritual, its efficient cause. This chiastic structure, reflecting back on the private erotic impetus behind Maud's conversion, gives special emphasis to Thomas's internal change: the "godly inspiration" that structures his vocation is an image of his mother's secret desire. Note that even the vocation itself is represented in terms not of the pastoral, institutional, or legal roles that in fact defined the office, but of private devotions: "prayor, wache & contemplacione." Like a late medieval layperson, Thomas adopts quasi-monastic devotions, cloistering them in the enclosed space of the self. Indeed, the reference to Thomas as a "mirror" points to his exemplary role, one who models a spirituality removed from the public arena not via retreat within a monastery, but within himself. He is, tellingly, a mirror to his "subjects all": "subjects" can refer to those under either ecclesiastical or secular authority, and it is their convergence that makes necessary an inward zone of devotion as an alternative.[55]

This interior devotion, as the complement to an ecclesio-political public, is defined through tropes of secrecy, especially in the passage that details Thomas's allegorical *mensae*. Thomas imitates Christ in the dark of night, a setting that elicits some of the legend's most self-consciously literary language:

Whene the sonne had wythdrawe his lyghte
Ande the mone by derke lyst shew hyse face,
In the dulle silence off the derke nyghte
Thyrtene powr mene hade oure Thomas,
Gyrt wyth ane apurne, in a secrete place (253–57)

[When the sun had withdrawn its light
And the moon by dark wanted to show his face,
In the dull silence of the dark night
Our Thomas served thirteen poor men,
Clothed in his vestment, in a secret place].[56]

Thomas performs relatively ordinary acts of charity, but their secret, night-time quality— that is, their separateness from a public arena—marks them as sacred.[57] Note that they are also marked as sacred by the aureate style of this passage, an echo of Lydgate and other Benedictine poets. As in earlier texts, aureation here indexes a sacred realm at a remove from the secular world, but this realm has been relocated from the institutional space— architectural or ideological—of the monastery to a private or secret one. Where Lydgate uses self-consciously literary language to mark the difference between secular and sacred jurisdictions, Wade uses it to mark the difference between private spirituality and a public culture in which these jurisdictions have merged.

Thomas thus becomes an example of a "devotione pure" that is practiced "Nyghtly," away from the public eye (281, 285). It is the privacy of his spiritual activities that marks a decisive break with his past life: as we have seen, Becket's first of three acts of charity represent "the thre masses done att the blissed fest Natiffe / Off oure redemere, swett Crist Jesus" (276–77), which in turn manifest his "neew lyffe" purified of the "fylthe off alle rusty vanyte" (filth of all rusty vanity) of public life (279). Such corporal *mensae*, the prelude to the "mensa Sacre scripture," further distance Becket's inner spirituality from the public ritual they shadow, as their figurative nature itself suggests. His secret nighttime practices include the gathering of "morcellys" of Scripture as "spiritual refectione" for his mind (293–94), followed by the "swete mele off goddys dyvyne seruyce" (sweet meal of God's divine service) (308). The metaphor is developed at some length in order to insist on a material, but countersecular, arena:

The brede off this meele, callyde divyne servyce,
Thus bakyne att the ovyne off bornynge devocioune;
Preparyde our prelatt in alle goddly wyse,
Goynge to the table off the blesed consecracione—
The hedde-table callyde off oure saluacione (309–13)

[The bread of this meal, called the divine service,
Thus baked in the oven of Thomas's burning devotion,
Our prelate prepared in an entirely holy manner;
Going to the table of the blessed consecration—
The head-table identified for our salvation].

Although the eucharistic bread is ultimately recognized as the product of sacramental ministrations, and so a reference point for the institutional authority and earthly role of the church, it begins as a material metaphor for "burning devotion"—a mystical fervor separate from Thomas's sacerdotal role, which is strikingly secondary here.

Indeed, the sacrament is associated with a private, interior devotion differentiated from, even the antithesis of, Thomas's office. While he necessarily dresses the part, his "pontificalle aray" (324) serves primarily as a contrast to his humility: during mass, Thomas "mekyde hyme inwardly alleway" (always meeked himself inwardly) (326). The reflexive verb underscores the centripetal quality of his spiritual life, pulled continually toward a private interior. As an action that has no external manifestation, this self-meeking parallels the sacrament that Thomas performs, and thus it seems to have a more intimate, essential connection to it than does his office, which is represented by showy material accoutrements. Thomas's inward devotion is privileged even over the liturgy itself, which it obscures: "So fervently one the passione off Cryst his myde layde, / That his devocione was more percevyde thene the wordys thatt hy sayde" (So fervently was his mind set on the passion of Christ, that his devotion was more evident than the words he said) (328–29).[58] When in the course of the mass his mind is distracted by "vaverynge thowghtys vayne / Thatt sodenly flyttyde" (wavering vain thoughts that suddenly flitted) (330–31), he directs his attention not to the words of the liturgy, which it is his role to perform, but to the "swete meditaciones" of Anselm, written "wndyr ane elegant style," that serves to "reconcyle" his mind (334, 336).[59]

Here again the aesthetic is associated with private devotion, rather than with an institution such as the Benedictine order, the association that obtains in Lydgate's Lives. This inward meditation is valued to such a degree that it warrants abbreviating the mass, restricting its duration in secular time: in fact, in order to limit his vulnerability to pernicious distractions, Thomas speeds through the rite:

> Att this hyghe sacryfice ffulle shortly wolde he bee,
> Feerynge ylle angellys thatt wer fulle pernycyous,
> As vayne thowghtys fflyttynge off prone ffragilitee
> In myende att thatt swete oblacione ffulle glorious.
> Thus ordyryde hymesilff this prelatt vertuous
> Wyth short devocione ther vayne corsys to subdue,
> Ande thus hastely he recevyde owr savyour Cryst Jesu (337–43)

> [At this high sacrifice, fully briefly would he be,
> Fearing evil angels that were very pernicious,
> As vain thoughts, on account of an inveterate fragility, flitting
> In his mind at that very glorious sweet oblation.
> Thus this virtuous prelate ordered himself
> To subdue their vain courses by means of short devotion,
> And thus hastily he received our savior, Christ Jesus].

Although the mass is a liturgical event, it nevertheless occurs in secular time ("the holy masse whyle," 331), and in its course Thomas is subject to the distractions that can afflict even the most devout mind. He models an ideal alternative to this potentially soul-threatening distraction: meditative language that is notable for its aesthetic effect, an association of sacred timelessness and the literary that was, as we saw in the last chapter, an established capability of aureate poetics.

"Vertuous Urbanitee": London in the *Life of St. Thomas*

Positioning the most consequential boundary between spiritual and secular arenas at the borders of the individual self, the legend represents the sacred as essentially placeless: like Maud escaping from her father's home for her clandestine love, it eludes territorial jurisdiction altogether. At the same time, however, the legend's identification of the sacred with the private self is facilitated by its focus on the city. As we saw in Chapter 4, the city sometimes served as an alternative to the jurisdictions of church and crown: it can thus—imaginatively, if not actually—suspend, defer, or complicate jurisdictional disputes between them. In Wade's legend, the city, as a crowded and lively public space where religious and political concerns are both in evidence, serves as a useful metonym for the res publica as a whole, as well as the antithesis of the private self.

In imagining the city in this way, the poem takes advantage of practical and conceptual affordances of the London cult of St. Thomas. Traditionally, on the day after the mayoral election (October 28), the new mayor, accompanied by some members of his company and the city's aldermen, visited the Church of St. Thomas of Acre in Cheapside, believed to be Thomas's birthplace.[60] From there, as the *Liber Albus* records, they proceeded to St. Paul's and then assembled in the Pardon Churchyard near the tomb of Gilbert and Matilda Becket.[61] Paul Alonzo Brown has suggested that the ritual is evidence that Thomas was "considered a champion of the rights of the people."[62] What is clear is that the ritual conflated the London cult of St. Thomas with citizenship and with London's distinctive jurisdiction: that is, with an urban alternative to the forms of community traditionally presented at debate in the Becket legend. This urban community enters Wade's poem through the romance plot of his parents' marriage, which is the very story commemorated in the civic rituals associated with the cult. Gilbert, as a "burgesse off Londone" (20), and Maud, the Saracen princess who follows him there, locate the narrative within the framework of urban forms of community and jurisdiction, just as Maud's desire and marriage are crucial to the conceptualization of the sacred as private experience.

London substitutes for the contested jurisdictions of the traditional Becket legend by representing England metonymically, as a more finite, discrete instantiation of the polity. So, in a small but significant revision, Wade's Maud knows the words "England, London, and Becket," in contrast to other versions in which she knows only "Becket" or "London."[63] The three proper nouns that constitute Maud's English vocabulary concatenate the nation, the city, and citizen (the latter in the form of Gilbert's proper name, which is also Thomas's). This is a graduated scale in descending order, in which London is a metonym for England, as Gilbert is for London. The narrative context in which they are linked suggests the city's scale and identifiable boundaries are especially important: London is a finite space, where it is possible to find a person, as Maud is discovered by Gilbert's servant Richard and as she in turn discovers Gilbert. In conceptualizing the larger notional community of England through the figure of the city, its knowability as a bounded place and the possibility of being known within it are attributed to the nation as well. If England itself provides earthly boundaries, and thus a relatively comprehensible scale, to a transcendent sacred, its own territorial definition and fictions of affiliation derive from its urban metonym.

As we have seen, London is also a key topos—that is, a rhetorical and conceptual place—for the poem's representation of a private spirituality, defined against a public arena. We can now see that the metonymic relationship between the city and the nation allows this opposition between private and public to substitute for the legend's traditional conflict between spiritual and sacred jurisdictions. Thus Maud's three English words also point simultaneously to Gilbert's public identity—in Maud's improbable ability to locate him across a vast spatial and cultural geography—and to his secret intentions, which make her journey necessary in the first place. When Maud first confesses her love to Gilbert, he lies in promising to marry her, as he later admits. "Ferynge the ffare subtyle caste off ffemynyne deception" (Fearing the fair subtle plot of feminine deception) (49), Gilbert had in turn deceived her about his future intentions. "London, England, Becket" are at once the key words of his private promise to her and the public coordinates with which she tracks him down when he violates this promise. Public urban culture and private identity are here complements: that city is, on the one hand, a place where a woman from a distant land, whom you once disingenuously promised to marry, might show up calling your name through the streets and, on the other hand, a place where you might cultivate a private self that is separate from public forms of identity and experience, in which such a promise may never register.

Gilbert's religious devotion is specifically represented as a private correlative of civic identity: usually identified as a crusader, in Wade's legend Gilbert is first introduced as a London burgess and then shortly afterward identified as a pilgrim, who travels to the Holy Land to "visett there the holy placys, *off deuocione inwarde*" (visit the holy places there on account *of inward devotion*) (25; emphasis added).[64] (Public) citizenship and "inward devotion" are complementary terms, even mutually constitutive ones. When Maud arrives in London, after the arduous journey that has left her in "vyle aray" (61), she wanders the streets, now calling "Londone, Bekett" (63). Her state—as a vulnerable and impoverished foreigner without adequate material markers of her social identity—is the antithesis of the status that Gilbert enjoys through the concatenation of his city, his citizenship, and his proper name.

London ultimately becomes a defining aspect of Maud's identity too, through the crucial role that it plays in her rehabilitation and conversion. Maud is subject to public view when she arrives in the city, and it is a specifically urban visibility that reunites her with Gilbert: she is spotted and rescued by Richard, Gilbert's man, who recognizes her despite her disheveled appearance, and Gilbert at once has her taken to the home of a matron, where Maud is "newly arayde" (77). The transformation of her appearance marks a decisive shift in Gilbert's inner disposition toward her: he immediately goes to St. Paul's to ask the bishops whether he can marry a non-Christian woman. In London, that is, Maud ceases to represent to Gilbert a foreign woman and is accepted by him as a possible wife, and she is then—in the third and culminating transformation—baptized, with six bishops in attendance (an urban surplus). The specifically urban social identities of both Gilbert and Maud define their corresponding religious interiority too as a phenomenon of city life.

Their child, Thomas, becomes the saintly guarantee of this reciprocal relationship between urban and religious identity. In an episode attested in neither of Wade's primary sources, the pregnant Maud has a dream in which the Thames runs into her lap (120), creating a punning association between the river, "Tamys," and the child she will bear.[65] Thomas's name is coincident with that of the river that was a defining feature of the city and the boundary of London identity. Maud's vision also contributes importantly to the thematic of an inward spirituality, identifying the interior location of the sacred with the womb, a bodily figure buttressed later in the poem by the identification of the church itself as a "womb" that is violated by Thomas's martyrdom. Indeed, as an inward phenomenon that finds a complement in the city as a public space, religion is ultimately defined in contrast to the territorial jurisdiction the city represents. Paradoxically, it is precisely as a correlative of urban territoriality that private spirituality is placeless, the theme of Thomas's sermon to the monks of the chapterhouse upon his return to England, which Wade identifies in Latin and English: "Non habemus hic ciuitatem manentem e.c.,— / Thatt is in owr mother tonge as moche thus to say: / here we have noo cytee to reste ws in alway" (1686–88).[66] This topic is inflected with the Augustinian opposition of the city of God and city of man, but it also reflects the poem's pervasive interest in locating the sacred in the inner lives of citizens.

As a phenomenon of inward feeling, spirituality is not compromised by worldly practices of any kind, allowing the poem to celebrate Thomas's refined "urbanitee," practices associated with, or derived from, citizenship. Although he is lauded as chancellor for cleansing the consistory court of avarice and bribery, the poem endorses Thomas's acceptance of small gifts of food, which is praised as evidence of his "vertuous vrbanytee" (358)—that is, elite urban etiquette appropriate to his public role and entirely unrelated to his inward spirituality. In this he follows his father, whose identity, as we have seen, comprises his public status as a citizen and the "inward devotion" that compels his two pilgrimages. Housed in the secret spaces of the self, the sacred is untouched by small luxuries and fine manners. These cannot compromise true devotion, manifest by private thought or private acts, done under the cover of night. Wade's praise for "virtuous urbanity" may be linked to the interests of Christ Church Priory, which had, for example, the benefice of All Hallows Lombard Street in their gift, a parish church in the center of London's banking district, not far from the Tower and Baynard's Castle, a parish "to which golden currents flowed from every part of the known globe," and whose benefice was lucrative enough to capture the interest of Edward IV, Elizabeth Woodville, and Richard, Duke of Gloucester.[67] But it must also be seen as part of the poem's general understanding of the sacred as sequestered from public practice by its categorically private quality, and of a public culture in which the tensions between secular and Christian ethics—by which "urbanity" and "virtue" might be contrasted—have been dissolved by the convergence of the separate authorities of crown and church that once underwrote their differences.

Wade's legend, then, shows none of the claustrophobia that Lydgate's does in response to a similar ecclesio-political culture, in which an energetic archbishop, closely involved with secular affairs as Lord Chancellor, embodied the integration of royal and ecclesiastical jurisdiction. By the end of the fifteenth century, the flattening of once-variegated forms of community perhaps did not pose the same sort of threat that it had at the beginning of the century. Or perhaps, as I suggested earlier, the difference reflects more narrowly the exceptional status of Christ Church Priory, which—as the community that tended Becket's shrine—had little need to make a case for its cultural importance or its privileges, which were already secured by its close relationship to the archbishop.[68] Whatever the reason, the legend endorses a vision of English community in which religious and secular jurisdictions are compatible and coextensive. These conjoined jurisdictions identify the nation as paradigmatic, even as England is, in turn, represented metonymically by London, an urban public that is both the forum for, and complement to, private devotion. The city at once offers an alternative jurisdiction that suspends the contest between church and crown, and it positions devotional identity within the inner precincts of the self.

*   *   *

The Becket legend enjoyed something of a vogue in the early sixteenth century, with several vernacular Lives circulating in print. In his entry on Becket in the *Kalendre of the Newe Legende of Englande* (1516), Richard Pynson, remarking that an abbreviated version cannot do justice to the story, sends his readers to other fully elaborated ones, confident—with good reason—that one would be readily accessible.[69] He himself printed the prose version from William Caxton's *Legenda Aurea* as an independent text in 1520.[70] John Rastell apparently anticipated a robust market for the verse legend that was discussed at the beginning of this chapter: he had eighty reams of the text warehoused when his goods were inventoried after his death in 1538—the year Thomas was demoted from saint to traitor by a royal proclamation that ordered the removal of all visual and textual representations of him from books, church fabric, and ritual.[71]

Wade's poem itself was never printed, nor is there evidence of its influence or dissemination beyond the single manuscript witness, whose textual location among other documents related to Christ Church Priory may suggest the limits of its circulation. While it may not itself have shaped the conceptualization of English community beyond its institutional home, the poem does suggest something about the resource that the Becket cult and legend could provide for thinking about civic and national community in a historical moment in which religious and secular authority were increasingly imbricated, on the eve of their complete merger in the person of the king. Evidence for this may be found in the legend's surprising resonance with an unlikely successor: Thomas More's *Utopia*. *Utopia* is explicitly presented under the aegis of Archbishop Morton, More's first patron and a formative influence, who plays an important role in the dialogue that frames the political allegory.[72] The most striking parallel to Wade's *Life of St. Thomas*, however, is to be found in *Utopia*'s simultaneous debts to the monastery and the city, and London in particular. The civic government of Utopia famously borrows specific offices and governing structures from London: the role of Utopia's syphrogrants is anticipated by London's Common Council, which drew its membership from householders, while the tranibors parallel London's aldermen, who served in advisory roles to the mayor.[73] Perhaps even more fundamental is the influence of the monastery on the social and political order of Utopia, grounded as it is in the idea of common property, which More links explicitly to the monastic *conventus*.[74] Utopia's debt to monastic community also registers in the imperative of regulated, daily labor—indeed in the value accorded to physical labor generally, which is granted a qualified equivalence to intellectual labor.

The conceptual genealogy of More's ideal polity in both the city and the monastery may seem to a modern reader to suspend *Utopia* between a medieval past and an early modern future. But this is a view from our own historical moment, indebted to our own historiographical conceits. Wade's poem reminds us that urban jurisdiction and citizenship are late medieval phenomena too. And Thomas Becket, a patron saint of London civic identity, whose devotions were represented as quasi-monastic and whose shrine was tended by Benedictine monks, was an important vector for their affiliation in the late Middle Ages. More was especially well positioned to appreciate this. He had an established relationship to Christ Church Priory through Morton, who sponsored More at Canterbury College, Oxford, the college affiliated with the priory.[75] More later became a member of the priory's confraternity, in recognition, suggests Peter Roberts, of "his reverence for its patron saint."[76] It is quite possible that More read Wade's *Life of St. Thomas*, which is bound with some Latin verses attributed to More that inaugurate a pageant that welcomed Charles V and Henry VIII to London in 1522.[77]

It is worth considering these pageants briefly by way of conclusion, both because they are a bridge between Wade and More and because like the *Life of St. Thomas* and *Utopia* they use urban space to develop a conceptualization of England in which religious and secular jurisdictions are fully compatible. On the drawbridge at the city gate, the two sovereigns were greeted by two giants, Sampson and Hercules, embodying religious and secular order, respectively, each holding tables identifying the lands over which the emperor claimed sovereignty (124r). Other pageants elaborate the relationship between secular or sacred authority by linking them through the larger formal structure of the series. One pageant, staged in the middle of London Bridge, represented Jason and Medea, along with a dragon and two bulls with the Golden Fleece, in honor of the emperor's position as the head of the Order of the Golden Fleece (124v). The authority of the classical past represented here (of importance to Henry VIII as well as the emperor) finds Christian analogues in other pageants, such as the one representing Charlemagne receiving the crown of thorns from the king of Constantinople and the patriarch of Jerusalem, and a pageant that honored Henry VIII as king of France and the emperor as Charlemagne's putative descendant (125r–125v).

As the pageant moved farther into the city, the focus narrowed more specifically to England but retained this dual attention to political and religious forms of community. The pageant at the conduit in Cornhill depicted Arthur and the Round Table, populated by figures representing all the kingdoms in his power (126r–126v), while the pageant at the Little Conduit in Cheapside—just outside of St. Paul's churchyard—recalled England's sacred history with a tableau of native saints: St. George; St. Edmund, king and martyr; Edward the Confessor; Henry VI; St. Dunstan; St. Erkenwald; and Thomas of Canterbury (128v).[78] The pageants thus underscored London's role as a forum capable of hosting various kinds of community, religious and secular, and as a metonym for England.[79]

These forms of community are differently integrated in *Utopia*, where secular public space has been thoroughly homogenized and rationalized, and where religion is correspondingly made a matter of private concern, as it is in Wade's legend. In Utopia, all forms of punishment are reserved to the secular leader and the secular legal order, while priests have only moral jurisdiction— the power to reprove and instruct—and the ability to alienate from church a person who has transgressed egregiously against social norms. The constitutive problem of the St. Thomas legend in its traditional form is thus resolved in *Utopia* through jurisdictional homogeneity—with the important, telling exception of Utopian priests, who are, as Becket had argued, exempt from secular punishment.[80] In *Utopia*, this exception highlights how the designation of religion as private, a matter of personal belief, facilitates the rationalization of political space— a more systematic version of the way that Wade's *Life of St. Thomas* links the interiorization of devotion and a hybrid ecclesiopolitical public culture. Read together, what may otherwise be taken as an effect of the secular nature of the polity More imagines—including Utopia's capacity to admit, even celebrate, religious pluralism—may rather be seen as an extension of the idea of religion as private already developed in Wade's *Life* in response to the coordination of ecclesiastical and royal jurisdiction.

For Wade as for More, the public culture of the city and the private experiences of the sacred are defined as complements. Whether or not Wade's poem influenced *Utopia*, composed not twenty years later, they both align the public with the secular and the private with religion, suggesting more continuity between late medieval and early modern social ideas than is often

credited, and pointing toward a more complicated genealogy for them, beyond Reformation ecclesiology and humanist selfhood or statecraft. On the
one hand, they remind us that some later formations of a "public" sphere may
be recognized more precisely as an effect of the coordination of political and
religious authority than as an effect of "secularization." On the other hand, in
their debt to the phenomena of urban life and ideas of citizenship, they also
remind us of the conceptual and practical resources provided by other experiences of community.

CHAPTER 7

St. Ursula and the Scale of English Community

In 1501, on the eve of her marriage to Prince Arthur, the fifteen-year-old Catherine of Aragon was welcomed to London with a series of pageants. The first was a tableau on London Bridge that featured Saints Ursula and Katherine of Alexandria. As we might expect, St. Katherine hails the Spanish princess as her name saint. More surprisingly, St. Ursula welcomes her as blood kin: the saint boasts that she herself is "of noble blood of this land," claiming a Lancastrian lineage, as Catherine of Aragon did. She thus recognizes the princess as a "second Ursula."[1] Catherine of Aragon is likely to have found the compliment as such less remarkable than the identification of Ursula, a virgin martyr celebrated widely across Western Christendom, as an English saint with a special relationship to the land and a genealogical relationship to the monarch. As Catherine no doubt knew, the center of the Ursuline cult was in Cologne, where the saint and her 11,000 companions were supposed to have been martyred.

The pageant does not invent Ursula's affiliation with England. She is traditionally British, and her earthly bridegroom Etherius is the son of the English king—details given wide currency through Jacobus de Voragine's *Legenda Aurea*. As may be recalled from the discussion of the *SEL Ursula* in Chapter 1, the legend in broad outline sounds much like a national myth, in which British and English communities are united though Ursula's prospective marriage and the formation of her retinue of British and English virgins, and then sanctified through their collective martyrdom. A Middle English prose legend found in Huntington Library MS 140, written some fifty years before the London pageant, underscores the legend's potential as a story of Christian origins and English cultural identity by adding a bizarre coda to the legend: after their martyrdoms, Ursula and Etherius are married in heaven, attended by Christ and the heavenly hosts.

The virgin martyr is conventionally understood to become the bride of

Christ upon her death, and traditional versions of the Ursula legend thus stage her martyrdom as an alternative to a secular marriage that would have violated her prior vow of Christian virginity. But in the Huntington legend, discussed further below, martyrdom relocates Ursula's earthly marriage to heaven, sacralizing it instead of staging its supersession by spiritual union. The London pageant follows a similar logic. In identifying Catherine of Aragon as a "second Ursula," who is to marry the second Arthur, the pageant stages their nuptials as the belated consummation of the saint's long-deferred engagement to another English prince. The pageant thus encodes a double temporality in which Ursula's betrothal is at once a foundational event in the past that is repeated in the marriage of her double, Catherine of Aragon, and, at the same time, an event that has not yet happened and is to be fulfilled at last in the marriage of the first Tudor prince.

Prior to the fifteenth century, Ursula's identification as British did not prompt any significant national, dynastic, or regional affiliations. As we saw in Chapter 1, the *SEL Ursula*, for example, does not construct a shared geographical or ethnic affiliation linking the saint and its Anglophone audience, as it does for the Anglo-Saxon saints and the British Alban. Rather than associating her with native saints, fourteenth-century vernacular textual culture, like contemporary visual traditions, represented Ursula primarily as a virgin martyr. Extant rood screens, for example, often group her with St. Margaret of Antioch, Catherine of Alexandria, Barbara, Agnes, Cecilia, and other female saints, which suggests that in a parish setting her sex was considered more significant than her ethnic identity or the geography of her legend.[2] Even in Osbern Bokenham's mid-fifteenth-century *Legendys of Hooly Wummen*, Ursula is still framed primarily in terms of her status as a female saint, even as small details register an increasing interest in her as a native one, as when Ursula's father, considering the English king's request for her hand, fears "*our* creuelnes."[3]

One vector for this emerging identification of Ursula as a native saint is the confusion of her legend with a similar narrative in Galfridian historiographic traditions.[4] In Geoffrey of Monmouth, Conanus Meriadoc, a British prince, wants Britain the Less, the colony that he founds on the Continent, to be racially pure, so he sends for girls of his own nation as brides for himself and his men. The 11,000 British girls embark, one of whom is to marry Conanus and is also the daughter of the Cornish king, Dionotus; they encounter a storm in which many drown and the rest are blown off course and slaughtered by Huns. It is not surprising that two stories featuring 11,000 virgins who travel by boat and are slaughtered by Huns were confused with one another, although the differences between them may seem to us as consequential as the parallels: where the hagiographic legend features both ethnic and religious difference—a princess who is British and Christian is compelled to marry a pagan English prince—the Galfridian narrative is about the desire for self-identity in the face of a traumatic rupture in the history of a community. In Geoffrey of Monmouth, the British Christian prince wants to marry a British Christian princess in order to replicate a British community on the Continent in the wake of the Roman conquest of Britain—a futile desire, as the double violence, natural and human, of the story's denouement makes clear.[5]

Nevertheless, Conanus's British bride, anonymous in the earliest redactions of the *History of the Kings of Britain*, ultimately comes to be identified as Ursula.[6] The *Brut*, for example, identifies the princess as St. Ursula, sometimes in image as well as in text: in Bodleian MS Laud Misc. 733, for example, the saint holding a heraldic shield appears in the margin of the text (see Figure 2).[7] Small details in the *Brut* bring the Galfridian story closer to the hagiographic legend: Ursula has "privelich" vowed her virginity to God, so that the sudden storm that blows the ships off course to Cologne is not merely an adventitious natural disaster but a miraculous event that guarantees her sacred virginity.[8] Ursula, moreover, "preaches" to her companions, exhorting them to die rather than be dishonored. So thoroughly does Galfridian history absorb the legend that Fabian's *Chronicle* (1516) is forced to confront the troubling differences between the hagiographic and historiographic traditions.[9]

Ursula's place in English historiography helped to balance the most obvious impediment to the adoption of Ursula as a native saint: the fact that her cult was centered in Cologne, site of her martyrdom. The basilica dedicated to the saint in that city displayed row upon row of head reliquaries, and its walls were decorated with innumerable bones forming repeating patterns, a macabre formal exploration of the cult's most distinctive feature: the mirroring of the saint's singular identity by the collective identity of her retinue. Cologne was a popular site of pilgrimage for English people and their fictional representatives, including the Wife of Bath.[10] Its priority as the center of the Ursuline cult persisted through the fifteenth century: William Caxton authorizes his departures from *Legenda Aurea* on the grounds that he learned details of the story while resident there.[11] Two other European cities also boasted close affiliation to the legend: Basel, which featured prominently in *Legenda Aurea* and other versions of the legend as the city from which the virgins disembark and begin their pilgrimage on foot to Rome, and which also claimed to possess Ursula's head;[12] and Bruges, where the Hospital of St. John possessed other

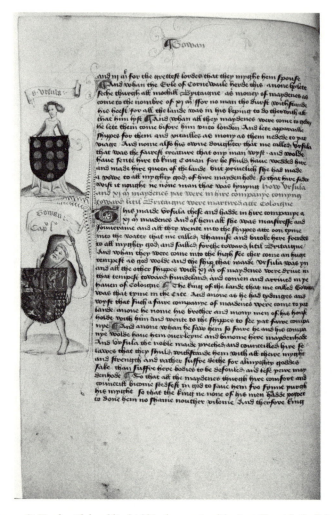

Figure 2. St. Ursula with heraldic shield in the margin of the *Brut Chronicle*. Bodleian MS
Laud Misc. 733, fol. 30v. By courtesy of the Bodleian Library, University of Oxford.

relics of St. Ursula, which were translated to Hans Memling's extraordinary
reliquary in 1489. The visual narrative presented by the six panels of Memling's
shrine begins with the virgins' arrival in Cologne and traces their affiliation
with Basel, Rome, and Cologne through realistic contemporary images of
these cities—notably ignoring her British homeland altogether.[13]

The cult's affiliations with these Continental cities point to an interurban network that might both inform the London pageant and undercut its dynastic claims.[14] Cologne and London were Hanseatic cities with an especially close trading relation: some of the London communities formed through this mercantile activity also shared devotion to St. Ursula, and the overlapping routes of pilgrimage and trade with which they were familiar pointed outward to the saint's pan-European cult. Given its staging on London Bridge, Ursula's speech suggests her identity as a London saint as much as a Tudor or English one. Indeed, from the perspective of its reception and production, the pageant must be understood within a series of multiple, overlapping categories of affiliation: Tudor, national, Continental, Christian, urban, and mercantile. If Catherine of Aragon was surprised to see St. Ursula claim a Tudor genealogy on London Bridge, she was surely not alone.

The communities at different scales associated with St. Ursula reinforced a key conceptual capability of the legend discussed in Chapter 1: as a narrative of marriage turned martyrdom, featuring a vast company of virgins who voyage by boat and on foot, the Ursula legend provided a forum for thinking about forms of community *in terms of* their scale, as well as for thinking about the *mobility of scale*. The Ursuline company is both a figure for and an alternative to the British and English kingdoms, just as the intimate company of virgins afloat at sea is a heterotopic reflection of the supranational Christian community represented by Rome and Pope Cyriacus. Given this capacity to negotiate the dramatic contraction and extension of a community, it is no wonder the legend was of such interest in a period during which England itself shifted dramatically in scale. As we will see in the first section of this chapter, the Ursula legend had connections to many of the phenomena that affected England's absolute and relative scale. To those already discussed throughout this study, the pageant's Tudor politics adds another: an emphasis on "Britishness" that had once, and soon would again, inform England's claim to sovereignty over Wales, Scotland, and Ireland. These affiliations, along with the legend's narrative images and relationships, provided a vocabulary for thinking about scale and the mobility of scale in the late Middle Ages not only as topical concerns but also as conceptual ones.

They are explored as such with particular energy by two versions of the legend written on the cusp of the sixteenth century: Edmund Hatfield's ambitious aureate verse *Lyf of Saynt Ursula*, addressed to Margaret Beaufort and written within some ten years of the London pageant, perhaps in 1509, and a prose Life included in Richard Pynson's 1516 *Kalendre of the Newe Legende of Englande*. Although both of these works promote Ursula as a native saint, and although both Hatfield and Pynson had royal patrons, neither of these legends are exclusively—or even primarily—concerned with Tudor or national forms of community. They are concerned instead with movement between and across communities that are either smaller or far larger than England, which they consider by exploring the narrative's themes of geographical mobility through formal vocabularies that enable them to represent movement across scales.

Hatfield's legend does this, above all, by using alliterative catalogs of proper names to explore the categories of sameness and multiplicity, the single and the plural. Like recent theoretical assessments of community as "inoperative," the legend uses these catalogs to suggest the paradox of community, necessarily caught between the heterogeneity of its members and the unified or collective identity embraced by, or imposed on, them. Hatfield's legend ultimately imagines community as an aggregation of discrete identities and affiliations, rather than a homeostatic communion that erases differences. Like the definition developed at the Council of Constance, Hatfield's *Lyf of Saynt Ursula* represents England as a nation that comprises discrete polities that retain their own specificity.

The exploration of scale in Pynson's prose legend, in turn, is developed by centering the story on pilgrimage, rather than martyrdom. The virgin company traverses an expansive terrain, moving between different levels of geographical specificity and generalization as they move between places, producing an elastic sense of the extension and conceptual scale of narrative space. For Pynson, the contradictions inherent in community—defined by the unstable threshold between the sameness and differences of its members and the attendant problem of boundaries, porous or impermeable—may find some resolution in the overlapping and unstable relationship *between* communities, and especially the mobility across scale these relationships often entail.[15] In the context of the dramatic re-scaling of English and Continental polities, contemporary debates about the spatial scale of national and religious community, and the stunning expansion of the known world, the Ursula legend figured movement not only from place to place, but also from scale to scale.

The first section of this chapter establishes some historical and analytical coordinates for these texts by parsing the relationship between Ursula and the several London communities with which she was affiliated at the end of the fifteenth century, especially in terms of events or phenomena that opened questions about their nature and scale. These are offered less as topical referents for the legends, however, than as historical instances of, and provocations to, the questions they explore about the nature of community and the relationship between communities at different scales. Ultimately, my interest lies in how Hatfield's and Pynson's legends explore such questions on the level of form. The kinds of social imaginings, economic practices, and political events surveyed here are significant because they condition—though they do not determine—the conceptual capabilities of the legends' formal qualities.

The Several St. Ursulas of the London Pageant

Dynastic and British St. Ursulas

From the moment her ship was in sight of the English coast, Catherine of Aragon herself may have been made to perform the dynastic allegory given explicit expression in the pageant on London Bridge. The ceremony of her arrival, accompanied by Henry VII's new barges and other well-appointed ships, might have recalled the narrative images of the Ursula legend then in vogue. Of course, the princess had perforce to arrive by boat, but the plans for her progress from Southampton to London suggest intentional citation of the legend. Catherine was to be accompanied by English ladies "all in a suyt" (all in one livery) for whom eleven palfreys were ordered, presumably one for each lady. An appendix to Pynson's *Boke of Cokery* that provides further details of the event includes a list of eleven noblewomen—four countesses and seven baronesses—who were to head a larger company of "knyghtes wyves."[16] Like St. Ursula, then, Catherine of Aragon was to be accompanied by eleven aristocratic women, with a still larger train following behind, dressed to identify them as a company. Pynson's pamphlet *A Remembraunce for the Traduction of the Princesse Kateryne* (1500), which outlines the ceremonies planned in honor of Catherine's arrival, announces in a rubric that the queen herself, Elizabeth of York, commanded that the ladies be thus arrayed.[17] Perhaps the representation of Catherine as a second Ursula was her idea too.[18] There was an established tradition of devotion to St. Ursula in the north, which had been actively cultivated by Archbishop Scrope from the beginning of the fifteenth century,[19] and this regional cult had been embraced by Yorkists. Richard of York and Cecily Neville, Elizabeth's grandparents, named their fifth daughter after the saint in 1454—incidentally the year that Richard was named protector of the realm, a key impetus to his accelerating political hopes.

Or perhaps the idea is to be attributed to her mother-in-law, Margaret Beaufort, who was, as noted above, the addressee of Hatfield's verse legend.[20]

This would make sense of the pageant's unlikely suggestion that St. Ursula and Catherine share Lancastrian blood (Catherine was the great-great-granddaughter of John of Gaunt), which also linked Catherine to her bridegroom. Although it was not the only lineage on which his claim to the throne was predicated, Henry VII's most immediate blood connection to the crown was through Gaunt: he was the great-grandson of John Beaufort, the eldest of Gaunt's children with Katherine Swynford. Catherine of Aragon and Arthur Tudor's shared Lancastrian genealogy is implicitly complementary to, even constitutive of, their shared Britishness. Arthur's very name identifies the accession of the Tudors as a return to a mythic British past, of course. The pageant reinforces this claim by underscoring the shared Britishness of Arthur and Ursula—implicitly calling on the status of St. Ursula in Galfridian historiography—and thus fashioning a union of religious and secular versions of the Tudor myth.[21] As its pairing with once and future Arthurs suggests, dynastic interest in St. Ursula is related to Tudor interest in a shift in scale from England to the archipelago.[22]

Native and International St. Ursulas

Although the Ursula pageant—a spectacle celebrating a royal wedding—is overtly concerned with a dynastic claim regarding the realm, it also creates an affiliation between the saint and the "land" that supplements royal genealogy with a geographical or spatial definition of English community. This may have been highlighted by Catherine's Ursula-like progress to London with her company of eleven noble attendants: the St. Ursula tableau on London Bridge identifies an association with English geography already performed in Catherine's own itinerary. Viewed as part of a performance that includes the princess's progress, the pageant may be seen to identify the city, on whose threshold this association is named, as a metonym for England.[23] Part of a long tradition of London civic performance that marked the conjunction of royal and urban interests, the pageant echoes the urban models for national community that, as we saw in the last three chapters, were important alternatives to the conceptualization of England as a realm.[24]

The pageant on the bridge, then, identifies London as a metonym for Britain and thus also maps this community on to a specific geography. And in this it highlights the distinctive re-scaling at work in fifteenth-century efforts to claim Ursula as a native saint: where the regional cult of St. Wenefred, for example, or the institutional one of St. Edith scaled up from local to national, the pan-European cult of St. Ursula had to be scaled down to claim her as an English saint. The London pageant, whose metonymic function highlights this downsizing, should thus also be understood in relation to supranational communities, as is suggested by its address to the Spanish princess who hailed from perhaps the most cosmopolitan court in Western Europe.[25]

Indeed, considered from this perspective, the pageant may be more fundamentally concerned with England's shrinking scale than with the Tudor fantasy of a British archipelago evoked in the verses. The London pageant marks a point of historical coincidence, in the person of Catherine of Aragon, between the recent identification of Ursula as a native saint and her expanding New World cult. Catherine was a girl of nine, resident at her parents' court, when Columbus returned in 1494 from his second voyage, on which he discovered an archipelago in the Caribbean whose islands were so numerous they seemed beyond count. As Bartolomé de las Casas recounts, Columbus named the largest one St. Ursula and lumped together the rest—"todos las otras"—as the Eleven Thousand Virgins: we still know the islands dedicated to "Santa Orsola y las onze mil virgenes" as the Virgin Islands.[26] Catherine's nuptial retinue included her tutor and confessor Alessandro Geraldini, well known for his support of Columbus and later the first bishop resident in the Caribbean.[27] For Catherine and some of her companions, St. Ursula may thus have represented itineraries well beyond the familiar geography of European Christianity.

Among its most obvious effects, New World exploration changed paradigms of space and scale. In its wake, England, a small island long positioned at the "edge of the world," was now located on a still more expansive map.[28] This massive shift was, moreover, accompanied by other more proximate and immediately consequential forces reconfiguring the scale of English community. England had recently lost much of its Continental territory, retracting to its own shores at a time when Continental polities amalgamated smaller realms, scaling up to roughly the size they have today as nation-states. Catherine's immanent wedding was itself directly related to England's newly insular status and this re-scaling of Continental polities: an important impetus for the alliance between England and Spain was their mutual desire to prevent France from annexing the sovereign duchy of Brittany after the death of Duke Francis II (d. 1488).[29]

As it happens, St. Ursula figures prominently in this contest as well. Anne of Brittany worked energetically to avoid marriage to Charles VIII and the loss of Breton sovereignty it would entail, and she enlisted Ursula as her patron

Figure 3. Anne of Brittany with her patron saints St. Anne, St. Ursula, and
St. Helen. Grandes Heures, Bibliothèque Nationale MS lat. 9474, fol. 3.
Reproduced by permission of the Bibliothèque Nationale.

saint in this effort. The stunning book of hours produced for her by Jean Bour-
dichon shows Anne backed by the saint, who carries the Breton banner of
arms, decorated with ermine (see Figure 3).[30] Hailing from the Galfridian legend, this Ursula represents a Britain that encompassed considerable Continental territories. Anne of Brittany, alas, was not as successful as St. Ursula in
eluding marriage to a neighboring king with superior military power: in 1491,
besieged at Rennes, she was compelled to marry Charles VIII and cede to him
sovereignty of her duchy.[31] Brittany had long been an urgent strategic concern
for England: the duchy was an important ally and bulwark against the French.
Indeed, before becoming duchess after the death of her father, Anne had been
betrothed to the ill-fated Edward, Prince of Wales, to advance the long-
standing alliance between England and Brittany. As duchess, she carefully

cultivated ties with Henry VII, who was as keen to retain Brittany as a friendly toehold on the Continent as Anne was to maintain its sovereignty.

The failure of Anne's efforts had significant implications for England, as well as for Brittany, and, as I noted above, the newly unified and enlarged France gave urgency to the long-discussed prospect of the Anglo-Spanish marriage.[32] Perhaps when the saint in the London pageant calls Catherine of Aragon a "second Ursula," some—including the savvy princess—would have understood that her affiliation with Ursula replaced Anne of Brittany's. Following close upon the annexation of Burgundy and Picardy in the 1470s, France's absorption of Brittany signaled, for all practical purposes, the end of England's Continental ambitions beyond the pale of Calais. Even its insular territory was threatened: France now controlled the southern coast of the Channel in its entirety, and England's border was suddenly its own shore.[33]

The failure to counter France's growing size and strength as it annexed smaller kingdoms and duchies is thus an immediate context for Catherine of Aragon's arrival in London, and so also for the London pageant's presentation of Ursula as a saint of "this land." Affiliated with and addressed by St. Ursula as a native saint, the Spanish princess connects the pageant's representation of England to the changing scale of European polities, as well as to the re-scaling of the world as a whole through Atlantic exploration, where the innumerable islands of another archipelago now also claimed an association with the saint.

Urban Ursulas

Shifts in the scale of English and European polities were important not only to the dynasties immediately involved. As a symbol of Brittany's sovereignty, St. Ursula represented geopolitical and economic concerns relevant to a broad swath of English merchants and aristocrats, concerns we have seen expressed in the *Libelle of Englyshe Polycye*, with its insistence on the importance of the Channel to English trade. The pageant Ursula also signifies in the context of London's place in an extranational web of port cities and trading communities, above all the Hanseatic League. If St. Ursula is associated with a nascent sense of national identity, that is, her cult also intersects with an important alternative to the nation, transurban networks of trade and law.[34] St. Ursula's primary cult site, the Hanseatic city of Cologne, was also home to London's largest and most important community of alien merchants, the Steelyard: their devotion to Ursula may have limited any particular claims that the Tudors made on the Ursuline cult, at least in London.[35] The staging of the Ursula pageant on London Bridge, the boundary of the city that conferred their privileges and status, may be significant in this regard as well.[36]

Trade between London and Cologne was so important to both cities that Cologne had in fact distanced itself from the Hanse, whose status in England deteriorated in the late fifteenth century.[37] The English revoked some of the Hanse's erstwhile privileges in 1447; in the period from 1468 to 1473, England and the Hanseatic League were effectively at war.[38] Cologne merchants, however, who conducted much of the international cloth trade in London, had forged a relationship with England independent of the league, and they were granted important exemptions from some of the legal actions taken against other members.[39] In 1468, for example, when the warehouses of other Hanseatic communities were sealed, those of Cologne merchants were exempt. Even after some of these tensions were resolved, Cologne retained elements of its separate status and special privileges.[40]

Some English merchants' interest in St. Ursula may be attributed to contact with their Steelyard colleagues and trade with Cologne.[41] There was a chapel devoted to St. Ursula "in the pultry," that is, Cheapside, a neighborhood of mercers.[42] The Confraternity of St. Ursula at St. Lawrence Jewry, which is unattested in the 1389 Guild returns, was of sufficient numbers and prominence by the early sixteenth century that it had a devotional image printed (see Figure 4).[43] Thomas Hutchen, citizen and mercer, left money in his 1524 will to have his name enrolled in the guild's bederoll, while Margaret Pynkton left a torch to the fraternity.[44] A London pewterer who left money to a "penny guild" of St. Ursula may have dealt with Steelyard merchants, who played an important role in the overseas pewter trade, or he may have been a merchant himself, a shift in vocation characteristic of pewterers in this period.[45]

London civic drama also reflects the economic affiliations of a thriving urban cult of St. Ursula.[46] The Drapers' Lord Mayors Show that welcomed the king of Denmark in 1522 included a new pageant of the legend, performed by the daughters of guild members. Ursula was played by "Child's eldest daughter," who was attended by six other "virgins," one of whom—"Gally's daughter"—seems to have gotten too close to one of the torches: the list of expenses includes a charge for her "fyn smok" that was damaged as a result.[47] The pageant was presented by the Drapers again in 1529, evidence that at that date the city's identification with the cult was still routed through merchant communities with strong ties to Cologne.[48] When Elizabeth of York gave three shillings and four pence to "the bretherhed of Saint Ursela in London"

Figure 4. Image of St. Ursula printed on behalf of the Confraternity of St. Ursula at St. Lawrence Jewry, dedicated to the saint (London, s.n.). © British Library Board. Shelfmark C.18.e.2.

in December 1502, she may have intended to advance Tudor affiliation with the saint, as the pageant honoring Catherine of Aragon the year before had done, but she also thereby acknowledged Ursula as a London saint, the saint of a city of English and Continental merchants and traders.[49]

This mercantile community may have had special access to the historical irony of Tudor appropriation of St. Ursula at precisely the moment that the cult expanded to the New World. The *London Chronicle* records that in 1498, just three years before the pageant, Henry VII supplied a fleet of ships at the "besy request and Supplicacion of a Straunger Venisian"—that is, the Genoese-born merchant John Cabot—"to seche an Iland, wheryn the said Straunger Surmysed to be grete comodities" (to seek an island wherein the stranger surmised that there were vast commodities).[50] The chronicler notes with condescension that Cabot had only armchair knowledge of the New World: he had "by a Caart made hym self expert in knowing of the world" (with a map made himself expert in knowing about the world). Although we cannot know whether this map identified the Caribbean archipelago of St. Ursula and the 11,000 Virgins, we can assume the presence in London of merchants and civic leaders whose growing interest in the cult as a local or a national phenomenon coexisted with a curiosity like Cabot's in faraway islands.[51]

As its dating by mayoral, not regnal, year signals, the *London Chronicle* tells the history of London as an urban node in an international network, located in the realm but not reducible to it, and it is in this framework that it presents the news of New World discovery. So too the London pageant, even as it explicitly addresses Tudor political authority, indexes St. Ursula's affiliation with the city and the networks of trade in which it participated. Organized and hosted by city officials—if under the watchful eye of some of Henry VII's commissioners—the pageant is poised between multiple forms of urban, national, and supranational community. The urban audience of the London pageant may have been especially alert to the shifts between these different scales of community, which had practical, economic, and imaginative consequences for them.

The pageant thus helps us see the dynamic relationship between several communities that Ursula might represent as a native "British" saint—London, English, or Tudor—and the other communities or spaces with which she was affiliated, whether Continental polities, the Hanseatic League, or the New World. Indeed, these forms of community are precariously and intricately related: as we have seen, the effort to proclaim Tudor legitimacy through the British saint is linked to the impact of Breton politics on English national concerns and therefore on their dynastic remedy, the alliance with Spain in the person of Catherine of Aragon, who in turn marks a point of intersection with England's relationship both to the Continent and to the New World. At the same time, the saint's affiliation with London points to supranational trading networks, such as the Hanseatic League and merchant communities in London, which also point outward to exploration across the Atlantic.

English Ursula in Huntington Library MS 140

If, as the London pageant suggests, St. Ursula could index a complex and changing system of communities, she could also represent a unified and stable community, much like her virgin company, as she does in the eccentric prose legend found in Huntington Library MS 140 and in the version that Caxton includes in his *Golden Legend*. As mentioned briefly above, the Huntington Ursula legend violates the expectations of the genre when the martyred Ursula marries her earthly bridegroom in heaven, rather than Christ, the divine Spouse. In a strikingly matter-of-fact sentence, the legend concludes, "And so she was wedded that day to the kyng of Englond full gloriously byfore the kyng of heven, wither she and all her felyship bring us all thurgh their vertues, merytes, and prayers" (359–60).[52] This bizarre revision of the story emphasizes the usefulness of the legend's nuptial vocabulary and marriage plot for representing a form of English community in which ethnic differences and historical change have been effaced—British and English, Christian and pagan, joined in a mystical marriage.

This nationalist project registers in the legend's manuscript context. The Huntington manuscript comprises two separate books dated between 1456 and 1467, both owned by one William Turner in the sixteenth century: the first contains Bokenham's *Mappula Angliae*, along with poems of topical political concern, and the second gathers together the *Libelle of Englysche Polycye*, a Latin prose *Apollonius of Tyre*, and the prose Ursula, as well as English and Latin poems in her honor (353).[53] In this textual company, small revisions to the story to develop its local import stand out. The English king is no longer simply an aggressor: his "many sore threatenynges" (many grievous threats) are softened by "many grete plesaunt promyssions" (many very pleasant promises). The legend's unusual reference to the dispersed origins of the virgin company—they have been "gadered and chosen oute of dyuers reames and came to-gyder in Brytayne" (gathered and chosen from diverse realms and came together in Britain)—echoes the definition of England as a nation formulated at the Council of Constance, where, as we have seen, England claimed its status as a "nation" on the grounds that it comprised several discrete polities. The audience that assembles to wonder at this "newe goostly chevalry" (new spiritual chivalry) also represents diverse polities, "many contrayes and kyngdomes," as well as a mix of religious and secular jurisdictions, represented by "worthy lordis and ladyes, both spirituell and temperall." Most striking, the virgin company collapses territorial or spatial difference: the community gathers in "Englond and Brytayne," as though these formed one coherent space (357). The virgins themselves, like the space they occupy, are undifferentiated, lacking even the number that traditionally offers some register of their plurality: against the weight of tradition counting Ursula's companions at 11,000, the prose legend claims that the number is not known: "the which number in all no creature knoweth, but oonly God" (which number in total no creature knows except only God) (359).

It is worth pausing here to consider the conceptualization of virginity that grounds this idea of corporate identity. Lydgate's short devotional poem addressed to St. Ursula and the 11,000 Virgins parses it with particular care: the poem reminds the Ursuline company that, having "avowyd in [their] tendir age / To persevere in virginal clennesse," they are granted entrance into an undifferentiated communion of saints, a community they already anticipate in their collective identity.[54] Hence the poem accounts for the virgin saints in groups of one thousand, the smallest unit of identity it recognizes: they are hailed as "O ye maidenys, of thousands ful helleuene" (O ye maidens, of thousands a complete eleven) (9). Lydgate underscores their shared, homeostatic identity through a pun: the roses and lilies with which the virgins are crowned, conventional symbols of martyrdom and virginity, are a "Fressh, undiffadid, tokne of your maydenheede" (16). "Undiffadid" means "unfaded" and forms a doublet with its near synonym, "fresh": the freshness of the flowers figures virginity as a form of purity so absolute that it exempts the girls from physical decay, indeed from time itself. But "undiffadid" is a *hapax legomenon*, the unique attested instance of the negative form of "diffadid," indeed perhaps a nonce word, and its rarity encourages us to hear a pun on "undivided" as well.[55] The pun marks the perpetual freshness of virginity as the condition of, and corollary to, their collective identity, and it thus recognizes virginity as a differently scaled form of a corporate identity that is likewise "sealed" off from others, like the community in which they participate, similarly understood as bounded, discrete, and unified.

The Huntington prose legend extends this conceptualization of virginity as the ground of a corporate identity by linking it more closely to the medieval paradigm of marriage as an absolute union of two persons. Rather than permanently forestalling the conjunction of British Christian and pagan English communities as it does in all other versions of the legend, Ursula's martyrdom-cum-marriage in the Huntington legend *precipitates* the most perfect form of this union in the sacralized marriage of two martyrs. Ursula and Etherius, after their apotheosis and marriage, represent the full eclipse of Ursula's Britishness by her English groom, as well as the full merging of spiritual and political authority, anticipated by the audience of "spiritual and temporal" lords and ladies who once gathered to witness the formation of the virgin company.

*   *   *

The only other copy of this prose legend is found in Southwell Minster MS 7, a late exemplar of Mirk's *Festial* that includes a selection of *Prose SEL* Lives of English saints, discussed above in Chapter 4. With its account of pilgrimage to Cologne and Rome, the Ursula legend, which precedes these other native saints' Lives, forms a narrative bridge between the *Festial*'s sanctorale, which ranges over Western Christendom, and the specifically English community figured by the *Prose SEL* legends. In this use of the Ursula legend as the narrative threshold for the Anglo-Saxon saints' Lives, Southwell Minster MS 7 imagines English national identity as a framework for participation in a larger Christian world: national affiliation registers here as a fundamental aspect of identity, one that structures even religious identification.[56] The scribe of the Southwell Minster manuscript nevertheless balked at the substitution of Etherius for Christ in Ursula's spiritual wedding. The narrative stutters into silence rather than recount Ursula's postmortem marriage to an earthly groom: she was, it reads, "weddyd that daye to the kyng of befor the kyng of hevyn."[57] The lacuna restores the suspension of Ursula's earthly marriage, and so also the legend's capacity to gesture ambivalently to both an idea of a discrete national identity and an expansive and open-framed Christian identity.

Although Ursula's heavenly marriage to Etherius is unique to the Huntington legend, it finds an echo in Caxton's version of the legend, which also emphasizes marriage as a figure for the dissolution of discrete identities into a single shared one. The English king wants Ursula "coupled to his sone by maryage" (336r): the turn of phrase, with its suggestion of both sexual coupling and a medieval theory of marriage in which two bodies are coupled in one will, underscores marriage as a form of communion that depends on the erasure of the wife's identity in the supervening structure of her husband's name and person.[58] This model of marriage, in turn, signals Caxton's interest in the creation of a homogeneous community, expressed in his most significant departure from the Ursula tradition: he identifies all of Ursula's companions as English, not British or a mixed company of the two. Rather than a relationship between Britain and England, they stand as a comprehensive sampling of England: "Thenne virgynes cam fro alle partyes / and men cam for to see this grete companye" (then virgins came from all the areas and men came to see this great company) (336v).[59]

*   *   *

If the London pageant and these nationalist versions of the Ursula legend imagine English community as a structure that subordinates particular or local differences to a putatively homogeneous corporate identity, other versions put such differences in dynamic, unresolved relation to one another. The legend facilitates both of these ideas of community through the figure of Ursula's virgin company, the 11,000 companions who either replicate or multiply Ursula's own virginal (intact, discrete) identity. As we will see, the second form of community, defined by its plural and thus diverse members, proved especially useful at the end of the century for thinking about both the complexity and the unstable scale of English community.

This is most strikingly the case in Hatfield's aureate verse *Lyf of Saynt Ursula*. In most versions of the legend, the 11,000 virgins differ from Ursula primarily in their namelessness, their lack of particularized identity. Hatfield's legend, in contrast, gives them proper names, along with family identities and geographical origins, in alliterative catalogs. The names, as marks of particular identity, point to a form of community defined by its internal heterogeneity. This desire for particularity and differentiation allows us to identity Hatfield's legend as "archipelagic," understood conceptually, if not necessarily topically: that is, it is a forum for representing local and discrete identities as they are aggregated into larger complex forms.

Archipelagic Ursula

Like the London pageant, Hatfield's *Lyf* is affiliated with Tudor politics. As has already been noted, Hatfield, a Benedictine monk of Rochester Abbey, specifically addresses this long verse legend to Margaret Beaufort, the imposing Lancastrian dowager and mother of Henry VII.[60] The poem reflects and advertises Margaret's vaunted personal devotion and keen interest in British saints and, implicitly, the Tudor affiliations of St. Ursula we saw heralded in the London pageant. Aside from the closing address to her, however, the legend does not develop Ursula's significance as a dynastic saint. It is more overtly concerned with the difficulty of claiming Ursula as an English saint against her long-standing association with Cologne, an effort that accounts at least partly for its length and strenuous display of a self-consciously literary vernacular. The competing claims of the English and Cologne cults quite literally structure the poem: Hatfield first tells a version of the legend from the "Chronicles of England"—that is, the historiographic tradition founded by Geoffrey of Monmouth's *History of the Kings of Britain*—before turning to the "Cologne" legend, which more closely parallels the *Legenda Aurea* version of the story.

Although narrative priority is given to the Galfridian version of the legend, Hatfield identifies the "Cologne legend' as the more accurate account. The "chefe cause of varyaunce" between the two versions, he avers, is the religious violence to which England, like the saint, has been victim.[61] The Huns who martyr Ursula and her company next invade England and destroy its written records: "all bokes of allegaunce," that is, all authoritative books, with a pun on allegiance to Britain as well as to the truth:

So was this londe replete with folkes extraneous
Whiche had the actes of brytayne in derysyon
And brente theyr bokes for false and erroneous

Also the cronycles in processe ben contryued
After the actes not made Immedyatly
But now of late tyme not perfytly dystryued
Wherfore the brytayns counted one company
The holy vyrgyns with the women innumerably
Whiche with the stormes by see were drowned all
Her hystory of Colen declareth the contrary
As shall ensewe the trewe memoryall (2r–2v)

[So was this land full of foreign peoples
Who had the deeds of Britain in contempt
And burned their books as false and erroneous

Also the chronicles as a result are invented
After the events, not made immediately
But now at a later time, not accurately recounted.

For this reason, the Britains counted as one company
The holy virgins indiscriminately with the women
Who were all drowned at sea by the storms.
Their history from Cologne declares the contrary,
The true record, as follows].

English cultural memory is forever corrupted by the violence of invasion. But rather than compromise the authority of the English cult, the lacuna—parallel to Ursula's martyrdom as another function of pagan violence—intensifies it. The association between the saint's story and the national historiography that (imperfectly) remembers it underscores England's vulnerability as an island nation: England is a figural double for Ursula's boat, alike menaced by marauding pagans.

As even this brief summary may suggest, the legend's interest in place and community exceeds the immediate topical concern about Cologne's precedence as home of the Ursuline cult. The Galfridian legend draws attention to the discontinuities in the geographic and ethnographic identity of Britain. Britain is, in Geoffrey's account of the Roman period, both the island occupied by Rome and a Continental colony led by a British prince. It is a story, that is, about the contingencies of place: Britain remade as a Roman colony, Brittany remade as a British one. It thereby disassociates geography and ethnic community, a theme expressed graphically in the deaths of the 11,000 British brides meant to ensure the ethnic purity of Conanus's colony. English community, defined in ethnographic or political terms, is unmoored from stable geographical referents, just as its cultural memory is unmoored from the past by a history of invasion.

The second section of the poem, the narrative according to the "Cologne" legend, shifts the terms of geographical displacement to something more abstract. Instead of movement across geographical space—such as Conanus forced to refound Britain on the Continent—Hatfield experiments with movement across geographical *scale*, dislocating the places of the legend through their magnification or particularization. This is accomplished especially through the lists of the proper names he supplies for members of Ursula's company. Hatfield devotes separate verse chapters to the names of the virgins, bishops, and kings in Ursula's retinue. By figuring discrete identities within a larger collective, the lists extend the legend's capacity for thinking about forms of community that preserve internal difference and identity.

The legend does not, of course, provide names for all 11,000 British girls. But the itemized catalog of proper names supplements the general representation of their anonymous plentitude—the unthinkably large number of 11,000—with a particularized figure of abundance. The list of virgins begins as follows:

> Aboue all other these fyue were pryncypall
> Ursula was fyrst to cryste that cast her courage
> The nexte Nynnosa of her orygynall
> Cordula the thyrde doughter of an erle sage
> Her legende sheweth she was of Ursulaes lygnage
> The fourthe Eleutheria doughter to Ursulaes aunt
> The fyfth Florencia ryght wyse but yonge of age
> Doughter of a kynge in the fayth of cryste flagraunt (fol. 4r)

> [Above all other these five were foremost:
> Ursula was first who cast her love on Christ
> The next, Ninnosa, of her ancestry,
> Cordula, the third daughter of a wise earl—
> Her legend shows she was of Ursula's lineage—
> The fourth, Eleutheria, daughter to Ursula's aunt,
> The fifth, Florencia, very wise though young in age,
> Daughter of a king fervent in the faith of Christ].

While Ninnosa, Cordula, and Eleutheria are identified as Ursula's kin, Florencia, daughter of a different king, represents both a separate lineage and another polity. As the list continues, the sense of a community as an aggregate of distinct kin groups becomes a defining feature, especially in contrast to the figure of homogeneous community that the 11,000 virgins usually represent. See, for example, the second stanza listing the eleven "chefe guydes," along with their sundry kin, who are next in precedence:

> The fourth Sapiencia doughter of a prynce prudent
> With her two systers Eulalia and Serene
> The fyfth Carpafora of a kynge procedent
> With Eutropped & Pallidore systers & virgyns clene
> The syxte Columba to a thousande dyde preuene
> With Cordula her syster of a kynge generate
> The seuenth Benedicta with her foure systers shene
> To her obedyence a thousand congregate (fol. 4v)

[The fourth, Sapiencia, daughter of a prudent prince,
With her two sisters, Eulalia and Serene,
The fifth, Carpafora, descended from a king,
With Eutropped and Pallidore, sisters and pure virgins,
The sixth, Columba, to a thousand did act as guide,
With Cordula, her sister, fathered by a king,
The seventh, Benedicta, with her four beautiful sisters,
A thousand gather under her authority].

Hatfield's legend thus replaces the homogeneity of the virgin company—
11,000 anonymous and undifferentiated virgin martyrs—with a new particularity. Although there is little individualizing detail in these lists, the
frequency of unusual names has a similar force: it produces the effect of historical specificity. This is true with the lists of kings and bishops as well, who
more categorically represent territorial jurisdictions and thus the variegated
nature of the Ursuline company.[62]

Another function of these lists is to address a material fact that troubled
the Cologne cult. In addition to the bodies of young women, the bonefield
where the Ursuline relics were unearthed contained the remains of older
women, men, and children. To save appearances, the legend came to include
kings and bishops, as well as married women and their children in Ursula's
retinue.[63] Caxton's *Golden Legend* version explains that the figure of 11,000
accounts only for the virgins: an additional 15,000 male members of the Ursuline retinue make a grand total of 26,000 martyrs.[64] Presumably to fortify
such claims, some legends in the Cologne tradition provide lists of proper
names: Hatfield's lists derive from this tradition, most likely from the *Epistola
ad vergines christi uniuersas super historia nova undecim milium virginum*,
also known as the *Passio sive historia undecim milium virginum*, printed in
Cologne as early as 1482 and several times thereafter.[65]

These catalogs of names approximate similar ones in historiographical
traditions, but they are nonce identities that cannot locate the legend in historical time.[66] Indeed, they are antithetical even to narrative time, insofar as
they displace a sequential account of events. The names instead magnify the
spatial coordinates of the legend by figuring a multitude of political spaces.
Note that they magnify in the mode of a microscope: through differentiation,
the increasing particularization of component parts, rather than through expansion. The legend figures extension in space as an effect not of expansive
territorial coordinates, but rather of increased specificity or localization.

Despite its Tudor affiliations, the legend does not understand Ursula's "Britain" as a warrant for English hegemony over other ethnic or political communities in the archipelago, but as a discrete polity that participates in a complex system of realms and religious jurisdictions, whose kings and bishops rival Ursula's virgins in number.

Spatial extension, that is, is mapped by individual bodies, represented by proper names. These names may be read both as a special instance of the trope by which the body figures a community, and—especially in the case of the virgins—as a counterweight to this trope. The virgins' proper names signal their individuated or finite identities: that is, the absolute particularity of their perfectly "intact" bodies. At the same time, this very quality links Ursula's companions: virginity is the category of identity on which their affiliation is predicated. Although this dynamic is especially pronounced in the case of the virgins, it informs the status of the kings and bishops too: tropes of virginal intactness are hyperbolic instantiations of a more general habit of thought in which the human body—as the location and limit of sensation, memory, and desire—figures the limits of an identity that distinguishes one person from another. All members of Ursula's retinue hover between the singular identity represented by individual embodiment and a collective one formed through pilgrimage and, ultimately, martyrdom.

Hatfield's legend thus identifies the individual body as the basic unit of community even as it explores the uncertain relationship the body has to corporate metaphors of community. Fantasies of national community and shared history—such as Galfridian history—are corruptible precisely because they extend beyond the cognitive, affective, and biological capacities of any one person. In the place of the *communal*, then, Hatfield's legend insists on the *aggregate*: the virgins, along with the kings and bishops who accompany them, hail from different kingdoms and different lineages—singular, finite communities within an England recognized as an aggregate of local places and identities.

The paradoxical and reciprocal relationship between singularity and community figured by the lists of proper names also impels Hatfield's pervasive use of alliteration, evident in the passages quoted above and, for example, in the introduction of Ursula herself:

A mayde Immaculate and chaste contynually
The prynte af pleasaunce in prudence prerogate
This vyrent vyrgyn in vertue venerable
Was named Ursula heyre apparent to the lande (fol. 2v)

[A maid immaculate and continually chaste,
The impress of (divine) love, absolute in prudence.
This verdant virgin, venerable in virtue,
Was named Ursula, heir apparent to the land].

The verse form of Hatfield's legend draws attention to measured intervals of time through its meter and the rhyme pattern of its stanzaic form. But this is secondary to the alliterative display in lines such as these. To a greater degree even than rhyme, alliteration is a prosodic technique based on proximity, and in Hatfield's poem, it reproduces on the level of the line the spatial logic that we have seen on the level of theme. This is especially true in the stanzas devoted to proper names, where their proximity—given aesthetic value precisely through alliteration—draws attention to the spatial relationships the names represent. At the same time, Hatfield identifies the rhythmic—which is to say temporal—constraints of prosody as antithetical to the legend's poetics of naming:

Theyr holy names to expresse I entende
Of all the pryncypall after the trewe hystory
Tho that I can not in ryme all comprehende
Labour the entent and lette the sounde passe by
Theyr holy names to the ryme may not applye
To vary the sense for soundynge of a syllable
I holde not best leste some wolde thynke contrary
And Iuge this wrytynge forged or fallyble (fol. 4r)

[I intend to express the holy names,
Of all the principals, according to the true history,
Even though I cannot encompass them all in rhyme.
Attend to the intention and let the sound pass by;
Their holy names to the rhyme might not correspond;
To vary the sense on account of the sound of a syllable
I hold not the best, lest some will think contrary,
And judge this writing forged or fallible].

While the names are difficult to fit into the rhyme scheme, they are amenable to alliteration, whose formal demands, in turn, encourage Hatfield's aureation: the poem's self-consciously literary and sometimes invented vocabulary—*lucydently, patefy, virent, prevene*—expands the number of alliterative possibilities. Just as the sameness or shared identity of the 11,000 virgins generates the particularity of proper names, the sameness demanded by alliteration—the repetition of an initial sound—is an impetus to a special kind of particularity: the production of a hyperspecialized literary vocabulary. The formal protocols of the poem, which work by the multiplication and particularization of sameness, mimic the narrative logic of the legend.

Hatfield registers his departure from established models of political community by worrying out loud that some readers will be suspicious of, or confused by, the long list of kings. He explains this as a matter of historical difference: there was "Not than as now one [king] in a londe reygnynge" (fol. 5r, unpaginated). This is true of the new geopolitical reality on the Continent where, as we have seen, France and Spain had annexed and unified smaller sovereign states into much larger ones. There actually *were* fewer kings in Hatfield's day, at least across the Channel, and this re-scaling of European polities informs England's relative scale, important to its cultural identity. Indeed we can provide a genealogy for the legend's thematic and formal interest in the aggregation of discrete elements—what we might call its archipelagic poetics—in the conjunction of England's new insularity and Tudor efforts to fashion a greater Britain through dynastic association with Wales and the alliance with Scotland through Princess Margaret's betrothal to James in 1502.[67] These were important factors in the emergence of an "archipelagic" idea of Britain, one paralleled by the definition of England as a "general nation" in the context of church councils. We might suspect that the appeal of the Cologne version of the Ursula legend at this moment, when England was being reimagined as an island within an archipelago, lies precisely in its shift away from the generic identity of the 11,000 virgins to their individuation within an aggregate community. The Cologne legend enters English literary culture in a poem, commissioned by Margaret Beaufort, that speaks to English insularity less in terms of finitude or isolation than in terms of the relations to other spaces that define any bounded place. Tellingly, it enters Welsh vernacular literature in this period as well: Hugh Pennant translated the Herman Joseph legend within a decade of Hatfield's poem, in what was perhaps the first Welsh-language version of the legend.[68] The model the legend posits for retaining a discrete identity within a larger composite evidently held some appeal too for other "British" communities, whose distinct cultural identity was at greater risk.

The poem's conceptual and formal interest in multiplication and particularization is also a corollary to the sudden, radical opening up of political, economic, and religious space through New World exploration with which

Hatfield's poem is contemporary. If the proper names representing bounded identities speak to a desire for national definition vis-à-vis Continental polities, they may also index a deeper desire for finitude within an expanding world. While on the Continent, small polities were consolidating into larger realms, producing a narrower set of political communities in a familiar geography, the scale of the known world was expanding dramatically as explorers returned from across the Atlantic, where there were innumerable islands to be named. Hatfield's *Lyf* writes the proliferation of names as a phenomenon of the past, but it was a phenomenon of the present too. Just as Columbus turned to the Ursula legend to name the Caribbean archipelago he discovered on his second voyage, Hatfield turns to it as a narrative structure for exploring the shifting scale of English community.

Such topical pressures, however, are less central to Hatfield's poem than their conceptual analogues. Like other works we have analyzed, Hatfield's poem is concerned with the fine line between being-in-common and communion, between singular and collective forms of identity, and between embodiment as the irreducible ground of community and its limit.

St. Ursula of Britain and the Mobility of Scale

In the Ursula legend that Richard Pynson included in the *Kalendre of the Newe Legende of Englande*, similar conceptual concerns are figured by infant members of the Ursuline company who miraculously do not encumber their mothers. The legend dwells on the infants' perfect self-enclosure: they receive insubstantial sustenance by sucking their own fingers, and so they have no need to nurse or, as the legend notes, to urinate or defecate. Exemplary virgins, they define the company in terms of hermetic self-identity, thus modeling a community defined by absolute communion. Significantly, this form of community is theorized by re-scaling the virgin's body from that of the marriage-age girl to the babe in arms. Through the narrative figures of the infants, the legend links the integrity of the body to its *finitude*, an especially striking emphasis in the context of the avowedly nationalist *Kalendre*, which seeks to re-scale Ursula's supranational cult as an English one. The *Kalendre* legend, however, also develops alternatives to this kind of perfectly insular community in its exploration of how even a bounded community is defined by its relationships to other communities. Even as its scale shrinks, the Ursuline community is oriented outward. Where the London pageant directs

Catherine of Aragon toward the heart of London, in a trajectory that traces England's own contraction within its insular boundaries, Pynson's Ursula legend is oriented toward a larger, more abstract space, a mobility of scale that is in part a paradoxical effect of the finite bodies of its members.

The *Kalendre of the Newe Legende of Englande* itself is an effort to re-scale little-known regional saints as English ones, and the Ursula legend—developing the conceptual resources the story provides for thinking about such shifts in scale—can be read as a meditation on, or reaction to, this project. In its preoccupation with finite spaces that render scale more flexible or elastic, the Ursula legend may serve especially as a useful tool for thinking about England's residual and recently renewed claims for sovereignty over Wales, Ireland, and Scotland. These claims are an avowed project of the *Kalendre*, which asserts that saints representing these communities are included in the volume on the grounds that they of "veray ryght owe to be subiecte & obedyent to this Realme of Englonde" (prologue, n.p.).[69] Printed just a few years after the defeat of James IV at Flodden Field, Pynson's legend is written at a moment of special elasticity in England's scale, at a moment when Tudor politics asserted such dominance anew, after a long period during which it languished in practice.

*   *   *

Simply by virtue of its inclusion in the 1516 *Kalendre of the Newe Legende of Englande*, Pynson's Ursula legend seems to represent a much stronger endorsement of Ursula's status as a national saint than Hatfield's. Pynson's introduction to the volume—which rivals earlier supranational legendaries in scope and heft with its 164 saints—argues for the special affiliation between native saints, "our auncestours neyghboures and frendes" and his Anglophone audience, who are "moche bounden to loue theym & honoure them" (prologue, n.p.). This nationalist agenda shapes some details of the Ursula legend: Ursula is identified as English, not British, while the English king is deprived of his geographical affiliation to become a placeless pagan, "a certen kynge beynge a paynym" (a certain king who was a pagan) (108v).[70] The conventional reference to how far Ursula's fame has spread—"into many countreys and landes so farre"—distances this pagan king from her homeland, identified as "moche Brytane nowe callyd Englonde (108r). Ursula's Britain is thus the earlier identification of a national community linked by geography and a continuous chronology to contemporary England.

But St. Ursula is not fully integrated into this collection. She stands out, in the first place, as a familiar saint among the unfamiliar Anglo-Saxon names, which blur together in the alphabetical index: Ursula appears late in the list of names beginning with "w" that includes Walburge, Walleno, Walstan, Wenefrid, Werburge, Wilfrid, Wyro, and so on.[71] More striking still is the difference in the legend's narrative style and length. The other legends are notably abbreviated—Pynson explains that this is why he calls it a calendar—many running fewer than fifteen lines in the modern edition, with longer entries generally limited to around fifty. Whereas entries for the Anglo-Saxon saints focus on historical, institutional, and geographical details, and offer only a cursory narrative of their lives, the Ursula legend, some four times the length of the other entries, gives an uncommonly full version of the narrative that includes details unprecedented in any other Middle English version.[72] Its difference from the rest of the volume signals a departure from the territorial and ethnographic understanding of English identity inherent in the idea that the Anglo-Saxon saints are "ancestors" to its Anglophone audience, as well as from the volume's presentation of "England" as the normative scale of religious identity.

Indeed, England serves primarily as a point of departure in a narrative of travel: to a far greater degree than any other Middle English version of the legend, this one is preoccupied with pilgrimage, which commands so much narrative attention that even the mass martyrdom of the Ursuline virgins seems secondary. Notably, in the pilgrimage story, specific locations are less important than mobility itself: the sacred nature of Ursula's company is evidenced above all by immunity from the material and practical concerns that usually attend travel. The virgins are miraculously spared the possibility and danger of getting lost and also the attendant anxiety about reaching the day's intended destination or finding a place to spend the night, as well as the usual challenges of traveling with small children. The company's wonderful mobility, which sometimes condenses and sometimes dilates distance and time, renders abstract the relationships between Cologne, Basel, and Rome, the legend's conventional geographical coordinates. Indeed, the absence of any of the friction—social, material, or epistemological—usually produced by movement through space effectively unmoors the narrative from geography.

The pagan prince whom Ursula is to marry and the persecutors who will slaughter them are, in contrast, encumbered by their own corporeality and the materiality of the space through which they move and so are entirely out of sync with the virgin company. Ursula and her virgins thus arrive at Cologne well in advance of the story's climax—"theyr tyme of tryumphe was not yet commen" (109v)—and they fill this temporal lag with a side trip to Basel and Rome. A hiatus within the three-year hiatus before Ursula is to marry Etherius, this ad hoc pilgrimage constitutes a kind of temporal *mise en abyme*: the interval of time in which the Ursuline company is to celebrate her nuptial virginity is further opened up by the dilation of the journey. The legend in this way presents the pilgrimage as correlative to Ursula's deferred marriage, and, like the long betrothal, its most basic function is to figure community as paradoxically both porous and inviolate. Along the way, Ursula and the 11,000 virgins are joined by kings and bishops, as well as ordinary Christians, such as the mothers with infants, even as the company as a whole remains identified by virgin perfection.

The infants are thus broadly emblematic of the pilgrimage, a form of travel that is miraculously immaterial and therefore extraterritorial, resistant to any form of emplacement. The women with babies in arms, Pynson explains, travel "as lyghtlye and as easely as dyd the other which bare none" (as lightly and as easily as did the others who bore none) (109v). This is, in part, because the children enjoy virtual entertainment: "The sayde yonge babes & chylderne were as well comfortyd by vysyon of aungellys & other sayntys as other were and made therof many euydent sygnes of ioye & gladnes in theyr maner as they coulde" (These young babies and children were as well comforted by visions of angels and other saints as others were, and made many clear signs of joy and gladness in their own way on account of them). Nor do their bodily needs encumber their mothers:

> Thyse innocentys and souckynge chylderne neyther greuyd nor noyed theyr kepers nor yet lettyd theym by souckynge vppon them as they were wont to doo, but thrught the grace & largesse of almyghtye God they put theyr fyngers in theyr owne mowthes and sowkyd out there full swete & delycate nourysshynge wherwyth they were full well fedde & susteynyd (109v)

> [These innocents and nursing children neither grieved nor annoyed their keepers nor hindered them by suckling upon them as they were accustomed to do, but rather through the grace and generosity of almighty God they put their fingers in their own mouths and there sucked out very sweet and delicate nourishment with which they were very well fed and sustained].

Children who need no earthly food make excellent travel companions for another reason: "they neuer wet theyrselfe with theyr uryne nor otherwyse after the maner as chylderne by course of nature be defoulyd, but euer pure and clene as they that were fedde with aungellys food" (they never wet themselves with their urine nor were defouled by course of nature in other ways, after the manner of children, but ever pure and clean, as ones who had been fed by angelic food) (109v-110r). The babies are carefully distinguished from the virgin company: they are not numbered among the 11,000, the legend is quick to insist, but—along with other pilgrims who join Ursula's original company—they supplement Ursula's vast company with another 5,000 members. As addenda, the infants gloss the virgins, and especially the virgin body's status as an image of community: they are super-virgins, models of an even more radical physical integrity. Although they witness the nonvirginal status of some of the women in Ursula's retinue, the babies more than compensate for this as virgins par excellence themselves: the borders of their bodies crossed not even by food or excreta, they embody a form of community characterized by absolute self-identity and completeness. The legend's abstract representation of place is a

Figure 5. Capital decorated with a fleur-de-lys marking the beginning of the legend of St. Ursula in the *Kalendre of the Newe Legende of Englande* (1516). © British Library Board. Shelfmark G.5936.

corollary of this form of community, which is bounded in such a total way that it does not really occupy space at all, but instead figures a kind of placelessness. This very much recalls the *SEL*'s heterotopic Ursula, discussed in Chapter 1, but in Pynson's legend placelessness is rooted in the (virginal or infantile) body itself, rather than in Ursula's rudderless boat.

This narrative detail about the infants has no precedent in English vernacular culture. Hatfield borrows it from Hermannus Joseph's *Undecim* or *Epistola ad vergines* or the Continental tradition established by it.[73] One possible clue for the provenance of Pynson's legend is the initial that marks the beginning of the legend (108r): unusually for the *Kalendre*, the capital T is decorated, albeit simply, with a single fleur-de-lys (see Figure 5).[74] The fleur-de-lys is so pervasive a symbol that no confident argument about textual relations can be based on it. But I want to hazard the suggestion that it points to some affiliation to

Figure 6. Detail of the lower register of Hans Burgkmair's painting of the Basilica of Santa Croce in Gerusalemme, Rome (1504). Staatsgalerie in Katharinenkirche, Bayerische Staatsgemäldesammlungen, Augsburg, Germany. Art Resource, NY.

Figure 7. Left wing of Hans Burgkmair's painting of the Basilica of Santa Croce in Gerusalemme, Rome (1504), depicting the legend of St. Ursula. Staatsgalerie in Katharinenkirche, Bayerische Staatsgemäldesammlungen, Augsburg, Germany. Art Resource, NY.

Figure 8. Right wing of Hans Burgkmair's painting of the Basilica of Santa Croce in Gerusalemme, Rome (1504), depicting the legend of St. Ursula. Staatsgalerie in Katharinenkirche, Bayerische Staatsgemäldesammlungen, Augsburg, Germany. Art Resource, NY.

one of the most stunning late medieval representations of the Ursula legend, the panels that frame Hans Burgkmair's painting of Santa Croce for the Dominican convent of St. Katherine's in Augsburg (1504). There is certainly a thematic parallel between them for Burgkmair's painting also emphasizes pilgrimage. The central image of Santa Croce is famous for its realistic depiction of pilgrims in Rome searching for lodging: one exhausted traveler rests on a stoop. This emphasis extends to the Ursula legend in the panels framing the image of the church, which—like Pynson's legend—represent it primarily as a story of mobility, rather than martyrdom (see Figures 6, 7, and 8).

Positioned precisely in front of Ursula's ship is a coat-of-arms featuring a single fleur-de-lys, and this one can be confidently identified: it belongs to the Welser family, the wealthy merchant princes of Augsburg. Veronica Welser was prioress of St. Katherine's, and the coat-of-arms memorializes her role in commissioning this triptych.[75] The nuns of St. Katherine's had been enclosed against their will in the mid-fifteenth century, and art historians have explored how the set of paintings from which this one comes—a series depicting the seven pilgrimage churches in Rome—compensated for their enclosure by allowing imaginative forms of travel. St. Katherine's had secured the privilege of having prayer stations count as full spiritual equivalents of their Holy Land referents.[76] Prevented from undertaking pilgrimage across the geography of Western Christendom, the nuns of St. Katherine's remade— re-scaled—the finite space of their house into a far more expansive one, through a visual and devotional program that magnified the space without increasing its extension.

There is good reason to assume that the nuns of St. Katherine's had access to the version of the Ursula legend on which Pynson's is based in their well-stocked library.[77] Rather more conjecture is required to posit that Pynson's legend was influenced by the Augsburg nuns who responded to their forcible enclosure by re-scaling the act of pilgrimage.[78] But regardless of precise lines of influence, the visual representation of the Ursula legend at St. Katharine's is a useful *comparandum* for Pynson's legend. It helps us to understand, in particular, how the legend speaks to shifts in geographical scale, including Pynson's re-scaling of regional saints as national ones in the *Kalendre* and the re-scaling of England relative to Continental polities and the New World. Both Pynson's and Burgkmair's Ursula legends respond to a marked contraction—the retreat of England to its insular borders, the confinement of the Augsburg nuns to their house—by imagining mobility across scales within those finite, bounded spaces. Just as the nuns' movement around the finite space of their convent stands for the larger-scale movement of pilgrimage to Rome, so Pynson's sacred infants, whose size and miraculous self-enclosure embody a principle of finitude, figure an intact community that can move across different spatial scales. In the case of St. Katherine's, Augsburg, this relationship to space may depend on the way that the (virginal) nun and the nunnery both figure community as separate, inviolable, whole: it may rely, that is, on the same ideological principle that motivated the nuns' enclosure. Pynson's legend, in contrast, depends on an idea of integrity that codes virginity as an image of finitude and separateness rather than sexual purity. These are preconditions for metaphorical (and conceptual) mobility in the legend, and thus for more flexible, contingent relationships to other communities, determined neither by emplacement nor extension.[79]

The Ursuline infants, set in motion across a vast, indefinite geography, are the smallest possible instantiations of the human body as a figure for community. In them, as in the Hatfield legend, we can see how the legend of St. Ursula, featuring a sacred community whose multiple members each represent an inviolate whole, witnesses at once a desire for finitude in an expanding world and a corollary desire for forms of community unmoored from both a fixed scale and fixed places. While Pynson's legend explores this desire by imagining a pilgrimage through geographical space that has been rendered abstract and insubstantial, Hatfield's legend, as we have seen, explores shifts in scale precisely by particularizing territorial space, filling the spatial field of "England" with the smaller political units embodied by the catalogs of virgins and minor kings. In their *Alice in Wonderland*–like disruption of normative scales, Hatfield and Pynson draw on the conceptual resources of the Ursula legend—explored as early as the *South English Legendary*—to respond to the sudden opening up of geographic, political, economic, and religious space at the end of the fifteenth century.

*　*　*

I have read these texts primarily in terms of England's diminishing scale in this period, but they may also be read, as I suggested above, in terms of renewed Tudor claims to overlordship of Wales, Ireland, and Scotland. The elastic scale theorized in the legend could authorize a more expansive archipelagic England, not just figure a shrinking insular one. It is worth noting, however, that in the early sixteenth century these political claims were as tenuous as the claim for Ursula as a native saint. Although Henry VII had invoked Britishness as a central part of Tudor kingship, it did not yet have practical force. The vulnerability of early Tudor kingship prevented effective enforcement of such nostalgic claims to overlordship.

Hatfield's poem, in particular, was composed not long after Arthur's death had left Henry VII with only one surviving male heir, a moment when James IV of Scotland could vaunt his own proximity to the English throne and openly imagine his own marriage to Margaret Tudor as the foundation for the union of England and Scotland.[80] Indeed, the poem develops its archipelagic model of political community during what might be identified as a hiatus in the history of "Britishness." It is significant that the poem makes no overt reference to Ireland, Scotland, or Wales, nor are the discrete polities represented by the members of Ursula's retinue organized into larger hierarchical structures of political power. Written long after the Norman Conquest and colonization, at the end of a long period during which political instability had all but suspended English overlordship in practice, and just shy of Tudor assertion of sovereignty in practice, Hatfield's poem imagines individual political communities participating collectively in a British nation, neither subordinated to it nor subject to the English king.

Pynson's *Kalendre*, in contrast, follows a watershed moment, the Battle of Flodden (1513), and its explicit assertion of English overlordship in the prologue heralds renewed English claims on the category of Britain. The Ursula legend, which misidentifies the saint as English, is nevertheless presented as a meditation on England's scale, not Britain's: in order to take advantage of the conceptual resource it provides for thinking about mobility of scale, Pynson's legend too avoids presenting the story as warrant or topical allegory for Tudor "Britain."

Fernand Braudel famously wrote that in this period England became an island "without realizing it at the time."[81] In Braudel's historical materialist account, England's consciousness of its insularity is ruled out because it becomes significant only with England's later maritime and commercial dominance. Hatfield's and Pynson's Ursula legends suggest otherwise. Like other texts in this study, they are preoccupied with a territorial and bounded definition of England, whose scale is nevertheless elastic in relation to other communities; they add to this a distinctive preoccupation with the scalar potential of an archipelagic form. But it is true that they are ignorant of the future significance of British insularity and imperialism. While it would be possible to read their archipelagic rhetorics in terms of that future, these works, written before Henry VIII's assertion of sovereignty over Wales and

Ireland in the 1530s and 1540s, are more significant for the wrinkle they represent in a history of British imperialism that would link the Norman Conquest of the Celtic nations to later Tudor assertions of sovereignty and beyond. These texts are interesting less because they can be considered part of that familiar discursive formation than because they stand outside it, just as other texts in this study are less interesting as part of a prehistory of English nationalism than as explorations of the complex system of communities that existed before the nation achieved indexical status.

This is also what it means to read them as literature: as texts that imagine and invent possible forms of community and potential relationships between them using, among other things, the special capacity of literary form to unsettle the scalar relationships that might seem to determine them.

NOTES

Introduction

1. James Clark, ed., *Chronica Maiora of Thomas Walsingham*, trans. David Preest, 276. Further citations to this text are given parenthetically. For the Latin, see Henry Thomas Riley, ed., *Thomæ Walsingham, quondam Monachi S. Albani, Historia Anglicana*, vol. 2, 195.

2. Important recent studies that address earlier Anglo-Latin and Anglo-Norman Lives of English saints include Virginia Blanton, *Signs of Devotion*; Susan Ridyard, *"Condigna veneratio"*; A. G. Rigg, *History of Anglo-Latin Literature*; and Jocelyn Wogan-Browne, *Saints' Lives and Women's Literary Culture*.

3. Scale has become an important category of analysis in cultural geography: see Clare Newstead, Carolina Reid, and Matthew Sparke, "Cultural Geography of Scale." As they explain, cultural geography is influenced by Neil Smith's idea of "scale jumping": Smith, in his widely cited study, *Uneven Development: Nature, Capital and the Production of Space*, argues that capitalism causes jumps in scale as modes of production, consumption, and investment shift. Recent work in cultural geography is interested in scale as constructed not only by capitalist production but also by many ideological and social formations, both consonant with and resistant to dominant institutions; see Newstead et al., "Cultural Geography of Scale," 486–87. See also Sally Marston, "Social Construction of Scale," which offers as a case study nineteenth-century women's construction of the scale of the "home" in order to argue that the production of scale happens through "social reproduction" as well as material production. The relationship between shifts in paradigms of geographical scale and shifts in temporal scale has not received comparable attention.

4. Jean-Luc Nancy, "Of Being-in-Common." See also Nancy, *Being Singular Plural*, esp. 28–41. Similar questions, in different forms, were already at the heart of vernacular literary production, e.g., the interest in "associational" and "absolutist" forms of polity in the *Canterbury Tales*, explored by David Wallace in *Chaucerian Polity*. Although Wallace focuses primarily on secular discourses, he notes that the theories of authority and community with which he is concerned are importantly informed by religious discourses.

5. In its broadest terms, my approach echoes other calls for macro-level analyses of literary form: in medieval studies see for example Christopher Cannon, "Form," and in the field at large Franco Moretti, *Graphs, Maps, Trees*. Cannon differs from Moretti in seeing macro-level analysis as complementary to "close reading" rather than an alternative to it, and in preferring interpretive rather than qualitative approaches even at the macro level.

6. In this way, this project may contribute to other efforts to theorize narrative and poetic

form in terms of the scalar relationships it helps to construct: see, e.g., Nirvana Tanouki, "The Scale of World Literature."

7. This study thus offers a thorough—though far from exhaustive—survey of fifteenth-century Middle English native saints' Lives. Significant texts that are not addressed substantially include the massive Middle English dossier of St. Cuthbert materials; the "Life of St. Walstan" (M. R. James, ed., "Lives of St. Walstan"); the prose *Life of St. Etheldreda*, preserved uniquely in Oxford, Corpus Christi College MS 120; and Henry Bradshaw, *Life of St. Werburge*, and the cluster of Lives of Anglo-Saxon female saints in Cambridge University Library MS Add. 2604. I offer a reading of Bradshaw's *Life of St. Werburge* in Catherine Sanok, *Her Life Historical*, 83–115.

8. On the important exception of Calais, held by the English until 1558, see David Wallace, *Premodern Places*, 22–90. The classic argument that England "became an island" between the mid-fifteenth century and the loss of Calais is made by Fernand Braudel, *Civilization and Capitalism*, vol. 3, 353–56.

9. Saskia Sassen contrasts the "centrifugal scalings" of the Middle Ages, to "the centripetal scaling of the modern nation-state marked by one master normativity," as well as "the centrifugal scalings of the global that disaggregate that master normativity [of the nation state]" (*Territory, Authority, Rights*, 10). The "centrifugal scalings" of the Middle Ages are not replicated in the era of modern globalization, nor do they anticipate modern versions: they represent configurations of a complex system widely separate in time and each is necessarily formed by proximate phenomena whose very complexity prevents simple analogies between them. As Sassen argues, medieval social formations have something to teach us not because they anticipate modern ones, but because their historical distance and the historical scope they make possible allow us to see complex relations and so help us avoid simplistic models of causality.

10. The foundational essays are Louise Loomis, "Nationality at the Council of Constance," and Loomis, "The Organization by Nations at Constance." See also J. P. Genet, "English Nationalism." For the significance of the council's definition for literary culture, see Lesley Johnson and Jocelyn Wogan-Browne, "National, World, and Women's History."

11. Jean Campan presented a full version of the French argument: Genet, "English Nationalism," passim.

12. France, in comparison, had six. Campan also compared England's two provinces and twenty-five bishoprics to France's eleven provinces and 101 bishoprics: Genet, "English Nationalism," 65.

13. Genet, "English Nationalism," 68.

14. Genet, "English Nationalism," 75.

15. "Hyponym" and its opposite, "hypernym," are terms used in linguistics to indicate a category shift, down or up, respectively, in conceptual or referential level: thus, "beagle" is a hyponym for "dog" and "animal" is a hypernym of "dog."

16. "Master normativity" is Sassen's term for the indexical work that the nation claims to do in the nineteenth and twentieth centuries: Sassen, *Territory, Authority, Rights*, 10 and passim. Caution against assuming the normative status of "England the nation" is offered by Derek Pearsall, "The Idea of Englishness in the Fifteenth Century." This is not, however, to deny the force of arguments that the "nation" was an available category in the period: on which see, inter alia, Kathy Lavezzo, *Imagining a Medieval English Nation*, and Thorlac Turville-Petre, *England the Nation*.

17. Wallace's work anticipates Sassen in its preference for a long diachronic historical frame

in order to avoid deterministic sequential causality, a key principle of Sassen's use of complex-systems theory.

18. Cf. Charles Taylor's tripartite taxonomy for modes of atemporality: a "Platonic" sense of timelessness, the Augustinian theory that time experienced by humans as chronological is present to God as a kind of macro-synchrony, and an immemorial mythic time, Mircea Eliade's "time of origins." Taylor's observation might be extended by attention to the many forms of secular time: Taylor, *Secular Age*, 55–57.

19. From this perspective, the "homogenization" of modern secular time is not only a democratic leveling, a time of horizontal community. It is also a form of total time, monolithic time, that may be better understood as an effect of the nation's status as "master normativity," rather than, as in Benedict Anderson's influential account, its precondition: Anderson, *Imagined Communities*. On modern secular time as empty or homogeneous, see also Taylor, *Secular Age*, 58–59 and passim.

20. Jacques Le Goff, *In Search of Sacred Time*, xiii.

21. Sherry Reames, "Standardization and Reform in the Sarum Lessons for Saints' Days," 115. Chichele's interest in St. Wenefred, along with the Welsh David and Chad, may have reflected his time in Wales as the bishop of St. David's: Robert Scully, "St. Winefride's Well," 208. The effort to accommodate these saints registers, for example, in Cambridge, Gonville and Caius College MS 146/196, a book produced for a Lincolnshire church in the early fifteenth century. Sts. Chad and David have been added to the calendar, although Wenefred has not (fol. 6r); and materials for Wenefred, David, and Chad have been squeezed into available space (see fol. 364v; fols. 376r–377r). See Kari Schmidt, *Manuscripts in the Library of Gonville and Caius College, Cambridge* (A.13.134R), and also M. R. James, *Descriptive Catalogue of the Manuscripts in the Library of Gonville and Caius College*, 164–66.

22. London, British Library MS Royal 2 A XVIII. I rely on the digital facsimile: http://www .bl.uk/manuscripts/FullDisplay.aspx?ref=Royal_MS_2_A_XVIII. The two parts of the book, originally separate, were owned by Margaret Beaufort. Previous owners include members of the Beauchamp and Neville families. On the ownership and provenance of the manuscript, see the British Library website cited here.

23. "I believe you can no where find the bodies of so many saints entire after death, typifying the state of final incorruption. I imagine this to have taken place by God's agency, in order that a nation, situated, as it were, almost out of the world, should more confidently embrace the hope of a resurrection from the contemplation of the incorruption of the saints": J. A. Giles, ed., *William of Malmesbury's Chronicle of the Kings of England*, 236. On this passage, see Robert Stein, "Making History English."

24. Ranging from Judith Butler's theoretical challenge to the a priori existence of the sexed body to, say, recent biomedical studies of the role that gut bacteria play in an appetite for specific foods: Judith Butler, *Bodies That Matter*; Vic Norris, Franck Molina, and Andrew Gewirtz, "Hypothesis: Bacteria Control Host Appetites."

25. Cf. romance, which also often explores the body's variability in relation to different communities through narrative tropes of bodily change or instability, as, for example, that of Lord Bercilak in *Sir Gawain and the Green Knight*, or the redescription of Criseyde's body upon her transfer to the Greek camp in Chaucer's *Troilus and Criseyde*.

26. A recent useful account of the limitations of a taxonomic approach to Middle English genres is Alfred Hiatt, "Genre Without System."

27. Again I am thinking especially of Sassen, who uses centrifugal/centripetal as key

analytical categories, but I suspect that other versions of systems theory—e.g., Bruno Latour, *Reassembling the Social*—would be equally helpful at the level at which I am borrowing it.

28. In this regard, the approach to form I outline here is compatible with others that emphasize a dialectic between form and history, on which see, e.g., Maura Nolan, "Making the Aesthetic Turn." It departs, however, from such approaches in preferring the model of the system to the binary structure of dialectic, and it thus also moves away from the identification of art as a separate "privileged space," produced by the dialectical relationship of form and history.

29. Carl Horstmann calls Wade's poem an "epische Legende": Horstmann, ed., "Thomas Beket." Lydgate's references to the Troy story self-consciously construct a relation to an epic tradition: see Chapter 5.

30. Lancastrian kings also celebrated St. George as an "English" saint, continuing a well-established tradition. I leave the cult of St. George aside as an exceptional case, outside of the boundaries of this study because there is no claim for geographical or blood relations that would mark George as a native saint. As Jonathan Good has argued, George's foreignness was important to the adoption of his cult at various historical moments: see Good, *The Cult of St. George in Medieval England*.

31. The arms are represented on the Wilton diptych, in one of the exterior images. Nigel Saul notes that Richard's devotion to Edward the Confessor—perhaps an effort to identify himself with the saint's association with peace—was more marked than that of any other late medieval monarch aside from Henry III and "perhaps" Henry V: Saul, *Richard II*, 311–12.

32. Edward I, Edward II, and Edward III all carried the banner of St. John into battle against the Scots. Royal promotion of the cult perhaps dates back to Athelstan. For the history of the cult, I rely on Susan E. Wilson, *The Life and Afterlife of St. John of Beverley*, 119–24. Vernacular culture witnesses little interest in the cult: an exception is the brief prose *Life of St. John of Beverley* included in Bokenham's Abbotsford legendary (fol. 102r–v), which celebrates him as a bishop, with no reference to his role as a patron of English kings in their campaigns against the Scots.

33. S. Wilson, *Life and Afterlife*, 122.

34. Cf. S. Wilson, who notes that Lancastrian kings fostered "social cohesion" and extended their own influence by "being intimately involved with the saints' own people" in *Life and Afterlife*, 123. Henry VI continued family devotion to John of Beverley with a week-long visit to the town in 1448: A. P. Baggs et al., "Medieval Beverley."

35. John of Beverley and John of Bridlington were linked as Yorkshire saints: a pilgrim badge, now in the collection of the Museum of London (item 88.84), depicts them together: Museum of London Collections Online (accessed April 23, 2014).

36. Alexander Neville, Archbishop of York, began to amass evidence of his sanctity soon after the prior's death, and the official papal inquiry began in 1391. On the early development of the cult, see Jonathan Hughes, *Pastors and Visionaries*, 303–5. The pope's attentive response to the dossier may have been a way to show support for Neville, recently accused of treason by Richard II for his affiliation with the Lords Appellant, but Richard II was himself devoted to the saint and had long shown marks of special favor to the priory: see Michael J. Curley, "John of Bridlington."

37. Curley, "John of Bridlington." Henry V went on pilgrimage to Bridlington in 1407.

38. Hughes, *Pastors and Visionaries*, 307; S. Wilson, *Life and Afterlife*, 123.

39. Writing about St. John's tomb in his entry for 1389, Walsingham records "miracles so

great and so manifest that astonishment fell upon almost the whole of England": Clark, *Chronica Maiora*, 273. Lancastrian support of the cult continued throughout the fifteenth century. In 1413, Henry V cited his devotion to St. John when he excused Bridlington priory from its financial obligation toward defense of the coast. Similarly on the grounds of the king's "great affection and singular devotion" to the saint, the priory was exempt from the Alien Priories Act in 1421, then from all tithes and clerical subsidies in the 1440s, as well as from an Act of Parliament requiring support for the king's debts in 1450. See J. S. Purvis, *St. John of Bridlington*, 49.

40. Scully, "St. Winefride's Well," 207. The story of Earl Richard of Chester's 1115 visit, sometimes identified as the earliest recorded pilgrimage to Holywell, seems to derive from Bradshaw's *Life of St. Werburge*, but his account, which also places Richard at the as-yet-unbuilt Basingwerk Abbey, is unreliable: Fiona Winward, "The Lives of St. Wenefred," 96. It is worth noting that the pilgrimage route to Holywell from the south passed through Ludlow, which may have made the cult visible to the royal household: see Thomas Wright, *History and Antiquities of the Town of Ludlow*, 181.

41. Saul, *Richard II*, 310.

42. On the new shrine, see A. T. Gaydon et al., "Houses of Benedictine Monks." The occasion must have been magnificent: the abbot of Shrewsbury had been granted the right to wear the mitre, ring, and other pontificalia just the year before. In November of that year, the abbey received from Pope Boniface IX the right to give indulgences to those who gave alms to maintain the church: significantly, the papal document identifies the church not only by its original dedication to Saints Peter and Paul, but also by its recent dedication to Saint Wenefred: W. H. Bliss and J. A. Twemlow, eds., *Calendar of Entries in Papal Registries Relating to Great Britain and Ireland*, vol. 5, 20 and 91. Richard's devotion to St. Wenefred may have encouraged Archbishop Walden to mandate observance of her feast in the Sarum rite: Richard Pfaff, *Liturgy in Medieval England*, 438. English bishops gathered at St. Paul's to mark the inclusion of Wenefred, along with David, Cedd, and Thomas of Canterbury, in March of 1398: Charles Joseph Hefele, *Histoire des concils d'apres les documents originaux*, vol. 10, 236.

43. For the Glyndwr revolt and the historical context for it, see R. R. Davies, *Conquest, Coexistence, and Change*, especially chap. 17. For Wales and England in the wake of the Glyndwr rebellion, see Glanmor Williams, *Recovery, Reorientation, and Reformation*.

44. Anne Sutton shows that the Holywell and Shrewsbury shrines represent different sociodevotional phenomena, attracting different sorts of pilgrims, and on this basis dismisses Adam of Usk's claim that Henry V made a pilgrimage to Holywell: Sutton, "Caxton, the Cult of St. Winifred, and Shrewsbury," 114. But the chapel that Bokenham attributes to Henry IV suggests otherwise, as does Bokenham's legend itself, which is evidence of actual or presumed interest on the part of the Abbotsford legendary's wealthy, perhaps aristocratic, owner. Audelay too, who was attached to Lord Strange, links the Holywell spring and the shrine in Shrewsbury in his Wenefred carol.

45. Henry IV supplied much of the endowment: see M. J. Angold et al., "Colleges of Secular Canons: Battlefield, St Mary Magdalene," 128–31. On the window, see Richard Marks, *Stained Glass in England During the Middle Ages*, 187.

46. There is a third possible motivation for royal promotion of the cult of St. Wenefred in this period: as a counter to growing interest in Lollard ideas in the region, not least among prominent Shrewsbury citizens. William Thorpe and a Shropshire canon named John Pollyrbatch were arrested in 1406 by the bailiffs and commons of Shrewsbury and then examined by the abbot, who sent the case on to Archbishop Arundel. Under a temporary statute, employed

only in this single case, Arundel, in his capacity as chancellor, interviewed Thorpe in anticipation of formal heresy proceedings before Parliament: Maureen Jurkowski has identified the writ outlining this episode, which is best known from Thorpe's own account. See Jurkowski, "The Arrest of William Thorpe in Shrewsbury and the Anti-Lollard Statute of 1406."

47. Adam of Usk records the pilgrimage from Shrewsbury to Holywell: E. M. Thompson, ed., *Chronicon Adae de Usk*, 313.

48. S. Wilson, *Life and Afterlife*, 123.

49. M. J. C. Lowry, "Caxton, St. Winifred, and the Lady Margaret Beaufort," 111. It is noteworthy that Welsh devotion to the saint also increases in this period, and the Wenefred legend becomes a subject of Welsh vernacular poetry. See Scully, "St. Winefride's Well," 220; Jane Cartwright, *Feminine Sanctity and Spirituality in Medieval Wales*, 73; also Glanmor Williams, *The Welsh Church from Conquest to Reformation*, 495. Winward notes the lack of interest in Wenefred in Wales before the fourteenth century: Winward, "Lives of St. Wenefred," 94.

50. Indeed, it may serve as an index of, and perhaps mechanism for, the territorialization of sovereignty in this period. As Sassen explains, earlier conceptualizations of sovereignty as rooted in the networks of obligation and affiliation ultimately give way to ones in which sovereignty is defined with reference to territorial boundaries, a gradual shift under way in this period (*Territory, Authority, Rights*, 32–45).

51. The visit to Shrewsbury may also have been an occasion to settle the promised reward for the capture of Oldcastle, while Henry's visit to the shrine of St. John of Beverley during this progress seems to have been undertaken with a view to shoring up support in Yorkshire for the French war: James Doig, "Propaganda and Truth," 169–70.

52. On Porter and Beauchamp, see also Sutton, "Caxton," 115.

53. Clark, *Chronica Maiora*, 426.

54. The Hours of William Porter, Pierpont Morgan Library MS M. 105, fol. 52r (John of Bridlington), fol. 73r (Wenefred), and fol. 51r (John of Beverley). A digital facsimile of the manuscript can be found at utu.morganlibrary.org.

55. Christine Carpenter, "Beauchamp, Richard, Thirteenth Earl of Warwick (1382–1439)."

56. Hugh Owen, *Some Account of the Ancient and Present State of Shrewsbury*, 103. Richard Beauchamp's daughter, Margaret, married John Talbot, first earl of Shrewsbury (officially earl of Shropshire), at Warwick castle in 1425, deepening his regional affiliation with Shrewsbury.

57. Richard Marks, *Image and Devotion in Late Medieval England*, 205, citing Nicolas, *Testamenta Vetusta* (London, 1826), vol. I, 240.

58. On the chapel, see Linda Monckton, "Fit for a King?" On the images of English saints in its visual program, see Marks, *Stained Glass*, 61. St. Wenefred also features in a window in Haseley, Warwickshire, which Sutton attributes to Beauchamp's devotion: Sutton, "Caxton," 115.

59. David Thomas, "Saint Winifred's Well and Chapel, Holywell," 24.

60. Scully, "St. Winefride's Well," 209. For the affiliation of Richard of York and Edward IV with Shrewsbury, see Hugh Owen, *History of Shrewsbury*, vol. 1, 219–33.

61. The final two stanzas of the poem praise the abbot, Thomas Pennant, for the work on the edifice that he oversaw, including a canopy over the well surmounted by the "crown of York." For the poem and an English translation, see H. W. L., "Roman Catholics at Holywell."

62. For Edward IV's grant, see H. C. Maxwell-Lyte et al., eds., *Calendar of the Patent Rolls*, 437. Thomas erroneously gives 1445 as the date of this grant: Thomas, "Saint Winifred's Well and Chapel, Holywell," 24. For Richard III's grant, see Richard Owen, *Catalogue of the Manuscripts*

Relating to Wales in the British Library, 141 (item 350). For Henry VII, see T. Duffus Hardy, *Thirty-sixth Annual Report of the Deputy Keeper of the Public Records*, 378.

63. Purvis, *St. John of Bridlington*, 49.

64. Richard Barrie Dobson, *Durham Priory*, 29, and James Raine, *Saint Cuthbert*, 159. Edward IV also worshipped at Cuthbert's shrine within a month of his accession. Raine, *Saint Cuthbert*, 163.

65. As witnessed, for example, by British Library MS Harley 955, a late fifteenth-century devotional handbook affiliated with Syon Abbey, which includes materials for Sts. Wenefred, John of Bridlington, and John of Beverley: *Catalogue of the Harleian Manuscripts*, vol. 1, no. 955.

66. Bodleian Library MS 779, fol. 189r. The legend is edited by Carl Horstmann in "Des Ms. Bodl. 779 jüngere Zusatzlegenden zur südlichen Legendensammlung," 331–33. See also note 21 above.

67. British Library MS Harley 2403, fols. 113r–116r. The opening of the legend states that the feast "is not ordeyned by holy churche to be halowed," but may be observed by those with devotion to the saint (fol. 113r). On the textual tradition of the *Festial*, see Susan Powell, ed., *John Mirk's Festial*, vol. 2, appendix I; see also M. F. Wakelin, "Manuscripts of the *Festial*."

68. Mirk was an Augustinian canon of Lilleshall Abbey, about twenty miles from Shrewsbury.

69. Powell, *John Mirk's Festial*, 1.162.

70. Wode was executed for treason: Marmaduke Prickett, *History of the Priory Church of Bridlington*, 32–33.

71. E.g., Ralph Taylor, a carpenter, left money for masses at an altar of St. John of Bridlington in the parish church of St. Peter in Sandwich in 1475: Purvis, *St. John of Bridlington*, 43. For further testamentary evidence of devotion to St. John, see Purvis, *St. John of Bridlington*, 43–44, and Prickett, *History of the Priory Church of Bridlington*, 25–26, 113–14.

72. The term is James Simpson's, who uses it to describe the broad thematic and discursive purview of late medieval English literature: Simpson, *Oxford English Literary History*, vol. 2. I echo Simpson's term to suggest that the phenomenon he identifies may be understood in part through the overlapping jurisdictions to which this corpus gives sustained attention.

73. Loomis, "Nationality at the Council of Constance," 526.

74. Genet, "English Nationalism," 69.

75. Genet, "English Nationalism," 74.

76. Jocelyn Wogan-Browne, "Outdoing the Daughters of Syon," 400. Wogan-Browne identifies the inclusion of the St. Denis legend in fifteenth-century versions of the *South English Legendary*, the *Gilte Legende*, and Caxton's *Golden Legend* as part of the English claim to France after Agincourt.

77. Sassen, *Territory, Authority, Rights*, 41.

78. Friedrich Brie, ed., *The Brut or Chronicles of England*, vol. 2, 381 and 456. See also Catherine Sanok, "Good King Henry and the Genealogy of Shakespeare's History Plays," 41–42.

79. The role that religion played in the efforts by Lancastrian kings to shore up their legitimacy is well established: see, e.g., Paul Strohm, *England's Empty Throne*. Devotion to native saints is an important, if as yet understudied, aspect of this phenomenon.

80. Cited by Taylor, *Secular Age*, 121.

81. Nicholas Watson, "Censorship and Cultural Change in Late-Medieval England." Important reconsiderations of the Watson thesis are offered by Kathryn Kerby-Fulton, *Books*

Under Suspicion, as well as several essays in Kantik Ghosh and Vincent Gillespie, eds., *After Arundel*.

82. Cf. Robert Meyer-Lee, "The Emergence of the Literary in John Lydgate's *Life of Our Lady*."

Chapter 1

1. Above all, David Wallace, *Chaucerian Polity*. As Anne Thompson and Christopher Cannon have argued, the centrality of the *Canterbury Tales* to our understanding of medieval English literature has effaced the contribution of earlier story collections, and the *SEL* in particular, to the idea of the collection as such: A. Thompson, *Everyday Saints*, 124, and Cannon, *Middle English Literature*, 160.

2. This is characteristic of legendaries, but not hagiography *tout court*: saints' Lives and affiliated texts do often highlight the persona of the narrator, a topic that has received considerable critical attention, especially regarding the Lives of holy women, for whom the mediating voice of a male cleric is often crucial to establishing the saint's authority. For the deployment of such tropes, see, especially, Lynn Staley Johnson, "The Trope of the Scribe and Literary Authority in the Works of Julian of Norwich and Margery Kempe." On the "outspoken" *SEL* poet, see the foundational essay by O. S. Pickering, "The Outspoken *South English Legendary* Poet."

3. See Thomas Liszka, "South English Legendaries." An important recent exception is A. Thompson, *Everyday Saints*. The fullest account of the textual tradition remains Görlach, *Textual Tradition of the SEL*.

4. Cf. Thomas Liszka, "The First 'A' Redaction of the *SEL*." The form of the work outlined by the *Banna sanctorum* is, broadly speaking, the one represented in the EETS edition of D'Evelyn and Mill, who present the earliest "orderly" text of the *SEL*: Charlotte D'Evelyn and Anna Mill, eds., *South English Legendary*, I. v. For practical purposes, my argument addresses the *SEL* as it is presented in this edition, the text to which most of the citations refer (by volume, page, and line numbers), but I attend to some of the particularities of the textual tradition in the notes.

5. Contributions to this debate include Virginia Blanton, "Counting Noses"; Sarah Breckenridge, "Mapping Identities in the *SEL*"; Jill Frederick, "The *SEL*"; Renee Hamelinck, "St. Kenelm and the Legends of the English Saints in the *SEL*"; Klaus Jankofsky, "National Characteristics in the Portrayals of English Saints in the *SEL*"; and Turville-Petre, *England the Nation*.

6. Blanton, "Counting Noses."

7. Re the prologue's title, see D'Evelyn and Mill, *South English Legendary*, 1.

8. This metaphor thus also embraces the temporale material. I suggest some of the ways this material is important to the representation of time and its relationship to community in the second section of this chapter, but I focus primarily on the sanctorale.

9. Manfred Görlach, ed., *The Kalendre of the Newe Legende of Englande*.

10. On the "vernacular heterogeneity" of the *SEL* and the "diversity of interests and polities" with which it is correlated, see Lesley Johnson and Jocelyn Wogan-Browne, "National, World, and Women's History," 106.

11. See Hamelinck, "St. Kenelm," 26–27, and Frederick, "*SEL*," 67.

12. E.g., its analysis of the causes of the Conquest (lines 75–80). I discuss the legend's representation of the Conquest's consequences later in the chapter.

13. Lines 1–4. On the role of genealogy, specifically with reference to the legend of St. Mildred, see Paul Acker, "Saint Mildred in the *SEL*," 143. Frederick also notes the emphasis on genealogy in the Aldhelm legend: "*SEL*," 68–69.

14. Lines 17–28. See also Frederick, who identifies Oswald's "symbolic value" as an English saint in the way that his story is prefaced by an account of Athelstan's victory over the Danes: Frederick, "SEL," 61.

15. On the parallel the SEL makes between Edmund's difficulties with Henry III and Thomas's contest with Henry II, see A. Thompson, Everyday Saints, 51.

16. All references are to the edition in Laurel Braswell, "Saint Edburga of Winchester," 325–29.

17. Cf. Hamelinck, "St. Kenelm," 22.

18. All references are to the edition in Michael Nagy, "Saint Aethelberht of East Anglia in the SEL," 165–68. This edition is not lineated; I give references by page and line number as represented on the page.

19. The incident occupies lines 5–20; Mark's martyrdom, lines 21–40 (I, 159–60); cf. the Legenda Aurea, in which it is a brief anecdote in a long legend.

20. This scene is significantly different in the version of the prologue to the Becket legend, found in Bodl. MS Laud 108, B.L. Stowe MS 949, Lambeth Palace MS 223, and the Vernon manuscript: there, the princesses asks Thomas all at once about his name, his faith, and his land: Thiemke, Die Me. Thomas Beket-legende des Gloucesterlegendars, 3.

21. In making this argument, I assume that Amiraud's use of "lawe" points primarily to secular law, as contrasted to the princess's interest in Christianity. But the term can also refer to religion, and the ambiguity here is thematically important: the Becket legend, of course, addresses precisely the question of religious and secular jurisdiction in England, as if an extended narrative response to the questions about English law raised in this scene.

22. Arjun Appadurai, Modernity at Large, esp. chap. 2, "Disjuncture and Difference in the Global Cultural Economy," 27–47.

23. Appadurai contrasts the scalar or spatial understanding of community to a "contextual" one, defined by intimate webs of sociality and "technologies of interactivity" (178). He suggests how a scalar understanding is essential to the nation, which produces local communities as "exemplars of a generalizable mode of belonging to a wider territorial imaginary" (191).

24. Cf. J. D. North's account of an analogous layering of different kinds of temporality for monks: North, "Monastic Time."

25. Turville-Petre, England the Nation, 66.

26. Jankofsky, "National Characteristics," 91.

27. Jacobus explains that the church "renews" the sequence of offices at Advent, the time of renewal, even though in "sequence of time" it is preceded by the time of "deviation," the period from Adam to Moses, represented in the liturgy by the interval between Septuagesima and Easter: Jacobus de Voragine, Golden Legend, I, 4. The SEL's deviance from the liturgical calendar supports Annie Sampson's argument that the SEL is not a liber festivalis: Sampson, "The SEL," 187–90.

28. Sampson also notes the unusual choice of January 1 and compares the SEL to the Hereford Breviary's sanctorale ("SEL," 189n). One intriguing possibility is that the SEL follows an earlier English tradition in this regard: Michael Lapidge notes that the Cotton Corpus Legendary, the collection with the "greatest influence on Anglo-Saxon observance," starts at January 1: Lapidge, "Saintly Life in Anglo-Saxon England," 263. Cf. Thomas Heffernan, "Additional Evidence for a More Precise Date of the 'South English Legendary,'" 348.

29. R. T. Hampson, Medii Aevi Kalendarium, 2, 409n, cited by Heffernan.

30. On the Circumcision and historical division, see Kathleen Biddick, Typological Imaginary.

31. The role of these two Christic feasts in establishing a framework for the relationship between the native and nonnative saints' Lives is one way we might recognize the significance of the A redactor's coordination of temporale and sanctorale material in the collection.

32. Alison Chapman, "Now and Then," 94.

33. Chapman bases her argument on Cranmer's nontypological structuring of readings in the Book of Common Prayer, 110–11. The *SEL*, whose calendar form also eschews typology as the structure of time, produces a similarly open temporality.

34. On the calendar tradition, see Hampson, *Medii Aevi Kalendarium,* 389–472.

35. Thompson's thesis is that the legendary's emphasis on the "everyday" correlates to the affective communities, family and parish, that inhabit that temporal framework. Cf. Anne Thompson, "Shaping a Saint's Life," on the *SEL*'s interest in "the satisfactions of a life fulfilled within time" (44).

36. Cf. Chapman, "Now and Then," which argues that such a conjunction makes space for secular time.

37. Exclusively, it must be noted, for Christians; Jews are projected by typology into a fixed past. Again, see Biddick, *Typological Imaginary.*

38. Liszka argues that the Becket legend was initially intended as the first item in the sanctorale section, with the Laud prologue serving as a supplement to it: Liszka, "MS Laud Misc. 108 and the Early History of the *SEL*," 80–83. Several manuscripts that do not now have Becket as the final legend nevertheless show evidence of its structural position as an end point: Cambridge, Corpus Christi College MS 145, ends with Thomas, his translation, then Guthlac, which is out of order (April 11). In British Museum MS Harley 2277, Becket is followed only by "Maledictorum Iude and Pilati." In Bodleian MS Ashmole 43, Becket is followed only by Edward the Confessor, very likely out of place, though perhaps related to his early January feast (January 5). British Library MS Cotton Julius D. ix. begins with "Yeres day," but its Becket legend is followed by many items. I rely on Görlach, *Textual Tradition,* passim, for this information about the contents and order of the *SEL* manuscripts.

39. Görlach, *Textual Tradition,* 217. Görlach notes that the legend of Silvester, celebrated on December 31, is not included in most of the A manuscripts and suggests that it is omitted because it would be an "anticlimax" after the Becket legend.

40. On the importance of St. Thomas of Acon to civic ritual in London, especially as a cult that connected London to the geography of crusade, see Laurence Warner, "Adventurous Custance," 46.

41. For the date and development of the Saracen legend, see Anne Duggan, "Lyell Version of the Quadrilogus Life of St. Thomas of Canterbury," 107, 112–13. On the story's relation to the London church affiliated with the order, see Laurence Warner, "Becket and the Hopping Bishops," 123–24. For a history of the order, see A. J. Forey, "The Military Order of St. Thomas of Acre."

42. The scene of martyrdom also develops this trope: see Cannon, *Middle English Literature,* 159.

43. "Dixit idem episcopus, quod esset miles Christi, et pro Deo et S. Thoma martyri, Cantuariensi archiepiscopo, in clericali ordine militaret," *AASS* October 1, col. 544D, cited by Anne Duggan, "The Cult of St. Thomas Becket in the Thirteenth Century," 44.

44. See, e.g., Charles Kingsford, ed., *The Song of Lewes,* 85n358. On the *SEL*'s political affiliation with the Barons' War, see Thomas Heffernan, "Dangerous Sympathies."

45. Hamelinck, "St. Kenelm," 24.

46. On the tradition of Becket's Tuesdays, see Kay Brainerd Slocum, *Liturgies in Honour of Thomas Becket*, 247–55.

47. Jean-Luc Nancy, "Of Being-in-Common."

48. The *SEL* also includes the legends of the Irish saints Brigit and Patrick, neither of which acknowledges proximate cultural or communal reference points. Bodleian MS Bodley 779 also includes a Life of St. Wenefred, as discussed briefly in the Introduction.

49. Britain is presumably Cornwall, as most scholars have supposed, although Brittany is also a possibility. Whether Cornish or Continental, the difference of Britain from "Engelonde" in the *SEL Ursula* is interesting evidence that the latter is not understood to include Cornwall or Brittany, both under the dominion of the English king when the *SEL* was composed.

50. Manuscripts with "fairhede" (variable spellings) include British Library MS Egerton 2891; Corpus Christi College Cambridge MS 145; British Library MS Cotton Julius D. IX; and Bodleian Library MS Bodley 779. Texts that read "ferrade" include Bodleian Library MS Laud 108, fol. 63; British Library Harley 2277; Bodleian Library MS Ashmole 43; British Library MS Stowe 949; Trinity College Oxford MS 57; Trinity College Cambridge MS R 325. I rely on Friedrich Schubel, *Die südenglische Legende von den elftausend Jungfrauen*, passim.

51. Michel Foucault, "Other Places," 24. This real—rather than purely imaginary—relationship to the more "structured" sites of a culture is what distinguishes a heterotopia from a utopia. The mirror metaphor clarifies the difference between them: the image in the mirror might be understood to figure a utopia, as a place I see myself where I am in fact absent, but it is better understood as a heterotopia "insofar," Foucault writes, "as the mirror does exist in reality, where it exerts a sort of counteraction on the position that I occupy" (24).

52. Foucault, "Other Places," 27.

53. Foucault defines a heterotopia as a "countersite" that features structures and norms that mirror those of real social and political spaces.

54. The legend's interest in a temporality other than national history is suggested both by its refusal to locate the story "here in England," and in its single reference to contemporary England, an antifeminist aside that suggests it would be impossible to rally the requisite number of virgins from contemporary communities: "Were me mighte nou as sone finde . as me mighte tho / I ne wene noght me ssolde in al this toun . finde ten mo" (Where could one find [virgins] as readily now as they could then? / I don't think you could find ten in this whole town) (I, 444, 57–58). In MS Ashmole 43, the legend is yet more skeptical: the narrator doubts that ten virgins can be found in "al acontrei," the whole region. The negative valence of the exemplary relationship linking past and present—contemporary England compares poorly with the virgin-rich kingdom of yore—is doubled by the genealogical rupture that separates Ursula's virgins from contemporary girls: as virgins, soon to be martyrs, they can have no genealogical link to the audience.

55. Kathleen Davis, "Hymeneal Alogic."

56. Relevant here is the elastic relationship between individual and collective identity: virgins are to honor their own virginity and Ursula's. That is, their behavior is both about individual ethical identity and the basis of their shared affiliation with Ursula, the paragon who defines their individual worth and grounds their collective identity.

Chapter 2

1. This manuscript is the unique witness for both poems. Unless otherwise noted, citations are to Mary Dockray-Miller, ed., *Saints Edith and Aethelthryth*; translations provided are my

own. Information regarding the presentation of the texts is based on my own inspection of the manuscript. Carl Horstmann's editions remain useful: Horstmann, ed., *S. Editha sive Chronicon Vilodunense* and "Vita S. Etheldredae Eliensis."

2. I adopt the term "morphology" generally from biological sciences to indicate the normative and category-level thinking implicit in these body metaphors.

3. Jocelyn Wogan-Browne, "Outdoing the Daughters of Syon," 396. On visitations of women's houses and other challenges to their institutional authority, see Nancy Bradley Warren, *Spiritual Economies*, 14–29; for Wilton Abbey in particular, see Dockray-Miller, *Saints Edith and Aethelthryth*, 7, and Wogan-Browne, "Outdoing," 406.

4. In a telling gambit, the *Life of St. Edith* pushes back the origin of the house—otherwise dated to the tenth century—to the eighth. On the history of Wilton Abbey, see R. B. Pugh and Elizabeth Crittall, eds., "Houses of Benedictine Nuns." According to this source, the poem's account of the original chantry, founded in the eighth century by Earl Weohstan of Wiltshire for his father-in-law, is otherwise unattested.

5. The Lives are now part of a larger manuscript containing thematically similar material—lists of kings and documents related to monastic institutions—but this grouping appears to be an early modern construct. The legends were, however, accompanied from the beginning by lists of the abbey's founders and the legend's sources, which follow the Edith legend: Dockray-Miller, *Saints Edith and Aethelthryth*, 29.

6. Addressed to the Wilton community, they also participate in the construction of female saints' lives as gendered reading for female audiences and as narrative frameworks in which women were encouraged to see themselves as historical subjects: on which see Catherine Sanok, *Her Life Historical*, 1–49.

7. Horstmann, *S. Editha*, vii. See also Wiesje Nijenhuis, "The Wilton Chronicle as a Historical Source."

8. Wogan-Browne, "Outdoing," 398. Wogan-Browne suggests that the legends' formal difference from Lydgate is evidence that they predate his English saints' Lives. On the legends' prosody, see also Dockray-Miller, *Saints Edith and Aethelthryth*, 31–32. Other lives of female saints in quatrains include a *Life of St. Anne* (Roscoe Parker, ed., *Middle English Stanzaic Lives of St. Anne*, 110–26); *Life of St. Margaret* (Sherry Reames, ed., *Middle English Legends of Women Saints*, III. a); and *Life of St. Dorothy*, in Cambridge University Library MS 4122. The Wilton manuscript shows some interest in the stanza form as such: in the first pages of the poem, the first and last lines are linked by a line of red ink (fols. 199r–200r), but this is not sustained across the whole text.

9. See the Introduction, p. 13–23. This is a trope that surfaces repeatedly: important articulations include Aelfric's *Life of St. Edmund*, and Lydgate's Lives, addressed in Chapter 5. The legend of Etheldreda's intact body goes back at least to Bede's *Ecclesiastical History*: see Virginia Blanton, *Signs of Devotion*, chap. 1.

10. Sarah Salih, *Versions of Virginity in Late Medieval England*.

11. Blanton, *Signs of Devotion*. See also Dockray-Miller, *Saints Edith and Aethelthryth*, 25–26. Later fifteenth-century Middle English legends are especially useful *comparanda* for the Wilton legend: they include a rhyme-royal legend in the Abbotsford legendary, almost certainly by Osbern Bokenham; a prose legend included in a legendary that comprises many female English saints, Cambridge University Library MS 2604; and an independent prose legend in Oxford, Corpus Christi College MS 120. The Corpus Christi life is being edited by Elena Sasu, forthcoming in *Textes Vernaculaires du Moyen Âge*, ed. Stephen Morrison (Brepols).

12. This brief reference is amplified in the legend's historical and geographical description of each of the Anglo-Saxon kingdoms (lines 5–102).

13. It is worth noting that this mutability characterizes England only as a secular polity; its ecclesiastical jurisdictions are very stable. So, for example, the two archbishoprics of Kent, Canterbury and Rochester, were configured in Anglo-Saxon England "ryght in the same manere they ben ther yytte" (in just the same way that they still are) (12).

14. *MED*, "mene," n. (3), definition 1, a course of action or means of attaining an end; also definition 2, (a) and (c), intermediary or agent, and definition 3, (a) and (b), an intermediate state and "something physically between two extremes."

15. The legend is not, however, especially interested in virginity as an ethical practice. It is not much interested in ethics at all, with the minor exception of humility, which is represented as Etheldreda's signature virtue, in the form of both her love of the poor and the vulnerability that she chooses to impose on herself: for example, as an exercise in meekness, she bathes in front of the other nuns and only after they have all bathed.

16. Cf. the bells that ring "wyth ouht touching of monnes hond" (825) during the translation of Etheldreda's body.

17. *MED*, "kindeli," (adv.), definitions 1 and 2.

18. Similar language is used to describe the sarcophagus later: in the story of the monks' anxiety about transporting it to Ely, it is said to be "so follych and so redy ydyght" (728).

19. So, to cite only one closely relevant example, Edith's body is referred to as "that golden vessel of the divine presence" in Goscelin's vita, the most important source of the Middle English legend: Michael Wright and Kathleen Loncar, eds., "Goscelin's Legend of Edith," 69.

20. This identity of tomb and body is given larger-scale narrative expression in the parallel between Etheldreda's translation, the ritual reburial of the saint's body in which it is recognized as a sacred object, and the miraculous transportation of the tomb to which she will be translated: in both, the sacred quality of the object is manifest in its original perfection and its miraculous mobility.

21. While there has been a great deal of critical attention to medieval representations of the sealed body, anxieties about the articulated body have been only recently explored, especially in work informed by disability studies: e.g., Christopher Baswell, "King Edward and the Cripple." The bibliography on the virginal body as a sealed container is too vast to account for here: still helpful is the foundational analysis in Clarissa Atkinson, "'Precious Balsam in a Fragile Glass.'"

22. Seeta Chaganti, *Medieval Poetics of the Reliquary*.

23. Dockray-Miller, *Saints Edith and Aethelthryth*, 26–27.

24. The legend explicitly remarks that the ring adorns the shrine at lines 950–54.

25. The offsite authority may be a mark of the fabricated nature of this episode, which is elsewhere unattested. Dockray-Miller suggests that it conflates two miracles that do have authority elsewhere: one in which one of the Vikings who attack the monastery breaks a hole in the tomb and one in which an Ely canon later pokes at the saints' relics through a hole in order to verify its status: Dockray-Miller, *Saints Edith and Aethelthryth*, 27.

26. Cf. "Hurre body is there [in Ely], bot hurre soule is in blys" (970).

27. Wright and Loncar, "Goscelin's Legend of Edith," 71.

28. Cf. the Middle English prose legend in Cambridge University Library MS 2604, which follows Goscelin in presenting Edith's body as hybrid witness to her sanctity and earthly sin: in her appearance before her translation, she announces that her eyes, hands, and feet will be found corrupt because she "mysused" them in her youth, but the rest of her body is incorrupt

because she was never guilty of gluttony or lechery (fol. 73v). She also announces a "tokyn" of her translation without analogue in the Wilton legend: that her body will be found "redy arysing upward out of the grounde." The brief legend in the *Kalendre of the Newe Legende of England*, perhaps influenced by the Wilton legend, represents her body as incorrupt, a sign that it was "uncorrupte fro Lybydiousnes & Glotony," even as her feet, hands, and eyes evince their misuse in her youth through their decay. The Edith legend was marked up for printing, presumably in London and thus potentially available even in this copy to Pynson. See John Ayto, "Marginalia in the Manuscript of the Life of St. Edith." On Goscelin's development of the legend, see Stephanie Hollis, "St. Edith and the Wilton Community," 248–50.

29. Her feeling is inspired specifically by the account of Jesus' baptism in the gospel of Matthew (3.16–17), in which the Holy Spirit appears as a dove to inform John of Jesus' salvific identity and to institute the sacrament of baptism (1121–30). The allusion is obscured in Dockray-Miller, where "yfolwyd" (1126) is mistranslated as "accompanied" (*sic* for "baptized").

30. A similar point is made by Wogan-Browne, "Outdoing," 404.

31. The claim is made again, a little differently, a couple of lines later: "Bot all the remanent of my body, as hole hit ys, / Excepte the organys of the lemys the whyche governede my wittes five, / and as clene with ougt ony corrupcione hit is, / as hit was whenne yche was on urthe alyve" (2471–74).

32. E.g., the discovery of Edith's incorrupt body (line 2572); the cure of the blind Beteric (2836); the cure of Syric, a mute peasant boy (3800); and the healing of Theodoric (4264–65). The ladies also sing the *Te Deum* to celebrate Wultrude's miracles, e.g., the healing of the child who was born crooked and blind (3221).

33. Cynthia Camp, *Anglo-Saxon Saints' Lives*, 47–48; Wogan-Browne, "Outdoing," 401. My reading is informed by Nancy Bradley Warren's observation that the convent wall was not, in practice or theory, an "impenetrable boundary" in late medieval England, which provides a way to understand the legend's celebratory attention to the presence of many men—Edulf and his fellow monks, King Etheldred and others—on this occasion: Warren, *Spiritual Economies*, ix.

34. Dockray-Miller's translation of the passage suggests a criminal desire for the relic: Edulf "thought then in his heart to steal some relic of that blessed body" (193). But the verb "kete" (line 2608), translated here as "steal," means to "get, obtain," with no necessary connotation of illegitimacy. Cf. line 2685, where a woman is said to have "kete" heavenly bliss through penitence.

35. But see Wogan-Browne, "Outdoing," 402–3, which argues that Edith's intact body is the antithesis of the "femininized anti-body" of the Jews.

36. Lisa Lampert, *Gender and Jewish Difference from Paul to Shakespeare*. Lampert borrows the idea of the "hermeneutical Jew" from Jeremy Cohen, *Living Letters of the Law* (1999).

37. This story is offered near the end of the poem as proof that Edith's frequent postmortem appearances to the sisters were not "fantomysliche ydo" (done as a phantom) (4558). "Fantomysliche" is a *hapax legomenon*. The *MED* gives as its definition "by deluding the senses; by illusion"; I read it as having a stronger sense of spectrality: e.g., in the manner of a specter. In line with the legend's emphasis on embodiment, the nuns see Edith in this miracle "bodyliche wyth hurre hyge sygt" (bodily with their eyesight) (4557): that is, they see her in embodied form with their own bodily senses.

38. Another Wilton resident, Alfildus, receives a closely related vision: it is thus a shared, not exceptional, experience and thus broadly representative of the community that Alfyne will head as abbess, rather than a sign of her particular authority over it.

39. It is significant in this regard that Alfyne's tenure as abbess bridges the massive historical break between Anglo-Saxon and Norman England (4664–68).

40. The nuns are referred to as ladies throughout; see, e.g., lines 1280, 1285, 1287, 1290, 1399, 1402, and 2985.

41. Tony Kushner, *Angels in America*: "The smallest indivisible human unit is two people, not one; one is a fiction" (333). Cf. Nancy on "being" as necessarily "being-with-one-another": Jean-Luc Nancy, *Being Singular Plural*, 3.

42. King Alfred founds Wilton "thorow preyer of Egwne the quene, / for Elflede that chyldys sake" (584–85).

43. In the legend as it survives the first reference to the relationship between Edith and Wultrude comes when Edith has become abbess of three houses—St. Mary's in Winchester, Barking, and Wilton—and decides to remain at Wilton in order to be under her mother's "chasteyssynge" (1606).

44. It may be that the legend can be read in terms of the nonprofessed girls at Wilton to be educated. In moments such as this, it defines the relationship between the girls and the nuns in familial terms, suggesting a naturalized concern for their education and well-being. Certainly Edith seems like a model for such a girl, in her various elegant accomplishments, her defense of nice clothing, and her dutiful relationship to her abbess/mother. Cf. V. A. Kolve on the familial paradigms employed to figure the relationship between oblates and monks: Kolve, "Ganymede/ Son of Getron."

45. Cf. Barbara Newman on sacrificial motherhood in *From Virile Woman to WomanChrist*, chap. 3.

46. As, for example, in the legend of St. Agnes, in which the saint chastises her parents for their grief at her grave. A similar dynamic obtains in *Pearl*: see Sanok, "Geography of Genre in the *Physician's Tale* and *Pearl*," 187–88.

47. Significantly in this regard, Wultrude's death is repeatedly identified as a union with Edith, rather than with Christ: God "ordeyned that he [Wultrude] shulde come hurre doughter tyll" (3049); again, in death she is brought "to Ede here doughter, that mayden clene" (3065); "for forsothe, wyth hurre doughter Seynt Ede he [Wultrude] is" (3072). The legend also twice notes that Wultrude is buried near her daughter (3075, 3083).

48. St. Elphege, who officiates at the ceremony, tells the child's parents about Edith's miraculous participation and exhorts them never to let her marry. The girl, Brightgifu, becomes Wilton's third abbess (2235–48).

49. She is identified as Saint Wultrude while still alive many times (2908, 2923, 2927, 2935, 2951, and, after her death, passim). "Saint" can be a general adjective indicating holiness, but it is employed in these examples as a title, and in the context of Wultrude's earthly miracle working, the term proleptically designates her future sanctity. In one of Wultrude's living miracles, for example, an escaped prisoner seeks sanctuary at St. Edith's church but is pursued by his jailers. When Wultrude prays that the thief be spared "hongur and wo, / and also to kepe hym from that derke place" (2925-26), they are blinded, until restored by Wultrude after the king had granted her the man. Wultrude continues to perform miracles after her death, as a saint and not as abbess. Her posthumous miracles account for a significant portion of the legend, from lines 3066 to 3238, when the narrator announces that the legend will resume its focus on Edith.

50. Dockray-Miller, *Saints Edith and Aethelthryth*, 136n88.

51. For medieval political theory that understood individual royal will as the expression of common interest, see John Watts, *Henry VI and the Politics of Kingship*, 27–31. As Watts shows,

this theory was put under pressure by Henry VI's infant accession and extended minority, in the period contemporary to the Wilton legends.

52. See Camp, *Anglo-Saxon Saints' Lives*, 40–42.

53. My thinking about this point has been advanced by Joshua Jenkins in his final essay for English 407, University of Michigan (Winter 2014).

54. Internal evidence throughout suggests that the legend anticipates an audience of Wilton nuns. Reference to the "first funders," for whom they are obligated to pray (315–16), initiates a list of royal support that continues to line 369. The story of Wilton's foundation is identified specifically as the story of "this abbay" (683). The founders' identities are elaborated so that the legend's audience can pray for them (686–89). References to "this place" (233) and to the stone laid by Alfred at the foundation of Wilton "that stonte *here* yet" (791) moreover insist on Wilton as the location of reading.

55. Dunstan exhorts Edith specifically to "for gete thy peple and eke thy fadur house" (2016).

56. Edith later calms a storm for the Archbishop of York, on pilgrimage to Jerusalem, in a miracle that the narrator compares to this one (4539).

57. Cf. Wogan-Browne, "Outdoing," which notes the "co-dependence of royalty and monasticism" in the legend (399).

58. The same point about the compatibility of Christian and royal ethics is made again implicitly in the narrative that follows, in which Alfred's charity to a poor man—who turns out to have been St. Cuthbert, as the saint explains in a second visionary appearance—is followed by his successful defeat of the Danes and conversion of their king (482–573).

59. Representations of affect as an expression and effect of kingship appear in a range of late medieval and Early Modern English texts, from the *Alliterative Morte Darthur* to *King Lear*.

60. It is worth noting that Robert Hallum, Bishop of Salisbury, who served as the head of the English delegation at Constance, was closely affiliated with Wilton and played an active role in the abbey's efforts to reestablish its authority. On Hallum, see R. N. Swanson, "Hallum, Robert (*d.* 1417)." Hallum had granted Wilton an indulgence, a prestigious and lucrative privilege, signaling ecclesiastical approval of the nunnery's recent efforts to reform. On the council and its definition of the "nation," see the Introduction, p. 7–8.

61. The passage is borrowed largely from Higden, *Polychronicon*, bk. 6, chaps. 13–17: see Dockray-Miller, *Saints Edith and Aethelthryth*, 230n136.

62. Cnut's conversion is a coup for Wilton Abbey. The Archbishop of Canterbury follows Cnut "evermore" and preaches to him "algate where ever he hede" (3287, 3288), but it is Edith who converts him: "Bot tho at Wyltone he was ycristonyd, for the grete fore / the whyche he had tho there of this virgyn Seynte Ede" (3289–90). The ecclesiastical hierarchy—so powerful in the fifteenth century—is presented here as well-meaning and assiduous, but less effective than the nunnery itself and its saint.

63. This miracle, in which the false Agamundus suffers a dreadful illness until he returns land he has seized from Wilton, recalls the miracles that demonstrate St. Edmund's attention to the property and jurisdiction of Bury St. Edmund's in Lydgate's *Edmund and Fremund*: on which see Chapter 5. See also the narrative of the theft of the monastery's land by Brixon, cousin to one of the nuns (lines 3917–4053), as well as the series of miracles in which Edith provides sanctuary to escaped prisoners (4378–4428, 4442–81, 4482–4517).

64. Lines 88–89, 113. Egbert is Edith's kinsman.

65. Cf. the perfunctory account of Harthacnut's accession and reign: "And anone after Kyng Haralde dyede tho, / And his brother Hardeknowde was made kyng tho anone, / The wheche

regnede here bot yeres two. / And Haralde regnede byfore hym foure yere and won. / Bot yet in Hardeknowdes tyme, a nother miracle was do / In the churche of Wylton by fore Seynt Ede, so full of grase" (3910–15).

66. Wogan-Browne, "Outdoing," 396.

67. See Talal Asad, *Formations of the Secular*.

68. This audience would have comprised nuns and girls in residence to be educated: see Dockray-Miller, *Saints Edith and Aethelthryth*, 7. As she notes, many of the well-born girls at Wilton to be educated would become laywomen.

69. Ayto, "Marginalia in the Manuscript of the Life of St. Edith."

70. There were fourteen professed nuns in 1485, down from forty-four in 1441: Pugh and Crittall, "Houses of Benedictine Nuns."

Chapter 3

1. Given the special prominence of St. Wenefred in the Lancastrian devotional program, we might expect Shrewsbury Abbey to have commissioned vernacular legends to commemorate the royal visits to the shrine and encourage other elite or nonelite audiences to follow suit. There is, however, no vernacular Life of St. Wenefred from Shrewsbury Abbey or from Basingwerk, the Cistercian monastery that oversaw her well shrine in Flintshire. Instead, the most ambitious vernacular Wenefred legends were written by poets who came to Shrewsbury as pilgrims.

2. See the Introduction for a fuller discussion and relevant bibliography.

3. Susanna Fein, ed., *John the Blind Audelay: Poems and Carols*, 5, 7, 8–22. All citations are to this edition.

4. I discuss the Abbotsford legendary as a whole in Chapter 4. In the context of the manuscript, the Wenefred legend is distinctive, but not unique, as a verse text.

5. The Middle English sermon included in Charles de Smedt, ed., "Documenta S. Wenefreda," and dated there to 1401 is rather a sixteenth-century manuscript copy of Mirk's legend. The manuscript, now Stonyhurst College MS A.11.8, also contains a list of miracles attributed to Wenefred dating from 1556 to 1668. I am grateful to Mrs. Jan Graffius of Stonyhurst College for assistance in identifying this manuscript, which is not provided with cataloging information in de Smedt.

6. The "new" Middle English Life of St. Wenefred announced by Curt Bühler is in fact a manuscript copy of the legend in Caxton's *Golden Legend*, with only small differences that are readily attributable to the process of transcription. The text, in a late sixteenth-century hand, concludes with a note that it was "drawen out of an ould pryntinge boocke word by word & cetera per Jo.P": Bühler, "A New Middle English Life of Saint Winifred?" The booklet, which also includes Welsh-language materials, is now Pierpont Morgan Library MS B. 26.

7. Ronald Pepin and Hugh Feiss, trans., *Two Mediaeval Lives of Saint Winefride*. On questions of authorship, dating, and sources of the Latin vitae, see Fiona Winward, "The Lives of St. Wenefred." See also Robert Scully, "St. Winefride's Well," 203. Each of these vitae, in redacted form, is included in later Latin legendaries of native saints: an abbreviated version of the anonymous legend is included in the Romsey collection, British Library MS Landsdowne 436, and Robert Pennant's vita is the basis for the legend included in *Nova Legenda Angliae*, as well as the Wenefred lections in the Sarum breviary: Winward, "Lives of St. Wenefred," 129. For the text and translation of the Romsey manuscript version, see James Ryan Gregory, ed. and trans., "The Life of St. Winifred."

8. MS Abbotsford, fols. 214v–218v: all references are to a microfilm copy of the manuscript. I am grateful to Andrea Longson, Senior Librarian, Advocates Library, for helping me gain

access to this work, and to Angela Heetderks for digitizing it. The book is now available in digital facsimile at http://lib1.advocates.org.uk/legenda/. The Wenefred legend itself is incomplete: a prayer for Wenefred's intercession to protect her devotees from fiends in the moment of their deaths breaks off mid-stanza. The manuscript lacks legends for the feasts that fall between Wenefred's day, November 3, and St. Andrew, November 30, with which the legendary, as per tradition, begins. For a description of the manuscript, see Simon Horobin, "A Manuscript Found in the Library of Abbotsford House." Horobin is preparing an edition of the legendary for EETS.

9. See Theresa Coletti, *Mary Magdalene and the Drama of Saints*, 73.

10. Parental lament is one of Bokenham's rhetorical specialties: compare St. Anne's lament for her childlessness in *Legendys of Hooly Wummen* (1763–76), on which see Catherine Sanok, *Her Life Historical*, 71–72.

11. Viz., "in hyre nosethyrls he blew softely" (216r).

12. There is evidence for the existence of a chapel at this time, but I have found no additional evidence identifying it with Henry IV. An indulgence was granted in 1427 to those who visit and give alms at the Holywell chapel on the principal feasts and other holidays: W. H. Bliss and J. A. Twemlow, eds., *Calendar of Entries*, vol. 7, 504. The reference to the chapel buildings as "collapsed" in this document leads David Thomas to suggest that the chapel was at least three hundred years old, but this is only conjecture: Thomas, "Saint Winifred's Well and Chapel, Holywell," 17. The current structure, which embraces but does not enclose the well, is believed to date to the reign of Henry VII, as is the chapel constructed over it; they have strong associations with the Stanley family and some connection to Margaret Beaufort, though her role has been questioned in recent scholarship: see Richard Marks, *Image and Devotion in Late Medieval England*, 205.

13. The well is said to have produced twenty tons of water a minute: Thomas, "St. Winifred's Well," 16.

14. Fol. 217r–217v. The friar's regional identification is important enough for Bokenham to mention it twice, bracketing the description of Henry IV's chapel.

15. Bokenham more generally revises the legend in ways that emphasize the kinds of violence made possible by royal military and political power. In most versions of the story, Caradoc is swallowed by the earth as soon as he has beheaded Wenefred; it is a mark of the enormity of the crime. In Bokenham's version, Caradoc waits by her body, in arrogant defiance of anyone who may challenge his deed. His act and remorselessness are explicitly linked to his identity as the son of a king, and they are generalized as characteristic behavior of men of his station: "as of swyche p[er]sonys yt ys the guyse / lytil or noon he held his trespass" (215v). It is only when Beuno prays that he be punished that the ground opens and swallows the prince in token of God's displeasure, not at the murder itself, but at Caradoc's "unrepentaunt obstynacye."

16. Richard of York's sometime residence at Ludlow gave him ample opportunity to cultivate favor in Shrewsbury, which provided him with men in 1452: see Ralph Griffiths, "Richard Duke of York and the Royal Household in Wales," 15–19, and James Winston, *English Towns in the Wars of the Roses*, 47–48. Yorkist ties to Shrewsbury are also noted in Scully, "St. Winefride's Well."

17. Cf. the miracle told in Mirk's *Festial* of a man's miraculous recovery from the bite of a spider so deadly it had already killed two of the man's companions. The bite, on the man's neck, caused his throat to swell to such proportions that his death seemed imminent. His mother offered a candle at Wenefred's shrine and fetched some of the water in which the saint's bones had

been washed, and these actions cured the afflicted area: Susan Powell, ed., *John Mirk's Festial*, 2.165. The bodily parallel between Wenefred and her devotee, who alike suffer a mortal wound in the neck, is unmediated by king or national identification; indeed, it is antithetical to such mediation. This miracle is also recounted in an unidentified manuscript, quite likely a copy of the *Festial*, mentioned in Thomas Wright, *History and Antiquities of the Town of Ludlow*, 181n, cited in Charlotte D'Evelyn and Frances Foster, "Saints' Legends," 634.

18. Cf. Pennant's *Life*: "In the western district of Great Britain there is a certain province called Wales, bordered on one side by the territories of the kingdom of Anglia and, on the other side, by the Ocean sea": Pepin and Feiss, *Two Mediaeval Lives of Saint Winefride*, 27. Bokenham omits the following sentence, which identifies Wales as a region "much honoured" due to the "countless prerogatives" of the many saints who once lived there.

19. The *occupatio*, which borrows from Higden's *Polychronicon*, touches on the origin of the name Wales, the commodities associated with the country, as well as "many other thyngys . . . Wich seyd Policronica declaryth opynly." Cf. Churchill Babington, ed., *Polychronicon Ranulphi Higden*, 396–98, 400.

20. In the prologue of the *Mappula*, Bokenham explains that the work is designed to clarify place-names in English saints' Lives. Bokenham also takes from the *Polychronicon* the detail, discussed below, that Caradoc's lineage thereafter "bark in the maner of dogs" as vengeance for the violence done to Wenefred (216v–217r). In that passage, Higden remarks that Wenefred is worshipped both at her well shrine and in the "cite of Shrewsbury where she rests now": Babington, *Polychronicon Ranulphi Higden*, 428–31.

21. The phrase "there present" is used again in the miracle of the white friar (217v).

22. Cf. Carolyn Dinshaw, *Getting Medieval*, 39.

23. Bokenham notes his source for this anecdote, which is not attested in any other vernacular legend.

24. It is the central theme of *ars moriendi*, as well as much homiletic writing.

25. Wenefred's resurrection is common to all versions of the legend. My argument is that Bokenham develops an idea of the importance of secular life, perhaps inspired by this narrative detail, to an uncommon degree.

26. Elsewhere, he refers specifically to Lydgate as a model (who exceeds his own poetic capacity): e.g., the prologue to the Life of St. Anne in the MS Arundel 327 version: "If I hadde cunnyng and eloquens / My conceytes craftely to dilate / Als whilom hadde the frysh rethoryens / Gowere, Chauncere, and now Lytgate" (lines 1–3).

27. The Arundel Castle MS of Lydgate's Lives, whose scribe Scott has identified as responsible for a number of Lydgate manuscripts: Kathleen Scott, "Lydgate's Lives of Saints Edmund and Fremund: A Newly-Located Manuscript in Arundel Castle," *Viator* 13 (1982): 333–66, cited by Horobin, "Manuscript Found in the Library of Abbotsford House," 153.

28. Caradoc's aureate speech is even more strongly correlated to his abuse of power over Wenefred than to the seductions of poetic language: it articulates a coercive social authority that parallels the physical power with which he ultimately overwhelms her. Bokenham explains Caradoc's failure to repent as a function of his political and social station: "Fle thens he serteyn wolde in no wyse / And for that he a kyngys sone was / As of swyche personys yt ys the guyse / Lytil or noon he held hys trespas" (215v). His false sense of privilege is, importantly, an effect of vertical structures of community and the relations of power they produce. We may read this as a general form of the legend's topical critique of Lancastrian appropriation of the saint.

29. Osbern Bokenham, *Legendys of Hooly Wummen*, line 89. "Embelish" is also a term of art

for Lydgate: see *MED*, "embelishen," definition 3.a, which gives only Lydgate and Bokenham as examples.

30. On this point, see also Catherine Sanok, "Calendar Time in *Balade* Form," 228–31.

31. My comments about the brackets take their cue from Jessica Brantley's work on the relationship between literary form and its manuscript presentation, especially her argument for the graphic tracing of rhyme in the *Tale of Sir Topas*: Brantley, "Reading the Forms of *Sir Topas*," 417–19.

32. This formal address to temporality complements and complicates the calendrical form of the legendary in which the narrative is found.

33. James Doig, "Propaganda and Truth," 167.

34. The chantry was ultimately established in 1449, at the behest of Henry VI; an entry in the papal register for 1462 confirming its establishment refers to Henry V's initial plans and notes that the chantry was to have one chaplain who could be either secular or regular: Bliss and Twemlow, *Calendar of Papal Registers, vol. 11*: "Vatican Regesta," vol. 491 (1463).

35. Given that the central thematic of the carol is Henry V's military triumphs, it may be that this poem was originally written for Henry V's 1421 pilgrimage to Shrewsbury and only lightly revised after Henry V's death to refer to the infant king.

36. In *Marcolf and Solomon*, Audelay uses "seculars" to refer to secular clergy (565, 601, 669), such as himself, as well as to the laity (716).

37. His residence there may or may not indicate that Audelay himself was a member of the order; see Fein, "Introduction," in *John the Blind Audelay*, 6.

38. Anthony Ilaria, "Canons and Canonesses Regular."

39. That is, they follow a secular liturgy in having nine lessons for major feasts rather than the twelve lessons of monastic practice: Richard Pfaff, *Liturgy in Medieval England*, 272.

40. See Susanna Fein, "Good Ends in the Audelay Manuscript," for a reading that suggests penitential themes as the basis for the collection's organization, that is, on the macro-level of the form of the book.

41. Fein, "Introduction," in *John the Blind Audelay*, 22.

42. E.g., the stanza that concludes "Our Lord's Epistle on Sunday," the epilogue to the *Counsel of Conscience*, and "On the World's Folly": Fein, *John the Blind Audelay*, 265.

43. Audelay may be productively compared in this regard to Thomas Hoccleve's self-presentation in the "Complaint." On self-naming and emergent ideas of the literary, see Robert Meyer-Lee, *Poets and Power from Chaucer to Wyatt*.

44. The twenty-five carols comprised by the sequence embrace a wide range of topics, from the hagiographic (carols on the feast of St. Stephen, John the Evangelist, Holy Innocents, Thomas Becket, all of which are Christmas season feasts, as well as St. Anne, which is not strictly linked to the season) to the topical/political (Henry VI) to assorted *pastoralia* (carols on the Ten Commandments, Seven Deadly Sins, Seven Works of Mercy, etc.). A rubric directs the audience to "syng these caroles in Cristemas" (175). Susanna Fein, who identifies the sequence as the third of four divisions in the manuscript, notes that the set of carols is a "forerunner to the lyric sequence": Fein, "Critical Overview and Major Issues," 6.

45. On the carol, see Seeta Chaganti, "Carol," and Chaganti, "Choreographing Mouvance."

46. My reading here is inspired by Eleanor Johnson's discussion of perpetual time in the *Revelations* of Julian of Norwich in "Julian of Norwich and the Comfort of Eternity."

47. Christopher Page, *Owl and the Nightingale*, 115. On dance, time, and performance, see also Seeta Chaganti, "Danse Macabre in the Virtual Churchyard."

48. Although the hagiographic carols in the Christmas sequence do not feature refrains with the striking continuous present of the Wenefred carol, they share an emphasis on the daily. St. Anne is invoked thus: "Pray fore us both nyght and day," for example, and St. Francis is asked to "Save thi breder both nyght and day."

49. Peter Osborne, *Politics of Time*, viii–x, passim.

50. Fein reads this phrase as "head's gesture," arguing that the well is a metonym for Wene-fred's head. My reading differs on philological grounds, but also depends on an alternative inter-pretation of the well as a figure for Wenefred. Although I agree that the well serves as a double for Wenefred in some way, I do not think that it is as an anthropomorphic figure. Rather, the well is a physical representation of Wenefred that is importantly different, in materiality and morphology, from a human body. As we have seen in Bokenham's version, the legend of St. Wenefred, through the central image of the well, offered a way to conceptualize community as dynamic and particular, in contrast to comparatively static and abstract corporeal models of community.

51. We may note that Audelay omits reference to its Lancastrian architecture: there is no reference to Henry IV's chapel, though it was standing in the 1440s, according to Bokenham's purportedly eyewitness account.

52. On the "drive towards the local" in fifteenth-century pilgrimage, see Eamon Duffy, "Dy-namics of Pilgrimage in Late Medieval England." Duffy reads local pilgrimage as a way medieval English people "mapped the familiar" (165–66).

53. The sense of discrete smaller units that informs the idea of the "translocal" is supported here by the way that "contre" often indicates a politically discrete community.

54. On St. Wenefred's bell, see Hugh Owen, *Some Account*, 104, 127.

55. Cf. Helen Barr on the "lyric present" in "'This Holy Tyme.'" Barr derives her under-standing of lyric time from George Wright, "The Lyric Present: Simple Present Tense Verbs in English Poems," *PMLA* 89 (1974): 563–79.

56. Cf. Robert Meyer-Lee, on Audelay as both a historically particular figure and an exem-plary model for all Christians: Meyer-Lee, "The Vatic Penitent."

57. On Shrewsbury Abbey as "unmistakably an urban institution," see Nigel Baker, *Shrews-bury Abbey*," 226.

58. Ben Nilson, *Cathedral Shrines of Medieval England*, 4. On Shrewsbury Abbey, see A. T. Gaydon et al., "Houses of Benedictine Monks."

59. In Chaucer's *Troilus*, the narrator bids his poem to "kis the steppes wher as thow seest pace / Virgile, Ovide, Omer, Lucan, Stace" (*Troilus and Criseyde*, 5.1791–92).

60. On literature as palliative, see Rebecca Krug, "*Piers Plowman* and the Secrets of Health." In identifying a theory of literature in vernacular practice (rather than in an explicitly program-matic text or *ars poetica*), I follow Jocelyn Wogan-Browne et al., eds., *Idea of the Vernacular*.

61. See the discussion of this point in the Introduction.

Chapter 4

1. Especially clear examples of personal devotion are provided by the references to patrons in Osbern Bokenham's *Legendys of Hooly Wummen*.

2. The *Gilte Legende* (abbreviated as *GiL* henceforth in the notes) is translated from Jean de Vignay's *Légende dorée*, a French translation of *Legenda Aurea*. All references are to Richard Hamer, ed., *Gilte Legende*, cited by volume and page number.

3. Hamer, *GiL*, I, xi. Some *Legenda Aurea* manuscripts include Latin legends of English

saints: e.g., Cambridge, Pembroke College MS 277; Oxford, Balliol College MS 228; and London Westminster Abbey Chapter Library MS XII: Manfred Görlach, *Studies in Middle English Saints' Legends*, 26. See also Virginia Blanton, *Signs of Devotion*, 236.

4. To signal their genealogy and formal translation, I refer to these works as the *Prose SEL Lives*, instead of the *Supplementary Lives*, the modern editorial title that emphasizes instead their inclusion in some manuscripts of *GiL*. References are to Richard Hamer and Vida Russell, eds., *Supplementary Lives*, cited by page number. The manuscripts containing the *Prose SEL* Lives are British Library MS Add. 11565, British Library MS Add. 35298, and Lambeth Palace Library MS 72. In addition, six of the legends—Edmund of Abingdon, Edmund king and martyr, Edward king and martyr, Oswald, Dunstan, and Faith—have been appended to a copy of Mirk's *Festial*, now Southwell Minster MS 7. There must have been at least two more copies of the *GiL* containing the *Prose SEL* legends: the book on which Caxton based the *Golden Legend*, and one for which a leaf of the table of contents survives, see Hamer and Russell, *Supplementary Lives*, xvii–xviii. See also Görlach, *Studies*, 93–123, which revises and updates Görlach, *The SEL, Gilte Legende and Golden Legend*. The *GiL* manuscripts that include the *Prose SEL* legends do not derive from a single exemplar: English saints' Lives were *separately* added to individual texts; on the lateral transmission of the *Prose SEL* legends, see Hamer and Russell, *Supplementary Lives*, xiv.

5. Late copies of *SEL* include Bodleian Library MS Bodley 779 (early or mid-fifteenth century); Bodleian Library Laud Misc. 463 (c. 1400); British Library MS Add 10301 (c. 1400); Cambridge Trinity College MS R. 3. 25 (c. 1400); Yale University Takamiya MS 54 (first half of fifteenth century). For the last, see O. S. Pickering and Manfred Görlach, "A Newly Discovered Manuscript of the *SEL*."

6. On this dating, see Görlach, *Studies*, 71.

7. See Sherry Reames, "*Legenda Aurea*," 197–210; see also the essays in Brenda Dunn-Lardeau, ed., "*Legenda Aurea*."

8. Görlach notes that the *SEL* itself is "amongst the earliest vernacular reflexes" of *Legenda Aurea*, but he has also convincingly established the late and limited influence that Jacobus's collection had on the *SEL*: by his calculation, only twenty-five of the *SEL* legends derive from the Latin legendary: Görlach, *Studies*, 30. For a detailed account of the *SEL*'s sources, see Görlach, *Textual Tradition*.

9. The *Speculum Sacerdotale*, a fifteenth-century sermon collection, also borrows somewhat from *Legenda Aurea*, and seven legends translated from *Legenda Aurea* into English couplets are found in the Vernon manuscript: Görlach, *Studies*, 58–59, 69.

10. See the Introduction for "capability" in systems theory, as formulated by Saskia Sassen, *Territory, Authority, Rights*, 27–28.

11. Henry VI was crowned in Notre Dame in 1431.

12. It is significant that neither Bokenham's collection nor the expanded version of the *GiL* evinces any particular interest in the saints promoted most actively by Lancastrian kings. Saints who were important to monarchical self-representation, e.g., Sts. Wenefred and Edmund, whose legends are included uniquely in the British Library MS Additional 35298, represent urban rather than royal forms of the cult, as discussed below.

13. On the *Libelle*, see John Scattergood, "The *Libelle of Englyshe Polycye*"; Sebastian Sobecki, *The Sea and Medieval English Literature*, 145–60; and Sobecki, "Bureaucratic Verse." On the sea and representations of an insular England, see the essays in Sobecki, ed., *The Sea and Englishness in the Middle Ages*, especially Kathy Lavezzo, "The Sea and Border Crossings in the

Alliterative *Morte Darthur*," which also uses scale as a key analytical category. While such concerns may have been especially acute in the middle decades of the century, they persist for much longer, as witnessed by the currency that the *Libelle* continued to enjoy. For its ample textual tradition, including several manuscript exemplars produced in the sixteenth century, as well as Hakluyt's 1598 edition, see Frank Taylor, "Some Manuscripts of the 'Libelle of Englyshe Polycye.'" See also Andrew Breeze, "Sir John Paston, Lydgate and the *Libelle of Englyshe Polycye*."

14. The image of England as a walled city under siege also finds a resource, broadly speaking, in the long-standing association between London and/or England and Troy.

15. Discussed in Caroline Barron, *London in the Later Middle Ages*, 113.

16. On urban trade, see Sassen, *Territory, Authority, Rights*, 55–58.

17. This is the poem's fiction; London jurisdictions were markedly heterogeneous, on which see Shannon McSheffrey, "Sanctuary and the Legal Topography of Pre-Reformation London" (with thanks to Elizabeth Allen for the reference), quotation at 484.

18. Osbern Bokenham, "Mappula Angliae," ed. Carl Horstmann.

19. See Kathy Lavezzo, *Angels on the Edge of the World*: see especially chap. 3, "Locating England in the *Polychronicon*," 71–92.

20. "The lengthe of this Ile, as seithe Solinus, is VIII C. Ml. paas, that is VIIIC myle, who-so wille metene hit frome the brynke of Totenese unto the angille of Calidonye" (7).

21. This too can be traced back to Bede.

22. Edward king and martyr is also an Essex saint.

23. The text notes also that Cedde, "by assent of kynge Oswy," left the monastery to become Bishop of York (28).

24. This chapter is incomplete due to the loss of a leaf.

25. The term, with a different but—I believe—related referent, is James Simpson's: Simpson, *Oxford English Literary History*, 1. See also the Introduction.

26. One effect of omitting saintly kings is that English geography is figured especially through its cathedrals. Ben Nilson notes that most major shrines at English cathedrals are those of bishops, who were "among very few people buried within cathedrals"; cathedrals are generally not the resting place of royal bodies: Nilson, *Cathedral Shrines*, 9–10. This is the case for several of the saints included in the *GiL* and the Abbotsford legendary: e.g., Dunstan and Alphege (Canterbury shrines); Indract [*sic*, for Ithamar] and Paulinus at Rochester; Erkenwald (London); Chad (Lichfield); Swithun (Winchester); Oswald (Worcester); and Cuthbert (Durham).

27. All that we know confidently about that book is that it contained the Lives of these four saints, and we can be certain of the identity of Cedde and Felix. We are on less certain ground with Oswald and Edward: there were two St. Oswalds, one a king and one a bishop, and two St. Edwards, Edward the Confessor and Edward the Martyr. The latter possibility would be more likely if Oswald is Oswald of Worcester, the bishop, an important advocate for Edward's claim to the throne.

28. The *Life of St. Wenefred*, itself incomplete, is the last extant legend: it was presumably followed by the Lives of saints whose feasts fell between that of St. Wenefred, November 3, and the feast of St. Andrew, November 30, with which the legendary begins. Horobin notes that the lost section of the manuscript very likely contained the verse legends of St. Katherine of Alexandria, Cecilia, and Elizabeth of Hungary, which are found in British Library MS Arundel 327. A missing quire accounts for the loss of some other legends, perhaps including Bokenham's *Life of St. Anne*. See Horobin, "Manuscript," 140. Horobin notes further that some legends align

particularly closely with our knowledge of Bokenham's professional life: the legendary includes the Life of the recently canonized Nicholas Tolentino, who was—like Bokenham himself—an Augustinian friar, and the *Life of St. Vincent*, drawn principally from *Legenda Aurea*, adds specific reference to the saint's chapel at Bokenham's own house, Clare priory (141).

29. Perhaps, as Horobin has proposed, this book was intended for Cecily Neville. The choice of native saints may have some bearing on the question. The inclusion of Wenefred could confirm Neville affiliations: see the account of the devotion of Richard de Beauchamp, the thirteenth Earl of Warwick and Cecily Neville's nephew and collaborator, in the Introduction, p. 23. On the other hand, the collection does not include some saints we would expect in a book produced expressly for Cecily, e.g., St. Cuthbert, the patron saint of the Nevilles of Raby: on that association, see Raine, *Saint Cuthbert*, 105–12.

30. The *Mappula* has been dated to the early 1440s, whereas the Abbotsford manuscript was probably produced sometime after 1460. Internal evidence for the date of the Abbotsford legendary includes a reference to Bokenham's pilgrimage to St. Wenefred's well in 1448, and a small revision to the prologue to the *Life of St. Margaret* regarding Lydgate—referred to as still living in the *Legendys of Hooly Wummen* but not here—points to a date after the monk's death in 1449 (the latter is noted in Horobin, "Manuscript," 144–45). There is a strong likelihood that the legendary dates at least ten years later than this: the legend of Nicholas of Tolentino suggests firsthand knowledge of the saint's tomb, and Bokenham may have traveled to Tolentino in 1459 for the general council of his order (Horobin, "Manuscript," 141). The *Mappula* itself may be later than the 1440s, the *terminus ante quem* posited by Carl Horstmann and taken as writ by subsequent scholars (Bokenham, "Mappula," 4). Horstmann's claim is a lateral one, based on the putative date of the *Libelle of Englyshe Polycye*, but the manuscript also contains works of much later date, including a poem attributed to Skelton on the death of Edward IV, which must date after 1483.

31. See note 27 above regarding the uncertain identity of these saints.

32. Horobin, "Manuscript," 140.

33. The "Deposition" of Edward the Confessor was observed in the York calendar—though not Sarum—so there is warrant for considering this as a possibility. But at York, too, it was a minor feast, and it would have been surprising to include a legend at this point in the calendar when there is not one for Edward's primary feast. It is not even entirely certain that the reference to "Edward" in the *Mappula Angliae* is to Edward the Confessor. It may be to Edward, king and martyr, whose feast fell on March 18. The martyred king Edward makes sense as a companion to the Essex saint Felix and Bishop Oswald. Cf. also *Prose SEL* Lives in Southwell Minster MS 7, which includes Edward, king and martyr, and not Edward the Confessor.

34. Horobin, "Manuscript," 139–40.

35. Miriam Gill, "Saint with a Scythe."

36. Simon Horobin, "Politics, Patronage, and Piety," 935.

37. *Kalendre of the Newe Legende of England*, fol. 61r.

38. Susan Wilson, *Life and Afterlife*, 118–24.

39. Guernes de Pont-Sainte-Maxence, *Vie de Saint Thomas le martyr*, ll. 171–75.

40. Görlach, *Studies*, 125.

41. Görlach, *Studies*, 126.

42. The essential work on the cult of St. Faith is Kathleen Ashley and Pamela Sheingorn, *Writing Faith*.

43. Relevant here is the identification of Edmund of Abingdon, whose shrine was at

Pontigny, as Edmund of "Pontenay" in British Library MS Additional 35298, fol. 72r. Although the explicit identifies the Michaelmas text as "the life of Seint Michael" (282), it in fact refers only briefly to the war in heaven between Michael and the archangel. Most of the legend rehearses lore related to demonology, the cosmos, and human physiology. In this period, St. Michael's association with visionary knowledge may have been shadowed for some English audiences by Joan of Arc's visions of the saint.

44. The inclusion of the Irish saints might also be read as a mark of Yorkist sympathies.

45. On this tradition, see Christopher Baswell, "King Edward and the Cripple."

46. On the basis of orthographic and dialectical differences, Görlach suggests that these legends were incorporated into the *GiL* earlier than the other Additional Legends: Görlach, *Studies*, 83. Read as a separate set, their London affiliations come into focus: Edward the Confessor and Erkenwald were enshrined in London, while Wenefred's London cult was perhaps strongest in the community of Shrewsbury merchants. The manuscript presentation of the Lives of Edward and Erkenwald suggests their particular importance: there is more frequent use of rubrication to mark subdivisions within the narrative: British Library MS Additional 35298, fols. 48r–53r, 53r–57r. Caxton includes all three legends in the *GiL*, evidence, as Görlach argues, that there was at least one other *GiL* manuscript that contained them: Görlach, *Studies*, 141.

47. See Hamer and Russell, *Supplementary Lives*, xxvi, and Görlach, *Studies*, 82 and 133n. Additional evidence for a London provenance of the *GiL* can be found in the Becket legend, which gives unusual attention to the saint's father, a London burgess, even identifying him as the legend's subject in the rubric, which refers to the text as "the life of Seint Thomas of Canturbury and of Gilbert Beket his fader" (285). In the legend, Thomas is said to work as a young man for a worshipful man "of *this* cite of London" (287; emphasis added).

48. The *Life of St. Alban* is by far the longest saint's Life in the collection: it runs 1,076 lines in Hamer's edition, while most legends run between 100 and 400 lines; it is rivaled in length only by the Assumption of the Virgin (1,002 lines). In British Library MS 630, the beginning and end of the text (154v, 168v) are outlined in a way that both sets it apart from the other saints' Lives and emphasizes its literally central position in the volume (the table of contents identifies it as the 89th of 168 chapters, 366r). Larissa Tracey notes that this mise-en-page is otherwise limited to major feasts: Tracey, "British Library MS Harley 630." Its prominence has led some scholars to suggest that the translator was affiliated with St. Alban's Abbey: see Richard Hamer, *Three Lives from the "Gilte Legende*," 16–18. His evidence has been challenged in Görlach, *Studies*, 79n117; and Tracey, "British Library MS Harley 630," 39.

Whether or not the translator was a monk or affiliate of St. Alban's, the legend may reflect London devotion to the saint. The abbey cultivated a close relationship to the city and fostered the cult, surely in part to increase pilgrimage from the metropolis. The abbey also had significant London properties: see William Page, "Houses of Benedictine Monks." In the early fifteenth century, the abbey's steward, John Barton, served as the city's recorder: Barron, *London in the Later Middle Ages*, 175. See also the Introduction, regarding the miracle recorded in James Clark, ed., *The Chronica Maiora of Thomas Walsingham*, of St. Alban's cure of a mad London woman.

49. This emphasis can be demonstrated by the many references to Verolamium, by name or as the "city." In the course of five pages of the modern edition (387–93), there are a dozen such references (lines 353, 370, 375, 382, 474, 488, 492, 496, 502, 526, 548, 553). It is notable that before his conversion to Christianity, Alban is identified not with his city but all of Britain: he is "prince of knyghtes thorugh all Bretaigne and steward of the same ile" (380).

50. See also lines 852, 869, and 890, where the Verolamium martyrs are called "citezenis with aungels."

51. Cf. Sarah Rees Jones on the role of local saints' cults in the formation of civic identity and ideas of citizenship in the twelfth and thirteenth centuries: Jones, "Cities and Their Saints in England."

52. Sassen, *Territory, Authority, Rights*, passim.

53. See McSheffrey, "Sanctuary and the Legal Topography of Pre-Reformation London." I am especially indebted to Elizabeth Allen's forthcoming work on sanctuary.

54. Urban space is also invoked, in a destructive key, by the fire that consumes the city when the people neglect to provide the saint with a worthy shrine. The fire consumes everything but the saint's tomb from Ludgate to Aldgate, without respect to jurisdiction: "it neither sparid churchis ne towris but devourid them fervently. As ye se that a smalle fyre consumyth anone stoble or towe, so this grete fyre consumyd and wastid petevouslye fulle ryalle byldyngis bothe of stone and of tre so cruelly and so hastely that thaye had no tyme to remeve and for to saue there goodis, but eche manne ranne aboute as people fro themselfe, for it semyd as God wolde take vengeaunce and distroye alle the cyte utterly for the synnes that reynid therein" (57–58).

55. See p. 53.

56. *MED*, "kindelen," (v.1 and v.2). The *MED* entry for "kindelen" (v.1) notes that both its "forms and senses show influence of *kindelen*, (v.2)."

57. Kathleen Davis, "Hymeneal Alogic." See pp. 57–58.

58. A great deal of the narrative of Edward's life focuses on the abbey and Edward's special relationship to it. There is an elaborate account of how Edward comes to build Westminster on the ruins of an abbey on Thorney Island in lieu of the pilgrimage he had vowed to take to Rome, which is also an etiological myth about the origins of St. Peter's special relationship to the enlarged institution. Cf. Görlach, who remarks that the legend includes "details of London-Westminster traditions": Görlach, *Studies*, 82.

59. There is a similar miracle in the Erkenwald legend: a man goes to tan skins on the saint's feast day rather than observe it; others say it is "grete foly with so lytle wynnyng of that pore crafte to displese almyghty God and that holye seinte that alle wel disposid men wurship and halowe in that daye." The skinner accidentally strikes himself in the eye with his tool; the narrative wryly observes that he was thus forced to observe the feast in the end (64–65).

60. They may be compared on these grounds to other works that define England in terms of its "enclosure," as analyzed by Lynn Staley, *Island Garden*, passim.

61. On the contemporary cultural value and institutional affiliations of prose in relation to poetry, especially aureate poetry, see Robert Meyer-Lee, "The Emergence of the Literary," 338–42.

62. Cf. Eleanor Johnson, *Practicing Literary Theory in the Middle Ages*, on prosimetrum as a pervasive mode of vernacular literary production.

63. Readers did not necessarily read the legends chapter by chapter, of course, but numbered chapters may nevertheless have altered their experience of the text by making it easier to track continuities and gaps in their reading.

64. The list of contents, preserved in a Paris manuscript, of a now lost copy lists the Additional Lives in calendar order: Görlach, *Studies*, 82.

65. Cf. Görlach, *Studies*, 85.

66. Görlach, *Studies*, 82–83.

67. In addition to the fragmentary table of contents that serves as flyleaves in Paris,

Bibliothèque Nationale MS nouv. acq. lat. II, 3075, tables of contents are found in British Library MS Additional 35298, British Library MS Harley 630, British Library MS Harley 4775, and Lambeth Palace Library MS 72 (this last in a sixteenth-century hand): Hamer, ed., *GiL*, III, 6, 10, 12, and 14; see also Görlach, *Studies*, 83, 85.

68. In an influential essay, Homi Bhabha refers to these as "pedagogical" and "performative" modes: Bhabha, "DissemiNation," 209–34.

69. The appendix to the *Festial* also includes prose legends of the British St. Ursula, discussed in Chapter 7, and St. Katherine, who is linked to England through her genealogy, on which see Catherine Sanok, *Her Life Historical*, 87–88.

70. This is the case even if Southwell Minster MS 7 was used for private rather than parish devotions: it would nevertheless index the liturgy through its selection of *Prose SEL* legends and their status as an appendix to a sanctorale.

71. Wenefred was, for Mirk, a regional saint like Alkmund, but she was well established as a national one by the time that the Southwell *Festial* was written.

72. It is possible that this reflects accidental loss rather than intentional omission. The Southwell *Festial* contains fewer than half of the *Prose SEL* legends, and almost all come from the first half of the group, which probably circulated in pamphlet form, as its variable position in the *GiL* manuscripts suggests. However, the legends are not in the order in which they are found in *GiL* manuscripts, and the *Life of St. Faith* falls in the second half of the collection. The likelihood that the *Prose SEL* circulated as a pamphlet, as this and the other manuscript witnesses together suggest, opens the intriguing possibility that it was originally compiled as a mini-legendary devoted to English saints, where the nation would have functioned more categorically as an organizing category. On the pamphlet circulation of saints' Lives, see A. S. G. Edwards, "Transmission and Audience of Osbern Bokenham's *Legendys of Hooly Wummen*."

73. On the inclusion of the Arundel legends in the Abbotsford legendary, see Horobin, "Politics, Patronage, and Piety," 941, and note 27.

74. On St. Vincent's chapel, see Horobin, "Manuscript Found," 141, and Christopher Harper-Bill, ed., *Cartulary of the Augustinian Friars of Clare*, 8, 12, and 74.

75. British Library MS Arundel 327 also embellishes the verse forms of some of Bokenham's legends in this way: see, e.g., the opening of the *Life of St. Margaret* (fol. 7r) (British Library, Catalogue of Illuminated Manuscripts, http://www.bl.uk/catalogues/illuminatedmanuscripts/ILLUMIN.ASP?Size=mid&IllID=7585, accessed June 16, 2015). Cf. Abbotsford MS, fol. 129v.

76. It may also signal ethical similarity: see Horobin, "Politics, Patronage, and Piety," 936.

Chapter 5

1. Arundel served in both offices in 1396, 1399, and 1407–10. On the tension between the idea of the *libertas ecclesiae* and the fact of the church's pervasive integration into late medieval political culture, see Benjamin Thompson, "Prelates and Politics from Winchelsey to Warham."

2. Richard G. Davies, "Thomas Arundel as Archbishop of Canterbury," 14.

3. R. L. Storey, "Episcopal King-Makers," 83.

4. Storey, "Episcopal King-Makers," 89.

5. Paul Strohm, *England's Empty Throne*, passim.

6. Catto suggests that the 1414 statute on Lollardy marks the decisive moment when religion was "established and enforced by public authority," in contrast to the separate jurisdictions of church and state before 1400; Jeremy Catto, "Religious Change Under Henry V," 97. On the limited effect of the Constitutions, see Kathryn Kerby-Fulton, *Books Under Suspicion*, 397–401.

7. For an extended account of the differences between ecclesiastical and secular political jurisdiction, see R. N. Swanson, *Church and Society in Late Medieval England*, chap. 4, "Two Laws, One Kingdom."

8. See Phyllis Roberts, "Prophecy, Hagiography, and St. Thomas of Canterbury," 73–74; T. A. Sandquist, "The Holy Oil of St. Thomas of Canterbury," 334–39; and Christopher Wilson, "The Tomb of Henry IV and the Holy Oil of St. Thomas," 181–82. Roberts notes that the oil continued to be used throughout the fifteenth century, perhaps as late as 1509: Roberts, "Prophecy," 75. See also Nigel Mortimer, *John Lydgate's Fall of Princes*, 139n.

9. Catto remarks that Chichele presided over what was in effect an "autonomous national church" while also playing an active role on the king's council, which he headed when Henry V was in France on campaign. After Henry V's death, Chichele served on Henry VI's minority council up through the 1430s: Catto, "Henry Chichele."

10. Perhaps in part, as Catto suggests, by borrowing music used in the king's chapel for liturgical celebration of these saints: Catto, "Henry Chichele."

11. British Library Additional MS 11565 and Lambeth Palace Library MS 72: Richard Hamer and Vida Russell, eds., *Supplementary Lives*, 283.

12. Readings of the *Life of Sts. Edmund and Fremund* that focus on its royal addressee include Jennifer Sisk, "Lydgate's Problematic Commission"; Fiona Somerset, " 'Hard Is with Seyntis to Make Affray' "; and Karen Winstead, *John Capgrave's Fifteenth Century*, 116–37.

13. Robert Meyer-Lee, "The Emergence of the Literary." On the literary status of these texts, see A. S. G. Edwards, "John Lydgate's *Lives of Ss Edmund and Fremund*," 141.

14. On the hypothesis that the *Gilte Legende* is a product of St. Alban's, see n48 of Chapter 4. Further association between Lydgate's work and the *Prose SEL* is witnessed by the fragmentary table of contents for a lost copy of the amplified *Gilte Legende*, preserved in the binding of Paris, Bibiliothèque Nationale MS nouv. acq. lat. 3075, which also lists Lydgate's *Life of Our Lady*: see Walter Sauer, "Manfred Görlach," 249.

15. For other genealogies for emerging ideas of literature and a specifically literary tradition in this period, see John Bowers, *Chaucer and Langland*; Robert Meyer-Lee, *Poets and Power*; Maura Nolan, *John Lydgate and the Making of Public Culture*; and Jennifer Summit, *Lost Property*.

16. First noted by Pierce Butler, cited in Manfred Görlach, *Studies in Middle English Saints' Legends*, 78.

17. Mary Jeremy, "Caxton and the Synfulle Wretche," *Traditio* 4 (1946): 424, cited in Görlach, *Studies in Middle English Saints' Legends*, 78n114. Görlach states that Jeremy's argument is "demonstrably false" and argues that the omission should be attributed to a copyist, not the translator, who would have "probably turned to a supplementary exemplar to fill the gap" (78). But the grammatical adequacy of the passage may point to intentional omission rather than eye skip. Jeremy's argument may seem more plausible if the patent evidence of the discontinuities in monarchical lineage available to any fifteenth-century English writer or reader, rather than patriotism, is adduced to explain the omission. Of particular interest to me is her observation that the resulting incoherence of the story was "apparently of secondary importance."

18. The *Life of Edmund of Abingdon* is missing from British Library Additional MS 11565, along with the other Lives that open the series, and it appears in a different position in Southwell Minster MS 7: see Hamer and Russell, *Supplementary Legends*, xv.

19. Cf. the *SEL Life of St. Alphege*, discussed in Chapter 1.

20. Another change from the *SEL*—the added detail that Alphege's body was first buried in

London, before its translation to Canterbury (167)—is further evidence of the London affiliations of the *Prose SEL*.

21. The ideological fiction of a monastic remove from secular concerns was belied in practice by the political stature and economic power of the Benedictine order. See Catto, "Religious Change Under Henry V," 102–3; Julian Luxford, *The Art and Architecture of English Benedictine Monasteries*, 118; and Kevin Shirley, *The Secular Jurisdiction of Monasteries*, passim. Luxford provides a useful overview of the ideological and material challenges facing the Benedictine order in the fifteenth century, pp. 115–50.

22. R. Davies, "Thomas Arundel as Archbishop of Canterbury," 14.

23. John Ganim, "Lydgate, Location, and the Poetics of Exemption," 169.

24. A. R. Myers, *English Historical Documents*, 784 (item 470). For the full text, see William Abel Pantin, ed., *Documents Illustrating the Activities of the General and Provincial Chapters of the English Black Monks*, 110–15. See also Phillip Stump, *The Reforms of the Council of Constance*, 158.

25. Michelle Still, *The Abbot and the Rule*, 8, 22–23.

26. The proposal was adopted in the *Decretales reformationis*: Stump, *Reforms*, 148 and 158. As the motive force behind the English delegation to Pisa, and a mentor to Thomas Spofford and Chichele, both leading members of the English delegation to Constance, Arundel played a key role in monastic reform, on which see Gerald Harriss, *Shaping the Nation*, 318.

27. Stump, *Reforms*, 148–49.

28. On Chichele's role, see E. F. Jacob, *Archbishop Henry Chichele*, 35.

29. The following paragraph relies throughout on Mortimer, *John Lydgate's Fall of Princes*, 135–44.

30. Mortimer, *John Lydgate's Fall of Princes*, 132–33n100.

31. Ganim, "Lydgate, Location, and the Poetics of Exemption," 167. The relationship between Lydgate's Lives and the debate about the status and privileges of Bury St. Edmunds and St. Albans is echoed almost a hundred years later in the publication of Bradshaw's *Life of St. Werburge*, at the behest of John Birchenshawe, Abbot of Chester, in the context of similar debates about his right to wear pontificalia and the monastery's exemption: see Tim Thornton, *Cheshire and the Tudor State*, 193–95.

32. Cf. Cynthia Camp, *Anglo-Saxon Saints' Lives*, 173–209, which reads the presentation manuscript of the *Life of Sts. Edmund and Fremund* as split between the text's interest in sacred time and a visual program that emphasizes the monastery's historical role as custodian of St. Edmund's shrine.

33. Recent critics have discussed this narrative as a didactic allegory for, and defense of, the pious king: Somerset, " 'Hard Is with Seyntis to Make Affray,' " and Sisk, "Lydgate's Problematic Commission."

34. Lydgate's investment in this hierarchical structure of political authority is underscored by the episode at Thetford, a town mercilessly attacked by the Danes. Its community of citizens—identified as such—models a horizontal form of community, in contrast to the corporate model of the realm over which the king presides as head, and this difference presumably accounts for its terrible fate.

35. Giorgio Agamben, *Homo Sacer*.

36. Lydgate has selected and reordered miracles recounted in his primary source, the *Vita et passio cum miraculis sancti Edmundi* in Oxford, Bodley MS 240, a text included in Carl Horstmann, ed., *Nova Legenda Anglie*, 575–647. On Lydgate's sources for the miracles, see Anthony

Bale and A. S. G. Edwards, "Introduction," in *John Lydgate's Lives of Ss. Edmund and Fremund*, 20–24, 169–72. All quotations of the *Life of Sts. Edmund and Fremund* are from this edition. On the order of the miracles, see James Miller, "Lydgate the Hagiographer as a Literary Artist," 280.

37. Somerset notes that this miracle was not traditionally linked to Edward's visit and donation: "'Hard Is with Seyntis to Make Affray,'" 265, citing James Miller Jr., "John Lydgate's Saint Edmund and Saint Fremund: An Annotated Edition" (PhD diss., Harvard University, 1967), 347.

38. For these events, see Mortimer, *John Lydgate's Fall of Princes*, 145–47, on which I rely.

39. "Lollardis" doubles the generic term "heretikes" (1.933) here, but it resonates with the close association of the term with contemporary Wycliffite challenges to the church (against which Edmund serves as a "strong wall") and heterodoxy ("false doctrine"). Somerset calls this passage the "poem's most blatant presentism": "'Hard Is with Seyntis to Make Affray,'" 267.

40. Cf. the attribution of a versified account of the abbey's privileges, the "Cartae Versificatae," to Lydgate: see Ganim, "Lydgate, Location, and the Poetics of Exemption," 170, and Mortimer, *John Lydgate's Fall of Princes*, 149.

41. Each of the eight stanzas of the final prayer ends with the line "Pray for thenherytour off Ingelond and France" or a close variation (3508–71).

42. Somerset, "'Hard Is with Seyntis to Make Affray,'" reads it as a corrective to a dangerously pacifist model of kingship; Sisk, "Lydgate's Problematic Commission," reads it as a failed attempt to combine incompatible genres.

43. The *MED* gives Lydgate's *Edmund and Fremund* as the first attestation of "prothomartir."

44. John Lydgate, *Saint Alban and Saint Amphibalus*. All further citations are given parenthetically.

45. On the efforts to present Henry VI as sovereign in 1439, see John Watts, *Henry VI and the Politics of Kingship*, 140–41.

46. While Lydgate's poem differentiates secular and sacred communities, partly through their separate etiologies, this doubling also opens the poem to readings that might insist on their identity. Indeed, this seems implied by the 1534 edition of the poem, printed by John Herford at the request of Robert Catton, Abbot of St. Alban's. The end of the poem has been lightly revised to address Henry VIII, his queen Katherine, and their infant daughter and is surely meant to suggest that the abbey and its patron saint can help to authorize the king's newly claimed status as head of the English church and perhaps—in the insistence on St. Alban's exempt status in the printer's explicit—even to model England's exemption from Roman authority. John Lydgate, *The Glorious Lyfe and Passion of Seint Albon Prothomartyr of Englande*, 1534.

47. The St. Alban's monk Matthew Paris had similarly developed an elaborated sense of the monastery as a microcosm of the nation, believing that these institutions "represented the same static pattern of government on a progressively large scale": Antonia Gransden, *History Writing in England*, 373.

48. In contrast, Britain as a secular political form remains tied to Rome through the administrative structure of the empire: the colonial administrators communicate regularly with Rome, and Alban's persecutors wait six months for instructions from the emperor, because they are terrified to punish his favorite without explicit permission.

49. Cf. Christopher Cannon, *Middle English Literature*, 173–86.

50. The category is Christopher Cannon's: Cannon, "Monastic Productions."

51. Lydgate's presentation of his style in the *Life of Sts. Edmund and Fremund* has received

important recent attention from Ruth Nissé, who understands it as an effect of the poem's "ideologically incoherent" praise for Henry VI, and from Alexandra Gillespie, who argues for its affiliation with poem's devotional claims: Gillespie, "The Later Lives of St Edmund," and Nissé, "'Was It Not Routhe to Se?'"

52. However mediated by Lydgate's own *Troy Book*.

53. My understanding of aureate style and Lydgate's conception of the literary has been significantly advanced by Meyer-Lee, "Emergence of the Literary."

54. Lois Ebin shows that terms such as "enlumyn" and "aureate" articulate Lydgate's poetics: Ebin, "Poetics and Style in Late Medieval Literature," 268–69.

Chapter 6

1. Audelay is especially concerned with heterodoxy, which we have seen was an important framework and warrant for the coordination of these two jurisdictions. Susanna Fein notes that Audelay seems to object especially to the punishment of heterodoxy by secular authorities, most strikingly in the refrain *Nolo mortem peccatoris*. Fein, ed., *John the Blind Audelay*, 24.

2. There is a unique stanzaic *Life of St. Thomas* in a mid-fifteenth-century copy of the *SEL*, Bodleian MS Rawl. poet 225. An excerpt of this version, the story of Becket's parents, has been edited: Paul Alonzo Brown, "Development of the Legend of Thomas Becket," 262–68. Like the carols, this version has a pronounced interest in London: e.g., it underscores Thomas's exceptional childhood through comparison with contemporary London children: "suylk a child levande has no burges now in lundun" (fol. 56r).

3. E.g., "The fyrst day of yole have we in mynd," found in Oxford, Bodleian MS Eng. poet. e. 1, and MS Sloane 2593: Thomas Wright, ed., *Songs and Carols Now First Printed*, 24; and "All holy chyrch was bot a thrall," in British Library MS Egerton 3307, in Richard Leighton Greene, ed., *Selection of English Carols*, 80. Both refer to Thomas's parents, which may suggest a London provenance. Audelay's St. Thomas carol is part of a Christmas sequence, which includes a Nativity carol (#6) and an Epiphany carol (#15), as well as carols for important feasts that fall between them.

4. Cf. "Pastor cesus in gregys medio": the second stanza of which begins "Hys moder be blyssed that hym bar, / And also hys fader that hym begatt": Richard Leighton Greene, ed., *Early English Carols*, 73 (item 115). The juxtaposition of London and Canterbury constitutes the second half of the very short carol "Clangat tuba, martir Thoma": "In London was bore this martir sothely; / Of Caunterbury hadde he primacy, / To whom we syng deuotely": Greene, *Early English Carols*, 74 (item 116).

5. See reference to his parents in Audelay's carol, which in this way is also representative of the St. Thomas carol tradition. Audelay is known to have been in London from records of the altercation there involving his patron, Lord Lestrange.

6. Brown, "Development," 20. Caroline Barron notes that the seal shows the city's patron saints, along with some of its architectural features, with the citizens imagined as supplicants in relationship to them, and she contrasts this to royal seals, which do not depict English subjects: Barron, "Political Culture," 113–14.

7. I am grateful to Andrea Bartelstein, librarian at Rauner Special Collections, Dartmouth, for supplying me with copies of the fragments, which retain slightly more of the text than the fragments themselves, which are now held by the British Library: "Verse Life of St. Thomas," London, John Rastell, c. 1520, Shelfmark C. 189. C. 17. On the text, see Ray Nash, "Rastell Fragments at Dartmouth."

8. All references are to Carl Horstmann, ed., "Thomas Beket, Epische Legende." A digital facsimile of the single extant manuscript, Cambridge, Corpus Christi College MS 298, is available through the Parker Library online; my notes regarding the manuscript and presentation of the text rely on this facsimile.

9. On Wade's sources, see Horstmann, "Thomas Beket," 407; and Brown, "Development," 36, 78n, 96, and 141n.

10. On the nature of the late medieval "public," see John Watts, "The Pressure of the Public." See also Maura Nolan, *John Lydgate*.

11. Cf. the exploration of this phenomenon in Hoccleve's *Complaint*.

12. Wade's legend is part of a late flowering of Lydgatean tradition that also includes Henry Bradshaw's *Life of St. Werburge* and Edmund Hatfield's *Lyf of Saynt Ursula*.

13. The term is also found in the Latin rubric, which closes with "ad laudem dei omnipotentis & laureate sui Martiris Thome" (411), and throughout the legend: e.g., the saint "gatt the laurealle" for establishing the church's right (line 19), and "Oure blessede patrone, laureate martyr Thomas" (line 97).

14. The poem's topical affiliation is not limited to its author: a rubric to the poem identifies Bosham, a key source, as a brother of the priory (*pace* modern historians), and the closing stanza presents a prayer for the community's "hede-fathere" (2294).

15. Cf. C. David Benson, *Chaucer's Religious Tales*, 22–23.

16. See Joseph B. Sheppard, ed., *Literae Cantuarienses*, III, 331–33 (document 1107). See also John Harvey, *English Cathedrals*, 138.

17. The manuscript copy of the legend apparently postdates its composition: whereas the poet explicitly refuses to name himself in the poem, the headnote identifies him as Lawrence Wade, a monk of the priory. The text itself is not ostentatious although it is carefully produced, with a generous mise-en-page of three stanzas per page and Latin rubrics that announce major plot points. The materials with which it is bound are certainly later than the composition of the poem: the list of archbishops (fols. 107r–113v) extends to William Warham (1503–32) and the list of priors (fols. 114r–120v) to Thomas Goldwell, who served in the office up until the priory was dissolved in 1539. The names of Thomas Cranmer, Reginald Pole, and Mathew Parker were added by a sixteenth-century hand.

18. According to a contemporary account of this event, the emperor and king were greeted by the archbishop and "ii other mytred"—one of whom is likely to have been the prior—upon their arrival at Canterbury, where they prayed at St. Thomas's shrine: Joycelyne Russell, *The Field of the Cloth of Gold*, 209 (appendix C). Positioned between Dover and Westminster, the priory had long served as a meeting ground or way station for foreign dignitaries, see, e.g., Joseph B. Sheppard, ed., *Christ Church Letters*, 57–58 (letter LIV), in which Henry VII requests that the prior entertain an ambassador from the king of Romania who was to deliver the livery of the Toison d'Or.

19. See Chapter 1 on this metaphor as it is used in the *SEL*.

20. That is, it presents sovereignty in terms of territorial boundaries, rather than bonds of obligation not confined to a specific geography.

21. Wade's account of the debate regarding spiritual and temporal jurisdiction follows Bosham. The poem records the specific provisions of the statute and the archbishop's response: the statute declared that disputes between secular authorities and clerks were to be adjudicated in secular courts, as should disputes within the church regarding benefices (the first article, at lines 946–59); that clerks accused of crimes were to be taken before secular judges (second

article, at lines 960–80); that archbishops could not leave the realm without license of the king (third article, lines 981–1015). Thomas recognizes these claims as the "subuersyone off alle spiritualle liberty" (973).

22. This is an argument advanced on the level of the manuscript as a whole in its attention to coronation, the ritual enactment of this hierarchy: in most instances the list of English kings includes the name of the archbishop who crowned the king, along with the identity of the king's father and his place of burial. See, for example, the entries for Richard II, Henry IV, and Henry V (105r–105v). This is followed by a list of the archbishops of Canterbury, presented similarly on the page.

23. The limits of the king's territory are also suggested in this passage by Thomas's concern that "owt-kyngys" (1099) will also claim this authority if the English king does.

24. E.g., priests should be obeyed "here" (1005); they should "be here putt aparte" from others by virtue of their office (1037).

25. Cf. the use of the same trope in the *SEL Life of St. Thomas*.

26. The involuted image depends on the idea of the monastery—one referent for "religion" here—as exempt from the secular order: Thomas is "belefte dede to the worlde" by virtue of entering the Cistercian house. Nevertheless, the anxiety it expresses about a sacred space distinguished from the "world" but still available as a refuge from persecution opens it beyond a specifically monastic context. While this passage is taken from Bosham's vita (bk. 4, chap. 20), it may have had topical significance in light of Morton's efforts to reform sanctuary practices, which depend on delimited and exceptional spaces of the sacred. See Christopher Harper-Bill, ed., *Register of John Morton*, I: xi, 2 (item 10), and 13 (item 49).

27. Wade takes this miracle from Herbert: Brown, "Development," 129–30. Cf. the miracle recounted in Richard Pynson's Life of St. Thomas, in which angelic choirs miraculously start singing the liturgy for martyrs during mass: Pynson, ed., *Here begynneth Lyfe of the Blessed Martyr Saynte Thomas*, fol. 1v.

28. Wade here distills this father/son conflict from the more complex history that is given greater acknowledgment in earlier versions of the story, most notably by omitting reference to the role of Henry's other sons and their mother.

29. This scene was depicted in the windows of St. Thomas of Acre in London: D. R. Woolf, "The Power of the Past," 24.

30. See lines 757–61.

31. It is unclear whether the speaker is Thomas himself or the collective voice of Thomas and his "comprovynciallys," as seems to be suggested later (767). In Herbert of Bosham, a rubric identifies this as Thomas's position, his insistence on the liberties of the church.

32. The martyred Becket is himself a Benedictine monk manqué: when the priory monks guard the body from the murderers, who return the next day with the intention of further desecrating the corpse, they discover Thomas's hair shirt, over which he was wearing "a coole hoodles suche as blake monkys were" (2168).

33. Frank Barlow, "Herbert of Bosham."

34. A *nota bene* in the margin marks this passage in the manuscript, fol. 56r.

35. It may be contrasted in this regard to the Rastell *Life of St. Thomas*, mentioned above, which includes discussion of the translation and the countless miracles it effects, as well as reference to Becket's Tuesdays, which informed contemporary devotional and pilgrimage practice.

36. Historians link these appointments with the critical role that Morton played in the

accession of Henry VII. See R. L. Storey, "Episcopal King-makers," and C. S. L. Davies, "Bishop John Morton, the Holy See, and the Accession of Henry VII." I rely throughout this paragraph on Harper-Bill, "Archbishop John Morton and the Province of Canterbury, 1486–1500."

37. *Pace* later Protestant historiography that represents Morton as ruthless, Harper-Bill argues for his fundamentally sound administration and sees him as a strong agent of reform: Harper-Bill, "Archbishop," 13, and Harper-Bill, "John Morton."

38. The resulting tensions were acute between the archbishop and St. Alban's under Abbot William Wallingford: see Harper-Bill, "Archbishop," 7. Morton's register includes several papal bulls authorizing the archbishop to reform exempt monastic houses: Harper-Bill, *Register of John Morton*, I, x, especially items 9, 48, 50, which command the reform of St. Alban's. See also M. D. Knowles, "The Case of St. Alban's Abbey in 1490," cited by Harper-Bill, "John Morton."

39. Harper-Bill, "Archbishop," 13.

40. On the tensions provoked by Morton's interest in *sede vacante* privileges, see Harper-Bill, *Register of John Morton*, II, ix–xvi. Morton's register provides several examples of revenues appropriated to the episcopal *mensa*, e.g., nearly £60 in tithes when the see of Worcester was vacant: Harper-Bill, *Register of John Morton*, II, 153 (item 506). The extensive record of the 1499 visitation of the see of Norwich is an indication of Morton's rigorous assertion of his jurisdiction over the material and spiritual fabric of the church: see, e.g., Harper-Bill, *Register of John Morton*, III, 160–68 (items 289–327). For records of the extended contest between the archbishop and the prior and convent of Winchester regarding the episcopal *mensa*, see Harper-Bill, *Register of John Morton*, I, 68–100 (items 221–66).

41. Harper-Bill, "Archbishop," 14.

42. The privilege, dating to 1331, was granted by Edward III and confirmed by Pope John XXII: Harper-Bill, "Archbishop," 15.

43. The dispute was finally resolved by the pope in 1499: Harper-Bill, "Archbishop," 15–17, quotation at 16.

44. Harper-Bill, "Archbishop," 20.

45. Wade borrows here from Herbert of Bosham, "Vita S. Thomae," 3.7–13.

46. See, e.g., the letter between the prior and Morton regarding the construction of the cathedral's central tower: Sheppard, *Christ Church Letters*, item 58.

47. Cf. Derek Pearsall, " 'If Heaven Be on This Earth.' "

48. Harper-Bill, "Archbishop," 17–20.

49. Harper-Bill, *Register of John Morton*, I, vii–viii.

50. Morton's role in Henry VII's accession and later in Parliament as the king's mouthpiece provides a topical framework for Wade's optimism about the coordination of church and crown. Harper-Bill, "Archbishop," 2.

51. Important studies include Jennifer Bryan, *Looking Inward*, and Nicole Rice, *Lay Piety and Religious Discipline in Middle English Literature*.

52. Wade draws attention to his suturing together of these two sources. In recounting Gilbert's imprisonment by the "Saracens," he identifies Grandison—"one Johne, bisshope off Excetere" (28)—as his source, remarking that Herbert of Bosham "dothe nott toche" this story (29).

53. Narrative mapping suggests an alternative reading in which the value accorded to Maud's love is more ambiguous: Maud has traveled to London in the company of pilgrims (59), presumably English pilgrims returning from the Holy Land, in a kind of reverse pilgrimage from the Holy Land to the object of her erotic desire.

54. Gilbert's dissimulation is thematically important here: although the legend identifies

inward change and disposition as the true forms of the sacred, it does not discount the power of sacramental language. The marriage promise—even of a Christian prisoner lying to a Saracen girl—has binding force. Indeed, precisely because it is not fully intended, it has the force of prophecy (see line 90, where the Bishop of Chichester addresses the question "in voice off prophecy").

55. *MED*, "subget," 2.b and d.

56. The secrecy of this practice is emphasized again at line 289.

57. Cf. Walter Hilton's representation of "a gode night and a lighti merkenesse," which contrasts with daylight and an attendant focus on the worldly, in *Scale of Perfection*. See Thomas Bestul, "Introduction," in *Scale of Perfection*.

58. This runs counter to the censure that a failure to enunciate liturgical language usually elicits, e.g., Titivillus, the demon responsible for collecting the syllables dropped by priests when performing the liturgy. Here, however, this failure is valued as evidence of sincere devotion as opposed to outward show.

59. Wade refers to Thomas's book as an "enchiridione," that is, a short treatise, in this case probably Anselm's *Orationes sive Meditaciones*, though possibly another selection of Anselm's devotional writings. On the manuscript tradition of Anselmian prayers and meditations, see Thomas Bestul, "The Collection of Private Prayers."

60. The mayor, sheriff, aldermen, and other citizens also heard mass or made processions from St. Thomas of Acre on November 1; Christmas Day; December 26, 28, and 29; January 1, 2, and 6; and May 6. See D. J. Keene and Vanessa Harding, "St. Mary Colechurch 105/18."

61. Caroline Barron and Marie-Helene Rousseau, "Cathedral, City and State, 1300–1540," 39; Brown, "Development," 21, citing *Liber Albus*, trans. H. T. Riley (London, 1861).

62. Brown, "Development," 21.

63. For examples of the first, see William Caxton, *Legenda aurea sanctorum sive Lombardica historia*, fol. 105r, and Pynson, *Lyfe of the Blessed Martyr Saynte Thomas*, fol. 1v. Maud knows only "London," in the *SEL* (II, 613). In the *Prose SEL Becket*, Gilbert tells Maud that he lives "In Englonde, in the cite of London." She responds, "To London wol I come for thi sake if thou wilte promyse to wedde me to thi wife"—a promise that seems to complete or extend her earlier promise to become Christian to secure his love. In this version, she must become a Londoner, as well as a co-religionist, to become a worthy wife, just as Gilbert's identity is linked intimately to the city. So too her wandering seems driven by her desire for the city as well as for Gilbert: she spends "so many yeres wanderyng aboute hedir and thedyr and euer she askyd aftir 'London, London,' and 'Beket, Beket'" (286).

64. The story of Gilbert's pilgrimage may lie behind the indulgence, printed by Pynson in 1515 for St. Thomas of Acre, addressed to English people who can "not conuenyently nor profytably" keep a vow to go on pilgrimage to Jerusalem. The indulgence offers dispensation from such vows for bequests left to St. Thomas's: see St. Thomas's Hospital, London, "Be it known to all cristen men and women, that thyse be the great indulgence." Gilbert's pilgrimage also finds a parallel in the indulgences granted to those present at the "house of Seynt Thomas of Acres in London," on certain feast days, which earned them "as great & lyke pardon and Indulgence with remyssyon of synnes as if they personally shuld vysyt the Churche at Rome named Scala Celi / and all other churches and holy places of Rome": see St. Thomas's Hospital, London, "Here after foloweth the newe pryuyleges and indulgences graunted by our holy Father Pope Leo X to the house of seynt Thomas of Acres in London." The small woodcut in the upper left corner of the folio closely resembles the one used by Pynson in his 1520 edition of the *Life of St. Thomas*, cited above.

65. The vision is found in neither of Wade's two primary and acknowledged sources, Grandison and Herbert of Bosham. There are, however, analogues in other Latin and vernacular legends, including Guernes de Pont-St.-Maxence and the Icelandic saga version of the legend: see Brown, "Development," 75. Compare Thomas's mother's vision as related by FitzStephen, in which she dreams that she "carried in her womb the whole church of Canterbury": George Greenaway, ed. and trans., *The Life and Death of Thomas Becket* (London: Folio Society, 1961), 35, cited in Phyllis Roberts, "Prophecy, Hagiography, and St. Thomas of Canterbury," 70.

66. Although the focus on London is largely confined to the beginning of the legend, the city is a key location and form of community throughout. Canterbury is also represented as an urban space, a pilgrimage city, especially in the account of Thomas's martyrdom, which includes a memorable scene of the people of the city collecting the saint's blood and marking themselves with it. Even in this section of the poem, the cathedral and monastic community are much less visible than the city as a locus of community.

67. Sheppard, *Christ Church Letters*, xxxv–xxxvi.

68. There had not been significant conflicts between the prior of Christ Church and the archbishop since the twelfth century. From the end of the fourteenth century, the priory was exempt from general chapters of the Benedictine order, an exemption granted by the archbishop, who reserved to himself and the pope the right to visit the priory: "Houses of Benedictine Monks: The Cathedral Priory of the Holy Trinity or Christ Church, Canterbury." Archbishop Morton also played an active role as a mediator between the priory and secular authorities: see, e.g., Morton's letter announcing to the prior the pardon from royal punishment he had secured for two of four monks (the prior was to choose which two): Sheppard, *Christ Church Letters*, 57 (letter LIII).

69. Pynson's *Kalendre* tells the story in a long *occupatio* ("how his moder being a pagan came to London fro fer countres and by the goodness of our Lorde was conuerted to the fayth; & how Seynt Thomas was in fauoure with the kynge and was made his Chaunceller"), on the grounds that the legend is "openly knowen to most people" and that abbreviating it for this context would "make the story the more darke & not to open as it shuld be." Pynson, ed., *Kalendre of the Newe Legende of Englande*, 97v.

70. As Brown notes, the close relation between the legend in Caxton's *Legenda Aurea* and this independent one renders moot the conjectural attribution of the latter to Alexander Barclay: Brown, "Development," 37. Brown notes that the only significant difference is the omission of Jacobus de Voragine's exposition of Thomas's name and Caxton's closing reference to the miracles to be found in the separate entry on the Translation of St. Thomas.

71. The inventory, Public Records Office Prob. 2/692, is edited by R. J. Roberts, "John Rastell's Inventory of 1538." Roberts identifies Rastell as an "ardent Protestant"; see also Russell, *Field of Cloth of Gold*, 33. But he was married to Thomas More's sister Elizabeth, and his son, the printer William Rastell, was a Catholic (he printed John Fisher's sermons in the 1530s). Even if John Rastell's stock of verse Lives of St. Thomas reflects a pragmatic interest in profit, it points to the often-overlooked complexity of private and public confessional identities in the period.

72. More was already Morton's protégé when Wade wrote his verse legend, and as a young lawyer in the mid-1490s, he would have observed the Chancery court at Westminster over which Morton presided as chancellor: Robert Keane, "Thomas More as a Young Lawyer," 44.

73. Dominic Baker-Smith, "Reading *Utopia*," 151. Sarah Rees Jones, noting More's self-representation as "citizen and sheriff of the famous city of London," in both the preface and end note to *Utopia*, argues that "the form of contemporary government uppermost in his

mind was not that of a kingdom, but that of a city": Jones, "Thomas More's Utopia and Medieval London," 117.

74. As Baker-Smith asserts, "monastic observance is never far from the surface" in *Utopia*. On the monastery as a kind of utopia in late medieval literary representations, see Pearsall, "'If Heaven Be on This Earth." Late medieval thinkers also anticipate More in considering the monastery a plausible social model: Reginal Pecock identified the Benedictine monastery as a "microcosm of society" because of its similarity to secular forms of community, in contrast to the eremitic emphasis of orders such as the Carthusians. Pecock, *Reule of Cristen Religion*, ed. Skeet, 416, cited in Jonathan Hughes, *Pastors*, 74.

75. Peter Roberts, "Politics, Drama, and the Cult of Thomas Becket in the Sixteenth Century," 206. On More's time at Oxford, see Howard Baker, "Thomas More at Oxford." Harpsfield notes Morton's patronage of More, and he is among those who identify Hithlodius in *Utopia* as a thinly veiled portrait of Morton: Nicholas Harpsfield, *Life and Death of Sir Thomas Moore*, 10–11, 12, 105.

76. More famously identified himself, and was identified, with Thomas Becket—an association advanced especially by Harpsfield's hagiographic *Life*. On the eve of his execution, More remarked in a letter to his daughter that it was the eve of Thomas's feast day and thus "very mete and conveniente" for his own circumstances: Peter Roberts, "Politics, Drama," 206. The association between Becket and More in Harpsfield is elaborated in Thomas Stapleton, *Tres Thomae* (Douai, 1588), which links Thomas the Apostle, Thomas of Canterbury, and Thomas More.

77. More's verses were performed outside of Deptford, where the mayor and aldermen met the sovereigns on their way to the city: Cambridge, Corpus Christi College MS 298, fol. 123v (Parker Library online). All citations are to this digital facsimile of the manuscript.

78. The one non-English saint included in this set was John the Baptist. The pageant also represented the Assumption of the Virgin, who was accompanied by the angels Michael and Gabriel (128v).

79. An analogous function is served by the way the pageants figure England as an island (126v–127r)—a place, like the city, that figures a finite and homogeneous space. The pageant's representation of London as a paradigm for England is underscored by Latin verses by William Lily, also given in English translation, included in the pamphlet that Pynson printed in honor of the occasion. The penultimate stanza, addressed to the city's mayor and "senators," praises the "noble cite" of London as the "flour of Christente," and it compliments the city officials for showing "what longeth to highe honours / To largesse / noblesse / and royall soueraynte" in the pageant, which is soon to be registered in the "house of fame . . . there it shall remayne euer without ende." Richard Pynson, ed., *Of the tryumphe*, 6v. The citizens themselves are lauded in the final stanza, congratulated for their devotion to Juno and Minerva, as well as their good fortune in counting Lily, the "flour of Poesy," in their midst.

80. This does not produce a problem in More's ideal polity, where that exalted state is well earned and where the economic and social structure eliminates the institutional privileges conducive to priestly immorality.

Chapter 7

1. Gordon Kipling, ed., *Receyt of the Ladie Kateryne*, 236.

2. E.g., at Litcham and Belstead, Suffolk: Eamon Duffy, *Stripping the Altars*, 171.

3. Osbern Bokenham, *Legendys of Hooly Wummen*, 87 (line 3186). The Abbotsford

legendary version shows no similar identification with the English king at this point: it reads "his cruelnesse" (206r).

4. The significant interest in the Ursula legend generated by the Galfridian story is notable compared to the relative lack of interest in St. Helen, whose British origin is explicitly promoted by Geoffrey. Aside from a version of the Helen legend added to fifteenth-century copies of the *SEL*, there is little evidence of interest in Helen as a British saint. An exception is the narrative sequence in stained glass at Ashton-Under-Lyne: Henrietta Reddish, "The Saint Helen Window Ashton-Under-Lyne," and Philip Nelson, "The Fifteenth-Century Glass in the Church of St. Michael, Ashton-Under-Lyne." On the Helen legend, see Antonia Harbus, *Helena of Britain in Medieval Legend*.

5. On the relationship between the hagiographic and historiographic versions of the Ursula legend traditions, see Marcelle Thiebaux, "Dameisele Ursula."

6. By at least the early fourteenth century, some manuscripts of the *History of the Kings of Britain* make the association.

7. The image is on fol. 30v; the story continues to fol. 31r: an online digital facsimile is found at http://bodley30.bodley.ox.ac.uk:8180/luna/servlet/view/all/what/MS.+Laud+Misc.+733.

The rubric to the right of the miniature reduces the story so that it accords with the Jacopean legend: "How Ursula and xi M° maydenes that were in hire companye comyng toward litil Britaigne were martired atte Coloigne" (30v). The manuscript belonged to George Neville, Lord Abergavenny, who was in attendance at the London pageant for Catherine of Aragon: Elizabeth Bryan, "Amazons and Ursulines," citing Kipling, *Receyt*, 12, 59.

8. Another small change made in this version of the legend is the narrative detail that Ursula and her virgins first go to London to be provisioned with ships and food—a reflection of Ursula's London cult: for the story, see *The Brut or Chronicles of England*, ed. Friedrich Brie, I, 43–44.

9. Robert Fabian, *Newe chronycles of Englande and of Fraunce*, 26v.

10. Cologne was also an important cult site for England's "protomartyr," St. Alban.

11. William Caxton, *Legenda aurea sanctorum*, fol. 337v.

12. The relic was not identified as Ursula when the Bishop of Basel acquired it in the thirteenth century, but it became identified as such when translated to a silver reliquary in the fourteenth century; it was housed in a chapel of the cathedral dedicated to Ursuline relics: Scott Montgomery, *St. Ursula and the 11,000 Virgins of Cologne*, 137–38.

13. The image of Cologne famously depicts the construction of the cathedral. Although these cities were the central cult sites, Western Europe was saturated with Ursuline relics, which had been dispersed in such great numbers in the fourteenth century that Pope Boniface IX banned further distribution in 1393: Montgomery, *St. Ursula*, 27. On the dispersal of bust reliquaries of the Ursuline virgins, see Anton Legner, *Kölner Heilige und Heiligtümer*, 71, and 267–400, passim.

14. On the city and trade networks such as the Hanse as sources for alternative models of secular community that "competed" with the nation, see Hendrik Spruyt, *Sovereign State and Its Competitors*, 59–150 passim.

15. Cf. Chapter 1's discussion of the *SEL Ursula* as an exploration of the paradoxical state that Jean-Luc Nancy calls "being-in-common," in which individual difference is not subsumed by a presumed, or imposed, shared identity, as they are in forms of "communion."

16. Richard Pynson, ed., *Boke of Cokery*, unpaginated [fol. 64r]. The list of "knyghtes wyves" seems to continue on the verso of this page, but it is not legible in the EEBO facsimile. The plans

for Catherine's arrival—revised several times in light of changing circumstances—were foiled by the fact that she landed at Portsmouth instead of Southampton: see Gordon Kipling, ed., *Triumph of Honour*, appendix I, 173–74.

17. Richard Pynson, *A Remembraunce for the Traduction of the Princesse Kateryne*, unpaginated [fol. 2v]. On this text, see Kate Harris, "Richard Pynson's *Remembraunce for the Traduction of the Princesse Kateryne*."

18. If the entry reflects some trace of Elizabeth's influence, she may have been responsible for borrowing elements of Anne of Brittany's use of the Ursula cult, on which see below: Elizabeth's aunt Margaret was one of Anne of Brittany's most important supporters and mentors.

19. Scrope established her feast day in 1401 and perhaps composed masses in her honor: see Pat Cullum, "*Virginitas* and *Virilitas*," 96, citing R. N. Swanson, ed., *Calendar of the Register of Richard Scrope, Archbishop of York, 1398–1405*, Borthwick Texts and Calendars, 11 (1985), vol. 2, n. 725. Merchants, especially those engaged in cloth trade, and hence linked to Cologne and other northern European cities, were another vector for regional promotion of the cult: in 1470, John Walker, the rector of Holy Trinity, Goodramgate in York, commissioned a set of windows that includes a St. Ursula light that is still extant. Walker's name, as Cullum suggests, suggests family ties to the cloth industry and thus indirectly to trade between York and Hanseatic cities.

20. The interest in Ursula among these women is also suggested by the naming of Margaret Pole's daughter Ursula (b. 1504). Pole enjoyed a close friendship with Catherine of Aragon and was half-sister to Margaret Beaufort, with whom she evidently shared an interest in a Tudor Ursula.

21. This corresponds to an emerging understanding of the legend's "Britain" as Wales rather than Cornwall or Brittany.

22. For the historical development of "an idea of a united realm of Britain" in this period, see R. B. Wernham, *Before the Armada*. Wernham points to Henry VII's attempt to forge peace with Scotland, especially in the 1497 truce of Ayton, renewed in 1499 and 1502, and in the marriage of Princess Margaret (60). Important analyses of the colonizing discourses and practices relevant to the representation of Ursula's Britishness include David Baker, *Between Nations*; David Baker and Willy Maley, eds., *British Identities and English Renaissance Literature*; Jeffrey Jerome Cohen, ed., *Cultural Diversity in the British Middle Ages*; R. R. Davies, *First English Empire*; and Simon Meecham-Jones, "Where Was Wales?"

23. On the pageant as a city production, with assistance from the king's household, and possibly also the Bishop of Winchester, see Kipling, *Receyt*, xviii–xxiii; and Sydney Anglo, "The London Pageants for the Reception of Katharine of Aragon," 54–55.

24. Cf. "London, thou art of towns a per se," another celebration of the city evidently occasioned by the royal wedding: the poem is identified in New York, Pierpont Morgan Library MA 717 as having been "made at London when my lorde prince Arthur was wed" (fol. 1): *Index of Middle English Verse* (DIMEV), item 3164. The poem is edited by Curt Bühler, "London Thow Art the Flowre of Cytes All," 8–9.

25. Catherine would surely have known about Ursula from her girlhood devotions. She was baptized by the Bishop of Palencia (Giles Tremlett, *Catherine of Aragon*, 27), whose cathedral boasted an especially important Ursuline relic: the head of Cordula, the one member of Ursula's retinue who hides to avoid death, only to repent and offer herself up for martyrdom the following day. A beautiful fifteenth-century altarpiece, sections of which are now housed at the Lady Lever Art Gallery in Liverpool and at the Prado, graced the Dominican church of San Pablo in

Palencia. On the extensive Ursuline relics in Spain, see Jaime Ferreiro Alemparte, *La leyenda de las once mil vírgenes*, 87–152.

26. Columbus was not the only explorer to express devotion to the saint, who spends a long time at sea until blown to her divinely ordained destinations: in 1520, the Portuguese explorer João Álvares Fagundes named islands off the eastern coast of Newfoundland after the legend, and Magellan named the eastern tip of the Straits of Magellan Cape Virgenes in its honor. Devotion to the saint in the maritime state of Venice also reflects Ursula's association with seafaring: e.g., Carpaccio's magnificent fresco cycle painted for an Ursuline guild in Venice in 1495, which represents Ursula as Venetian and the Huns who martyr the saint and her virgin company as Turks. The saint's association with seafaring accounts at least in some measure for the expansion of the cult to India, East Asia, Brazil, etc., in the sixteenth century: see Alemparte, *La leyenda*, 169–85, and Maria Cristina Osswald, "The Society of Jesus."

27. Garret Mattingly, *Catherine of Aragon*, 12, 38.

28. Kathy Lavezzo, *Angels on the Edge*, passim.

29. After the death of Duke Francis II, Brittany was ruled by his daughter. On this period in Anne's life, see Didier Le Fur, *Anne de Bretagne*, 11–16, and Georges Minois, *Anne de Bretagne*, 155–272.

30. Paris, Bibliothèque Nationale MS Latin 9474, fol. 3. St. Ursula is flanked by St. Anne, the duchess's namesake, and St. Helen, also a British saint. The image of St. Ursula later in the manuscript (fol. 199v) also encodes the association of Anne, with the Breton coat of arms displayed on the bow of Ursula's boat, in the background to her martyrdom. The images are reproduced in Émile Mâle et al., eds., *Les heures d'Anne de Bretagne*.

31. Anne had married the Holy Roman Emperor, Maximilian, by proxy in the hopes of securing military backing against France, but little help was forthcoming. She later married Charles's successor, Louis XII, which further cemented France's claim on Brittany: Minois, *Anne de Bretagne*, 275–78, 400ff.

32. Philip Edwards, *The Making of the Modern English State*, 93.

33. R. B. Wernham, *Before the Armada*, 11.

34. Spruyt, *Sovereign State*, 61–76; David Wallace, *Premodern Places*, 60.

35. It is worth noting that there is reciprocal interest in English cults in Cologne, especially the cult of St. Alban, to whom a parish church in Cologne was dedicated: Hugo Stehkämper, *Bürger und Kirchen in Köln im Hochmittelalter*, 116, 118.

36. On the bridge as the limit of London's jurisdiction, see Caroline Barron, *London in the Later Middle Ages*, 36. St. Ursula appears in this liminal zone also in the form of a brotherhood dedicated to her at St. Olave's in Southwark, which stood at the foot of the bridge, and to which one Elizabeth Bekingham granted a bequest in 1510: London, National Archives, PRO Prob.11/16/465 (Bekingham), with thanks to Katherine French for the reference and a copy of the document. For St. Olave's, see H. E. Malden, ed., "The Borough of Southwark," 4, 151–61.

37. The Hanse encountered increasing opposition from London merchants from the late fourteenth century on. See John Fudge, *Cargoes, Embargoes, and Emissaries*, 11–12, and T. H. Lloyd, *England and the German Hanse*, 53–55. On the relationship between England and Cologne more generally in this period, see Horst Buzello, "Köln und England."

38. Fudge, *Cargoes*, 13. Henry VI reopened negotiations in 1449, in response to the ongoing Burgundian boycott and the war with France, which made trade with the Hanse crucial to the English economy. Edward IV, in an effort to shore up London support, took a harder line with

the Hanse, and he gained a significant advantage when Charles the Bold succeeded Philip the Good and once again allied England with Burgundy: Fudge, *Cargoes*, 14–15, 22, 25.

39. See Fudge, *Cargoes*, 19, 26. On the dominant role of Cologne in London markets in the fifteenth century, see Stuart Jenks, *England, Die Hanse und Preussen Handel und Diplomatie*, I, 330–63. Jenks claims that "die englische Hauptstadt war im 15. Jahrhundert eine Kölner Hochburg" (357).

40. Fudge, *Cargoes*, 68.

41. The association between the Ursula cult and merchants, especially those dealing in the wool trade or with Hanseatic connections, obtains elsewhere in England as well. Thomas Dalton, a merchant of Hull, invokes St. Ursula in his will of 1497: Peter Heath, "Urban Piety in the Later Middle Ages," 214. William of Wigston, a wool merchant and mayor of Leicester, built a new chapel in 1512 dedicated to Mary, St. Ursula, and St. Katherine in the Church of the Annunciation of Our Lady of the Newarke; he founded the Hospital of St. Ursula as well: Charles Billson, *Medieval Leicester*, 81, 85. St. Ursula appears along with a maidenhead representing the Mercer's Company on the license for the Holy Trinity guild at Saffron Walden in Essex, a wealthy wool town. The guild, which held its fair on the feast of St. Ursula, enjoyed the patronage of Joan Bradbury, widow of Thomas Bradbury, mayor of London at his death in 1510 and formerly master of the Mercers: Anne Sutton, "Lady Joan Bradbury," 227.

42. Included in a list of "The nombre and the names of the perishe chirches and of alle odur chirches within london and the suberbis," in Richard Arnold, *In this booke is conteyned the names*, unnumbered page. Arnold's book is a compendium of historical information about London with an emphasis on the rights and liberties of the city and rules governing commerce.

43. Single-page image of St. Ursula, with the text "The Confraternyte of seynt Ursula in seynt Laurence in the Jury. Sancta vrsula cum sodalibus tuis ora pro nobis" (British Library MS C. 18e 2 [33]): Rudolph Kapp, *Heilige und Heiligenlegenden in England*, 172. Kapp is surely right that the print is earlier than 1550, the conjectural date given by EEBO.

44. London, National Archives, PRO Prob.11/24/176 (Hutchens) and Prob.11/21/399 (Pynkton), with thanks to Katherine French for references and copies of the documents. On bequests by merchant testators of St. Laurence Jewry to the parish guild of St. Ursula, see also Anne Sutton, *The Mercery of London*, 193.

45. H. S. Cobb, ed., *Overseas Trade of London*. Cologne pewterers had a special affiliation with the cathedral, as donors of the transverse support of the rood screen. The London pewterer is mentioned by Sylvia Thrupp, who takes his vocation to indicate humble status: Thrupp, *Merchant Class of Medieval London*, 38. But pewterers profited from the rising demand for domestic wares in the fourteenth century, and many became merchants: Ronald Homer, "Tin, Lead, and Pewter," 72–73.

46. Interest in the Ursula legend in this period is also related to the connections that English printers, including Caxton and Wynkyn de Worde, had to Cologne.

47. William Herbert, *History of the Worshipful Company of Drapers of London*, 455–57; Ian Lancaster, *Dramatic Texts and Records of Britain*, 969; Jean Robertson and D. J. Gordon, eds., *A Calendar of Dramatic Records in the Books of the Livery Companies of London*, 13–19.

48. Robert Withington, *English Pageantry*, I, 40n3. One Andrew Wright was paid for "a new pageant of St. Ursula," as well as for repairs to the Assumption pageant: Herbert, *History of the Worshipful Company*, 455. Herbert notes that the Drapers' records point to the involvement of the London sheriff in the selection of the pageant.

49. Nicholas Harris Nicolas, ed., *Privy Purse Expenses of Elizabeth of York*, 77.

50. Charles Kingsford, ed., *Chronicles of London*, 224.

51. Elizabeth Bryan, "Amazons and Ursulines," 30n, notes that the *London Chronicle* account of the pageant is prefaced by this anecdote, followed by a reference to the men that Cabot brought back from a second voyage in 1502, who are described as "clothid in Beestes Skynnes, and ete Raw fflessh, and Rude in their demeanure as Beestes": Kingsford, *Chronicles*, 258.

52. G. N. Garmonsway and R. R. Raymo, eds., "A Middle English Prose Life of St. Ursula." All references are to this edition. My discussion is also based on examination of the manuscript.

53. Garmonsway and Raymo, "Middle English Prose Life of St. Ursula," 353.

54. John Lydgate, "Ye Briton Martyrs famous in perfectness" (DIMEV 6816), in Lydgate, *Minor Poems*, 144, lines 2–5.

55. See the online *MED* entries for "defaden" and "undiffadid." According to the *MED*, "undivided" comes into use only in the fifteenth century but is well attested in Lydgate: the *MED* gives quotations from numerous works, including the *Life of Sts. Alban and Amphibalus* and the *Life of Sts. Edmund and Fremund*. The most resonant for my purposes here is its use in Lydgate's *Procession of Corpus Christi*: "this hoost is hole in ech partye, Bothe God and man, Cryste Jhesus verraily In eche partycle hoole and vndevyded" (174).

56. There is a striking parallel in another *Festial* manuscript, Cambridge University Library MS Ee.2.15, which includes "Dame Custance" and Lydgate's *Life of Sts. Edmund and Fremund*. Like the Ursula legend, the Custance story involves a devout Christian woman who wanders about in a boat in a plot that links marriage to sacred trial, and in both manuscripts these stories preface native saints' Lives. For a description of the manuscript, see M. F. Wakelin, "Manuscripts," 108–9.

57. Southwell Minster MS 7, fol. 173v. I am grateful to Brian Whitehouse, of Southwell Minster Historic Chapter Library, for providing me with digital facsimiles of the manuscript by permission of the Dean and Chapter of Southwell.

58. See Karma Lochri, *Covert Operations*, and Emma Lipton, *Affections of the Mind*. Cf. the definition of matrimony as "to cupyll two persons in one wyll" in the York rite: W. G. Henderson, ed., *Manuale et processionale*, given as a quotation for *MED* "couplen," 1.a.

59. This homogeneous national community is complemented by an international one: Ursula's father writes to the queen of Sicily, who gathers virgins "fro dyuerse Royammes" and counsels the "knyghtes of her companye"—Caxton's literalization of the trope of Ursula's military "company"—to embrace "this newe chyualrye" of Christianity. These non-Christian knights "make dyuerse playes and games of bataylle," eagerly observed by barons and great lords, who "had ioye and playsyre in beholding them ans also meruaylle" (fol. 336v). After this diversion, they are converted to Christianity by Ursula and set sail the next day, transforming the pilgrim company into something much more closely resembling a Crusading order.

60. Margaret owned a Life of St. Ursula: Rebecca Krug, *Reading Families*, 103. We can assume but not confirm that it was a copy of Hatfield's legend. Hatfield's affiliation with Margaret and his access to one of the poem's primary sources, a version of the vita that circulated in Cologne, discussed in note 65 below, may have been through John Fisher, Bishop of Rochester, later an important advocate for Catherine of Aragon, or through John Alcock, Bishop of Ely. Fisher, who was raised and educated in Beverley, a city in the Hanseatic network, was Margaret's confessor. Alcock, Bishop of Rochester in the 1470s, was Lord Chancellor from 1485 to 1487, as well as the prelate who baptized Prince Arthur, and an intimate of Margaret. His interest in St. Ursula is attested by his address to the synod at Barnwell in 1498, in which she is singled out for

special veneration, partly on the grounds that she was a queen of the "southern shores" (*austri a finibus*) of Britain: John Alcock, *Gallicantus Iohannis alcok epi Eliensis ad confratres suos curatos in sinodo apud Bernwell*, unpaginated (fols. 25v–26r). Wynkyn de Worde was associated with Fisher and Alcock, both of whose works he printed. The career of Thomas Rotherham, Bishop of Rochester from 1468, who negotiated with Cologne merchants on behalf of the crown in 1469, may also be relevant to Hatfield's access to Continental Ursula narratives: see Lloyd, *England and the German Hanse*, 204; and Rosemary Horrox, "Rotherham, Thomas (1423–1500)."

61. Edmund Hatfield, *Here begynneth the lyf* of *saynt Vrsula after the cronycles of englonde*, fols. 2r–2v. All citations are to this edition. The poem is also available as the "Lyf of Saynt Ursula," in the English Poetry Database.

62. See, e.g., the second stanza devoted to the list of kings:

> The nexte Oliuers with his spouse called Oliua
> The thyrde was Crophorus wt Cleopatra his spouse
> The fourth was Lucius fader to ye pryncypall Yotha
> And her two systers / the fyfth was Clodoueus
> His quene Blandina and Eugyn beauteous
> The syxte was Canutus with Balbina his quene
> The seuenth with Margaret quene was Pyppinus
> With theyr foure sones & doughters virgyns clene. (fol. 5v)

63. Elisabeth Schönau played a crucial role in identifying the bonefield with the relics and giving proper names to some of Ursula's companions. The vision of St. Ursula was the most popular part of Elisabeth's *Revelations*, to judge by extant manuscripts, of which there are some seventy: Anne Clark, *Elisabeth of Schönau*, 37–38. Elisabeth's catalog was then amplified by Hermann Joseph.

64. "And as I haue ben enformed in Colyen / that there were men besyde wymmen / that thylke tyme suffryd martirdome fyften thousand / So the nombre of this hooly multitude as of the hooly vyrgyns and men were xxvj M": Caxton, *Legenda aurea sanctorum*, fol. 337v.

65. The earliest edition was printed by Arnold ter Hoernen in Cologne in 1482, with subsequent editions by Johann Guldenschaff (Cologne, 1490 and 1494) and Hermann Bumgart (Cologne, 1500 and 1503). An affiliated text, *Historia undecim milium virginum breviori atque faciliori modo pulcerrime collecta*, was published in Cologne by Martin von Werden in 1500, 1504, 1507, and 1509; and reprinted in 1512 in Cologne by Heinrich von Neuss. Heinrich Quentell's edition, printed in 1503 and 1507, reprinted by J. de Sollingen in 1517, more conspicuously advertises Cologne itself in its title: *Historia vndecim milium virginum breuiori atque faciliori modo pulcherrime collecta: cum capitalium ecclesiarum tam collegiatarum que parochialium atque monasteriorum felicis Civitatis Coloniensis, Et item principalium Reliquiarum in singulis contentarum annotatione.* For this text, I use the 1482 edition held by the Newberry Library, cataloged as *Epistola ad Vergines* (Newberry Inc. 950). I have also consulted the Cologne editions of 1503 and 1512 in digital facsimile.

66. Many versions of the legend, including Jacobus de Voragine's, recount that the name of the British pope Cyriacus is expunged from church history when he abandons his seat to follow Ursula. The nonce identities in the Hatfield legend extend the opposition between a hagiographic and a historiographic discursivity already suggested by this detail in the traditional legend.

67. The poem's alliterative poetics could also be considered "archipelagic" in this context

too: Welsh, Scottish, Irish, and English literary cultures all use alliteration. Often considered a mark of nationalist nostalgia in Middle English textual traditions, alliteration as a prosodic feature common to archipelagic literary communities provides an especially interesting formal "capability" for thinking about their relation.

68. The Life is found in the Book of Sir Hugh Pennant, dated to 1514. Peniarth MS 182, National Library Wales, fols. 261–312: J. G. Evans, ed., *Report on Manuscripts in the Welsh Language*, vol. 1:3, 1007. The Latin poem that follows the Life on fol. 301, *O vernantes christi rose*, is also by Hermann Joseph. For Joseph's authorship of the poem, see François Petit, *Spirituality of the Premonstratensians*, 182. See also Cartwright, *Feminine Sanctity and Spirituality*, 84–85.

69. Citations are to Richard Pynson, ed., *Kalende of the Newe Legende of Englande*, for which I have used the copy held by Ushaw College (shelfmark XVIII C 4 7), and the EEBO facsimile. I thank Mathew Watson of Ushaw College for his kind assistance. The work is also edited by Manfred Görlach, *Kalendre of the Newe Legende of Englande*.

70. In the EEBO facsimile, this page is out of order: it follows folio 112.

71. Pynson remarks that many of the saints he includes were likely unknown to his audience, whose ignorance of English saints he seeks to remedy with the volume: Pynson, *Kalendre*, n.p.

72. Görlach notes the absence of a close source or analogue in Middle English. He also remarks that the legend's length and "aureate" style suggest a different translator from the rest of the volume, from which it departs also in not deriving from *Nova Legenda Anglia*: Görlach, *Kalendre*, 228.

73. In the Newberry edition (1482), "Porro lactentes infantule que vberum lacte nutriri solebant . iam nullo prorsus mammillarum nutrimento alebantur . sed digitos in ora mittebant et statim de ipsis digitis rorem sibi celitus ministratum sugebant. cuius vigore sustentabantur. Nunquam in eodem itinere vt paruulorum mos est et natura. sordebant se madefacientes. sed nec plorantes vagiebant. alijs inferentes molestiam" (not paginated, fol. 9v; cf. bk. 2 of *Revelationes seu imaginations B. Hermanni Iosephi canonici regularis Steinfeldensis*, *AASS* Oct. 9, p. 173).

74. EEBO image 123.

75. See the Book of Hours made in 1501 for Veronica Wesler by Albrecht of Breslau, now Cambridge, Fitzwilliam Museum MS 157. The Welser arms, held by an angel, is on fol. 1r: Nigel Morgan and Stella Panayotova et al., eds., *Catalogue of Western Book Illumination*, item 118. The Welser family devotion to Ursula registers also in the name of one of Veronica's sisters: an Ursula Welser is named in the *Augsburger Klosterchronik* (fol. 37v): Sabine Jansen, "Die Texte des Kirchberg-Corpus," 59.

76. Marie-Luise Ehrenschwendtner reads the paintings as a pointed act of resistance to enclosure, half a century after the fact. Chronicles record the nuns' energetic physical resistance in 1441. They jabbed workmen in the belly as they tried to close off windows and doors. With the paintings, the nuns, long confined to the house, found another form of escape: Ehrenschwendtner, "Virtual Pilgrimage?"

77. I have found no specific record of the Hermannus legend among the extant books or book lists from the nunnery. For a list of books associated with St. Katherine's Augsburg, see Jansen, "Die Texte des Kirchberg-Corpus," 56–59. Jansen notes that Veronica Welser had served as a convent scribe in 1496. The nunnery's chronicle records that she had inherited "etliche teütsche biehlein" of the cloister library (*Augsburger Klosterchronik*, fol. 57r): Jansen, "Die Texte des Kirchberg-Corpus," 60. One late fifteenth-century manuscript owned by the nunnery, now Leipzig Universitätsbibliothek Cod. 1552, contained a vernacular legend of St. Ursula, little of

which is extant due to the loss of a quire (personal communication, Dr. Christoph Mackert, Leipzig University Library). The incipit reads "Es was ein kunig in Britania, der hies Maurus, der was ein cristen. Der hett ein tochter, die hieß Vrsula, die was gar schon vnd weyß vnd behielt ir keusch durch got. Nun was zuo der zeit ein kunig" (Mackert, personal communication). This is different from vernacular legends cataloged by Werner Williams-Krapp, *Die Deutschen und Niederländischen Legendare des Mittelalters*, 466.

78. Such re-scaling is not original or unique to St. Katherine's. It finds an important precedent in the remaking of urban space in Western Europe as replicas or "mementos" of Jerusalem: see Robert Ousterhout, "The Church of Santo Stefano: A 'Jerusalem' in Bologna," *Gesta* 20 (1981): 311–21, with thanks to Jessica Brantley for this reference.

79. Cf. the relationships between communities theorized in the *SEL Ursula*, discussed in Chapter 1.

80. James IV and Margaret named their son Arthur, born in 1509 shortly after Henry VII's death and seven years after the death of Prince Arthur, as part of a broader claim that the future of Arthurian Britain lay with the Stuarts and Scotland: see Katie Stevenson, "Chivalry, British Sovereignty, and Dynastic Politics," 605–7, 610–12. See also David Armitage, "Elizabethan Idea of Empire," 272–73.

81. Braudel, *Civilization and Capitalism*, 3.353.

WORKS CITED

Primary Works

MANUSCRIPTS

Cambridge, Cambridge University Library
    Add. MS 4122
    Add. MS 2604
    MS Ee.2.15
Cambridge, Corpus Christi College MS 298 (Parker Library on the Web)
Cambridge, Gonville and Caius College MS 146/196
Edinburgh, Advocates Library, MS Abbotsford (Osbern Bokenham, *Legenda Aurea*)
London, British Library
    MS Additional 35298
    MS Cotton Faustina B. III
    MS Harley 630
    MS Harley 955
    MS Harley 2403
    MS Harley 4011
    MS Royal 2 A XVIII (British Library Digitized Manuscripts)
    C. 189. C. 17: "Verse Life of St. Thomas." London: John Rastell, c. 1520.
London, National Archives: Public Records Office, Prob. 11
New York, Pierpont Morgan Library
    MS B. 26
    MS M. 105
Oxford, Bodleian Library
    MS 779
    MS Laud Misc. 733 [LUNA]
    MS Rawl. poet 225
Oxford, Corpus Christi College MS 120
San Marino, CA, Huntington Library MS 140
Southwell, Southwell Minster MS 7

EARLY PRINTED BOOKS

Alcock, John. *Gallicantus Iohannis alcok epi Eliensis ad confratres suos curatos in sinodo apud Bernwell*. London: Richard Pynson, 1498. [EEBO]
Arnold, Richard. *In this booke is conteyned the names of ye baylifs custos mairs and sherefs of the*

cite of london from the tyme of king richard the furst. Antwerp: A. van Berghen, 1503? [EEBO]

Blakman, John. *Collectarium mansuetudinum et bonorum morum regis Henrici VI* (Robert Copeland, 1523) and *Kalendre of the Newe Legende of Englande.* London: Pynson, 1516. [Durham, Ushaw College, XVIII C 4 7]

Bradshaw, Henry. *The holy lyfe and history of saynte werburge.* London: R. Pynson, 1521. [EEBO]

Bumgart, Hermann, ed. *Passio sive historia undecim milium virginum.* Cologne, 1503. [Münchener Digitalisierungszentrum]

Caxton, William. *Legenda aurea sanctorum sive Lombardica historia.* London, 1483. [EEBO]

Confraternyte of seynt Ursula in seynt Laurence in the Jury. Sancta vrsula cum sodalibus tuis ora pro nobis. London, s.n., n.d. [EEBO]

Epistola ad Vergines. Cologne: Arnold ter Hoernen, 1482. [Chicago, Newberry Library, Newberry Inc. 950]

Fabian, Robert. *Newe chronycles of Englande and of Fraunce.* London, Pynson, 1516. [EEBO]

Hatfield, Edmund. *Here begynneth the lyf of saynt Vrsula after the cronycles of englonde.* London: Wynkyn de Worde, 1509? [EEBO]

Heinrich von Neuss, ed. *Historia undecim milium virginum breviori atqe faciliori modo pulcerrime collecta.* Cologne, 1512 [Münchener Digitalisierungszentrum]

Lydgate, John. *The Glorious Lyfe and Passion of Seint Albon Prothomartyr of Englande.* London: John Herford, 1534. [EEBO]

Pynson, Richard, ed. *Boke of Cokery.* London, 1500. [EEBO]

——, ed. *Here begynneth Lyfe of the Blessed Martyr Saynte Thomas.* London, 1520. [EEBO]

——, ed. *Kalendre of the Newe Legende of Englande.* London, 1516. [EEBO]

——, ed. *A Remembraunce for the Traduction of the Princesse Kateryne.* London, 1500. [EEBO]

——, ed. *Of the tryumphe, and the verses that Charles themperour, & the most myghty redouted kyng of England, Henry the. viii. were saluted with, passyng through London.* London, 1522. [EEBO]

St. Thomas's Hospital, London. "Be it know[n to all c]risten men and women, that thyse be the great indulgence." London: R. Pynson, 1515. [EEBO]

——. "Here after foloweth the newe pryuyleges and indulgences graunted by our holy Father Pope Leo X to the house of seynt Thomas of Acres in London." London: Pynson, 1517. [EEBO]

MODERN EDITIONS

Babington, Churchill, ed. *Polychronicon Ranulphi Higden.* London, 1865.

Bale, Anthony, and A. S. G. Edwards, eds. *John Lydgate's Lives of Ss. Edmund and Fremund and the Extra Miracles of St. Edmund.* Heidelberg: Universitätsverlag Winter, 2009.

Bliss, W. H., and J. A. Twemlow, eds. *Calendar of Entries in Papal Registries Relating to Great Britain and Ireland.* Vols. 5, 7, and 11. London: Her Majesty's Stationery Office, 1904, 1906, 1921.

Bokenham, Osbern. *Legendys of Hooly Wummen.* Ed. Mary Serjeantson. EETS 206. London: Oxford University Press, 1938.

——, "Mappula Angliae." Ed. Carl Horstmann. *Englische Studien* 10 (1887): 1–34.

Bradshaw, Henry. *Life of St. Werburge of Chester.* Ed. Carl Horstmann. EETS o.s. 88. London: Oxford University Press, 1887.

Brie, Friedrich, ed. *The Brut or Chronicles of England.* 2 vols. EETS 131 and 136. London: Oxford University Press, 1960.

Bühler, Curt. "London Thow Art the Flowre of Cytes All." *Review of English Studies* 13 (1938): 1–9.

Clark, James, ed. *The Chronica Maiora of Thomas Walsingham*. Trans. David Preest. Woodbridge, Suffolk: Boydell, 2009.

de Smedt, Charles, ed. "Documenta S. Wenefreda." *Analecta Bollandiana* 6 (1887): 306–10.

D'Evelyn, Charlotte, and Anna Mill, eds. *South English Legendary*. EETS 235 and 236. London: Oxford University Press, 1956.

Dockray-Miller, Mary, ed. *Saints Edith and Aethelthryth: Princesses, Miracle Workers, and Their Late Medieval Audience: The Wilton Chronicle and the Wilton Life of St. Aethelthryth*. Turnhout, Belgium: Brepols, 2009.

Fein, Susanna, ed. *John the Blind Audelay, Poems and Carols (Bodleian Library MS Douce 302)*. Kalamazoo, MI: Medieval Institute, 2009.

Fowler, J. T., ed. *Life of St. Cuthbert in English Verse, c. A.D. 1450*. Durham, UK: Surtees Society, 1891.

Garmonsway, G. N., and R. R. Raymo, eds. "A Middle English Prose Life of St. Ursula." *Review of English Studies* n.s. 9 (1958): 353–61.

Giles, J. A., ed. *William of Malmesbury's Chronicle of the Kings of England*. Trans. John Sharpe. London, 1866.

Görlach, Manfred, ed. *The Kalendre of the Newe Legende of Englande*. Heidelberg: Universitätsverlag C. Winter, 1994.

Gregory, James Ryan, ed. and trans. "The Life of St. Winifred: The Vita S. Wenefrede from BL Lansdowne MS 436." *Medieval Feminist Forum*. Subsidia series 4 (2016): 1–57.

Greene, Richard Leighton, ed. *Early English Carols*. Oxford: Clarendon, 1935.

———, ed. *Selection of English Carols*. Oxford: Clarendon, 1962.

Guernes de Pont-Sainte-Maxence. *Vie de Saint Thomas le martyr*. Ed. Emmanuel Walburg. Lund: C. W. K. Gleerup, 1922.

Hamer, Richard, ed. *Gilte Legende*. 3 vols. EETS 327, 328, and 339. Oxford: Oxford University Press, 2006, 2007, and 2012.

———, ed. *Three Lives from the "Gilte Legende."* Heidelberg: Universitätsverlag Winter, 1978.

Hamer, Richard, and Vida Russell, eds. *Supplementary Lives in Some Manuscripts of the Gilte Legende*. EETS 315. Oxford: Oxford University Press, 2000.

Harper-Bill, Christopher, ed. *Cartulary of the Augustinian Friars of Clare*. Woodbridge, Suffolk: Boydell, 1991.

———, ed. *Register of John Morton, Archbishop of Canterbury, 1486–1500*. 3 vols. Canterbury and York Society. Rochester, NY: Boydell, 1987–2000.

Harpsfield, Nicholas. *Life and Death of Sir Thomas Moore*. Ed. Elsie Vaughan Hitchcock. EETS 186. London: Oxford University Press, 1932.

Henderson, W. G., ed. *Manuale et processionale ad usum insignis ecclesiae Eboracensis*. Surtees Society 63, 1875.

Herbert of Bosham. "Vita S. Thomae." In J. C. Robertson, ed., *Materials for the History of Thomas Becket, Archbishop*. Vol. 3. London: Longmans, 1875–85. 198–219.

Hilton, Walter. *Scale of Perfection*. Ed. Thomas Bestul. Kalamazoo, MI: Medieval Institute, 2001.

Horstmann, Carl, ed. "Des Ms. Bodl. 779 jüngere Zusatzlegenden zur südlichen Legendensammlung." *Archiv für das Studium der neueren Sprachen und Literaturen* 82 (1889): 307–422.

———, ed. *Nova Legenda Anglie*. Oxford: Clarendon, 1901.

———, ed. *S. Editha sive Chronicon Vilodunense*. Heilbronn, 1883.

———. "Thomas Beket, Epische Legende, von Laurentius Wade (1497)." *Englische Studien* (1880): 409–69.

———, ed. "Vita S. Etheldredae Eliensis." In *Altenglische Legenden: Neue Folge*. Heilbronn, 1881. 282–307.

Jacobus de Voragine. *Golden Legend*. Trans. William Granger Ryan. 2 vols. Princeton, NJ: Princeton University Press, 1993.

James, M. R., ed. "Lives of St. Walstan." *Norfolk Archaeology* 19.3 (1916): 238–67.

Kingsford, Charles, ed. *Chronicles of London*. Oxford: Clarendon, 1905.

———, ed. *The Song of Lewes*. Oxford: Clarendon, 1890.

Kipling, Gordon, ed. *Receyt of the Ladie Kateryne*. EETS 296. Oxford: Oxford University Press, 1990.

———, ed. *Triumph of Honour: Burgundian Origins of the Elizabethan Renaissance*. Leiden: Leiden University Press, 1977.

Lydgate, John. *Minor Poems of John Lydgate*. Ed. Henry Noble MacCracken. EETS 107. London: Oxford University Press, 1911.

———. *Saint Alban and Saint Amphibalus*. Ed. George Reinecke. New York: Garland, 1985.

"Lyf of Saynt Ursula." Cambridge: Chadwyk-Healey, 1994. [English Poetry Database]

Mâle, Émile, et al., eds. *Les heures d'Anne de Bretagne: Bibliothèque Nationale (Manuscrit Latin 9474)*. Paris: Éditions Verve, 1946.

Maxwell-Lyte, H. C., et al., eds. *Calendar of the Patent Rolls, Preserved in the Public Record Office: Edward IV, 1461–1467*. London, 1897.

Myers, A. R., ed. *English Historical Documents, 1327–1485*. London: Routledge, 1969. Repr. 1996.

Pantin, William Abel, ed. *Documents Illustrating the Activities of the General and Provincial Chapters of the English Black Monks, 1215–1540*. London: Royal Historical Society, 1931–37.

Parker, Roscoe, ed. *Middle English Stanzaic Versions of the Life of St. Anne*. EETS 174. London: Oxford University Press, 1928.

Pepin, Ronald, and Hugh Feiss, trans. *Two Mediaeval Lives of Saint Winefride*. Toronto: Peregrina, 2000.

Powell, Susan, ed. *John Mirk's Festial*. 2 vols. EETS 334 and 335. Oxford: Oxford University Press, 2009, 2011.

Reames, Sherry, ed. *Middle English Legends of Women Saints*. Kalamazoo, MI: Medieval Institute, 2003.

Riley, Henry Thomas, ed. *Thomæ Walsingham, quondam Monachi S. Albani, Historia Anglicana*. 2 vols. London: Longman, 1863.

Sheppard, Joseph B., ed. *Christ Church Letters*. Camden Society 19. Westminster, 1877.

———, ed. *Literae Cantuarienses: The Letter Books of the Monastery of Christ Church Priory*. Vol. 3. Rolls Series 85. London, 1889.

Thompson, E. M., ed. *Chronicon Adae de Usk, 1377–1421*. London: H. Frowde, 1904.

Wright, Thomas, ed. *Songs and Carols Now First Printed*. London: Percy Society, 1847.

Secondary Works

Acker, Paul. "Saint Mildred in the *SEL*." In Jankofsky, *South English Legendary*, 140–53.

Agamben, Giorgio. *Homo Sacer: Sovereign Power and Bare Life*. Trans. Daniel Heller-Roazen. Stanford, CA: Stanford University Press, 1998.

Alemparte, Jaime Ferreiro. *La leyenda de las once mil vírgenes: Sus reliquias, culto e iconografía.* Murcia: Universidad de Murcia, 1991.

Anderson, Benedict. *Imagined Communities: Reflections on the Origin and Spread of Nationalism.* London: Verso, 1983.

Anglo, Sydney. "The London Pageants for the Reception of Katharine of Aragon." *Journal of the Warburg and Courtauld Institutes* 26 (1963): 53–89.

Angold, M. J., et al. "Colleges of Secular Canons: Battlefield, St. Mary Magdalen." In *History of the County of Shropshire: Volume 2.* Ed. A. T. Gaydon and R. B. Pugh. London: Victoria County History, 1973. 128–31. [British History Online]

Appadurai, Arjun. *Modernity at Large: Cultural Dimensions of Globalization.* Minneapolis: University of Minnesota Press, 1996.

Armitage, David. "Elizabethan Idea of Empire." *Transactions of the RHS* 14 (2004): 269–77.

Asad, Talal. *Formations of the Secular: Christianity, Islam, Modernity.* Stanford: Stanford University Press, 2003.

Ashley, Kathleen, and Pamela Sheingorn. *Writing Faith: Text, Sign, and History in the Miracles of Sainte Foy.* Chicago: University of Chicago Press, 1999.

Atkinson, Clarissa. "'Precious Balsam in a Fragile Glass': The Ideology of Virginity in the Middle Ages." *Journal of Family History* 8 (1983): 131–43.

Ayto, John. "Marginalia in the Manuscript of the Life of St. Edith: New Light on Early Printing." *Library* 32 (1977): 28–36.

Baggs, A. P., et al. "Medieval Beverley: Beverley and St. John." In *History of the County of York East Riding: Volume 6, the Borough and Liberties of Beverley,* ed. K. J. Allison. London: Victoria County history, 1989. [British History Online]

Baker, David. *Between Nations: Shakespeare, Spenser, Marvell, and the Question of Britain.* Stanford, CA: Stanford University Press, 1997.

Baker, David, and Willy Maley, eds. *British Identities and English Renaissance Literature.* Cambridge: Cambridge University Press, 2002.

Baker, Howard. "Thomas More at Oxford." *Moreana* 43–44 (1974): 6–12.

Baker, Nigel, ed. *Shrewsbury Abbey: Studies in the Archaeology and History of an Urban Abbey.* Birmingham, UK: Shropshire Archaeological and Historical Society, 2002.

Baker-Smith, Dominic. "Reading *Utopia.*" In George Logan, ed., *Cambridge Companion to Thomas More.* Cambridge: Cambridge University Press, 2011. 141–67.

Bale, Anthony, ed. *St Edmund, King and Martyr: Changing Images of a Medieval Saint.* Woodbridge, UK: York Medieval Press, 2009.

Barlow, Frank. "Herbert of Bosham." [*ODNB*]

Barr, Helen. "'This Holy Tyme': Present Sense in the Digby Lyrics." In Ghosh and Gillespie. 307–23.

Barron, Caroline. *London in the Later Middle Ages: Government and People, 1200–1500.* Oxford: Oxford University Press, 2004.

———. "Political Culture of Medieval London." In Clark and Carpenter. 110–33.

Barron, Caroline, and Marie-Helene Rousseau. "Cathedral, City and State, 1300–1540." In D. Keene, A. Burns, and A. Saint, eds., *St. Paul's: The Cathedral Church of London, 604–2004.* New Haven, CT: Yale University Press, 2004. 33–44.

Baswell, Christopher. "King Edward and the Cripple." In Donka Minkova and Theresa Tinkle, eds., *Chaucer and the Challenges of Medievalism.* Frankfurth: Peter Lang, 2003. 15–29.

Benson, C. David. *Chaucer's Religious Tales.* Woodbridge, Suffolk: Boydell, 1990.

Bestul, Thomas. "The Collection of Private Prayers in the Portoforium of Wulfstan of Worcester and the *Orationes sive meditationes* of Anselm of Canterbury." In R. Foreville, ed., *Les Mutationes socio-culturelles au tourant des XIe-XIIe siècles*. Paris: Centre National de la Recherche Scientifique, 1984. 357–60.

Bhabha, Homi. "DissemiNation: Time, Narrative, and the Margins of the Modern Nation." In *Location of Culture*. New York: Routledge, 1994. 199–244.

Biddick, Kathleen. *Typological Imaginary: Circumcision, Technology, History*. Philadelphia: University of Pennsylvania Press, 2003.

Billson, Charles. *Medieval Leicester*. Leicester: Edgar Backus, 1920.

Blanton, Virginia. "Counting Noses and Assessing the Numbers: Native Saints in the South English Legendaries." In Blurton and Wogan-Browne. 233–50.

———. *Signs of Devotion: The Cult of St. Æthelthryth in Medieval England, 695–1615*. University Park: Penn State University Press, 2007.

Blurton, Heather, and Jocelyn Wogan-Browne, eds. *Rethinking the South English Legendary*. Manchester: Manchester University Press, 2011.

Bowers, John. *Chaucer and Langland: The Antagonistic Tradition*. Notre Dame, IN: University of Notre Dame Press, 2007.

Brantley, Jessica. "Reading the Forms of *Sir Topas*." *Chaucer Review* 47 (2013): 416–38.

Braswell, Laurel. "Saint Edburga of Winchester: A Study of Her Cult, a.d. 950–1500, with an Edition of the Fourteenth-Century Middle English and Latin Lives." *Mediaeval Studies* 33 (1971): 292–333.

Braudel, Fernand. *Civilization and Capitalism, 15th–18th Century*. Trans. Sian Reynolds. Vol. 3. Rprt., Berkeley: University of California Press, 1992.

Breckenridge, Sarah. "Mapping Identities in the *SEL*." In Blurton and Wogan-Browne. 329–46.

Breeze, Andrew. "Sir John Paston, Lydgate and the *Libelle of Englyshe Polycye*." *Notes and Queries*, n.s., 48.3 (2001): 230–31.

Brown, Paul Alonzo. "Development of the Legend of Thomas Becket." PhD thesis. University of Pennsylvania, 1930.

Bryan, Elizabeth. "Amazons and Ursulines." In Bonnie Wheeler, ed., *Mindful Spirit in Late Medieval Literature*. New York: Palgrave, 2006. 21–30.

Bryan, Jennifer. *Looking Inward: Devotional Reading and the Private Self in Late Medieval England*. Philadelphia: University of Pennsylvania Press, 2007.

Bühler, Curt. "A New Middle English Life of Saint Winifred?" In Jess Bessinger and Robert Raymo, eds., *Medieval Studies in Honor of Lillian Herlands Hornstein*. New York: New York University Press, 1976. 87–97.

Butler, Judith. *Bodies That Matter: On the Discursive Limits of Sex*. New York: Routledge, 1993.

Buzello, Horst. "Köln und England, 1468–1509." *Mitteilungen aus dem Stadarchiv von Köln* 40 (1971): 431–67.

Camp, Cynthia. *Anglo-Saxon Saints' Lives as History Writing in Late Medieval England*. Woodbridge, Suffolk: Boydell, 2015.

Cannon, Christopher, "Form." In Paul Strohm, ed., *Middle English: Oxford Twenty-first Century Approaches to Literature*. Oxford: Oxford University Press, 2007. 177–90.

———. *Middle English Literature: A Cultural History*. Cambridge: Polity Press, 2008.

———. "Monastic Productions." In Paul Strohm, ed., *Cambridge History of Medieval English Literature*. Cambridge: Cambridge University Press, 2002. 316–48.

Carpenter, Christine. "Beauchamp, Richard, Thirteenth Earl of Warwick (1382–1439)." [*ODNB*]

Cartwright, Jane. *Feminine Sanctity and Spirituality in Medieval Wales*. Cardiff, UK: University of Wales Press, 2008.

Catalogue of the Harleian Manuscripts in the British Museum. 4 vols. London, 1808–12.

Catto, Jeremy, "Henry Chichele." [*ODNB*]

———. "Religious Change Under Henry V." In G. L. Harriss, ed., *Henry V: The Practice of Kingship*. Oxford: Oxford University Press, 1985. 97–115.

Chaganti, Seeta. "Carol." In Roland Greene et al., eds., *Princeton Encyclopedia of Poetry and Poetics*. 4th ed. Princeton, NJ: Princeton University Press, 2012. 208–9.

———. "Choreographing Mouvance: The Case of the English Carol." *Philological Quarterly* 87 (2008): 77–103.

———. "Danse Macabre in the Virtual Churchyard." *postmedieval* 3 (2012): 7–26.

———. *Medieval Poetics of the Reliquary*. New York: Palgrave Macmillan, 2008.

Chapman, Alison. "Now and Then: Sequencing the Sacred in Two Protestant Calendars." *JMEMS* 33 (2003): 91–123.

Clark, Anne. *Elisabeth of Schönau, a Twelfth Century Visionary*. Philadelphia: University of Pennsylvania Press, 1992.

Clark, Linda, and Christine Carpenter, eds. *Political Culture in Late Medieval Britain*. Woodbridge, Suffolk: Boydell, 2004.

Cobb, H. S., ed. *Overseas Trade of London: Exchequer Customs Accounts, 1480–81*. London: London Record Society, 1990. [British History Online]

Cohen, Jeffrey Jerome, ed. *Cultural Diversity in the British Middle Ages: Archipelago, Island, England*. New York: Palgrave Macmillan, 2008.

Coletti, Theresa. *Mary Magdalene and the Drama of Saints: Theater, Gender, and Religion in Late Medieval England*. Philadelphia: University of Pennsylvania Press, 2004.

Cullum, Pat. "*Virginitas* and *Virilitas*: Richard Scrope and His Fellow Bishops." In P. J. P. Goldberg, ed., *Richard Scrope: Archbishop, Rebel, Martyr*. Donington: Shaun Tyas, 2007. 86–99.

Curley, Michael. "John of Bridlington (c. 1320–1379)." [*ODNB*]

Davies, C. S. L. "Bishop John Morton, the Holy See, and the Accession of Henry VII." *English Historical Review* 102 (1987): 2–30.

Davies, Richard G. "Thomas Arundel as Archbishop of Canterbury, 1396–1414." *Journal of Ecclesiastical History* 14 (1973): 9–21.

Davies, R. R. *Conquest, Coexistence, and Change: Wales 1063–1415*. Oxford: Clarendon, 1987.

———. *First English Empire: Power and Identities in the British Isles, 1093–1343*. Oxford: Oxford University Press, 2002.

Davis, Kathleen. "Hymeneal Alogic: Debating Political Community in the *Parliament of Fowls*." In Lavezzo. 161–87.

Derrida, Jacques. "The Law of Genre." Trans. Avital Ronell. *Critical Inquiry* 7 (1980): 55–81.

D'Evelyn, Charlotte, and Frances Foster. "Saints' Legends." In J. Burke Severs, ed., *Manual of the Writings in Middle English, 1050–1500*. Hamden, CT: Archon, 1970.

Digital Index of Middle English Verse. www.dimev.net

Dinshaw, Carolyn. *Getting Medieval: Sexualities and Communities, Pre- and Postmodern*. Durham, NC: Duke University Press, 1999.

Dobson, Richard Barrie, ed. *Church, Politics and Patronage in the Fifteenth Century*. Gloucester: Alan Sutton, 1984.

———. *Durham Priory, 1400–1450*. Cambridge: Cambridge University Press, 1973.

Doig, James. "Propaganda and Truth: Henry V's Royal Progress in 1421." *Nottingham Medieval Studies* 40 (1996): 167–79.

Duffy, Eamon. "Dynamics of Pilgrimage in Late Medieval England." In Colin Morris and Peter Roberts, eds., *Pilgrimage: The English Experience from Becket to Bunyan*. Cambridge: Cambridge University Press, 2002. 164–77.

——. *Stripping the Altars: Traditional Religion in England, 1400–1580*. New Haven, CT: Yale University Press, 1992.

Duggan, Anne. "The Cult of St. Thomas Becket in the Thirteenth Century." In Meryl Jancey, ed., *St. Thomas Cantilupe, Bishop of Hereford*. Hereford: Friends of Hereford Cathedral, 1982. 21-44.

——"Lyell Version of the Quadrilogus Life of St. Thomas of Canterbury." *Analecta Bollandiana* 112 (1994): 105–38.

——. *Thomas Becket: Friends, Networks, Texts and Cult*. New York: Routledge, 2007.

Dunn-Lardeau, Brenda, ed. *"Legenda Aurea": Sept Siecles de Diffusion*. Montreal: Editions Bellarmin, 1986.

Ebin, Lois. "Poetics and Style in Late Medieval Literature." In Lois Ebin, ed., *Vernacular Poetics in the Middle Ages*. Kalamazoo, MI: Medieval Institute, 1984. 263–93.

Edwards, A. S. G. "John Lydgate's *Lives of Ss. Edmund and Fremund*: Politics, Hagiography and Literature." In Bale. 133–44.

——. "Transmission and Audience of Osbern Bokenham's *Legendys of Hooly Wummen*." In Alastair Minnis, ed., *Late Medieval Religious Texts and Their Transmission: Essays in Honour of A. I. Doyle*. Woodbridge, Suffolk: Brewer, 1994. 157–67.

Edwards, Philip. *The Making of the Modern English State, 1460–1660*. New York: Palgrave, 2001.

Ehrenschwendtner, Marie-Luise. "Virtual Pilgrimage? Enclosure and the Practice of Piety at St. Katherine's Convent, Augsburg." *Journal of Ecclesiastical History* 60 (2009): 45–73.

Evans, J. G., ed. *Report on Manuscripts in the Welsh Language*. Vol. 1:3: *Peniarth*. London: Historical Manuscripts Commission, 1905.

Fein, Susanna. "Critical Overview and Major Issues." In Fein. 3–29.

——. "Good Ends in the Audelay Manuscript." *Yearbook of English Studies* 33 (2003): 97–119.

——, ed. *My Wyl and My Wrytyng: Essays on John the Blind Audelay*. Kalamazoo, MI: Medieval Institute, 2009.

Forey, A. J. "The Military Order of St. Thomas of Acre." *English Historical Review* 92 (1977): 481–503.

Foucault, Michel. "Other Places." *Diacritics* 16 (1986): 22–27.

Frederick, Jill. "The *SEL*: Anglo-Saxon Saints and National Identity." In Donald Scragg and Carole Weinberg, eds., *Literary Appropriations of the Anglo-Saxons from the Thirteenth to the Twentieth Century*. Cambridge: Cambridge University Press, 2000. 57–73.

Fudge, John. *Cargoes, Embargoes, and Emissaries: The Commercial and Political Interaction of England and the German Hanse, 1450–1510*. Toronto: University of Toronto Press, 1995.

Ganim, John. "Lydgate, Location, and the Poetics of Exemption." In Lisa Cooper and Andrea Denny-Brown, eds., *Lydgate Matters: Poetry and Material Culture in the Fifteenth Century*. New York: Palgrave Macmillan, 2008. 165–83.

Gaydon, A. T., et al. "Houses of Benedictine Monks: Abbey of Shrewsbury." In *A History of the County of Shropshire: Volume 2*. Ed. A. T. Gaydon and R. B. Pugh. London: Victoria County History, 1973. 30–37. [British History Online]

Genet, J. P. "English Nationalism: Thomas Polton at the Council of Constance." *Nottingham Medieval Studies* 28 (1984): 60–78.

Ghosh, Kantik, and Vincent Gillespie, eds. *After Arundel: Religious Writing in Fifteenth-Century England*. Turnhout, Belgium: Brepols, 2011.

Gill, Miriam. "Saint with a Scythe: A Previously Unidentified Wall Painting in the Church of St. Andrew, Cavenham." *Proceedings of the Suffolk Institute of Archaeology and History* 38.3 (1995): 245–54.

Gillespie, Alexandra. "The Later Lives of St. Edmund: John Lydgate to John Stowe." In Bale. 163–85.

Good, Jonathan. *The Cult of St. George in Medieval England*. Woodbridge, Suffolk: Boydell and Brewer, 2009.

Görlach, Manfred. *The South English Legendary, Gilte Legende and Golden Legend*. Braunschweig: Technische Universität Carolo-Wilhelmina, 1972.

———. *Studies in Middle English Saints' Legends*. Heidelberg: Universitätsverlag Winter, 1998.

———. *Textual Tradition of the SEL*. Leeds: University of Leeds, 1974.

Gransden, Antonia. *Historical Writing in England, c. 550–c. 1307*. Ithaca, NY: Cornell University Press, 1974.

Griffiths, Ralph. "Richard Duke of York and the Royal Household in Wales, 1449–1450." *Welsh Historical Review* 8 (1976): 14–25.

Hamelinck, Renee. "St. Kenelm and the Legends of the English Saints in the *SEL*." In N. H. G. E. Veldhoen and H. Aertsen, eds., *Companion to Early Middle English Literature*. Amsterdam: Free University Press, 1988. 21–30.

Hampson, R. T. *Medii Aevi Kalendarium*. 2 vols. London, 1841.

Harbus, Antonia. *Helena of Britain in Medieval Legend*. Woodbridge, Suffolk: Brewer, 2002.

Hardy, T. Duffus. *Thirty-Sixth Annual Report of the Deputy Keeper of the Public Records*. London, 1876.

Harper-Bill, Christopher. "Archbishop John Morton and the Province of Canterbury, 1486–1500." *Journal of Ecclesiastical History* 29 (1978): 1–21.

———. "John Morton." [*ODNB*]

Harris, Kate. "Richard Pynson's *Remembraunce for the Traduction of the Princesse Kateryne*: The Printer's Contribution to the Reception of Catharine of Aragon." *Library*, 6th ser., 12.2 (1990): 89–109.

Harriss, Gerald. *Shaping the Nation: England, 1360–1461*. Oxford: Clarendon, 2005.

Harvey, John. *English Cathedrals*. London: Batsford, 1956.

Heath, Peter. "Urban Piety in the Later Middle Ages: The Evidence of Hull Wills." In Dobson, Church. 209–34.

Hefele, Charles Joseph. *Histoire des concils d'apres les documents originaux*. Paris, 1869. Vol. 10. [Internet archive]

Heffernan, Thomas. "Additional Evidence for a More Precise Date of the 'South English Legendary.'" *Traditio* 35 (1979): 345–51.

———. "Dangerous Sympathies: Political Commentary in the *SEL*." In Blurton and Wogan-Browne. Reprint. 295–312.

Herbert, William. *History of the Worshipful Company of Drapers of London*. London, 1837.

Hiatt, Alfred. "Genre Without System." In Paul Strohm, ed., *Oxford Twenty-First Century Approaches to Literature: Middle English*. Oxford: Oxford University Press, 2007. 277–94.

Hollis, Stephanie. "St. Edith and the Wilton Community." In Hollis. 245–80.

——, ed. *Writing the Wilton Women: Goscelin's Legend of Edith and Liber Confortatorius*. Turnhout, Belgium: Brepols, 2004.

Homer, Ronald. "Tin, Lead, and Pewter." In John Blair and Nigel Ramsay, eds., *English Medieval Industries: Craftsmen, Techniques, Products*, London: Hambledon, 1991. 57–80.

Horobin, Simon. "A Manuscript Found in the Library of Abbotsford House and the Lost Legendary of Osbern Bokenham." In A. S. G. Edwards, ed., *English Manuscript Studies, 1100–1700*, vol. 14: *Regional Manuscripts 1200–1700*. London: British Library, 2008. 130–64.

——. "Politics, Patronage, and Piety in the Work of Osbern Bokenham." *Speculum* 82 (2007): 932–49.

Horrox, Rosemary. "Rotherham, Thomas (1423–1500)." [*ODNB*]

Horrox, Rosemary, and Sarah Rees Jones, eds. *Pragmatic Utopias: Ideals and Communities, 1200–1630*. Cambridge: Cambridge University Press, 2011.

"Houses of Benedictine Monks: The Cathedral Priory of the Holy Trinity or Christ Church, Canterbury." In William Page, ed., *History of the County of Kent*, vol. 2. London, 1926. 113–21. [British History Online]

Hughes, Jonathan. *Pastors and Visionaries: Religion and Secular Life in Late Medieval Yorkshire*. Woodbridge, Suffolk: Boydell, 1988.

Ilaria, Anthony. "Canons and Canonesses Regular." In *Catholic Encyclopedia*. Vol. 3. New York: Robert Appleton, 1908. [Online]

Jacob, E. F. *Archbishop Henry Chichele*. London: Nelson, 1967.

James, M. R. *Descriptive Catalogue of the Manuscripts in the Library of Gonville and Caius College*. Vol. 1. Cambridge: Cambridge University Press, 1907.

Jankofsky, Klaus. "National Characteristics in the Portrayals of English Saints in the *SEL*." In Renate Blumenfeld-Kosinski and Timea Szell, eds., *Images of Sainthood in Medieval Europe*. Ithaca, NY: Cornell University Press, 1991. 81–93.

——, ed. *South English Legendary: A Critical Assessment*. Tübingen: Francke, 1992.

Jansen, Sabine. "Die Texte des Kirchberg-Corpus: Überlieferung und Textgeschichte vom 15 Bis zum 19 Jahrhundert." PhD dissertation. University of Cologne, 2005.

Jenks, Stuart. *England, Die Hanse und Preussen Handel und Diplomatie, 1377–1474*. Vol. 1. Cologne: Böhlau Verlag, 1992.

Johnson, Eleanor. "Julian of Norwich and the Comfort of Eternity." Paper delivered at the New Chaucer Society, Siena, 2010.

——. *Practicing Literary Theory in the Middle Ages*. Chicago: University of Chicago Press, 2013.

Johnson, Lesley, and Jocelyn Wogan-Browne. "National, World, and Women's History: Writers and Readers in Post-Conquest England." In David Wallace, ed., *Cambridge History of Medieval English Literature*. Cambridge: Cambridge University Press, 2002. 92–121.

Jones, Sarah Rees. "Cities and Their Saints in England, Circa 1150–1300: The Development of Bourgeois Values in the Cults of Saint William of York and St. Kenelm of Winchcombe." In Caroline Goodson, Anne Lester, and Carol Symes, eds., *Cities, Texts, and Social Networks, 400–1500*. Burlington, VT: Ashgate, 2010. 193–215.

——. "Thomas More's Utopia and Medieval London." In Horrox and Jones. 117–35.

Jurkowski, Maureen. "The Arrest of William Thorpe in Shrewsbury and the Anti-Lollard Statute of 1406." *Historical Research* 75 (2002): 273–95.

Kapp, Rudolph. *Heilige und Heiligenlegenden in England*. Halle (Saale): Max Niemeyer Verlag, 1934.

Keane, Robert. "Thomas More as a Young Lawyer." *Moreana* 41 (2004): 41–71.

Keene, D. J., and Vanessa Harding. "St. Mary Colechurch 105/18." *Historical Gazetteer of London Before the Great Fire*. London: Centre for Metropolitan History, 1987. 490–517. [British History Online]

Kerby-Fulton, Kathryn. *Books Under Suspicion: Censorship and Tolerance of Revelatory Writing in Late Medieval England*. South Bend, IN: University of Notre Dame Press, 2006.

Knowles, M. D. "The Case of St. Alban's Abbey in 1490." *Journal of Ecclesiastical History* 3 (1952): 144–58.

Kolve, V. A. "Ganymede/Son of Getron: Medieval Monasticism and the Drama of Same-Sex Desire." *Speculum* 73 (1998): 1014–67.

Krug, Rebecca. "*Piers Plowman* and the Secrets of Health." *Chaucer Review* 46 (2011): 166–81.

———. *Reading Families: Women's Literate Practice in Late Medieval England*. Ithaca, NY: Cornell University Press, 2002.

Kushner, Tony. *Angels in America: A Gay Fantasia on National Themes*. New York: Theatre Communications Group, 2013.

L., H. W. "Roman Catholics at Holywell." *Bye-gones Relating to Wales and the Border Counties*, ser. 1. Oswestry, 1874–75. 290–92.

Lampert, Lisa. *Gender and Jewish Difference from Paul to Shakespeare*. Philadelphia: University of Pennsylvania Press, 2004.

Lancaster, Ian. *Dramatic Texts and Records of Britain: A Chronological Topography to 1558*. Toronto: University of Toronto Press, 1984.

Lapidge, Michael. "Saintly Life in Anglo-Saxon England." In Malcolm Godden and Michael Lapidge, eds., *Cambridge Companion to Old English Literature*. Cambridge: Cambridge University Press, 243–63.

Latour, Bruno. *Reassembling the Social: An Introduction to Actor-Network-Theory*. Oxford: Oxford University Press, 2007.

Lavezzo, Kathy. *Angels on the Edge of the World: Geography, Literature, and English Community, 1000–1543*. Ithaca, NY: Cornell University Press, 2006.

———, ed. *Imagining a Medieval English Nation*. Minneapolis: University of Minnesota Press, 2003.

———. "The Sea and Border Crossings in the Alliterative *Morte Darthur*." In Sobecki, *Sea and Englishness*. 113–32.

Le Fur, Didier. *Anne de Bretagne*. Paris: Librairie Edition Guénégaud, 2000.

Le Goff, Jacques. *In Search of Sacred Time: Jacopus de Voragine and the Golden Legend*. Trans. Lydia Cochrane. Princeton, NJ: Princeton University Press, 2014.

Legner, Anton. *Kölner Heilige und Heiligtümer*. Cologne: Greven, 2003.

Lipton, Emma. *Affections of the Mind: The Politics of Sacramental Marriage in Late Medieval English Literature*. South Bend, IN: University of Notre Dame Press, 2007.

Liszka, Thomas. "The First 'A' Redaction of the *SEL*: Information from the Prologue." *Modern Philology* 82 (1985): 407–13.

———. "MS Laud Misc. 108 and the Early History of the *SEL*." *Manuscripta* 33 (1989): 75–91.

———. "South English Legendaries." In Thomas Liszka and Lorna Walker, eds., *The North Sea World in the Middle Ages*. Dublin: Four Courts, 2001. 243–82.

Lloyd, T. H. *England and the German Hanse, 1157–1611*. Cambridge: Cambridge University Press, 1991.

Lochri, Karma. *Covert Operations: The Medieval Uses of Secrecy*. Philadelphia: University of Pennsylvania Press, 2011.

Loomis, Louise. "Nationality at the Council of Constance." *AHR* 44 (1939): 508–27.

——. "The Organization by Nations at Constance." *Church History* 1 (1932): 191–210.

Lowry, M. J. C. "Caxton, St. Winifred, and the Lady Margaret Beaufort." *Library*, 6th ser. (1983): 101–17.

Luxford, Julian. *The Art and Architecture of English Benedictine Monasteries, 1300–1540*. Woodbridge, Suffolk: Boydell, 2005.

Malden, H. E., ed. "The Borough of Southwark: Churches." In *History of the County of Surrey*. Vol. 4. London, Victoria County History, 1912. 151–61. [British History Online]

Marks, Richard. *Image and Devotion in Late Medieval England*. Stroud: Sutton, 2004.

——. *Stained Glass in England During the Middle Ages*. Toronto: University of Toronto Press, 1993.

Marston, Sally. "Social Construction of Scale." *Progress in Human Geography* 24 (2000): 219–42.

Mattingly, Garret. *Catherine of Aragon*. Boston: Little, Brown, 1941.

McSheffrey, Shannon. "Sanctuary and the Legal Topography of Pre-Reformation London." *Law and History Review* 27 (2009): 483–514.

Meecham-Jones, Simon. "Where Was Wales? The Erasure of Wales in Medieval English Culture." In Ruth Kennedy and Meecham-Jones, eds., *Authority and Subjugation in Writing of Medieval Wales*. New York: Palgrave Macmillan, 2008. 27–55.

Meyer-Lee, Robert. "The Emergence of the Literary in John Lydgate's *Life of Our Lady*." *Journal of English and Germanic Philology* 109 (2010): 322–48.

——. *Poets and Power from Chaucer to Wyatt*. Cambridge: Cambridge University Press, 2009.

——. "The Vatic Penitent: John Audelay's Self Representation." In Fein. 54–85.

Middle English Dictionary. Ann Arbor: University of Michigan Humanities Text Initiative, 2001. http://quod.lib.umich.edu/m/med.

Miller, James. "Lydgate the Hagiographer as a Literary Artist." In Larry Benson, ed., *The Learned and the Lewd: Studies in Chaucer and Medieval Literature*. Cambridge, MA: Harvard University Press, 1974. 279–90.

Minois, Georges. *Anne de Bretagne*. Paris: Fayard, 1999.

Monckton, Linda. "Fit for a King? The Architecture of the Beauchamp Chapel." *Architectural History* 47 (2004): 25–52.

Montgomery, Scott. *St. Ursula and the 11,000 Virgins of Cologne*. New York: Peter Lang, 2010.

Moretti, Franco. *Graphs, Maps, Trees: Abstract Models for Literary History*. New York: Verso, 2007.

Morgan, Nigel, and Stella Panayotova et al., eds. *Catalogue of Western Book Illumination in the Fitzwilliam Museum and the Cambridge Colleges*. Vol. 1. Pt. 1. London: Harvey Miller, 2009.

Mortimer, Nigel. *John Lydgate's Fall of Princes: Narrative Tragedy in Its Literary and Political Contexts*. Oxford: Clarendon, 2005.

Nagy, Michael. "Saint Aethelberht of East Anglia in the *SEL*." *ChR* 37 (2002): 159–72.

Nancy, Jean-Luc. *Being Singular Plural*. Trans. Robert Richardson and Anne O'Byrne. Stanford, CA: Stanford University Press, 2000.

——. "Of Being-in-Common." Trans. James Creech. In Miami Theory Collective, ed., *Community at Loose Ends*. Minneapolis: University of Minnesota Press, 1991. 1–12.

Nash, Ray. "Rastell Fragments at Dartmouth." *Library*, 4th ser., 24 (1943): 66–73.

Nelson, Philip. "The Fifteenth-Century Glass in the Church of St. Michael, Ashton-Under-Lyne." *Archaeological Journal* 70 (1913): 1–10.

Newman, Barbara. *From Virile Woman to WomanChrist*. Philadelphia: University of Pennsylvania Press, 1995.

Newstead, Clare, Carolina Reid, and Matthew Sparke. "Cultural Geography of Scale." In Kay Anderson et al., eds., *Handbook of Cultural Geography*. Thousand Oaks, CA: Sage, 2002. 485–97.

Nicolas, Nicholas Harris, ed. *Privy Purse Expenses of Elizabeth of York: Wardrobe Accounts of Edward the Fourth*. London, 1830.

Nijenhuis, Wiesje. "The Wilton Chronicle as a Historical Source." *Revue Bénédictine* 115 (2005): 370–99.

Nilson, Ben. *Cathedral Shrines of Medieval England*. Woodbridge, Suffolk: Boydell, 1998.

Nissé, Ruth. "'Was It Not Routhe to Se?' Lydgate and the Styles of Martyrdom." In Scanlon and Simpson. 279–98.

Nolan, Maura. *John Lydgate and the Making of Public Culture*. Cambridge: Cambridge University Press, 2005.

———. "Making the Aesthetic Turn: Adorno, the Medieval, and the Future of the Past." *JMEMS* 34 (2004): 549–75.

Norris, Vic, Franck Molina, and Andrew Gewirtz. "Hypothesis: Bacteria Control Host Appetites." *Journal of Bacteriology* 195.3 (2013): 411–16.

North, J. D. "Monastic Time." In James Clark, ed., *Cultures of Medieval English Monasticism*. Woodbridge, Suffolk: Boydell, 2007. 203–11.

Osborne, Peter. *Politics of Time: Modernity and Avant-Garde*. London: Verso, 2011.

Osswald, Maria Cristina. "The Society of Jesus and the Diffusion of the Cult and Iconography of Saint Ursula and the Eleven Thousand Virgins in the Portuguese Empire During the Second Half of the 16th Century." *Via Spiritus: Revista de História da Espiritualidade e do Sentimento Religioso* 12 (2005): 601–9.

Owen, Hugh. *History of Shrewsbury*. 2 vols. London: Harding, Lepard, and Co., 1825.

———. *Some Account of the Ancient and Present State of Shrewsbury*. England, 1808.

Owen, Richard. *Catalogue of the Manuscripts Relating to Wales in the British Library*. London, 1900.

Page, Christopher. *Owl and the Nightingale: Musical Life and Ideas in France, 1100–1300*. Berkeley: University of California Press, 1990.

Page, William. "Houses of Benedictine Monks, St. Alban's Abbey After the Conquest." In *History of the County of Hertford*. Vol. 4. Victoria County History. 372–416. [British History Online]

Pearsall, Derek. "The Idea of Englishness in the Fifteenth Century." In Helen Cooney, ed., *Nation, Court and Culture: New Essays on Fifteenth-Century English Poetry*. Dublin: Four Courts, 2001. 15–27.

———. "'If Heaven Be on This Earth, It Is in Cloister or in School': The Monastic Ideal in Later Medieval English Literature." In Horrox and Jones. 11–25.

Petit, François. *Spirituality of the Premonstratensians: The Twelfth and Thirteenth Centuries*. Ed. C. Neel. Trans. V. Szczurek. Collegeville, MN: Liturgical Press, 2011.

Pfaff, Richard. *Liturgy in Medieval England*. Cambridge: Cambridge University Press, 2009.

Pickering, O. S. "The Outspoken *South English Legendary* Poet." In Alastair Minnis, ed., *Late Medieval Religious Texts and Their Transmission: Essays in Honour of A. I. Doyle*. Woodbridge, Suffolk: Brewer, 1994. 21–37.

Pickering, O. S., and Manfred Görlach. "A Newly Discovered Manuscript of the *SEL*." *Anglia* (1982): 109–23.

Prickett, Marmaduke. *History of the Priory Church of Bridlington.* Cambridge, 1836.

Pugh, R. B., and Elizabeth Crittall, eds. "Houses of Benedictine Nuns: Abbey of Wilton." *History of the County of Wiltshire,* Vol. 3 (1956): 231–42. [British History Online]

Purvis, J. S. *St. John of Bridlington.* Bridlington Augustinian Society, 1924.

Raine, James. *Saint Cuthbert, with an Account of the State in Which His Remains Were Found.* Durham, 1828.

Reames, Sherry. *"Legenda Aurea": A Reexamination of Its Paradoxical History.* Madison: University of Wisconsin Press, 1985.

——. "Standardization and Reform in the Sarum Lessons for Saints' Days." In Margaret Connolly and Linne Mooney, eds., *Design and Distribution of Late Medieval Manuscripts in England.* Woodbridge, Suffolk: Boydell, 2008. 91–117.

Reddish, Henrietta. "The Saint Helen Window Ashton-Under-Lyne: A Reconstruction." *Journal of Stained Glass* 18 (1986/7): 150–61.

Rice, Nicole. *Lay Piety and Religious Discipline in Middle English Literature.* Cambridge: Cambridge University Press, 2008.

Ridyard, Susan. "*Condigna veneratio*: Post-Conquest Attitudes to the Saints of the English." *Anglo-Norman Studies* 9 (1987): 179–206.

Rigg, A. G. *History of Anglo-Latin Literature, 1066–1422.* Cambridge: Cambridge University Press, 1992.

Roberts, Peter. "Politics, Drama, and the Cult of Thomas Becket in the Sixteenth Century." In Colin Morris and Peter Roberts, eds., *Pilgrimage: The English Experience from Becket to Bunyan.* New York: Cambridge University Press, 2002. 199–237.

Roberts, Phyllis. "Prophecy, Hagiography, and St. Thomas of Canterbury." In J. A. Burrow and Ian Wei, eds., *Medieval Futures: Attitudes to the Future in the Middle Ages.* Woodbridge, Suffolk: Boydell and Brewer, 2000. 67–80.

Roberts, R. J. "John Rastell's Inventory of 1538." *Library,* 6th ser., 1 (1979): 34–42.

Robertson, Jean, and D. J. Gordon, eds. *A Calendar of Dramatic Records in the Books of the Livery Companies of London, 1485–1640.* Malone Society Collections 3. Oxford: Oxford University Press, 1954.

Russell, Joycelyne. *The Field of the Cloth of Gold: Men and Manners in 1520.* London: Routledge, 1969.

Salih, Sarah. *Versions of Virginity in Late Medieval England.* Woodbridge, Suffolk: D. S. Brewer, 2001.

Sampson, Annie. "The *SEL*: Constructing a Context." In P. R. Coss and S. D. Lloyd, eds., *Thirteenth Century England: Proceedings of the Newcastle Upon Tyne Conference.* Woodbridge, Suffolk: Boydell, 1985. 185–95.

Sandquist, T. A. "The Holy Oil of St. Thomas of Canterbury." In T. A. Sandquist and M. R. Powicke, eds., *Essays in Medieval History Presented to Bertie Wilkinson.* Toronto: University of Toronto Press, 1969. 330–44.

Sanok, Catherine. "Calendar Time in *Balade* Form." In Anke Bernau and Eva von Contzen, eds., *Sanctity as Literature in Late Medieval Britain.* Manchester: Manchester University Press, 2015. 228–44.

——. "Geography of Genre in the *Physician's Tale* and *Pearl*." *New Medieval Literatures* 5 (2002): 177–201.

——. "Good King Henry and the Genealogy of Shakespeare's History Plays." *Journal of Medieval and Early Modern Studies* 40 (2010): 37–63.

————. *Her Life Historical: Exemplarity and Female Saints' Lives in Late Medieval England.* Philadelphia: University of Pennsylvania Press, 2007.

Sauer, Walter. Review of *The South English Legendary, Gilte Legende, and Golden Legend,* by Manfred Görlach. *Anglia* 93 (1975): 247–50.

Saul, Nigel. *Richard II.* New Haven, CT: Yale University Press, 2008.

Sassen, Saskia. *Territory, Authority, Rights: From Medieval to Global Assemblages.* Princeton, NJ: Princeton University Press, 2008.

Scanlon, Larry, and James Simpson, eds. *John Lydgate: Poetry, Culture, and Lancastrian England.* Notre Dame, IN: University of Notre Dame Press, 2006.

Scattergood, John. "The *Libelle of Englyshe Polycye*: The Nation and Its Place." In Helen Cooney, ed., *Nation, Court and Culture: New Essays on Fifteenth-Century English Poetry.* Dublin: Four Courts, 2001. 28–49.

Schmidt, Kari. *Manuscripts in the Library of Gonville and Caius College, Cambridge.* Woodbridge, Suffolk: Boydell, 2001.

Schubel, Friedrich. *Die südenglische Legende von den elftausend Jungfrauen.* Greifswald, 1938.

Scully, Robert. "St. Winefride's Well: The Significance and Survival of a Welsh Catholic Shrine from the Early Middle Ages to the Present Day." In Margaret Jean Cormack, ed., *Saints and Their Cults in the Atlantic World.* Columbia: University of South Carolina Press, 2007. 202–28.

Shirley, Kevin. *The Secular Jurisdiction of Monasteries in Anglo-Norman and Angevin England.* Woodbridge, Suffolk: Boydell, 2004.

Simpson, James. *Oxford English Literary History.* Vol. 2: *Reform and Cultural Revolution.* Oxford: Oxford University Press, 2004.

Sisk, Jennifer. "Lydgate's Problematic Commission: A Legend of St. Edmund for Henry VI." *Journal of English and Germanic Philology* 109 (2010): 349–75.

Slocum, Kay Brainerd. *Liturgies in Honour of Thomas Becket.* Toronto: University of Toronto Press, 2004.

Smith, Neil. *Uneven Development: Nature, Capital and the Production of Space.* Athens: University of Georgia Press, 2008.

Sobecki, Sebastian. "Bureaucratic Verse: William Lyndwood, the Privy Seal, and the Form of *The Libelle of Englyshe Polycye.*" *New Medieval Literature* 21 (2010): 251–88.

————, ed. *The Sea and Englishness in the Middle Ages: Maritime Narratives, Identity and Culture.* Cambridge: D. S. Brewer, 2011.

————. *The Sea and Medieval English Literature.* Woodbridge, Suffolk: Boydell, 2007.

Somerset, Fiona. "'Hard Is with Seyntis to Make Affray': Lydgate the 'Poet-Propagandist' as Hagiographer." In Scanlon and Simpson. 258–78.

Spruyt, Hendrik. *Sovereign State and Its Competitors.* Princeton, NJ: Princeton University Press, 1996.

Staley, Lynn. *Island Garden: England's Language of Nation from Gildas to Marvell.* South Bend, IN: University of Notre Dame Press, 2012.

Staley Johnson, Lynn. "The Trope of the Scribe and Literary Authority in the Works of Julian of Norwich and Margery Kempe." *Speculum* 66 (1991): 820–38.

Stehkämper, Hugo. *Bürger und Kirchen in Köln im Hochmittelalter.* Cologne: SH Verlag, 2007.

Stein, Robert. "Making History English: Cultural Identity and Historical Explanation in William of Malmesbury and Laymon's *Brut.*" In Sylvia Tomasch and Sealy Gilles, eds., *Text and*

Territory: Geographical Imagination in the European Middle Ages. Philadelphia: University of Pennsylvania Press, 1998. 97–115.

Stevenson, Katie. "Chivalry, British Sovereignty, and Dynastic Politics: Undercurrents of Antagonism in Tudor-Stewart Relations, c. 1490–c. 1513." *Historical Research* 86.234 (2013): 601–18.

Still, Michelle. *The Abbot and the Rule: Religious Life at St. Albans, 1290–1349*. Aldershot, UK: Ashgate, 2002.

Storey, R. L. "Episcopal King-makers in the Fifteenth Century." In Dobson, *Church*. 82–98.

Strohm, Paul. *England's Empty Throne: Usurpation and the Language of Legitimation, 1399–1422*. South Bend, IN: University of Notre Dame Press, 2006.

Stump, Phillip. *The Reforms of the Council of Constance*. Leiden: Brill, 1994.

Summit, Jennifer. *Lost Property: The Woman Writer and English Literary History, 1380–1534*. Chicago: University of Chicago Press, 2000.

Sutton, Anne. "Caxton, the Cult of St. Winifred, and Shrewsbury." In Linda Clark, ed., *Of Mice and Men: Image, Belief and Regulation in Late Medieval England*. Woodbridge, Suffolk: Boydell, 2005. 109–26.

———. "Lady Joan Bradbury (d. 1530)." In Caroline Barron, ed., *Medieval London Widows, 1300–1500*. London: Hambledon, 1994. 209–38.

———. *The Mercery of London: Trade, Goods, and People, 1130–1578*. Aldershot, UK: Ashgate, 2005.

Swanson, R. N. *Church and Society in Late Medieval England*. Oxford: Blackwell, 1989.

———. "Hallum, Robert (d. 1417)." [*ODNB*]

Tanouki, Nirvana. "The Scale of World Literature." *New Literary History* 39 (2008): 599–617.

Taylor, Charles. *Secular Age*. Cambridge, MA: Harvard University Press, 2007.

Taylor, Frank. "Some Manuscripts of the 'Libelle of Englyshe Polycye.'" *Bulletin of the John Rylands Library* 24 (1940): 376–418.

Thiebaux, Marcelle. "Dameisele Ursula: Traditions of Hagiography and History in the *SEL* and Layamon's *Brut*." In Jankofsky, *South English Legendary*. 29–48.

Thiemke, Herman. *Die ME. Thomas Beket-legende des Gloucesterlegendars*. Berlin: Mayer and Müller, 1919.

Thomas, David. "Saint Winifred's Well and Chapel, Holywell." *Journal of the Historical Society of the Church in Wales* 8 (1958): 15–31.

Thompson, Anne. *Everyday Saints and the Art of Narrative in the SEL*. Burlington, VT: Ashgate, 2003.

———. "Shaping a Saint's Life: Frideswide of Oxford." *Medium Aevum* 63 (1994): 34–52.

Thompson, Benjamin. "Prelates and Politics from Winchelsey to Warham." In Clark and Carpenter. 69–95.

Thornton, Tim. *Cheshire and the Tudor State: 1480–1560*. Woodbridge, Suffolk: Boydell, 2000.

Thrupp, Sylvia. *Merchant Class of Medieval London*. Ann Arbor: University of Michigan Press, 1989.

Tracey, Larissa. "British Library MS Harley 630: St. Alban's and Lydgate." *Journal of the Early Book Society* 3 (2000): 36–58.

Tremlett, Giles. *Catherine of Aragon: Henry's Spanish Queen*. London: Faber and Faber, 2010.

Turville-Petre, Thorlac. *England the Nation: Language, Literature, and National Identity, 1290–1340*. Oxford: Oxford University Press, 1996.

Wakelin, M. F. "Manuscripts of the *Festial*." *Leeds Studies in English*, n.s., 1 (1967): 93–118.

Wallace, David. *Chaucerian Polity: Absolutist Lineages and Associational Forms in England and Italy*. Stanford, CA: Stanford University Press, 1997.

———. *Premodern Places: Calais to Surinam, Chaucer to Aphra Behn.* Malden, MA: Blackwell, 2004.

Warner, Laurence. "Adventurous Custance." In Laura Howes, ed., *Place, Space, and Landscape in Medieval Narrative.* Nashville: University of Tennessee Press, 2007. 43–59.

———. "Becket and the Hopping Bishops." *Yearbook of Langland Studies* 17 (2003): 107–34.

Warren, Nancy Bradley. *Spiritual Economies: Female Monasticism in Later Medieval England.* Philadelphia: University of Pennsylvania Press, 2001.

Watson, Nicholas. "Censorship and Cultural Change in Late-Medieval England: Vernacular Theology, the Oxford Translation Debate, and Arundel's Constitutions of 1409." *Speculum* 70 (1995): 822–64.

Watts, John. *Henry VI and the Politics of Kingship.* Cambridge: Cambridge University Press, 1996.

———. "The Pressure of the Public on Later Medieval Politics." In Clark and Carpenter. 159–80.

Wernham, R. B. *Before the Armada: The Emergence of the English Nation.* New York: W. W. Norton, 1972.

Williams, Glanmor. *Recovery, Reorientation, and Reformation: Wales, c. 1415–1642.* Oxford: Clarendon, 1987.

———. *The Welsh Church from Conquest to Reformation.* Fayetteville: University of Arkansas Press, 1993.

Williams-Krapp, Werner. *Die Deutschen und Niederländischen Legendare des Mittelalters.* Tübingen: Niemeyer, 1986.

Wilson, Christopher. "The Tomb of Henry IV and the Holy Oil of St. Thomas." In Eric Fernie and Paul Crossley, eds., *Medieval Architecture and Its Intellectual Context.* London: A&C Black, 1990. 181–90.

Wilson, Susan. *The Life and Afterlife of St. John of Beverley.* Burlington, VT: Ashgate, 2005.

Winstead, Karen. *John Capgrave's Fifteenth Century.* Philadelphia: University of Pennsylvania Press, 2007.

Winston, James. *English Towns in the Wars of the Roses.* Princeton, NJ: Princeton University Press, 1921.

Winward, Fiona. "The Lives of St. Wenefred (BHL 8847–8851)." *Analecta Bollandiana* 117 (1999): 89–132.

Withington, Robert. *English Pageantry: An Historical Outline.* Vol. 1. Cambridge, MA: Harvard University Press, 1918.

Wogan-Browne, Jocelyn. "Outdoing the Daughters of Syon: Edith of Wilton and the Representation of Female Community in Early Fifteenth-Century England." In Jocelyn Wogan-Browne, ed., *Medieval Women: Texts and Contexts in Late Medieval Britain.* Turnhout, Belgium: Brepols, 2000. 393–409.

———. *Saints' Lives and Women's Literary Culture, c. 1150–1300: Virginity and Its Authorizations.* New York: Oxford University Press, 2001.

Wogan-Browne, Jocelyn et al., eds. *Idea of the Vernacular: An Anthology of Middle English Literary Theory, 1280–1520.* University Park: Penn State University Press, 1999.

Woolf, D. R. "The Power of the Past: History, Ritual and Political Authority in Renaissance England." In Paul Fideler and Thomas Mayer, eds., *Political Thought and the Tudor Commonwealth.* London: Routledge, 1992. 19–49.

Wright, Michael, and Kathleen Loncar, eds. "Goscelin's Legend of Edith." In Hollis. 15–93.

Wright, Thomas. *History and Antiquities of the Town of Ludlow and Its Ancient Castle.* Ludlow, 1826.

ACKNOWLEDGMENTS

This book explores medieval ideas of community on the premise that, as Tony Kushner has it, "the smallest indivisible human unit is two people, not one." It is itself a testament to this truth in that, like all books, it is written not only for, but also *with*, others. It is a genuine pleasure to be able to thank some of them here.

It is my great good fortune to have so many colleagues at the University of Michigan (UM) who are so generous with their interest, expertise, and feedback. Among them, I owe particular thanks to Alison Cornish, Sara Blair, Anne Curzan, Hussein Fancy, Karla Mallette, Scotti Parrish, Helmut Puff, Xiomara Santamarina, Michael Schoenfeldt, Megan Sweeney, Valerie Traub, Patsy Yaeger (who is much missed), and Andrea Zemgulys. Kit French has shared her own research with remarkable selflessness, and Peggy McCracken, ever astute and always encouraging, has been a crucial interlocutor at every stage of the writing of this book. I began this project during a year at the UM Institute for the Humanities, and the lively interdisciplinary discussion there, led by Daniel Herwitz, shaped some of its central concerns. I'm especially grateful to Sara Forsdyke and Steven Mullaney, whose offices flanked mine that year, for conversations about what we were working on and for advice about getting that work done. Karla Taylor, Theresa Tinkle, and the members of the Medieval Reading Group offered valuable feedback on an early version of Chapter 7, as well as ongoing conversations that have clarified or helped me orient this project. A series of wonderful research assistants—Stephanie Batkie, Maia Farrar, Angela Heetderks, and Elizabeth Mathie—have contributed not only by identifying and researching materials for the project, but also by bringing their own interests and perspectives to it. Megan Behrend provided indispensible assistance with the index.

Many other colleagues and friends have generously read and discussed parts of this project with me or have invited me to present it: I am especially grateful to Heather Blurton, Lisa Cooper, Patricia Dailey, Andrea Denny-Brown,

Bruce Holsinger, Jennifer Jahner, Rebecca Krug, Kathy Lavezzo, Emma Lipton, Robert Meyer-Lee, Laura Miles, and Leah Schwebel. Conversations with Jennifer Bryan, Susan Crane, Pat Cullum, Susanna Fein, David Wallace, and Jocelyn Wogan-Browne have pointed me in helpful directions, as have audiences at Columbia, Northwestern, Texas State San Marcos, UC Irvine, University of Iowa, University of Minnesota, University of Virginia, Yale, and many conferences. Marie-Luise Ehrenschwendtner provided very useful information in response to an email from a stranger in a different field. I am glad for the opportunity to thank Patricia Ingham for crucial feedback on the manuscript at an important juncture. The intellectual support and inspiration of Elizabeth Allen, Jessica Brantley, Seeta Chaganti, Susie Phillips, and Claire Waters—the first audience for much of this book—have been essential from its beginning to its end.

Part of Chapter 1 appeared as "Saints' Lives and Forms of Community in the *South English Legendary*," in Heather Blurton and Jocelyn Wogan-Browne, eds., *Rethinking the South English Legendaries* (Manchester: Manchester University Press, 2012), 211–32. Part of Chapter 5 appeared as "Saints' Lives and the Literary After Arundel," in Kantik Ghosh and Vincent Gillespie, eds., *After Arundel: Religious Writing in Fifteenth-Century England* (Turnhout, Belgium: Brepols, 2012), 469–86. I am grateful to the editors of these collections for the opportunity they provided for the initial exploration of arguments developed here, and I am grateful to Manchester University Press and Brepols for permission to use this material.

Librarians at several institutions were instrumental in answering queries or making materials available to me. I am especially grateful to Andrea Bartelstein, Rauner Special Collections Library at Dartmouth College; Harriet Fisher, Corpus Christi College, Oxford; Andrea Longson, Senior Librarian at Advocates Library; Christoph Mackert, Universitätsbibliothek Leipzig; Matthew Watson, Ushaw College; and Brian Whitehouse, Southwell Minster Historic Chapter Library. I am grateful for assistance I received at the British Library; Cambridge University Library; Durham University Library; Gonville and Caius College; the Newberry Library; and York Minster Library.

I thank the National Endowment for the Humanities, which supported this project with a Summer Stipend when it was just getting under way; the UM for support from the Associate Professor Support Fund and a Michigan Humanities Award; and especially the UM Institute of the Humanities, for the great luxury of a year in which to immerse myself in the project and, in the fellows' seminar, to be drawn outside its historical and disciplinary boundaries. A subvention from the UM Office of Research and support from the UM English Department (with particular thanks to Gaurav Desai) have facilitated the publication of the study.

Finally, this book is in no small part a product of the love, patience, and support of my family, Basil, Will, and Sylvie. In addition to the many practical and emotional forms their support has taken, this book has benefited incalculably from the way they have expanded the communities in which I participate and from what I've learned from watching them create and participate in communities of their own. This book is offered as a tribute to my parents and siblings, my first teachers about the delicate balance between singular and shared forms of identity.